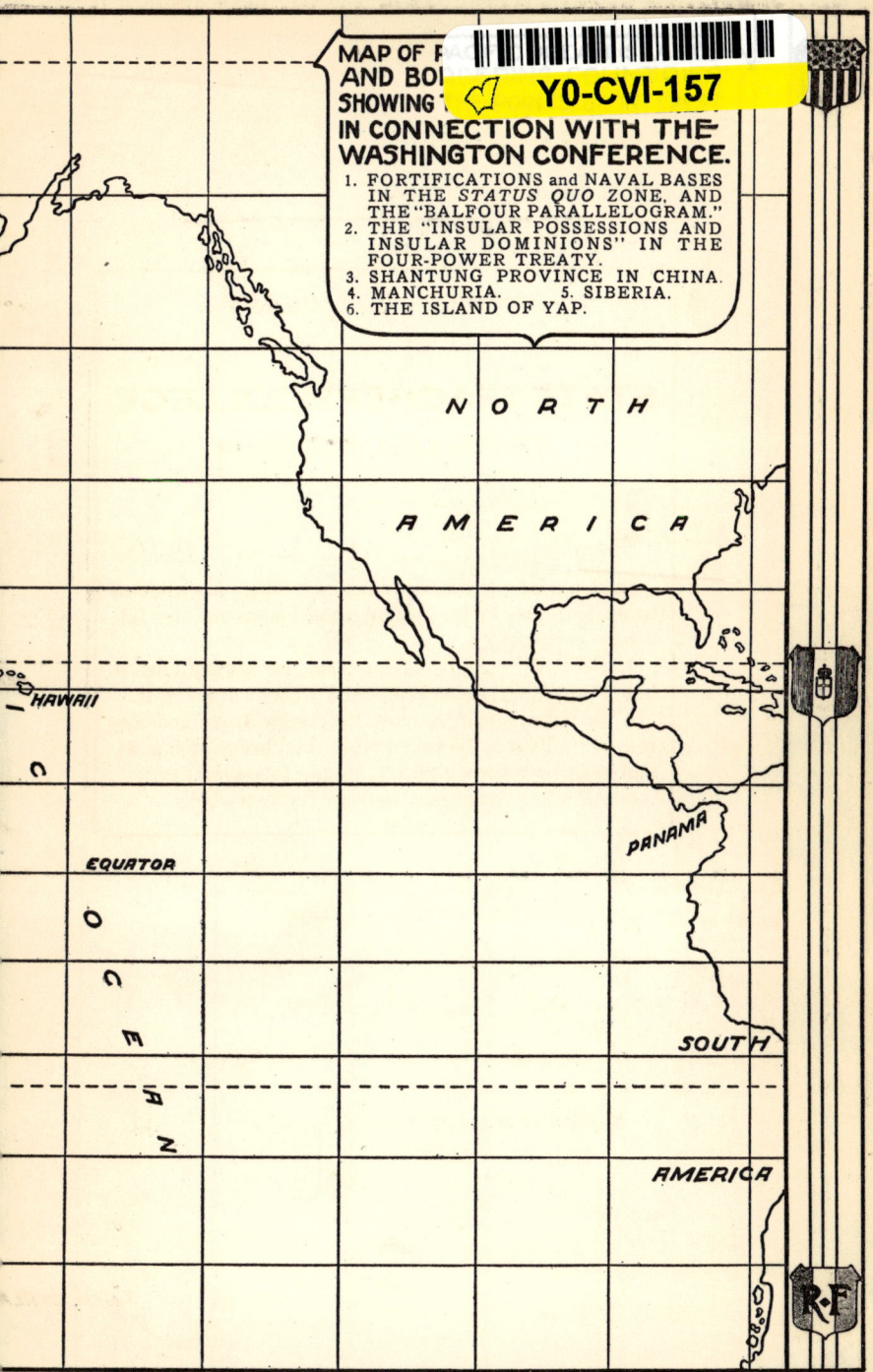

THE WASHINGTON CONFERENCE AND AFTER

STANFORD UNIVERSITY PRESS
STANFORD UNIVERSITY, CALIFORNIA

LONDON: HUMPHREY MILFORD
OXFORD UNIVERSITY PRESS

THE MARUZEN-KABUSHIKI-KAISHA
TOKYO, OSAKA, KYOTO

THE BAKER & TAYLOR COMPANY
55 FIFTH AVENUE, NEW YORK

THE
[**WASHINGTON CONFERENCE AND AFTER**]

A Historical Survey

By YAMATO ICHIHASHI, Ph. D.
Associate Professor of Japanese History in Stanford University; formerly Secretary to the Late Viscount Kato, Senior Delegate of Japan to the Washington Conference

1928
STANFORD UNIVERSITY PRESS
STANFORD UNIVERSITY, CALIFORNIA

COPYRIGHT 1928 IN THE UNITED STATES AND
IN GREAT BRITAIN BY THE BOARD OF TRUSTEES
OF THE LELAND STANFORD JUNIOR UNIVERSITY
ALL RIGHTS RESERVED—PUBLISHED 1928

PRINTED AND BOUND IN THE UNITED STATES OF AMERICA
BY STANFORD UNIVERSITY PRESS

DEDICATED
TO
DAVID STARR JORDAN

PREFACE

The purpose of this work is to present a historical survey of matters discussed and achievements made by the Washington Conference. In addition post-conference events of international importance in the Far Eastern and the Pacific region are summarized.

The aims of the conference were twofold: first, to bring about a limitation of armaments on the part of the Principal Allied and Associated Powers; and, second, to solve Pacific and Far Eastern problems by a concerted effort on the part of nine nations, including the United States, the British Empire, France, Italy, Japan, Belgium, China, the Netherlands, and Portugal. Thus, in reality, the Washington Conference was composed of two distinct conferences each with its special tasks.

The Five-Power Arms Conference constitutes the subject-matter of Part I of the book. At the outset an attempt is made to trace the origin of the conference; this is followed by a description of its organization, procedure, and personnel. The work of the conference began with the presentation, by the United States, on November 12, 1921, of a plan for a limitation of naval armament. The more salient aspects of this plan are analyzed. The story is then told of the trying task of the "Big Three" (Balfour, Hughes, and Kato), in effecting a provisional agreement on capital-ship ratio, which was the first and foremost achievement of this conference. Then follows an account of the opposition of France to America's proposed capital-ship ratio plan; of the British-French conflict over the question of submarines; of Japan's demand for the maintenance of the *status quo* on certain naval bases and fortifications in the Pacific, and of the French refusal to accede to the American proposal for a limitation on auxiliary craft.

In spite of these difficulties a naval treaty was attained. Its important stipulations are analyzed and discussed. The conference also achieved a Four-Power Pact whereby, among other things, the Anglo-Japanese Alliance which had existed for nearly twenty years was terminated. In the concluding chapter is presented a critical estimate of these treaties and of the treaty concerning submarines and poisonous gases, and also a brief discussion of the failure of the Geneva Conference of 1927 and of subsequent related occurrences.

In Part II is given a history of the Pacific and Far Eastern Conference, with China as its central problem. To enable general readers to approach this subject with a knowledge of the background, the modern history of China is briefly sketched. This conference effected two treaties, one on the Chinese tariff and the other on the "open door." Besides, it adopted a number of resolutions on important matters affecting the interests of China and other nations. All these are discussed in some detail. Two other problems were of special interest to China and Japan, namely, Shantung, and the Twenty-one Demands. The former was settled by a treaty, and as to the latter Japan offered concrete modifications. In addition there were two matters vitally affecting the United States and Japan: the question arising out of the Inter-Allied Siberian expedition, and that of the Island of Yap. The first was completely solved by a treaty between Russia and Japan, while the second was satisfactorily settled by an American-Japanese treaty. Each chapter is brought up to date in order to indicate post-conference development on the subject dealt with. In the concluding chapter an attempt is made to give a critical estimate of the achievements of this conference from a retrospect of nearly eight years.

The author wishes to express his gratitude to Professor Paul H. Clyde, who has read the manuscript and offered valuable suggestions and criticisms. However, the responsibility for the interpretation here presented rests wholly with the author.

Finally, he must acknowledge his indebtedness to the Hoover War Library for certain materials used in the present book.

YAMATO ICHIHASHI

STANFORD UNIVERSITY, CALIFORNIA
    September 10, 1928

CONTENTS

PART I. THE CONFERENCE ON LIMITATION OF ARMAMENT

CHAPTER	PAGE
I. The Origin of the Conference	3
II. The Conference Machinery	24
III. The American Proposal: A Great Diplomatic Adventure	34
IV. The "Big Three" on Capital-Ship Ratio	46
V. The "Décapitation" of the French Navy	60
VI. The Submarine Question	72
VII. Japan and Pacific Fortifications	83
VIII. France Refuses Auxiliary Limitation	94
IX. The Naval Treaty	104
X. The Four-Power Pacific Treaty and the Anglo-Japanese Alliance	113
XI. An Estimate of the Washington Arms Treaties, and the Aftermath at Geneva	138

PART II. THE PACIFIC AND FAR EASTERN CONFERENCE

XII. China, the Problem of the Pacific	155
XIII. The Question of Tariff Autonomy	167
XIV. The Open-Door Policy	178
XV. China Challenges Extraterritoriality, Foreign Troops, and Foreign Post Offices	202
XVI. The Powers Make Concessions to China	230
XVII. Principles versus Realities	248
XVIII. The Shantung Treaty	267
XIX. The Twenty-one Demands	289
XX. The Siberian Expedition	306
XXI. The Yap Settlement	323
XXII. The Pacific Conference and After—Conclusions	340

DOCUMENTS AND BIBLIOGRAPHY

APPENDIX

I. The Proposal of the United States for a Limitation of Naval Armaments 353

II. Provisional Agreement between the United States, British Empire, and Japan . . . 362

III. A Treaty between the United States of America, the British Empire, France, Italy, and Japan, Limiting Naval Armament . . 365

IV. A Treaty in Relation to the Use of Submarines and Noxious Gases in Warfare . . . 386

V. Treaty for the Settlement of Outstanding Questions Relative to Shantung . . . 389

VI. The Chinese Tariff Treaty 398

Bibliography 403

INDEX

Index 429

PART I

THE CONFERENCE ON LIMITATION OF ARMAMENT

CHAPTER I

THE ORIGIN OF THE CONFERENCE

The idea of limiting armaments did not originate with America alone, and certainly not with the Washington Conference. The evil of competitive armament had been recognized for centuries.[1] As early as 1713 the Abbot Charles Irénée de Saint-Pierre drew an important plan for a federation of States and emphasized that "the success of his proposal would render it possible to the various States to decrease materially their military expenses."[2] Many similar attempts have been made since then down to the outbreak of the Great War, including the two conferences at The Hague in 1899 and 1907.[3] By the treaties concluding the Great War the victorious powers reduced to a minimum the national forces of their former enemy states.[4] Concerning these reductions, Wheeler-Bennett says:

They are also the first steps towards that general reduction and limitation of armaments which they seek to bring about as one of the most fruitful preventives of war, and which will be one of the first duties of the League of Nations to promote.[5]

We find in Article 8 of the Covenant of the League of Nations the following item:

The Members of the League recognize that the maintenance of peace requires the reduction of national armaments to the

[1] See Hans Wehberg, *The Limitation of Armaments* (Washington, 1921).

[2] *Ibid.*, p. 5.

[3] *Ibid.*, pp. 6–94.

[4] Germany by the Treaty of Versailles, Austria by the Treaty of St. Germain-en-Laye, Bulgaria by the Treaty of Neuilly-sur-Seine, and Hungary by the Treaty of Trianon.

[5] J. W. Wheeler-Bennett, *Information on the Reduction of Armaments* (London, 1925), p. 27.

lowest point consistent with national safety and the enforcement by common action of international obligations.

Accordingly the League created a special machinery for armament limitation, and has spared no effort to attain results in this regard. But by 1921 neither the prewar international attempts nor the activities of the League had as yet been able to accomplish anything substantial toward reduction of armaments.[6]

Moreover, contrary to the ideal expressed in the Covenant, as soon as the calamitous war was ended, the victorious powers, especially the British Empire, the United States, and Japan, entered into a new, mad naval race, and France increased her military establishment, thus causing nationals of all these powers to stagger under an apparently ever growing burden.[7] But the folly as well as danger of these gigantic naval and military programs did not long remain unrealized by the civilized world, and consequently there sprang up everywhere popular movements to bring about reduction of armaments. Naturally these

[6] See Wehberg, *op. cit.*, and A. H. Abbott, "The League's Disarmament Activities and the Washington Conference," *Political Science Quarterly*, XXXVII, 1–24.

[7] For instance, in Japan the "eight-eight" program of 1914 had been given up in 1916 for financial reasons, and an "eight-four" plan was substituted for it. But in the United States the famous Naval Service Appropriation Act had been passed, on August 29, 1916, by both Houses of Congress, increasing naval expenditures from $155,029,000 for 1915–16 to $1,268,000,000 for 1917–18. And in 1919 America embarked on a new three years' program designed to make its navy second to none. Whereupon Japan decided (1919) to build eight battleships and six dreadnoughts; moreover, in April 1921 the Japanese Minister of the Navy insisted upon the necessity of carrying out the original "eight-eight" plan. In Great Britain the first of the "Hood" class had been laid down in 1917, but by 1921 she had three more ships of this type under construction. See further the American plan for reduction of naval armament discussed on pages 35–37.

movements were more vigorously agitated in the countries most involved. It was in response to these popular desires that the United States was led to take the initiative in inviting to a conference the British Empire, France, Italy, and Japan, with a view of seeking limitation of armaments by international agreements.

Unfortunately, from the published official records it is impossible to state just when the American Government began to entertain the idea of convening such a conference. But it may not be without interest to trace as far as possible, from these as well as from unofficial sources, the more important happenings that are suggestive of its origin.

In the 1920 session of the American Congress, Senator Borah suggested, by offering a resolution, that an international conference be held for the purpose of discussing armament questions. In the session of the following year he offered (February 24, 1921) an amendment to the Naval Bill, as follows:

> The President is authorized and requested to invite the Governments of Great Britain and Japan to send representatives to a conference which shall be charged with the duty of promptly entering into an understanding or agreement by which the naval building program of each of said Governments, to wit, the United States, Great Britain, and Japan, shall be substantially reduced during the next five years to such an extent and such terms as may be agreed upon, which understanding or agreement is to be reported to the respective Governments for approval.[8]

The Bill so amended was passed by the Senate in May and by the House in June, and was approved by the President on July 12, 1921.[9]

---

[8] *Congressional Record,* 66th Congress, 3d Session, Vol. LX, Part 3, p. 3740.

[9] *U.S. Senate Document,* 66th Congress, 3d Session, XV, 233.

6   THE WASHINGTON CONFERENCE AND AFTER

A suggestive article appeared in the *New York Times* of June 1, 1921, saying, among other things, that "President Harding has instituted 'informal feelers' with the object of ascertaining whether it would be feasible to bring about an international conference to provide means for the limitation of naval armaments," and that "these feelers have been entrusted to Colonel George Harvey, Ambassador to the Court of St. James, in his capacity as the American representative on the Allied Supreme Council." It added that this action was taken without any reference to the Borah amendment.

While sojourning in London during the month of August 1921, the writer learned from the naval attaché of an Embassy to the British Court what is briefly narrated below. Early in June conversations had taken place between a high American naval officer and the British Admiralty on the subject of a conference on naval armament limitation. The attaché had gathered this information from a high authority of the Admiralty, and had at once informed his own Admiralty, adding that such an international gathering would be forthcoming. Bearing this information in mind, it may be recalled that Admiral Sims was in England during May and June of the same year for the purpose of receiving an honorary degree from Cambridge University. On May 31 such a degree was conferred on the Admiral, and in response to this honor he said, "co-operation in time of war was formerly the problem; the present problem is co-operation in time of peace."[10] It is superfluous to state how enthusiastically he was entertained by the Government and people of England. Of course, the writer cannot verify a con-

---

[10] *The London Times*, June 1, 1921.

nection between the presence of the American Admiral and the statement of the naval attaché, although the attaché himself entertained no doubt on this point.

Again, when Mr. Lloyd George, the British Prime Minister, was asked in the House of Commons on July 7, 1921, whether he could not attempt to settle the controversies threatening the peace of the Far East by inviting the United States, Japan, and China to a conference, and also whether he would not state the Government's views on the subject of renewal of the Anglo-Japanese Alliance, he replied:

I hope soon to be in a position to make a statement on those important subjects (I am fairly hopeful of being in a position to make a statement on Monday, but it depends upon whether replies are received from the United States, Japan, and China)—but premature declarations would interfere with the success of negotiations and proceedings.[11]

The status of the Anglo-Japanese Alliance was soon made clear by Lord Chancellor Birkenhead, who expressed the legal view that "a decision was not immediately urgent since the Alliance, not having been formally denounced, would automatically continue in force until it were denounced."[12]

On Monday, July 11, the Prime Minister made a lengthy speech in answer to the foregoing questions:

The broad lines of Imperial policy in the Pacific and the Far East were the first subjects to which we addressed ourselves at the meetings of the Imperial Cabinet, having a special regard to the Anglo-Japanese agreement, the future of China, and the bearing of both those questions on the relations of the British Empire and the United States. We were guided in our deliberations by three main considerations. In Japan, we have an old

[11] *Ibid.*, July 11, 1921. [12] *Ibid.*

and proud Ally; the Agreement of twenty years' standing between us has been of very great benefit not only to ourselves and her, but to the peace of the Far East. In China there is a very numerous people with great potentialities, who esteem our friendship rightly, and whose interest we, on our side, desire to assist and advance. In the United States we see today, as we have always seen, the people closest to our aims and ideals with whom it is for us not merely a desire and an interest but a deeply rooted instinct to consult and co-operate.

I have already explained that the first principle of our policy is friendly co-operation with the United States. We are all convinced that upon this, more than upon any other single factor, depends the peace and well-being of the world. We also desire, as I have already stated, to maintain our close friendship and co-operation with Japan. The greatest merit of that valuable friendship is that it harmonizes the influences and activities of the two greatest Asiatic Powers, and thus constitutes an essential safeguard to the well-being of the British Empire and the peace of the East.

In addition to these considerations, we desire to safeguard our own vital interests in the Pacific and to preclude any competition in naval armaments between the Pacific Powers. All the representatives of the Empire agreed that our standpoint on these questions should be communicated with complete frankness to the United States, Japan, and China, with the object of securing an exchange of views which might lead to more formal discussions and conference.[13]

In pursuance of the expressed desire of Premier Lloyd George, Lord Curzon, the Foreign Secretary, was instructed to communicate those views to the American, Japanese, and Chinese representatives in London, so that they, in turn, might inform their respective governments concerning the same.

He [Lord Curzon] expressed at these conversations a very strong hope that this exchange of views might, if their Govern-

[13] *The London Times,* July 12, 1921.

ments shared our desire in that respect, pave the way for a Conference on the problems of the Pacific and the Far East.[14]

It seems evident from the remarks above that the idea of holding a conference on the Far Eastern problem had been seriously considered by the meetings of the Imperial Cabinet, and steps had actually been taken by the British Empire to interest the United States, Japan, and China to that end.

It was at this juncture that the American Government approached the governments of the four powers on the subject of a conference to discuss limitation of armaments and the Pacific and the Far Eastern questions. The actual approach to these powers was made on July 8, according to the American Secretary of State.

It would be highly interesting to establish, if possible, the exact positions of the United States and Great Britain as regards the convocation of the conference before the former took the initiative. But no documents are accessible to show this interesting point, and it must be passed with the observation that it was frankly stated by some writers in France and in Japan that the British were just as responsible as the Americans for the American initiative.[15] This belief had no small influence in shaping public opinion in France and Japan, as will be shown presently.

The general public learned nothing from official sources about the proposed conference until the evening of July 10, when the White House issued a communiqué stating that the American Government had approached the governments of Great Britain, France, Italy, and Japan

[14] *Ibid.*

[15] See Pertinax in *L'Echo de Paris,* quoted in the *New York Times* July 13, 1921, and the article entitled "Beikoku Teigi-no Rimen" ["Behind the American Proposal"], in the *Jiji,* July 15, 1921.

as to the advisability of holding a conference on armament limitation and the Far East and Pacific problems. We later learned from Mr. Hughes that on July 8, 1921, by the direction of the President, the Department of State had addressed an informal inquiry to the group of powers known as the Principal Allied and Associated Powers—that is, Great Britain, France, Italy, and Japan—to ascertain whether it would be agreeable to them to take part in a conference on the subject of limitation of armament, to be held in Washington at a time to be mutually agreed upon. In making this inquiry, it was stated to be manifest that the question of limitation of armament had a close relation to Pacific and Far East problems, and the President suggested that the powers especially interested in these problems should undertake in connection with the conference the consideration of all matters bearing upon their solution with a view to reaching a common understanding with respect to principles and policies in the Far East.[16]

The text of the communiqué referred to above is substantially the same as the quotation above except that the latter adds: "This has been communicated to the Powers concerned and China has also been invited to take part in the discussion relating to Far Eastern Problems."[17]

It seems from Mr. Hughes' statement that the Chinese Government was not approached simultaneously with the four powers. However, the formal invitations to the Principal Allied and Associated Powers and to China bear the same date, namely, August 11, 1921. Belgium, the

[16] *Senate Document No. 126,* 67th Congress, 2d Session, p. 783. Hereafter cited as *Document.*

[17] *Review of the Conference on Limitation of Armament* by the *Boston Evening Transcript* (Boston, 1922), p. 2.

Netherlands, and Portugal, on the other hand, were not invited until October 4.

The White House communiqué was unanimously and in the main enthusiastically received by the American press. Its reception abroad was neither unanimous nor enthusiastic except in the British Empire, if the writer's personal observation in Europe be correct. The European public in those days paid but little attention to international conferences of any kind; they had been very common since the signing of the Versailles Treaty, and for the most part quite unfruitful. However, when the news of the American initiative for another international assembly was announced there was a stir in European political and diplomatic circles, and the general public was naturally affected by it. Still, for the moment, the European public was unable to account for the sudden change in the attitude of the American Government on matters of international interest. Frankly, Europe was at a loss to understand the enthusiastic reception which the American public gave to their President's proposal in view of America's continual refusal to associate herself with the League of Nations. There existed in connection with the League two special commissions on disarmament, yet America had manifested no interest in these. Thus in general the European public showed little confidence in and no enthusiasm for the American proposal.[18]

But there was in France one warm journalist-supporter of the proposed conference, namely, Stephane Lauzanne, a well-known advocate of America and things American.

[18] See further: for Italian views, *The London Times,* July 14, 1921; for French views, the *New York Times,* July 13 and 15; and for the world at large, *The Outlook,* August 10, 1921 (article entitled "A Poll of the Press"), p. 680.

In his *Le Matin* he bitterly assailed the British Premier, who, he held, had been responsible for all the diplomatic defeats of France in all the international conferences since November 11, 1918:

> Et c'est vous, ami David, qui cette fois serez assis sur le tabouret. ... Allons à Washington la tête haute et le cœur en paix. Nous y trouverons des bras pour nous y accueillir, des oreilles pour nous écouter, des regards pour nous consulter et pas de mains pour soupeser nos pauvres tranées.[19]

A similar view was expressed, though in less vigorous language, in Lauzanne's article which appeared in *The Outlook*:

> The President's invitation has been received with real favor by the whole of France. .... There are numerous reasons for this. First of all, the invitation comes from America. To the great majority of the French this means that there are no underhand doings, no intrigues, no desire to effect a political success at the detriment of such and such a nation. Secondly, the invitation is intended to lead to something practical. There is nothing the French hate more than to be working in the clouds, for experience has taught them that one always ends by falling down to earth and that one is hurt in the falling. The study of disarmament by the so-called League of Nations is a study in the clouds. .... But the study of disarmament by the three greatest naval powers of the globe, and by one of the greatest military powers of Europe, can eventually meet with something tangible. Finally, for the first time since the Versailles Treaty of Peace, France has been invited to an international conference at which there will be no intention of requesting her to give up any one of the advantages she has obtained by the Treaty to the greater glory and greater benefit of England. .... Whatever the case may be, the line of conduct of France at the Conference of Washington is regulated in advance. She will back up America with her heart and power.[20]

[19] *Le Matin*, July 17, 1921.
[20] *The Outlook*, August 24, 1921, pp. 640–41.

When the White House statement reached Tokyo the Japanese public was skeptical.[21] It expected the proposed conference to confine itself to the discussion of armament limitation and consequently was surprised to find the proposal including the discussion of Far East and Pacific problems. The combination of these two subjects did not strike the Japanese as logical. It is interesting to note in this connection that the majority of Japanese writers soon began to characterize the proposed conference as the "Pacific Conference." To them armament limitation required no argument, the only requisite being an international understanding fixing a simultaneous action on the part of the interested powers. The invitation failed to receive an enthusiastic reception simply because of the combination of the two subjects.[22]

In England the invitation was received enthusiastically as is evidenced by the expressions given below:

The *London Daily Mail* declares that "the President's message surpasses in importance all other current doings of whatever moment." The *Daily Express* says that "it is a bright augury for the peace of the whole world that the President has dissolved the fog of mystery which has hung over the question of international disarmament. This country will gladly respond to the call." The *London Evening News* assures us that "if the President's desires are realized by a fair and perfectly possible limitation of armaments, the British people will be as ready as America to do him honor." *The London Times* informs us that the statement is both "momentous" and "timely," that it opens "a new and hopefully fruitful phase of the Pacific Problem," and that "the task of the proposed Conference will be as delicate and, unless dis-

[21] The communiqué was the first news on the proposed conference as far as the Japanese public was concerned. No intimation had been made by its Government concerning the informal American inquiry.

[22] The American opinion was also divided on this point. See *The New Republic*, July 20, 1921, pp. 202–3.

cerningly approached, as dangerous as any Conference ever essayed to discharge. Not even the Peace Conference at Paris had to face issues vaster or fraught with greater possibilities of good and evil to the world."

The English press has been "pouring superlatives," as the *New York Times* says, over President Harding's plan. .... They speak of it as an "earth-shaking event," a "turning point in history," and so on. These characterizations, the *Times* thinks, "are only partly born of the enthusiasm and eagerness which now exists in England for co-operation with the United States. They reflect also the pervading concern over the failure, up to the present, of the Great War to make an end of war." In this attempt, as the *Times* concedes, "time is on the President's side," and "a standard has been raised to which all who long for peace with security will repair."

Not only this Independent Democratic paper, but the dyed-in-the-wool Democratic *New York World* praises the President and his Secretary of State—who is doubtless the real author of the Conference—as highly as do the journals of his own party, and that is saying a great deal. The *World* even asserts that the proposal for the Conference, "is not only the most important action yet taken by this Administration, but it is the most important undertaking in the way of international relations since the signing of the Treaty of Versailles." Despite the fact that our Senate has rejected the League, Mr. Harding is working with four of the principal members of the League to carry out one of the League's great objects. .... To the *World* Mr. Harding's invitation "is doubly gratifying." "There are times when it seemed as if the President failed to appreciate the gravity of the issue or to understand the seriousness of the question of competitive armament in respect to the associated economic life of the world. .... He did nothing to further the general cause of disarmament until it was plain that Congress could not longer be restrained. .... The President has now generously atoned for any mistakes that he made in the earlier stages of the discussion. .... Mr. Harding's invitation is a manifestation of statesmanship of the first order. It is world leadership."[23]

[23] "The Arms Conference at Washington," in *The Outlook*, August 31, 1921, pp. 678–81.

The official attitudes of the invited nations showed a more marked enthusiasm. The Quai d'Orsay was first to speak. Jules Sauerwein wrote in the July 11 issue of *Le Temps:*

The intention of M. Briand is not only to accept the participation by France in a conference at which the very important questions of the Far East and disarmament will be discussed under the presidency of the United States but also to go himself to America in order that he may collaborate in person in these tasks as the head of the French Government.[24]

On July 12 the French Premier submitted to the Parliament his response to President Harding's invitation, which reads in part as follows:

Mr. Harding has taken the noble and generous initiative to convoke at Washington a conference in which the great, friendly, and associated Powers will seek the basis of an accord to assure the continuity and the stability of peace in the region of the Pacific. France has important interests in that part of the world; she cannot remain indifferent to the pourparlers and entente which have for their object to prevent all conflict. I believe I am interpreting your unanimous sentiment in thanking the President of the great Republic for having invited our country to that conference.[25]

It was reported from Rome on the 13th that Italy had officially accepted Mr. Harding's invitation.[26]

On July 14 the Japanese Foreign Office issued a communiqué to the press stating that it had replied to the American Government on the previous day. It reads in part as follows:

[24] See the article entitled "La réponse française à l'invitation de M. Harding," in *Le Temps,* July 11, 1921.
[25] *Le Matin,* July 13, 1921.
[26] *The London Times,* July 14, 1921.

The ideals of the Government and the people of Japan seek to secure an enduring peace of the world and to promote advancement of human welfare. They, therefore, welcome any plan that will help in realizing their ideals. The Government would gladly accept the American invitation to participate in a conference of the five Powers to discuss limitation of armaments. But in regard to a conference on the Pacific and Far Eastern questions the Government, before it would express its views, would desire to know the nature and scope of the American proposal in order to ensure the success of such a conference.[27]

On the same day Premier Hara gave an interview to the Reuter agent at Tokyo, remarking that it was impossible to say much with regard to President Harding's conference proposal, as it involved not only the armament question, on which the public opinion of Japan was entirely in accord with that of America, but also many other points requiring careful consideration by the Government. But he could say that the Japanese Government had received President Harding's proposal with the greatest sympathy. It was the earnest wish of the Japanese Government to do all in its power to help remove existing doubts and misunderstandings in order that peace and good-will might reign throughout the world.[28]

The Secretary of State and the Japanese Ambassador held informal interviews as regards the Japanese inquiry, and, as a result, the American Government delivered on July 23 its reply to the Japanese Government, which reads in part:

The Secretary of State is willing to proceed with exchanges of opinion regarding the agenda prior to the meeting of the Conference. He considers it inadvisable, however, at the present moment to hamper the programme and in particular to delay the

[27] See the *Jiji*, July 15, 1921. This is the writer's own translation.
[28] *The London Times*, July 18, 1921.

THE ORIGIN OF THE CONFERENCE 17

arrangements for the Conference pending an agreement regarding this matter.[29]

Japan was satisfied with this view, and her note of acceptance was received by the American Government on July 27. It says:

The Japanese Government, on that understanding, are happy to be able to inform the American Government that it is their intention gladly to accept an invitation for a Conference which shall embrace the discussion of the Pacific and Far Eastern questions. .... In order to ensure the success of the Conference, the Japanese Government deem it advisable that the Agenda thereof should be arranged in accordance with the main object of the discussions as above defined, and that introduction therein of problems such as are of sole concern to certain particular Powers or such matters that may be regarded as accomplished facts should be scrupulously avoided.[30]

With this decision of the Japanese Government the necessary preliminaries were completed.

Let us, for a moment, turn to the general reaction upon Japan's first note of her conditional acceptance. The note gave rise to the wildest speculations in America. Here is an example:

Is Japan the victim of a gigantic international conspiracy of white nations? Is the invitation that she attend the Disarmament Conference to be called at Washington merely a diabolically clever scheme whereby she will be placed in a position where she must either make various concessions in respect to the present troublesome Asiatic and Pacific questions or must see herself forced into a position of absolute isolation as a nation? Ever since Japan received the inquiry from the United States as to whether she would attend the Conference, these questions have

[29] *Review of the Conference on Limitation of Armament* by the *Boston Evening Transcript* (Boston, 1922), p. 2.
[30] *Ibid.*, p. 3.

been agitating the minds of all Japanese who think on international questions at all. If matters had gone no further than the delivery to the Foreign Office of the American inquiry, the results thereof would nevertheless have been tremendous in their effect on Japanese thought.[31]

Here is another example:

Japan, however, the fourth of the allied powers addressed, presented an unexpected obstacle, the tone of the Japanese press indicated that the invitation had come as somewhat of a shock. The outstanding difficulties between Japan and the United States, involving the Conference issue; the objection of the United States to the Pacific mandates north of the Equator accorded Japan by the Peace Conference, especially as regards the cable rights of the island of Yap; the disapproval of Japan's policy toward China and Siberia, and the alleged tendency of the United States to encourage the Chinese in their anti-Japanese campaign—all these, complicated by mutual distrust and the increase of naval armaments on both sides, made President Harding's invitation a not altogether agreeable surprise for Japan. The Japanese Government delayed its decision for some days, holding secret conferences as to what answers should be returned.[32]

Speaking more directly of the Japanese note, this article continues:

Though the underlying intent of the last paragraph was obviously to exclude the Japanese Pacific Mandates, including Yap, and the Shantung Controversy from the contemplated discussion, the fact remained that Japan had consented to sit in the conference called by the American President specifically for the purpose of effecting a mutual obligation to cease the financially ruinous and war-breeding competitive increase of armaments.

[31] H. W. Kinney, "Puzzled Japan," in *The Outlook*, August 24, 1921, p. 642.
[32] "The Disarmament Conference," *Current History*, September 1921, p. 917.

THE ORIGIN OF THE CONFERENCE 19

This was considered alike in the United States and Europe as a most encouraging augury. Following receipt of the last acceptance, the Washington Government proceeded to complete the arrangements for the Conference.[33]

These statements do not satisfactorily explain the hesitation of Japan. Of course, it is childish to assert that her reluctance was caused by her fear of the alleged conspiracy of white nations against her. One must try to understand the attitudes of the various governments invited, according to their respective positions on the subjects proposed for discussion by the American Government. It was understood from the beginning that the proposed conference on armament limitation was to be primarily concerned with naval armament; from the naval point of view, America, England, and Japan alone were vitally involved. These nations possessed the power to complete their respective gigantic building programs. But they were also in the best position to realize the grave danger of competitive construction. Baron Kato, Minister of the Navy, said as early as March 1921, in an interview given to the Tokyo correspondent of the Associated Press, that if the naval powers of the world agree to stop the construction of ships, Japan would willingly give up her "Double-Eight Program." He must have realized that the carrying out of the program would have meant a tremendous expenditure, almost ruinous to Japan's general interests. The position of Japan in this respect was somewhat that of England, which would not build ships except to maintain her superiority to the American navy. Financially America commanded the greatest advantages, but she too did not care to spend limitless treasure for her navy in view of her other needs. Neither France nor Italy

[33] *Ibid.*

enjoyed the prestige of great naval powers, and they were financially so handicapped as to leave them no hope of becoming such. The interest of these two nations in limiting naval armaments was largely negative. They would gain, should the great naval powers reduce their forces; but they were not so vitally interested as America, England, and Japan. Hence neither France nor Italy manifested real interest in the proposed armament conference.

Again, the interests of France in the Pacific and Far Eastern questions were very meager in comparison with those of the United States, Great Britain, or Japan. French interests in Indo-China were never seriously involved in the international questions of the Pacific, and likewise her interests in China. Italy had next to no interest in that region of the world. If, therefore, these two powers failed to show enthusiasm for the conference, it was largely explained by the reasons indicated above.

On the other hand, the British Empire, America, and Japan had larger and more vital interests in the Pacific and the Far East because of their territorial possessions, their geographical propinquity, and above all because of their financial and commercial positions. Of course, politically Japan was most vitally interested in that region because she was located there. Thus it should be evident that of the great powers Japan occupied a unique position so far as the Pacific and Far Eastern questions were concerned, be they in China, Siberia, or elsewhere. Besides, Japan was a new international power and as such she had been subjected to severe criticisms by the more established nations. Her activities had been looked upon with suspicion. Her recent blunders had been magnified beyond their merit. In short, Japan had been made the "goat" of all international ills in the Pacific region and, in particular,

THE ORIGIN OF THE CONFERENCE

of those which had obtained in China. Of this attitude of the Occidental powers Japan was wholly conscious. In these circumstances it was but natural for her to manifest anxiety to a degree unwitnessed either in England or America when the American proposal for a Pacific conference was proclaimed. Westerners were not lacking, however, who appreciated Japan's position, as the following editorial indicates:

Japan's reluctance is easy to understand. Her position as the dominant naval and military Power of the Far East is in many respects uncomfortable. She is very close to the seat of trouble. Passive China and cumbersome Russia have long been and continue to be sources of temptation to rapacious Powers and of danger likewise. Japan has been where she can see very clearly the effect of the contact between the Occidental and the Oriental. The nearness to these problems gives her a special interest in them. Her national safety is involved in them. Her concern at the suggestion that she engage with four other Powers, all of them Occidental, in a discussion of these problems ought to surprise nobody.

What is surprising is that any one should suppose that Japan would jump at the chance to discuss matters vital to her with nations to which they are not in the same sense vital. Americans ought to appreciate this well.[34]

At any rate, Japan's hesitation was only temporary and as soon as she discovered the nature and scope of the proposed Pacific Conference, she heartily accepted the American invitation. The formal invitation of President Harding was issued on August 11, 1921:

The President is deeply gratified at the cordial response to his suggestion that there should be a Conference on the subject of Limitation of Armament, in connection with which Pacific and Far Eastern questions should also be discussed.

[34] "Disarmament and the Far East," *The Outlook*, July 27, 1921, pp. 501–2.

Productive labor is staggering under an economic burden too heavy to be borne unless the present vast public expenditures are greatly reduced. It is idle to look for stability, or the assurance of social justice, or the security of peace, while wasteful and unproductive outlays deprive effort of its just reward and defeat the reasonable expectation of progress. The enormous disbursements in the rivalries of armaments manifestly constitute the greater part of the encumbrance upon enterprise and national prosperity; and avoidable or extravagant expense of this nature is not only without economic justification but is a constant menace to the peace of the world rather than an assurance of its preservation. Yet there would seem to be no ground to expect the halting of these increasing outlays unless the Powers most largely concerned find a satisfactory basis for an agreement to effect their limitation. The time is believed to be opportune for these Powers to approach this subject directly and in conference; and while, in the discussion of limitation of armament, the question of naval armament may naturally have first place, it has been thought best not to exclude questions pertaining to other armament, to the end that all practicable measures of relief may have appropriate consideration. It may also be found advisable to formulate proposals by which in the interest of humanity the use of new agencies of warfare may be suitably controlled.

It is, however, quite clear that there can be no final assurance of the peace of the world in the absence of the desire for peace, and the prospect of reduced armaments is not a hopeful one unless this desire finds expression in a practical effort to remove the causes of misunderstanding and to seek ground for agreement as to principles and their application. It is the earnest wish of this Government that through an interchange of views with the facilities afforded by a Conference, it may be possible to find a solution of Pacific and Far Eastern problems, of unquestionable importance at this time; that is, such common understandings with respect to matters which have been and are of international concern as may serve to promote enduring friendship among our peoples.

It is not the purpose of this Government to attempt to define the scope of the discussion in relation to the Pacific and Far East, but rather to leave this to be the subject of suggestions to be exchanged before the meeting of the Conference, in the expectation that the spirit of friendship and a cordial appreciation of the importance of the elimination of sources of controversy will govern the final decision.

Accordingly, in pursuance of the proposal which has been made, and in the light of the gracious indication of its acceptance, the President invites the Government of Japan to participate in a Conference on the subject of Limitation of Armament, in connection with which Pacific and Far Eastern questions will also be discussed, to be held in Washington on the 11th day of November, 1921.[35]

An identical invitation was addressed to France, to Italy, and to Great Britain. Moreover, under the same date a similar note with the exception of the second paragraph was sent to China. The remaining three nations, however, were not invited until October 4. These various nations signified their acceptance between August 15 and October 19. Such then were the preliminaries of the Washington Conference.

[35] *Conference on the Limitation of Armament, Washington, November 12, 1921—February 6, 1922* [*Conférence de la Limitation des Armements, Washington, 12 Novembre 1921—6 Février 1922*], Vol. I, pp. 4, 6; hereafter cited as *Official Record*, I.

CHAPTER II

THE CONFERENCE MACHINERY

Before we take up the work of the conference, its organization, procedure, personnel, and program should be briefly described. The aims of the Washington Conference were indicated in general terms in the American invitation; namely, to bring about a limitation of armaments on the part of the five Principal Allied and Associated Powers, and to solve the Pacific and Far Eastern problems by concerted efforts on the part of the nine participating nations. The conference was provided with a definite agenda for which a tentative suggestion was submitted by the American Government as early as September 10. This agenda included the following items, and was adopted by the conference with only the qualification that new questions might be introduced, should that be deemed advisable:

LIMITATION OF ARMAMENT

I. Limitation of Naval Armament, under which shall be discussed:
   a) Basis of limitation
   b) Extent
   c) Fulfillment
II. Rules for control of new agencies of warfare
III. Limitation of land armament

PACIFIC AND FAR EASTERN QUESTIONS

I. Questions relating to China
  1. Principles to be applied
  2. Application
     a) Territorial integrity
     b) Administrative integrity
     c) Open door—equality of economic and industrial opportunity

   d) Concessions, monopolies, or preferential economic privileges
   e) Development of railways, including plans relating to Chinese Eastern Railway
   f) Preferential railroad rates
   g) Status of existing commitments
 II. Siberia
   [Similar headings]
 III. Mandated Islands
   [Except questions earlier settled]

ELECTRICAL COMMUNICATIONS IN THE PACIFIC

Under the heading of "Status of existing commitments" it is expected that opportunity will be afforded to consider and to reach an understanding with respect to unsettled questions involving the nature and scope of commitments under which claims of rights may hereafter be asserted.[1]

The nature and scope of the agenda make it obvious that the Washington Conference was in reality composed of two distinct conferences each with its special tasks; and its organization was effected accordingly.

The machinery of the conferences may next be described in some detail. The inaugural session, November 12, 1921, was presided over by Mr. Hughes and was open to the public. The President of the United States welcomed the conferees with an address. At the close of this speech, Mr. Hughes was elected permanent chairman of the conference. Thereupon he presented his memorable scheme for limiting naval armaments. At the end of his speech, he nominated Mr. John W. Garret for the position of Secretary-General. His election followed by a unanimous vote. This open session was followed by six similar ones during the conference. These sessions were

[1] *Official Record,* I, 10.

hailed as a mark of complete departure from obsolete, secret diplomacy: "The period of open diplomacy was ushered in." "The people's diplomacy was substituted for diplomacy by diplomats." "Nothing was to be kept secret from the public." These open sessions were held for the purpose of acquainting the public with the general progress of the conference work by presenting, more or less oratorically, a survey of the things accomplished. These open sessions proved to be interesting, and instructive as well as entertaining to the public. The people welcomed them. Thus, they added to the popularity of the Washington Conference.

First, as to the conference on Limitation of Armament. The organization of the conference began on November 14. The Committee on Program and Procedure was formed, composed of the senior delegates of the five nations. That committee met and fixed the rules of procedure, the method of organizing various committees which the development of the conference might necessitate, and the manner and means of keeping records of various meetings as well as of making public such parts of the records as might be deemed advisable. When that was done, this committee was automatically dissolved, but the Committee of Senior Delegates came into being. This committee constituted the chief directing and controlling board of the conference. On the 19th it created a Subcommittee of Naval Experts to examine and report on the American proposals. On the previous day the Committee of the Whole, composed of all the delegates of the five nations, had been organized. This committee by reason of its large membership was confined to the work of listening to, examining, amending, and rejecting or accepting such reports as were presented to it by the various subordinate committees. It was the exclusive plenary session of the delegates.

On November 19 Mr. Hughes asked Mr. Balfour and Baron Kato to meet him informally at his office in the State Department. The purpose was to go over the American proposals. These three men continued to meet informally and soon became known as the "Big Three" of the conference. Probably they had the most difficult tasks to perform. They struggled day after day with such questions as an agreement on the ratio of capital ships. On December 15 the "Big Three," after a month's arduous work, emerged with a provisional agreement on the 5-5-3 ratio of capital ships as well as an agreement upon the maintenance of the *status quo* on certain fortifications and naval bases in the Pacific region. At their first meeting Baron Kato suggested that the naval experts of the three nations should be given an opportunity to examine the technical aspects of the American scheme. This was agreed upon, and on the same afternoon a Subcommittee of Naval Experts of America, Great Britain, and Japan was organized. Its function was to examine and report to the "Big Three" on the technical aspects of the American plan for limitation. It was given no authority to pass judgment upon matters of policy. The experts were to be advisers and nothing more.

The Committee of Naval Experts examined the American proposals, and, as might be easily anticipated, it was unable to reach any agreement. However, the members separately reported to their respective delegates. The "Big Three" were in no way affected by these reports.

On December 15 another committee was created and was called the Committee of Fifteen from the fact that in this committee the senior delegate of each nation was aided by two naval experts. It continued the work of the "Big Three" and attempted to obtain the consent of France and Italy upon the ratio of capital ships assigned to them by the American proposals. At the committee's fourth meeting (on the 20th) France offered a conditional acceptance.

On the 22d the so-called Joint Committee came into being. It was composed of all the delegates of the participating nations plus two naval experts for each delegation. The Joint Committee took up the question of abolishing submarines, and the question of limiting auxiliary craft, airplane carriers, etc. On the 28th the Subcommittee of Aviation was created to study and report on what could be done in regard to aeroplanes. On January 2, 1922, the Committee of Naval Experts was joined by a committee of legal authorities and was named the Committee of Naval and Legal Experts. Its function was to study the details of matters upon which provisional agreements had been secured. It also undertook the work of drafting treaties, resolutions, etc. Then on the 10th the Committee of Senior Delegates resumed its meeting for the purpose of examining and passing upon the provisional drafts as well as of discussing the uncompleted parts of the treaty. It continued this work until the results were ready to be presented to the Committee of the Whole.

Thus there were instituted ten committees and subcommittees exclusive of the plenary session. They are indicative of the complicated character of the tasks which were before the Arms Conference. The minutes contained in the *Official Record* already referred to are only those of the Committee of the Whole, the Committee of Fifteen, and the Joint Committee, and thus do not give full evidence of the work of the Arms Conference.

The Conference on the Far Eastern and Pacific Problems was similarly organized into several committees. On November 14 the Committee on Program and Procedure composed of the Senior Delegates of the nine nations came into being. It performed a similar function to the one in the Arms Conference and was dissolved as soon as its work was done. The Committee of the Whole and the Committee of the Senior Delegates were created on the 16th. In addition the following subcommittees were formed: on foreign post offices in China (26th); on extraterritoriality in China (28th); on Chinese tariffs (29th); and, lastly, Draft Committee (December 3).

It is not necessary to mention the details of the work of these committees, inasmuch as their names indicate the nature, scope, and character of their tasks. It should be clearly stated, however, that the Committee of the Whole of this conference met very regularly and achieved the main part of the work.

The reason why this was possible is very simple. The attention of this conference was practically confined to the problems of China, and in the solution of these all the participating nations were similarly interested. The question of Yap, however, concerned only the United States and Japan. The question of evacuating Siberia was solvable by Japan alone. It may be mentioned here in passing that Japan and China reached an agreement on the Shantung question at this time, but not as a part of the conference discussion, and that the United States and Japan also negotiated on the question of Yap, reaching an agreement immediately following the conference.

Such then was the machinery of the conferences.

The Washington Conference is said to have been characterized by people's diplomacy, informality, and open diplomacy hitherto unknown in the history of international relations. The plenary sessions in connection with the Washington gathering were responsible for this outburst of enthusiasm. But the idea of plenary sessions did not originate with the Washington Conference. These open sessions are now a part of all the modern international gatherings of larger scope. Except those of the Supreme Council, the meetings of the League of Nations have been and will be in part open to the public. Nor have the galleries been silent onlookers. The public now participates in all international gatherings wherever and whenever these are convoked. Thus the plenary sessions in connection with the Washington Conference were not unique in character. They were a response to a universal demand of the modern public. The public likes to see and hear the "big" men of the world.

As to the alleged substitution of people's diplomacy for diplomats' diplomacy, the writer has carefully checked up the career of every delegate at the conference, and he is obliged to conclude that the delegates were very largely chosen from among the diplomats and statesmen prominent in the executive branches of their respective governments. A very few were, indeed, strictly members of legislatures or of the judiciary. The personnel of the Washington gathering does not show any marked departure from the character of previous international assemblies. The conference was pre-eminently one of diplomats.[2]

As a conspicuous example of informality, the happenings at the first plenary session are often cited. According to the official program for the day, President Harding

[2] A brief description of the official positions held by the delegates is given in *Document,* pp. 21–36.

and Secretary Hughes alone were to speak, and no responses were to be made by foreign delegates. But when Mr. Hughes closed his memorable speech embodying the American proposals for limiting naval armament, the galleries cried out, "Briand." So the French Premier, a veteran speech-maker, responded to the call. When he sat down, the cry came, "Japan." Prince Tokugawa answered with a prepared speech. The cry continued until all the nations represented there spoke. Speaking of Balfour in this connection, an American journalist wrote, "I am sure it has not lain in his [forty years'] experience to sit publicly in an international assemblage to consider the peace of the world where the public galleries participated to the extent of interrupting the fixed program by calling aloud and by name upon the foreign delegates to make impromptu addresses, and cheering them heartily when they sat down."[3] But the speeches made were not "impromptu"; they had been carefully prepared to fit the occasion, for contrary to the journalist's imagination, the foreign delegates, one and all, were quite at home in informal America.

The social functions at Washington were far from being informal. The official invitations often requested the guests to appear in their official uniforms. Gold-braided uniforms and decorations were abundantly utilized at informal Washington, though the practice has been largely given up even in old countries.

Such expressions as "open diplomacy," "people's diplomacy," "informal diplomacy," are yet to be defined. But from what has been said in connection with the description of the machinery of the conferences, it ought to be

[3] E. G. Lowry in the *Philadelphia Public Ledger,* November 20, 1921.

tolerably clear that with the exception of the plenary sessions none of the meetings of the committees was open to the public, not even to the members of the delegations unless they were properly designated as members of such committees. Not only that, but many of the meetings are without minutes and some of these unrecorded meetings were very important. Furthermore, in no case were verbatim records permitted to be kept of the remarks of the various speakers in order to facilitate "free and frank" discussions. Thus even when the minutes were kept, they were more or less edited by the speakers themselves. Perhaps it is nearer to the truth to say that drafts were written out afterward by the speakers. The communiqués issued for the press were confined absolutely to those meetings on which minutes were officially kept, and these were always carefully edited. Very often they were abridged notes of the minutes, but with important omissions. Thus the official records render but an incomplete story of the work of the conferences, still less the communiqués. Besides, remarks, when printed even exactly as they were, will not always convey the proper emphasis made at the time they were spoken.

However, a unique practice was introduced at Washington as regards the treatment of the newspaper correspondents. At first, the delegates made special efforts to meet members of the press and talked to them rather freely but, of course, within the scope agreed upon among the conferees. It soon developed that these private individual interviews had to be given up, for there were more than four hundred correspondents present at Washington seeking "stories." The "group" interviews were substituted. Each delegation maintained an office for this purpose, and regularly gave interviews on the progress of the conference. The delegates allowed themselves to be questioned on any subject, though they were not able always to answer. These frequent contacts resulted in a close personal relationship between the newspapermen and the conferees. It was by these interviews that the delegates became evaluated among the journalists, and popularity of individual delegates was largely determined by the judgment rendered by the press.

CHAPTER III

THE AMERICAN PROPOSAL: A GREAT DIPLOMATIC ADVENTURE

It was on November 12, 1921, that the Washington Conference was inaugurated. The session was held in the spacious, simple, but beautiful room of the Daughters of the American Revolution Building; its white panels shone brilliantly, the more so because they were left unrelieved by colorful decoration. Aside from the portraits of George and Martha Washington, the national emblems of the powers attending the conference alone were displayed, and these very appropriately at the head of the hall, against a background of rich green ornamental plants. The delegates sat around green-covered tables forming an open square in the center of the floor. The seats immediately back of those around the square were assigned to other members of the delegations, arranged according to nationality, while the seats behind these were filled with members of the press. The boxes were occupied by ladies of prominent American officials and of the diplomatic corps. The galleries too were packed to capacity by members of Congress and other guests. The air was serene. Peace and tranquillity reigned as a prayer was offered.

Then President Harding extended his official welcome to the delegations in an address concluding with the following words:

I can speak officially only for the United States. Our hundred millions frankly want less of armament and none of war. Wholly free from guile, sure in our own minds that we harbor no unworthy designs, we accredit the world with the same good intent. So I welcome you, not alone in good will and high purpose, but with high faith. We are met for a service to mankind. In all simplicity, in all honesty and all honor, there may be written here the avowals of a world conscience refined by the consuming fires of war, and made more sensitive by the anxious aftermath. I hope for that understanding which will emphasize the guaranties of peace, and for commitments to less burdens and a better order which will tranquilize the world. In such an accomplishment there will be added glory to your flags and ours, and the rejoicing of mankind will make the transcending music of all succeeding time.[1]

These soothing words were soon turned into realities when Mr. Hughes laid down a bold plan for sweeping reduction of naval armaments. It electrified the calm session; some were shocked, some were even alarmed, but others were pleased. It made the day a memorable one in history. The scheme called, among other things, for the scrapping, by the United States, Great Britain, and Japan, of sixty-six battleships existing and in course of construction, aggregating 1,876,000 tons.

To be more specific, the American proposals involved several important matters. The first and foremost of these related to the abandonment by the three naval powers of their capital-ship building programs then in contemplation, and the scrapping of their capital ships just launched or in course of construction, as well as certain of their older ships. Under this plan the United States was to scrap 9 battleships (two of these just launched), 6 battle cruisers in course of construction, and 15 old battleships. In other words, she was to scrap 30 (new and old) ships with a total tonnage of 845,740. Great Britain was to abandon the 4 new "Hoods" not yet laid down, but upon which money had been spent. The tonnage of these four ships, if completed, would have amounted approximately to 170,000. She was to scrap, in addition, 19 older battleships, with an aggregate of 411,374 tons, or a grand total

[1] *Document,* p. 40.

of 581,375 tons. Japan was to abandon her contemplated program of 4 battleships and 4 battle cruisers. She was to scrap 3 new capital ships, one just launched and two in course of construction, and 4 battle cruisers, two in course of construction and two not yet laid down, but upon which certain material had been assembled. In addition, 10 older ships were to be scrapped. Japan was therefore to abandon or scrap, in all, 17 ships, with an aggregate of 448,928 tons.

Thus these three powers were to reduce their capital-ship strength by scrapping, in all, 66 ships with an aggregate of 1,876,043 tons.[2] Moreover, the scrapping of these ships was to be completed within three months after the date of agreement. However, neither France nor Italy was required by the American plan to scrap any of its capital ships. If these proposals were agreed to, the United States would have in service 18 capital ships with a total of 500,650 tons, Great Britain 20 ships with 604,450 tons, and Japan 10 ships with 299,750 tons, while France would have her existing 10 capital ships with 221,170 tons and Italy her 10 ships with 182,800 tons.[3]

The second proposal concerned replacement tonnage of capital ships and related matters. Replacement was to be limited to a maximum of capital-ship tonnage for the various powers as follows: for the United States and Great Britain, 500,000 tons each; for Japan, 300,000 tons; and for France and Italy, 175,000 tons each. But no new

[2] Note that these 66 ships include 2 Japanese battle cruisers not yet laid down, but not 4 British "Hoods" likewise not yet laid down, and that the aggregate tonnage given includes the 170,000 tons assigned to the "Hoods." In reality therefore these 66 ships possessed a total of 1,706,043 instead of 1,876,043. See also Appendix I.

[3] See further, Appendix I, pp. 353–54, and for the French and Italian ships see Appendix III, pp. 371–72.

ship was to be built during the life of the agreement, viz., for ten years, the proposed "naval holiday." Capital ships twenty years old might be replaced by new ones, whose keels, however, were not to be laid until the ships were seventeen years old, provided such construction did not lie within the "holiday." Moreover, no new capital ships whose displacement tonnage exceeded 35,000 tons were to be built. In other words, this second proposal fixed the ratio of replacement for capital ships at 5 each for the United States and Great Britain, 3 for Japan, and 1.75 each for France and Italy. It declared a naval holiday for ten years, and limited the maximum size of individual capital ships to be built at 35,000 tons.

On the basis of this capital-ship ratio, the third of the American proposals planned reduction of auxiliary combatant craft (which were classified as auxiliary surface combatant craft, submarines, airplane carriers and aircraft). But no limitation was effected on these classes, except airplane carriers whose case will be dealt with later, and further details of this third group of the proposals may be omitted.

We will now return to the conference and survey how these bold and drastic proposals impressed the assembly and, in particular, the members of the various delegations.

The foreign delegations were taken completely by surprise. The American proposals were radical in character, and the method of their presentation, if not unusual, was at least contrary to all expectation. It was expected that the inaugural session would proceed no farther than the usual exchange of diplomatic formalities.[4] The world

[4] It was officially pre-arranged that the President of the United States and his Secretary of State alone were to speak on this occasion. Their speeches were expected to be in the nature of a welcome.

seeking relief from the staggering burden was pleasantly shocked. Here is a description of the reception that was given to Mr. Hughes' plan by those who were present at the session:

> When the Secretary really settled down to his job the representatives of foreign Governments shed their air of indifference and became suddenly attentive. They looked at each other with something approaching amazement. . . . . This declaration was greeted with a storm of applause from the members of Congress, which in itself was so unusual a feature of international gatherings that the delegates from both European and Asiatic countries looked with something suggestive of alarm at the statesmen above them, who had risen to their feet and were clapping their hands with resounding force. Mr. Balfour alone appeared to hold to his habitual poise. Premier Briand appeared to find gratification in the statements of the American Foreign Secretary, which he followed in the French text placed before him. There was no discounting the surprise of Prince Tokugawa, Baron Kato, and Baron Shidehara, the delegates from Japan. The Italian, Portuguese, and Belgian envoys appeared to be greatly pleased, if a trifle startled, at the directness with which Mr. Hughes was stating the case.[5]

When the meeting was about to adjourn, the gallery shouted for M. Briand. He rose and said:

> If it is possible to obtain the security which she is entitled to expect, if it is only a question of making sacrifices, France is ready to consent. France has defended her liberty, and, I think, at the same time, the liberty of the world, and, if the necessary precautions are taken in order to insure her life and safety, France, like you, gentlemen, is ready to say, Down Arms![6]

Cries came for Japan, and Prince Tokugawa responded with these words:

[5] Louis Seibold in the *New York Herald,* quoted in *Current History,* December 1921, pp. xii–xiii.

[6] *Document,* p. 51.

THE AMERICAN PROPOSAL

The Japanese Delegation is happy to feel that the Presidency of this important Conference has now been placed in the hands of a statesman who enjoys the respect and confidence of the whole civilized world. All humanity is interested in the great purpose for which this meeting has been called. We are here to compose difficulties—not to create them. We mean seriously to promote true and honest friendship among nations—not to impair it. We propose, not to prescribe terms or to dictate a constitution to a dubious world—but to carry out the plain dictates of common sense. The world needs peace. It calls for political and economic stability. And to co-operate with the Powers here so worthily represented for the accomplishment of such a lofty end, under the guidance of the distinguished Presiding Officer, will be for Japan a source of the greatest pleasure.[7]

Cries continued until the representatives of all the participating nations had spoken. But none touched directly upon the proposed plan. Nevertheless that same afternoon the foreign delegations gave out their views on the American proposals. Mr. Balfour was quoted as saying that "it was a bold and statesmanlike utterance, pregnant with infinite possibilities. I am most hopeful of results."[8] Baron Kato characterized the American scheme as "a most concrete and logical plan," and said, "I am glad to accept it, in principle, as a basis of discussion."[9] M. Briand was reported as saying, "Mr. Hughes faces the problem with a great courage and nails the parley down to business."[10] A "symposium" of American Congressmen's views gave an almost unqualified approval to the scheme.[11]

[7] *Ibid.*, pp. 51–52.

[8] J. W. Griggs, in the *New York World*, November 13, 1921.

[9] The writer's notes in the press interviews, November 12, 1921. Hereafter cited as "Notes."

[10] R. Courtney, in the *New York Herald*, November 12, 1921.

[11] See the *New York Times* and the *Philadelphia Public Ledger*, November 13, 1921.

On the 13th the Japanese delegates gave a reception to the newspaper correspondents, and on that occasion Baron Kato said:

The costs of armament have now become so heavy that they are a burden hampering productive activity throughout the world, and Japan, like other countries, rejoices at the prospect of relief that is now offered. The limit of reduction to which Japan will go is marked only by the necessities of her security. With that security provided, she is prepared to agree to whatever limitations are acceptable to the other naval powers. Up to the present Japan has had fears which have caused her to continue building. Her government and people had hoped that the conclusion of the Great War would bring a cessation of construction, but as the United States, with her unassailable position, deemed it necessary to continue her naval development, no alternative was permitted to Japan.

It has never been the policy or intention of Japan to attempt to rival the two greatest navies of the world. Our program has always been defensive and must continue to be such. We long for a complete understanding that will terminate distrust and suspicion, and we shall strive at this Conference for an agreement on the limitation of navies so that we need fear no longer. Assurance from us is unnecessary; the great distance that lies between our shores and those of America, and the supremacy of the United States in wealth, size, and resources, make needless any words that we could pledge.[12]

These utterances reflect the immediate general reactions toward the American plan.

The official responses, however, were not made until the 15th when the conference sat at its second plenary session. Mr. Balfour was the first to rise. He began by saying that statesmen of all countries were beginning to discover that the problems of peace required almost as great qualities as were demanded for the conduct of a suc-

[12] Notes.

cessful war. These statesmen were interested in restoring the world to a condition of equilibrium. He congratulated Mr. Hughes for his armament limitation proposals, characterizing them as adding a new anniversary henceforth to be celebrated in connection with the Armistice. Mr. Balfour counted himself among the fortunate of the earth in that he was present and had a share in the proceedings of the inaugural session. They were memorable indeed. The secret was admirably kept. He hoped that all the secrets, so long as they ought to be secret, of the discussion would be as well kept. He thought that Mr. Hughes' speech was eloquent and appropriate, in every way a fitting prelude to the work of the conference which had been opened by the American President.

Touching upon the naval situation in general, Mr. Balfour continued by stating that the nation he represented was more profoundly concerned with all that touched matters naval than it was possible for any other nation to be, and this not for any reasons of ambition, not for any reasons drawn from history or tradition, but from the hard brutal necessities of plain and obvious facts. He then faced the American audience, and called their attention to the relative position of their country and his own with these words, "You are wholly immune from the particular perils to which, from the nature of the case, the British Empire is subject." After these preliminary remarks, he spoke on the American plan as follows:

> We have had to consider, and we have considered, the great scheme laid before you by our Chairman. We have considered it with admiration and approval. We agree with it in spirit and in principle. We look to it as being the basis of the greatest reform in the matter of armament and preparation for war that has ever been conceived or carried out by the courage and patriotism of statesmen. I do not pretend, of course—it would be

folly to pretend—that this or any other scheme, by whatever genius it may have been contrived, can deal with every subject; can cover the whole ground of international reconstruction. It would be folly to make the attempt and it would be folly to pretend that the attempt has yet been made in any single scheme, as was clearly explained by the Secretary of State on Saturday. The scheme deals, and deals only, with three nations which own the largest fleets at present in the world. It therefore, of necessity, omits all consideration for the time being of those European nations who have diminished their fleets, and who at present have no desire, and I hope never will have any desire, to own fleets beyond the necessities that national honor and national defense require.

Again, it does not touch a question which every man coming from Europe must feel to be a question of immense and almost paramount importance. I mean the heavy burden of land armaments. That is left to one side, to be dealt with by other schemes and in other ways.

I think it would be ill-fitting on such an occasion as this if I were to attempt to go into any details. There are questions—and I have no doubt that the Secretary of State, our Chairman, would be the first to tell us that there are details—which can only be adequately dealt with in committee. At the first glance, for example, and I give it merely as an example, our experts are inclined to think that perhaps too large an amount of tonnage has been permitted for submarines.[13]

Baron Kato, the next speaker, presented the official view of the Japanese Government:

Japan deeply appreciates the sincerity of purpose evident in the plan of the American Government for the limitation of armament. She is satisfied that the proposed plan will materially relieve the nations of wasteful expenditures and cannot fail to make for the peace of the world.

She cannot remain unmoved by the high aims which have actuated the American project. Gladly accepting, therefore, the

[13] *Document,* pp. 66–70.

proposal in principle, Japan is ready to proceed with determination to a sweeping reduction in her naval armament.

It will be universally admitted that a nation must be provided with such armaments as are essential to its security. This requirement must be fully weighed in the examination of the plan. With this requirement in view, certain modifications will be proposed with regard to the tonnage basis for replacement of the various classes of vessels. This subject should be referred to special consideration by naval experts. When such modifications are proposed, I know that the American and other delegations will consider them with the same desire to meet our ideas as we have to meet theirs.

Japan has never claimed or had any intention of claiming to have a general establishment equal in strength to that of either the United States or the British Empire. Her existing plan will show conclusively that she never had in view preparations for offensive war.[14]

M. Schanzer of Italy followed Baron Kato, and spoke at length, but what he said can be summed up in these words: "We only wish to express in a general way, in the name of the Italian Delegation, our great satisfaction with the proposals."[15]

As we introduce the last speaker, M. Briand, the reader should recall the remarks made in the first chapter, concerning French sentiment toward the British. The French delegates availed themselves of every opportunity to acquaint the conference with their hostile feeling toward Britain. So on this occasion M. Briand began his remarks by sarcastically referring to Mr. Balfour's speech.[16] On the other hand, he uttered with his masterful oratory profuse epithets in praise of Mr. Hughes. But in respect to the American plan, he was rather vague. He merely said:

[14] *Ibid.*, pp. 70–71.
[15] *Ibid.*, p. 71.
[16] See *ibid.*, pp. 72–73.

I, for my part, have noted the broad-minded and complete adherence in principle, by Great Britain and Japan, to the proposals of the American Government. But this does not mean that in the naval question France has nothing at stake. At the proper time, we shall have the opportunity of stating what we have already accomplished. We shall set forth in figures how, as a consequence of the war, our navy is today reduced to proportions quite inadequate for the defense of our national interests and geographical position.[17]

Such were the declarations of the foreign delegates, and these were widely commented upon by the journalists. The American impression may be seen from the following:

The utterances of the spokesmen of Great Britain, France, Japan, and Italy were not only in complete harmony with the principle of the American proposal for limitation of armament, but were even more important in their unmistakable fraternalism. There was a true meeting of national wills, and a cordial interchange of national feelings.

Any critic can find material in these utterances, if he wishes to pick flaws and carp at the spirit which moves the conference. It may be said truly, for example, that no nation has unconditionally accepted the American proposal. It may be added that suggestions are beginning to multiply, indicating that the proposal will probably be amended in some respects. Novel alternatives are coming out of formal and informal discussions. But no critic can truthfully show that the spirit of the British Empire, as expressed by Mr. Balfour, is not in harmony with the spirit of the United States, as expressed by Mr. Hughes; or that the spirits of France and Japan, each jealously watching national interests, are antagonistic to the proposal now under consideration. The simple truth is that each nation's representatives are supporting the purpose of the American plan and endeavoring to study out how the plan can be adopted without imperiling the national security. The desire of all is to see how far they can go

[17] *Document,* p. 73.

THE AMERICAN PROPOSAL

toward executing the plan, not how little they can do in that direction.[18]

One thing was absolutely certain. All the delegations agreed, "in principle," to accept the American scheme as the "basis of discussion." What these words in quotation meant will be made clear, it is hoped, in the following pages.

[18] Editorial, *Washington Post,* November 16, 1921.

CHAPTER IV

THE "BIG THREE" ON CAPITAL-SHIP RATIO

The most important task before the Washington Conference was to effect an agreement on the ratio of capital ships, the backbone of the fleet; America's proposed solution involved a sweeping reduction on the part of the United States, Great Britain, and Japan. These three powers would have to destroy many tons of their capital ships in order that the desired ratio might be established, while no such sacrifice was required of France or Italy. In other words, an agreement between the three great naval powers was of foremost importance; and, for this reason, Mr. Hughes asked, on November 19, Mr. Balfour and Baron Kato to meet him informally. Thus the "Big Three" commenced the difficult task which was not completed until December 15 when a provisional agreement was reached on the ratio of capital ships according to the American plan, namely, on the basis of 5-5-3. But, as a condition of her acceptance of the proposed ratio, Japan demanded an agreement for the maintenance of the *status quo* on the more important Pacific fortifications and naval bases, and for permission to substitute the "Settsu" for the "Mutsu." The admission of the second of the Japanese demands required proper compensation to the American and British navies. In this connection a special difficulty arose over the British desire to build two "Super-Hoods" of about 50,000 tons each. The American proposals it will be recalled contained a provision limiting the maximum size of capital ships to 35,000 tons. The seriousness of all these problems can be easily surmised from the fact that the "Big Three" spent nearly a month before they were able to bring their task to a harmonious conclusion. It was thought absolutely necessary to settle these problems before other matters of armament limitation could be taken up. In view of the importance attached to the solution of the ratio problem, it is proposed now to analyze the processes through which the agreement was finally achieved.

The negotiations were conducted through more than twenty informal interviews. The first of these was held on November 19, and the last on December 15. At the first meeting Mr. Hughes urged that the world was expecting a quick result, and he thought that the work necessary could be facilitated by informal discussions by the chief delegates of the three nations which were vitally concerned with the problems of limiting naval armaments. Of these problems, the most important was an agreement on the ratio of capital ships of the three greatest navies. He was exceedingly anxious to learn how the British Empire and Japan regarded the American proposal on that particular point. Baron Kato replied that what Mr. Hughes had suggested in regard to the method of negotiations was excellent and he was glad to accept it, if agreeable to Mr. Balfour. The British delegate concurred. Baron Kato then proposed that naval experts of the three nations be given an opportunity to examine the technical aspects of the American plan. This was agreed to by the American and British colleagues. It was understood that the naval experts were in no way authorized to pass judgment upon matters of policy. Their function was merely to examine the technical points in the plan and to report their views to the delegates.

On November 19 Admiral Coontz and Captain Pratt of the United States, Admiral Beatty and Rear-Admiral Chatfield of the British Empire, and Vice-Admiral Kato and Captain Uyeda of Japan were designated to form this subcommittee of experts. As might be easily anticipated these experts failed to agree. On the 28th Vice-Admiral Kato made a public statement:

> Owing to her geographical situation and to her peculiar national conditions, the imperative need of a navy is recognized by Japan in no less degree than by any other country; but Japan has resolved not to possess armaments in excess of the minimum strength for the bare necessity of insuring her national security. Japan is unable to accept the ratio of 60 per cent, because she considers it impossible to provide for her security and defense with any force less than 70 per cent. She desires to have the proposed ratio modified so that the relative strength of the three navies will be 10-10-7.

This deadlock between the Japanese and the American naval experts was looked upon as a very serious matter in journalistic circles.[1] Pessimism began to be manifest. But one Japanese journalist expressed the opinion: "there is not the slightest doubt as to the amicable and satisfactory settlement of the naval question."[2] On December 1 Mr. Balfour made a personal call on Baron Kato and expressed his regrets upon the inability of the American and Japanese experts to agree on the question of capital-ship ratio. He inquired of Baron Kato whether he could do anything to reconcile the disagreement so as to find a way to proceed with the work of the conference. Baron Kato replied that he would not obstruct the progress of the conference, but that the proposed ratio created difficulties for him, inasmuch as the ratio of 10-10-7 was not only the desire of his naval experts but also that of the Govern-

---

[1] See especially the newspapers for November 28, 29, 30, and December 1, 1921.

[2] K. K. Kawakami, *Japan's Pacific Policy* (New York, 1922), p. 16.

ment and the people of Japan. In these circumstances, he would not be able to make a satisfactory explanation to them, should he accede to the ratio proposed by the American plan. Moreover, it was highly important to avoid any intimation that he accepted the ratio under the pressure of American opinion, especially in view of the unfortunately strained relations which existed between America and Japan. One of his chief aims in coming to this country was to allay such a situation. Thus he found himself in the midst of great difficulties; but, of course, he was prepared to face all attacks and was ready to shoulder the responsibility. He was not worried about his personal difficulties. Only he was seeking some valid reasons to explain satisfactorily to the Government and the people of Japan, should he decide to accept the proposed ratio. Whereupon Mr. Balfour inquired whether Baron Kato had any definite suggestions upon which he might be able to accept the American ratio. Baron Kato then stated his desire to substitute the "Settsu" for the "Mutsu" and to effect an agreement on Pacific fortifications. Mr. Balfour expressed his appreciation and requested that he might be authorized to approach Mr. Hughes on those matters.

The day following the Balfour-Kato meeting, the "Big Three" met for the first time since the report of the naval experts had been made known to the delegates. Mr. Hughes briefly reviewed the report of disagreement of the experts and concluded that he saw no serious conflict in the disagreement. He then asked Baron Kato if he had any suggestions to offer. Baron Kato replied that movements for limitation of armament had begun to be agitated more vigorously the previous year in Japan and elsewhere. In March 1921, when he had been asked by the Tokyo agent of the Associated Press, "Would Japan give up her Double-Eight Programme, if an international agreement should prove possible?" he had said, "Yes." His attitude had not changed. He still approached the subject with the same spirit of effecting a sweeping reduction. He would do all he could to lead the conference to a successful conclusion.

There appeared, he continued, to be a difference of opinion as regards the definition of "existing naval strength." Of course, there was no universally accepted definition. The position of Japanese naval experts on this point was quite reasonable as he understood it. But to argue on such a technical matter from the technical point of view would get them nowhere. Therefore it was best not to introduce technical arguments. He would say, however, that the ratio of 10-10-7 was the result of a careful study and the Japanese Government and people were convinced that it was a fair ratio. Then referring to the latest addition to the Japanese fleet, Baron Kato said:

A word as to the "Mutsu." She was completed a month ago and is fully equipped and manned. She was commissioned yesterday and has joined the fleet. But according to the American proposal she is in the list of ships to be scrapped. I must have good reasons for scrapping her. I face a situation at once serious and difficult: on one hand, I desire a harmonious conclusion on the limitation; and, on the other hand, I must be equipped with reasons which will enable me to explain to the satisfaction of Japan. So far, I have been unable to find any means whereby mutual satisfaction can be obtained.

However, I said yesterday to Mr. Balfour, should it be possible for the Powers situated in the Pacific, particularly the United States and Japan, to maintain the *status quo* on their Pacific fortifications and naval bases, that would give me a reason to satisfy the Japanese people.

Finally, I must state emphatically to you, Mr. Hughes, that during the past several years the relations between the United

THE "BIG THREE" ON CAPITAL-SHIP RATIO 51

States and Japan were not what they should have been. Since last spring a new tendency has begun to manifest itself for the betterment of the situation. This very happy turn should be in no way changed; on the contrary, everything should be done to promote it. This makes me very anxious. Should I do anything at the conference to create any hostile sentiment in Japan against the United States, that would produce a very bad result. After all, to guard against such a possibility is far more important than anything else.

These are the difficulties I am now facing and I hope that you will help me in finding means to achieve our aims with satisfaction to all.

Mr. Hughes thanked Baron Kato for his candid statement, and, in turn, tried to answer each of the several points brought out by the Japanese delegate. He concluded by promising that the question of fortifications would be considered. Mr. Balfour then exposed the British views by saying that the acceptance of the American proposals made the position of the British Empire most insecure. But he was willing to meet the demand of the world. He should say, too, that Japan's desire for the maintenance of the *status quo* on Pacific fortifications was quite reasonable. She should have a guaranty that no superior navy would take advantage of her.

Baron Kato promised that he would communicate to his Government the views exchanged and would report to his colleagues as soon as he received instructions.

The next meeting was held on December 12. Following is an extract of the substance of Baron Kato's statement:

I received yesterday from my Government instructions on the question of the limitation of armament. There are three specific matters on which I should like to have your kind attention. These are the questions of ratio, of Pacific fortifications, and of the "Mutsu."

The Japanese Government feels that the ratio of 10 to 7 is necessary for the maintenance of national security, and the opinion of Japanese naval experts as regards the method of calculation arriving at the said ratio is in my judgment quite reasonable. But in view of the American and British desire I would consent to the ratio of 10 to 6 as proposed in the American plan.

For that, I would like to obtain from you a clear understanding in regard to the principle of maintaining the *status quo* on the fortifications and naval bases in the Pacific. If those islands are allowed to be fully developed, without restriction, into bases where the entire fleet can be concentrated and properly supplied, I am afraid that the Japanese Government would not be able to allay fear and suspicion of her people. From the Japanese point of view, in expressing her willingness to accept the ratio of 10 to 6, it is impossible to do so independently of the question of fortifications and naval bases. I consider it necessary that these two questions should be dealt with together.

Now, as to the case of the "Mutsu," according to the American proposal this ship is ninety-eight per cent complete and is reckoned in the list of ships under construction. The fact is, however, that she is one hundred per cent complete and should be included in the list of new ships. She was completed toward the end of October and was fully paid for. She is manned and has already cruised 2,500 miles. The American proposal confines ships to be scrapped to those either in the course of construction or old ones. I fail to find any valid reasons for scrapping a new ship already completed. Thus, should the "Mutsu" be included in the list of ships to be scrapped, neither I nor my colleagues can explain this act to the satisfaction of Japan. It is needless to explain to you what an effect the scrapping of a new ship is likely to produce upon the sentiment of the people. Neither is it necessary to explain how the morale of our naval men will be affected when you order the scrapping of the "Mutsu," a full-fledged new member of the fleet.

Now, the American proposal will leave 18 capital ships to the United States, 22 to the British Empire, and 10 to Japan. However, if the "Mutsu" is not scrapped, Japan will have 11 capital ships. But in order to retain the original number of 10 ships assigned to her, Japan will not object to scrapping the "Settsu." [Readers may be interested to learn that Japanese school children had contributed toward the construction of the "Mutsu," a fact which increased the sentimental aspect of the case.]

The first subject taken up was the question of fortifications. Mr. Hughes made it clear at once that he could not consider the case of Hawaii but was able to understand Baron Kato's view on the Philippines and Guam. He was, therefore, prepared to agree to the maintenance of the *status quo* on these latter. He assumed that Japan would do the same as regards her outlying islands. Baron Kato affirmed this view. Mr. Balfour thought so far as Great Britain was concerned the only place in question was Hongkong, which might be considered in Japan's neighborhood. He was prepared to agree to the inclusion of that island in regard to the maintenance of the *status quo*. An agreement was reached, and with it Japan accepted the naval ratio of 10-10-6.

The question of the application of the ratio was next considered, and naturally the question of the "Mutsu" was discussed. Mr. Hughes stated that the American proposals in regard to the application of the ratio had been guided by the principle of proportionate sacrifice. It was thought fair to include the "Mutsu" in the list of ships to be scrapped. He called the attention of his colleagues to the fact that the scheme did not deal with the question of ships constructed versus ships not constructed. America had two ships over ninety per cent completed. The Japanese demand to retain the "Mutsu" and to substitute the "Settsu" involved the naval program. Therefore he was unable to proceed farther with this question until he could discover from his experts what might be done by way of compensation for the American navy in case the

"Mutsu" was allowed to be retained. Mr. Balfour expressed a similar view. However, he remarked that the addition of the "Mutsu," a post-Jutland capital ship, affected Great Britain. She was relatively strong in pre-Jutland capital ships much worn by four years of war service; she was weak in post-Jutland ships. Consequently Great Britain would have to build if the "Mutsu" were retained. Mr. Hughes continued the debate. He understood that Great Britain had only one post-Jutland ship, the "Hood," which was in reality only partly post-Jutland in character. Japan, on the other hand, had the "Nagato" and some battle cruisers. Under the circumstances, Great Britain would be compelled to build if the "Mutsu" were retained. He asked Baron Kato to consider the fact that the retention of the "Mutsu" would dislocate the whole scheme. In regard to his own Government, he thought it would not be willing to scrap the two ships near completion; it would insist upon the principle of proportionate sacrifice. He reminded his colleagues that this question of the application of the principle was interdependent with the questions of the ratio and the fortifications. But Baron Kato did not give up his desire to retain the "Mutsu." Whereupon Mr. Hughes said it would be necessary to try to re-arrange the American scheme so as to balance the navies on the ratio of 10-10-6, the "Mutsu" being included in the Japanese list.

The interview resulted in two agreements, namely, one on the ratio of capital ships, and another on the maintenance of the *status quo* on fortifications and naval bases. But the question of the application of the ratio remained unsettled.

In a later interview, Mr. Hughes proposed a provisional agreement to accept the substitution of the "Settsu" for the "Mutsu" and added the following as compensation for the American navy: He would keep the "Colorado" and the "Washington" and would scrap the "North Dakota" and the "Delaware." These changes would alter the total tonnage of American capital ships from 500,650 to 525,850, and that of Japanese capital ships from 299,700 to 303,320. In these proposals he aimed to reach a replacement limit of 525,000 tons for the United States and 315,000 tons for Japan, as that would preserve the exact ratio and give America 15 ships and Japan 9 ships, with the maximum limit of 35,000 tons each. This was the American proposal, if Japan desired to retain the "Mutsu" and to scrap the "Settsu."

It was Mr. Balfour's turn to state the case for Great Britain. He said that his country had already taken a holiday for five years so far as capital ships were concerned and had laid down none since the close of the war. Consequently she had no complete post-Jutland capital ship, and, as was known to his colleagues, the "Hood" had been designed before the battle of Jutland. Though alterations had been made to embody the lessons of this engagement, she was not by any means the ship which would have been built if the design had been made after it. That was the original difficulty of the British delegation. This was made worse now by the retention of the "Mutsu." Japan would possess two post-Jutland capital ships, and the United States by her new proposal would have three such ships. Consequently, Great Britain now had to do something to reach equality with the American navy. Two new ships, embodying all the lessons of Jutland, had been designed at considerable cost. A good deal of material had been collected, contracts had been placed, and the contractors had carried out the necessary changes in their plant to build the ships. Hence the proper way in which to meet the proposals in regard to the American and Japanese navies was for Great Britain to complete these two ships, but for this she would scrap more than two of her older ships.

The two ships which the British proposed to build were to be "Super-Hoods" of about 50,000 tons each. This fact created a new problem for the "Big Three," because the original American plan had contained a provision to limit the maximum size of capital ships to 35,000 tons. In this connection Mr. Hughes pointed out that the "Mutsu" was finished and the American ships were within a few months of completion. The difference in Great Britain's case was that she would have to build almost from the start. The largest ship which America and Japan would possess would be of less than 35,000 tons, which was the limit proposed in the American plan. The greater the tonnage that was put into the new ships at the top of the list, the larger the tonnage that would have to come off at the end of the list.

Mr. Balfour answered that, owing to the fact that these were ships of an entirely novel type, they had required a great deal of effort in their design. If sacrificed, the whole of that labor would be lost. This was a very serious matter. A year would be lost in making fresh designs and other preliminary work. Meanwhile the United States would be in possession of three post-Jutland ships and Japan of two similar ones. Whatever conclusion might eventually be reached, these were considerations of substance and force. He would admit, however, Mr. Hughes' counter-argument that if Great Britain were to build big ships she would have to sacrifice more than their numerical equivalent.

Mr. Hughes recalled that the new standard aimed at was 525,000 tons for the United States and Great Britain and 315,000 tons for Japan. In working out the original program the figures for Great Britain had resulted in 600,000, of which 100,000 tons had been allowed on account of the greater age of the British ships. If, however, Great Britain was now to have two ships of 43,000 tons (in reality about 50,000 tons), the difficulties would be greater at the time of replacement than if each was willing to be content with ships of 35,000 tons. It was true that Great Britain possessed one "Hood" of 43,000, but she was admittedly not a complete post-Jutland ship, and in fact allowance had been made in the American calculation of her efficiency. But the situation would be changed by the British proposal to build two "Super-Hoods." It would be a great advantage, therefore, if Mr. Balfour could see his way to reduce the tonnage of the proposed ships and thereby eventually save the scrapping of one ship. Thus the debate continued.

Mr. Balfour now proposed to scrap four ships of the "King George V" type, a rough equivalent in tonnage to the two "Super-Hoods." But Mr. Hughes would not accept this. He said that the possession of the two "Super-Hoods" would not entitle Great Britain to enjoy the large excess in tonnage over that of the American navy which had been originally allowed because of the inferior quality of her old ships. But, after an extended debate, the British delegate was able to say that he would have to choose between two ships of 35,000 tons, with a sacrifice of two "King George V" ships, or two "Super-Hoods," with a sacrifice of four "King George V" ships and the "Tiger."

Mr. Hughes took up the first of the two propositions. He said that the two new ships of 35,000 meant a total of 70,000 tons while two "King George V" ships meant a total of 48,000 tons. Consequently, if Great Britain were allowed to carry out this plan, she would not only obtain the advantage of two new ships but also secure an addition of 22,000 tons. This would obviously create a serious problem. He suggested, therefore, that Great Britain scrap four "King George V" ships. The aggregate tonnage of those four ships would be 96,000 and would thus leave Great Britain with 587,000 tons of capital ships as against the 525,000 tons of American ships. This American proposal was finally accepted by the British, though they were allowed to increase the individual tonnage of the two "Super-Hoods" from 35,000 to 37,000. Thus ended the task of the "Big Three" on December 15, producing a provisional agreement on the ratio of capital ships and upon the maintenance of the *status quo* in the Pacific fortifications and naval bases. That was probably the most important of the achievements of the Arms Conference, and, therefore, the text[3] of the agreement is given in full in Appendix II.

This agreement is described as "provisional" because the position of France and Italy had not yet been determined. The important points are as follows: First, the three powers accept the ratio of capital ships on the basis of 5-5-3 as proposed by the original American plan, and agree to the maintenance of the *status quo* with respect to the Pacific fortifications and naval bases, excluding Hawaii, Australia, New Zealand, the islands along the coasts of the United States and Canada, and the islands composing Japan proper. Secondly, Japan is allowed to

[3] Reported to the first meeting of the Subcommittee on Limitation of Armament, held on December 15, 1921, and made public on that day. See *Document,* pp. 252–54.

retain the "Mutsu" and to substitute the "Settsu"; the United States is to complete the "Colorado" and the "Washington," and to scrap the "North Dakota" and the "Delaware"; and Great Britain is to construct two new ships of 35,000 legend tons each, and to scrap four ships of the "King George V" type. Thirdly, the maximum tonnage of individual capital ships to be built is fixed at 35,000 legend tons or the American equivalent of 37,000 tons; and the total replacement tonnage of capital ships allowed is, for the United States and Great Britain, 525,000 each, and for Japan 315,000. Lastly, a naval holiday for ten years is declared. These points in the agreement show that they closely adhere to the original American plan on capital ships, and, with the exception of the fortification provision, lay down a formula to be applied to France and Italy; but the story of how these two nations responded to this tripartite agreement will be our theme in the following chapter.

CHAPTER V

THE *DÉCAPITATION* OF THE FRENCH NAVY

Simultaneously with the attainment of the provisional agreement between the three powers, the so-called Subcommittee of Fifteen[1] was instituted for the purpose of securing French and Italian consent to the ratio of capital ships assigned to their navies by the American plan, namely, 1.75. It was generally known that France would not accept the ratio and that Italy would insist upon a navy equal to that of France. For instance, the Associated Press reported that France would ask for an allotment of 315,000 tons of capital ships, or nearly double the assigned tonnage of 175,000.[2] Such a demand was fully anticipated by the conference before any meeting of the committee was summoned.

When the committee held its first meeting on December 15, Mr. Hughes reported on the tripartite agreement; but before he touched upon it, he was impelled to answer the current rumor that France was bitter because of her exclusion from the meetings of the "Big Three." He called the attention of the committee to the fact that the American plan asked the United States, Great Britain, and Japan alone to make sacrifices, whereas France and Italy were not asked to do so. In other words, the first and foremost problem of the Arms Conference was to effect an agreement among the powers asked to scrap many tons of ships. He then presented the terms of the agreement,

[1] The committee was composed of Mr. Hughes, Colonel Roosevelt, and Admiral Coontz for the United States; Mr. Balfour, Lord Lee, and Admiral Chatfield for Great Britain; MM. Sarraut, Jusserand, and Admiral de Bon for France; MM. Schanzer, Albertini, and Admiral Acton for Italy; and Baron Kato, Admiral Kato, and Captain Uyeda for Japan.

[2] The *Baltimore Sun,* December 15, 1921.

THE "DECAPITATION" OF THE FRENCH NAVY 61

frankly stating, for instance, that the Japanese demand for the retention of the "Mutsu" required readjustments all around but without disturbing the original ratio proposed by the American plan. The importance he attached to this accord may be understood from his statement that he did not think that anything had been done since the Armistice of such importance to the whole world—nothing which meant such relief from financial burdens or held such promise for future peace.[3] He concluded by paying his tribute to his British and Japanese colleagues, saying that the success attained had been due to a remarkable spirit of good will and that the friendly desire on the part of Great Britain and Japan to co-operate had elicited his constant admiration. He had been deeply touched, in all his relations with their delegates, to note the unselfishness, cordiality, and determination with which all had endeavored to reach a successful conclusion.[4]

He called upon the French and Italian representatives for their views on the ratio allotted to them by the American plan. M. Sarraut was the first to respond. He complimented Mr. Hughes relative to his eloquent report on the provisional agreement. He could only express the highest satisfaction in respect to the accord, but France had not participated, before this meeting, in the negotiations on armament limitation, and she had never had the opportunity of exposing her exact condition. The conference, therefore, did not fully realize the needs of France, and for this reason he begged his colleagues to listen to Admiral de Bon.[5]

---

[3] "Subcommittees," *Conference on the Limitation of Armament* (Washington, 1922), p. 10. See further, pp. 4, 6, 8, and 12. Hereafter cited as *Official Record*, II.
[4] *Ibid.*, p. 10. [5] See *ibid.*, p. 12.

The French Admiral delivered a carefully prepared speech which was in the main an introduction to the French views on the whole subject of armament limitation. It, however, contained some specific references to the ratio of capital ships. The more salient points in the speech may be stated as follows: France has a population of 39,000,000 and 60,000,000 in her colonies. She depends, for raw materials, more and more upon her colonies. This means that France must have a navy in accordance with these considerations. At present she has ten capital ships, which she will use as long as they will last; but they will be useless in 1930, and they must be replaced. Suppose the committee allows 220,000 tons of capital ships (the American plan allotted to France the replacement tonnage of 175,000); this will give her too small a number of ships of 35,000 tons each. France is desirous of replacing the existing ten capital ships with ten ships of 35,000 tons each. Below this number she cannot go. Moreover, as her existing ships will become obsolete between 1930 and 1933 or 1934, France will have to begin to replace them before that date.[6]

M. Schanzer of Italy expressed the great satisfaction of the Italian delegation regarding the triple accord and concurred with his colleagues in considering this a great event for all future time. Leaving technical details to his naval expert, he stated the position of Italy, in very precise terms. Two principles must, according to the Italian point of view, govern the solution of the naval problem. First was the principle of parity of the Italian fleet with the French fleet. This principle had been admitted by M. Viviani and M. Briand, and it need not therefore give rise

[6] See *Official Record*, II, 12, 14, 16, and 18.

THE "DECAPITATION" OF THE FRENCH NAVY 63

to discussion. The second principle was the limitation of naval armament to the quantity strictly necessary for a purely defensive policy. The Italian delegation must support this second principle through the necessity of relieving their people of the economic consequences of war.[7] He concluded by saying that, as long as these principles were adhered to, Italy was willing to proceed as far as possible along the lines of the project set forth by the American plan in regard to the naval holiday for capital ships.[8]

Admiral de Bon made it very clear that France desired to possess the right to build 350,000 tons of capital ships at the time of replacement and that her replacement work must begin in 1926 or 1927. Needless to add, both these demands seriously conflicted with the American proposals. The difficulties thus created were complicated by the Italian demands. It appeared that Italy was willing to reduce her navy to any point so long as she was allowed to maintain the principle of parity with France. Leaving aside any attempt at interpreting the Italian diplomacy, it should be noted that her stand made the situation very disagreeable to France. The success or failure of the conference was made absolutely dependent upon what France would be willing to do. She was put on the defensive, and the struggles that ensued between her delegates and the others often ended to her disadvantage. The situation was a severe test of France's pre-conference enthusiasm.

But to return to the French counter-proposals, Mr. Hughes, although he was sympathetic with the aspirations of France, insisted that the entire problem must be considered from the point of view of realities. Thus far the three nations had dealt with the ratio question in a spirit

[7] *Ibid.*, p. 18.
[8] See *ibid.*, pp. 18 and 20.

of conciliation, and the same spirit must continue to guide the discussion of the conference. National pride must be put aside if armament limitation were to be made possible. America was in a position to build any navy she wanted; so were Great Britain and Japan. But these powers, putting aside the beautiful dream of national pride, had agreed to put a stop to competitive construction of ships in order that they might facilitate economic recuperation. Touching upon the French counter-proposals more specifically, he recalled the consideration given by the American plan to the peculiar situation of France. She was not called upon to scrap as the other powers were scrapping. But if France should insist that she should not only not scrap certain ships but should build new ships, as she had suggested, an appropriate recognition of the existence of a special situation would be lacking; it would create an entirely new situation of very serious import.[9] Mr. Hughes also severely criticized the French proposal to begin replacement before the date proposed by the American plan, namely, 1931. He concluded his remarks with the observation that Europe was confronted by a difficult economic situation of which those whom he addressed were better aware than he. He added that no reflection was intended in the use of the word "poverty," for the Allied nations of Europe had become impoverished in the best of causes.[10]

The Italian delegate reminded the conference that Italy had made no proposals concerning new naval construction, and reiterated that Italy fully associated herself with Mr. Hughes' remarks as to the aims to be attained by the conference. He emphatically stated that the conference

[9] *Official Record,* II, 28.
[10] *Ibid.,* p. 30. See also pp. 24, 26, 28, and 32.

THE "DECAPITATION" OF THE FRENCH NAVY 65

had been convoked for the limitation of armament, and, if the Italian delegation, on its return from Washington, were to bring back to its country an increase of armament, it would be confronted with the disapproval of public opinion.[11]

Mr. Balfour, too, concurred in no uncertain terms in the views of the American and Italian delegates. He pointed out to Admiral de Bon that he was in error in regard to the number of capital ships allowed to France under the American plan, namely, five, instead of four as the French Admiral seemed to think. In reply to the French statement that France was at a disadvantage as regards the ratio between the French and other navies because at this time the French navy was depleted, Mr. Balfour pointed out that in 1914 the ratio between the British and French fleets had been 3 to 1. The American plan allotted the ratio of 5 to 1.75. The French Admiral claimed that four capital ships did not constitute a useful unit, but the British delegate replied that the British Mediterranean Squadron consisted of four such ships. He added that the United States of America had proposed to cut down its fleet, and Great Britain and Japan had immediately agreed to follow suit. If the French nation were to take the opposite course, it would cause a repercussion among all the naval powers. Italy could never consent to be left behind; how could she be expected to do so? Hence, if France insisted on maintaining a large navy, Italy would follow suit. Would it stop with Italy? Certainly not. The process would be continued among all the powers.[12]

Thus the French counter-proposals were assailed on

[11] *Ibid.*, p. 32.
[12] *Ibid.*, pp. 38, 40, and 42.

all sides; Japan alone remained discreetly silent. Nevertheless, the French delegates, accepting the challenge, continued to fight. M. Sarraut said that as the head of the French delegation he could not pass unanswered certain criticisms of a political and moral nature by the American and British delegates, for they held serious implications. The first of these was to imply responsibility on the part of France for an attitude which might dislocate the general agreement for the reduction of naval expenditures so as to start again the competition in armaments. Thus there was left the cruel alternative from which she had to choose: should she accept what had been offered her, amounting, as far as she was concerned, to the ruin (*décapitation*) of the French navy? or refuse, and assume the responsibility of having frustrated a great pacific and humanitarian work? This alleged responsibility, he felt, was thrust upon France by the American press campaign of that very morning.

Furthermore, the French people had their responsibilities to the world, to insure order, peace, and tranquillity, as well as to insure the interests of their own nation. It was far from the intention of France to make war on any nation, and that was why she had accepted the principle of parity with Italy, whose colonies were less extensive than those of France.[13] But M. Sarraut offered no modification on the counter-proposals.

Mr. Hughes was profoundly depressed by what the French delegate had said. He regretted too that the American plan should have been characterized by the French colleagues as a "device," something concocted in secret and made to have a pleasant appearance. He could not understand the French suggestion that capital ships

[13] *Official Record,* II, see pp. 46, 48, 50, 52, 54, 56, and 58.

THE "DECAPITATION" OF THE FRENCH NAVY

limited to 175,000 tons amounted to nothing and that it was *décapitation* of the fleet." The proposal was that France should scrap none of her dreadnoughts, while Great Britain, the United States, and Japan were scrapping over forty per cent of their capital ships other than pre-dreadnoughts. The proposal thus involved a direct saving to France of forty per cent of her strength in dreadnoughts as compared with the other powers. This could not be described as "nothing"; it was forty per cent. There seemed to be a feeling expressed with eloquence and fervor that there existed a magic purse and that it was only necessary to conjure up a fleet for national needs, and, presto! a fleet would appear.[14]

At this juncture M. Sarraut reminded the committee that he was awaiting further instructions from his Government. Thus the situation had now reached the point of desperation. There was no hope of reconciling the French demands with the general aims of the conference. Mr. Hughes must have realized this, for, over-riding the French delegates, he instructed the American Ambassador at Paris to approach the French Premier for a favorable decision on the subject. That was done on December 16, and on the 20th he was able to report on the result of these direct negotiations with M. Briand. First, he read the letter that he had sent to M. Briand, which in part was as follows:

You will observe the attitude of France will determine the success or failure of these efforts to reduce the heavy burden of naval armament . . . .
We are entirely willing that France should have the benefit of an increased tonnage which would preclude the necessity of her scrapping her dreadnoughts; that is to say, her present

[14] *Ibid.*, p. 60.

strength in dreadnoughts is about 164,000 tons, and there is not the slightest objection to allowing this and an increase over this, or a total of 175,000 tons, which would be more than 70,000 tons over what she would have on the basis of relative strength as it exists.

If it be said that France desires a greater relative strength, the obvious answer is that this would be impossible of attainment. If such an agreement as we are now proposing were not made, the United States and Great Britain would very shortly have navies of over a million tons, more than 6 to 1 as compared with France, and France would not be in a position to better herself, much less by any possible endeavor to obtain such a relative strength as has been suggested. In short the proposed agreement is tremendously in favor of France by reducing the navies of Powers who not only are able to build but whose ships are actually in course of construction to a basis far more favorable to France than would otherwise be attainable. The proposed agreement really doubles the relative strength of the French Navy.

In these circumstances, I feel that the suggestion that has been made that France should build 10 new capital ships in replacement with a tonnage of 300,000 tons or more suggests a program of such magnitude as to raise the greatest difficulties. In fact, I regret to say that, after canvassing the matter thoroughly and taking the best information I can obtain, I am compelled to conclude that it would not be possible on this basis to carry through the agreement.[15]

M. Briand sent his reply from London on the 18th, which was in part as follows:

You fear that the maintenance of this French request may have as its effect to hinder the agreement between the five Powers.

The will of the French Government is to do everything which is compatible with the care of the vital interests of France with a view to reconcile our points of view.

[15] *Document*, pp. 254–57.

THE "DECAPITATION" OF THE FRENCH NAVY 69

In the question of naval armament, the preoccupation of France is not the offensive point of view but uniquely the defensive point of view.

With regard to the tonnage of capital ships, that is to say, attacking ships, which are the most costly, I have given instructions to our delegates in the sense which you desire. I am certain that I shall be sustained by my Parliament in this view.

But so far as the defensive ships are concerned (light cruisers, torpedo boats, and submarines) it would be impossible for the French Government, without putting itself in contradiction with the vote of the Chambers, to accept reductions corresponding to those which we accept for capital ships under this formal reserve which you will certainly understand.[16]

The French Premier's letter was a source of gratification to Mr. Hughes, for he understood that the words "instructions to our delegates in the sense which you desire" meant that the ratio of capital ships, namely, 175,000 tons for France, should be accepted.[17] But the French delegation objected to this interpretation. Admiral de Bon said that the acceptance of the said ratio was conditioned by the consent, on the part of the other delegations, to the French proposal of commencing the replacements in 1927 and also by an agreement upon all the other problems of naval limitation. Not only that, but he still expressed the desire that France would be allowed six capital ships instead of five. In other words, he still demanded 210,000 tons instead of 175,000 tons.[18] Once more the conference was threatened by an impasse.

Mr. Balfour took up the debate at this point and said that M. Briand's letter could not mean anything but an assent to the American scheme in regard to capital ships

[16] *Ibid.*, p. 257.
[17] *Official Record*, II, 72.
[18] See *ibid.*, pp. 72, 74, 76, and 78.

while it made a specific reserve as to auxiliary craft, light cruisers, torpedo boats, and submarines. This position of the French Premier was satisfactory to him because that was precisely in accord with the British stand. The British Empire had come to the provisional agreement with the United States and Japan as to capital ships but with a reserve in regard to all other classes of craft. That being clearly the case, there was no need for the French delegation to insist upon this reserve as a condition in accepting the ratio of capital ships. Moreover, Admiral de Bon's interpretation clearly indicated that the French acceptance of the ratio was also conditioned on France being permitted to commence her replacement building in 1927. But he understood that M. Briand had accepted the naval holiday proposed by the American plan, which permitted no replacement construction before 1931. Obviously there was disagreement between the letter and the interpretation of it by Admiral de Bon. He, therefore, asked the French delegation to clarify this ambiguity.[19]

Mr. Hughes concurred with the British understanding of the proposals contained in the letter of M. Briand, and reiterated that the conference, at this point, was interested in the ratio question of capital ships. But the position of Admiral de Bon was that the conference had to deal with auxiliary craft, etc., before dealing with capital ships. If this was the case, then it was necessary for the conference to know what was the exact proposal that the French delegation was contemplating in regard to various craft other than capital ships. He begged the French delegation to make a statement to that effect as soon as possible.[20]

[19] *Official Record,* II, 80 and 82.
[20] *Ibid.,* pp. 84 and 86.

Replying to these remarks M. Sarraut said that there was no discrepancy between the terms of his premier's letter to Mr. Hughes and the instructions received by the French delegation. In neither was it stated that the allowance of 175,000 tons was accepted; no mention was made of any figures. The observations of Admiral de Bon were technical conclusions in the spirit of M. Briand's letter. The letter and the instructions clearly showed that the question of capital ships and other craft was absolutely bound together, that is to say, that, before solving the problem of capital ships, indisputable guaranties were imperatively needed in regard to the other component parts of the fleet.[21]

The debate was continued, but without any agreement on the ratio question. As a matter of fact, the committee was forced to abandon, for the time being, the subject. In conclusion of the present chapter, it may be observed that no communiqué for the press was issued. But alert newspapermen guessed what was happening behind the doors, and their papers devoted large space to the French stand, and severely criticized France.[22] It cannot be said whether this public pressure had a wholesome effect upon the progress of the conference, but it certainly made the French delegates very sensitive and more defiant in their general attitude.

[21] *Ibid.*, pp. 86 and 88.

[22] See newspapers between December 17 and 20. Articles were written under titles such as these: "French Naval Ambitions Expected to Bring Crisis in Conference"; "French Demand for 10 Battleships Imperils Holiday Program"; "French Ambitions at Sea Stir British"; "Admiral Ballard Says Demand Might Scrap Treaty"; "French Ire Roused"; "French Naval Plan Unofficial"; "Grave View Taken of French Claim"; "French Angling for Guarantee"; etc.

CHAPTER VI

THE SUBMARINE QUESTION

We have seen in the previous chapter that the capital-ship ratio allotted to France and Italy remained still unsettled; but the discussion of this subject had elicited a good deal of hard feeling and plain speaking, and when the question of submarines was later introduced in the conference a prolonged discussion took place in which the French and British delegates exchanged bitter words. In fact, because of opposition and new demands on the part of the French delegates, the public was soon to learn of other obstacles to the practical application of the fair principles which had been so generously voiced at the second plenary session. The only further thing that the conference accomplished was a treaty relating to the rules governing the use of submarines and the prohibition of the use of poisonous gases. In the following pages we shall survey the views expressed by the various delegations on submarines and discuss the failure of the conference to limit these vessels.

The original American plan proposed to allot 90,000 tons each to the United States and Great Britain, 54,000 tons to Japan, and 35,000 tons each to France and Italy. The British position had been made clear on November 15, when Mr. Balfour said that submarines were a class of vessels most easily abused in their use, one which, in fact, in the late war, had been most grossly abused. He admitted that probably the submarine was the defensive weapon, properly used, of the weak, and that it would be impossible, or, if possible, it might well be thought undesirable, to abolish it altogether. But the amount of submarine tonnage permitted by the new scheme was far in excess, he believed, of the tonnage possessed by any nation at the present moment, and he only threw it out as a suggestion that it might be well worth considering whether that tonnage should not be further limited, and whether, in addition to limiting the amount of tonnage, it might not be practicable, and, if practicable, desirable, to forbid altogether the construction of those submarines of great size which were not intended for defense, which were not the weapon of the weaker party, and the whole purpose of which was attack by methods which civilized nations would regard with horror.[1] In other words, the British delegate, considering the proposed limitation to be insufficient, offered two suggestions: first, to effect a more drastic reduction, and, secondly, to forbid construction of large-sized submarines.

When the subject was brought before the committee on December 22 for discussion, Lord Lee of the British Empire called the attention of the committee to the existing submarine tonnage of the five nations, namely, 83,500 tons for the United States, 80,500 for Great Britain, 32,200 for Japan, 28,300 for France, and 18,500 for Italy. It seemed to him very strange to put before a conference on the limitation of naval armaments proposals designed to foster and increase the type of war vessels which, according to the British view, was open to more objection than surface capital ships. Moreover, it would be a certain consequence, if submarines were retained, that the powers which possessed large mercantile marines would be compelled to increase the numbers of their antisubmarine craft. This would give but little relief to the overburdened taxpayer, and would provide scant comfort to those who wished to abolish war and to make it less

[1] *Document,* p. 68.

inhumane.[2] He therefore reiterated the British desire for their abolition or reduction, and he explained that this desire was not motivated by any selfish reasons on the part of the British Empire. He tried to answer, at this point, the argument for submarines as the legitimate weapon of the weaker powers and an effective and economical means of defense for an extensive coastline and maritime communications, by saying that such argument could be shown to be groundless technically as well as by recent history. He stated that Great Britain possessed one hundred submarines of 80,000 tons total, and she was prepared to scrap them all. He knew, however, that the conference could not be convinced of the British view, and he would, therefore, request the committee to effect a reduction of these undersea vessels. He invited the French delegation, in particular, to expose its views on this subject.[3]

Mr. Hughes took up the criticism directed against the American proposal, and replied that according to the American figures the existing submarine tonnage possessed by the various powers was as follows: the United States, 95,000; Great Britain, 82,464; France, 42,850; Italy, 20,228; and Japan, 31,400. The United States was willing to reduce from 95,000 to 90,000 tons;[4] but obviously this was a weak answer, because by the American scheme Great Britain, Italy, and Japan were allowed to increase their tonnage.

M. Sarraut reviewed the French stand on submarines, covering the international discussions preliminary to the Treaty of Versailles down to the most recent ones in connection with the League of Nations. France held the view that the submarine was the only weapon for a nation not

[2] *Document,* p. 265.   [3] *Ibid.,* pp. 264–69.   [4] *Ibid.,* pp. 269–70.

abundantly supplied with capital ships. For France it was an essential means of preserving her independence. Moreover, as far as abuse was concerned, that might be true of every method of warfare, and there was nothing peculiar about the employment of these vessels. The inhuman and barbarous use made of submarines by a belligerent in the late war was a reason for condemning that belligerent but not for condemning these vessels. They could be used in keeping with the laws of humanity. The French Government would not abolish or reduce its total tonnage or the size of individual craft beyond what it deemed necessary to assure the safety of its territories.[5] This was a plain refusal of both British proposals.

M. Schanzer also disagreed with Lord Lee's characterization of submarines, and insisted that these were necessary to protect the lines of communication of his country. He added that the conference, in which only five powers were represented, could not settle the question of submarines, which concerned many other powers.[6] Japan agreed with both France and Italy, but her delegate insisted upon more vigorous international rules governing the proper use of these vessels.[7]

Whereupon Mr. Hughes summarized the views of the various delegations and said that, as had been indicated by the remarks of the delegates, he thought that all could not fail to be deeply impressed by the statement of Lord Lee, supported as it was by the very definite statement of facts as to the use of submarines. He thought that one clear and definite point of view emerged on which all were agreed, i.e., that there was no disposition to tolerate, on any plea of necessity, the illegal use of the submarine as practiced in the late war, and that there should be no diffi-

[5] *Ibid.*, pp. 270–71.   [6] *Ibid.*, p. 271.   [7] *Ibid.*, pp. 271–72.

culty in preparing and announcing to the world a statement of the intention of the nations represented at the conference that submarines must observe the well-established principles of international law regarding visit and search in attacks on merchant ships. Much could be done in clarifying this position and in defining what uses of submarines were considered contrary to humanity and to the well-defined principles of international law.[8]

The discussion made it evident that outside the British Empire no nation was prepared to abolish the submarine. Thus the British proposal was doomed from the beginning. Nevertheless, the British persisted and the debate continued.

Admiral de Bon refuted, at length, the British views on the merit of submarines as defensive weapons, and concluded that the French delegation could not reasonably limit submarine tonnage since they had before them an entirely new weapon concerning which no one of them could foresee the possible transformation and growth, perhaps in the near future. This idea was a menace to no one, first, because he thought that no one here could consider that any one of them could become the enemy of any other; and, secondly, because they could agree, in mutual confidence, to keep each other informed of their future construction. He believed that 90,000 tons was the absolute minimum for all the navies that might want to have a submarine force.[9]

Mr. Balfour realized that the United States and Japan were relatively safe from submarine blockade, but he seriously questioned the views presented by the French and Italian delegates. He pointed out that during the late war Great Britain had had to provide all the defense against

[8] *Document*, p. 272.   [9] *Ibid.*, p. 285.

the enemy submarines for France and Italy, and if the same circumstances came again she would again have to provide it. He concluded by saying that, if the powers represented in this room set themselves resolutely to the task, the submarine could be banned.[10] M. Schanzer of Italy and Admiral de Bon and M. Sarraut of France continued the debate, but without reaching any agreement.

On December 24 Mr. Hughes proposed to modify his original scheme so as to allow the United States and Great Britain only 60,000 tons each, Japan, France, and Italy to retain their existing tonnage, namely, 31,452 tons, 31,391 tons, and 21,000 tons, respectively.[11]

This new proposal had apparently no logical basis. The original allotment of submarine tonnage was based on the principle of 5-5-3-1.75-1.75. The newly proposed allotment, if reduced to ratio, was 5-5-2.62-2.61-1.75, and thus it violated the fundamental principle upon which the original American plan was based and upon which it was still proposed to limit capital-ship strength. On the ground of principle, therefore, Japan could raise objection to the amended proposal. Italy could not accept it on the ground of parity with France. Besides, the plan was far from meeting the British desire for abolition, even putting aside the French demand for 90,000 tons. Was it a piece of diplomacy to cater to public sentiment at the expense of the foreign delegations? There was such a feeling among some of the delegates.

At any rate the Italian delegation lost no time in reminding the conference that its principle of parity with France, which had been applied to the limitation of capital ships, must govern the reduction of other categories of naval armament. He must demand 31,000 tons as allowed

[10] *Ibid.*, pp. 285–90.   [11] *Ibid.*, pp. 302–3.

to France, should the latter decide to accept this newly proposed tonnage.[12] Mr. Hughes declared that he was willing to agree to this Italian demand.[13] The Japanese delegate stated that Japan had accepted the ratio of capital ships on the basis of 5-5-3 at a considerable sacrifice, and that she was prepared to accept the same ratio relative to submarines as originally proposed by the American plan; that would have given her 54,000 tons. The newly proposed tonnage of 31,000 was regarded by the Japanese Government as wholly inadequate; therefore, he felt constrained to insist upon the original allotment of 54,000 tons.[14]

On the 28th M. Sarraut acquainted the committee with the instructions which he had received from his Government by stating that France accepted, as regards capital ships, the sacrifice which she must face in order to meet the views of the conference and which represented an important reduction of her normal sea power. She limited the program of the future constitution of her fleet to 330,000 tons for auxiliary craft and to 90,000 tons for submarines. While regretting that she could not possibly, under the present circumstances, entirely carry out the reduction and limitations contemplated in the American proposal, she at least felt quite certain that she was taking an important share in the work of the conference by reducing the French naval power in capital ships, a weapon specifically offensive and particularly costly, and by accepting a limitation for craft of other categories.[15]

Thus, on the face of the French stand, no agreement to limit submarine tonnage seemed possible. But that did not end the debate, which culminated in the exchange of

[12] *Document,* pp. 304–5.   [13] *Ibid.,* p. 305.   [14] *Ibid.,* p. 306.
[15] *Ibid.,* p. 310.

THE SUBMARINE QUESTION

some bitter words, particularly between the British and French delegates. At the session held on the 30th, Lord Lee exposed the views of Captain Castex of the French Navy, which he interpreted as the likely attitude of the naval authorities of France on the utilization of submarines in time of war. According to Lord Lee, Castex declared that before criticizing the Germans the French should recall the fact that torpedo warfare was the application of an idea essentially French in its origin. No torpedo commander would tell the captain of the liner about to be attacked that he would do so. In the dead of night, quietly, silently, it would send to the abyss the liner, cargo, passengers, and crew; then, with a mind not only serene but fully satisfied with the result achieved, the captain of the torpedo boat would continue his cruise. One could see nothing in the attitude of the Germans which, militarily speaking, was not absolutely correct. Thanks to the submarine, after many centuries of effort, thanks to the ingenuity of man, the instrument, the system, the martingale was at hand which would overthrow for good and all the naval power of the British Empire. Lord Lee concluded that these were the utterances of a responsible member of the French naval staff, and were, of course, known to British naval men. The British were justified in feeling apprehensive and even bitter in the thought that their late comrades in arms in the greatest war the world had ever known should contemplate the possibility of warfare of that kind.[16]

The French delegates, in reply to Lord Lee, characterized the views of Captain Castex as those of a "literary" man. Nevertheless they gave assurances to their British colleagues by officially repudiating his views. It seemed to

[16] *Ibid.,* pp. 348–50.

the writer a bit unsportsmanlike for the British delegate to put the French delegates in such an embarrassing position. They had been already subjected to merciless attacks by the press. But it was freely expressed at Washington that blows between the British and the French were inevitable. Each nation was looking for the opportunity. They had not been particularly friendly since the signing of the Versailles Treaty. Reference may again be made to what M. Stephane Lauzanne had said about the British Premier (see page 12).

Be that as it may, if Lord Lee was sincere in his belief of the hostile attitude of Captain Castex, it is clear that the British fight for submarine abolition was not actuated solely by humanitarian motives, as it had been made to appear. Apparently the chief reason for the British plea was their apprehension of the craft in the hands of the French navy. The British Empire, it would seem, was guided on this question by its national interest. At any rate, the official repudiation of Castex by the French delegation was officially accepted by the British as satisfactory, and the matter should have rested there. But for unknown reasons, M. Jusserand revived the case toward the end of the conference (January 31), and it naturally resulted in another diplomatic defeat for the French delegation.[17]

To recapitulate: the British were dissatisfied with the original American proposal and offered as counter-proposals, first, to go beyond the American plan in limiting total tonnage to be allotted to each of the five nations, and, secondly, to limit the maximum size of individual vessels so as to make of them weapons merely of defense, or, thirdly, to abolish them altogether. The Americans were

[17] *Document,* pp. 425–29.

willing to meet the first of these, and modified their original scheme accordingly; but this new plan was rejected by Japan, France, and Italy. Japan insisted upon the original plan, and Italy on her principle of parity with France. France not only rejected the modified plan which allowed her to retain what she then possessed, but, ignoring the new allotment of 60,000 tons each to the United States and the British Empire, she now demanded 90,000 tons as a minimum for submarines and 330,000 tons for other auxiliary craft. These demands made it impossible for the conference to effect any limitation either on submarines or on auxiliary craft.

Before leaving this subject, it would be interesting to discover the reasons which underlie the two divergent views on submarines, one represented by the British and the other by the United States, Japan, France, and Italy. The British seem to hold that the submarine is an offensive weapon, while the others consider it a defensive weapon; and consequently the former desire to abolish this craft, while the latter wish to retain them. Beyond this no information was given by any nation at the conference unless it be the British apprehension of the unlimited tonnage of this craft in the hands of the French nation.

Be that as it may, the conference was able to effect a treaty embodying the rules governing the use of submarines as well as the prohibition of poisonous gases in future wars.[18] The rules for the protection of neutrals and non-combatants at sea in time of war are: (1) a merchant vessel must be ordered to submit to visit and search after warning or to proceed as directed after seizure; and (2) no merchant ship must be destroyed unless

[18] See Appendix IV.

the crew and passengers have been first placed in safety. Belligerent submarines must observe these rules, and if a submarine cannot capture a merchant ship without violating these rules the latter must be allowed to proceed unmolested. The violation of these rules by any person is made liable to punishment as an act of piracy. The signatory powers agree not to use submarines as commerce destroyers. Finally, the treaty prohibits the use in war of asphyxiating, poisonous, or other gases, and analogous liquids, materials, or devices. Non-signatory powers are to be invited to adhere to this treaty.

Mr. Root said that this treaty was an attempt to crystallize, in simple and unmistakable terms, the opinion of civilization that already existed. This treaty was an appeal to that clear opinion of the civilized world, in order that henceforth no nation should dare to do what had been done when the women and children of the "Lusitania" had gone to their death by wanton murder upon the high sea.[19]

[19] *Document,* p. 161.

CHAPTER VII

JAPAN AND PACIFIC FORTIFICATIONS

It has already been pointed out that the acceptance by Japan of the capital-ship ratio proposed by the American plan was, in part, conditioned by her desire for an agreement on the maintenance of the *status quo* on some of the Pacific fortifications and naval bases, and that this demand was favorably received by both the United States and Great Britain as indicated in the provisional agreement of December 15. But the language employed in the agreement concerning this matter was unfortunately very vague, and gave rise to unexpected difficulties. Nearly a month was consumed before the "Big Three" were able to reach a definite agreement, which now appears as Article XIX of the Naval Treaty. The negotiations leading to this Article were important, and, therefore, a somewhat detailed statement of them may not be without interest.

The provisional agreement covering the point in question reads:

It is agreed that with respect to fortifications and naval bases in the Pacific region, including Hongkong, the *status quo* shall be maintained, that is, that there shall be no increase in these fortifications and naval bases except that this restriction shall not apply to the Hawaiian Islands, Australia, New Zealand, and the islands composing Japan proper, or, of course, to the coasts of the United States and Canada, as to which the respective powers retain their entire freedom.

Accordingly, with the exception of Hongkong, the islands to which the *status quo* was to be applied were not specifically designated, though the places to which it was not to be applied were more or less definitely described. This faulty character of the agreement must be admitted; but it was entirely due to the great haste in which it was composed. The "Big Three," especially Mr. Hughes, were very anxious to let the public know the result of their work. Of course, there was a general understanding among the negotiators as to which of the islands were to be included, where the *status quo* was to be maintained. Why, then, did they not specify them instead of resorting to the expressions "fortifications and naval bases in the Pacific region" and "the islands composing Japan proper"? It is hard to explain this, especially in view of the difficulty which had already arisen over the loose language used in the Four-Power Pact (discussed below in chapter x), namely, the expression "insular possessions and insular dominions in the region of the Pacific Ocean."[1]

The agreement, as it was written, was communicated to the governments concerned, or at least it was sent to the Japanese Government and by it made public. Now the interpretation given by the Japanese Government to the expression, "the islands composing Japan proper," included Amami-Oshima and the Bonin Islands, on the ground that those islands were within the administrative jurisdiction of the Home Government. But Mr. Hughes and Mr. Balfour regarded these islands as within the zone in which the *status quo* was to be maintained. Baron Kato himself also subscribed to the latter interpretation, but evidently without authorization of his Government.

These conflicting views created a situation particularly embarrassing to Baron Kato when he received instructions that he must adhere to the original agreement and have the Bonin Islands and Amami-Oshima excluded from the zone. These instructions reached him early in Janu-

[1] See chapter x.

ary, just when the Naval Treaty began to be drafted; and thus he found himself, for the second time, in an impossible position. One Japanese writer offered an explanation by saying that he was inclined to think that the Government at Tokyo took this attitude mainly because the United States reserved the right to strengthen the fortifications and naval bases in the Hawaiian Islands. Fair-minded critics admit that this Japanese contention was not devoid of plausible reason. Hawaii was 2,100 sea miles from San Francisco, while the Bonin group was only 500 sea miles from Japan. If America must keep on increasing the fortifications and naval bases on islands whose distance from the Pacific Coast was about four times as great as the distance between Yokohama and the Bonin group, Japan could reasonably advance strong arguments for the exclusion of that group from the *status quo* zone. Moreover, Pearl Harbor at Hawaii had already been converted into a magnificent naval base. If America really wished to be a harbinger of peace and looked forward to an age of amity and friendliness in the Pacific Ocean, why should she be so eager to keep on strengthening a naval base already well developed?[2]

But the present writer is inclined to think, at the same time, that the instructions from the Japanese Government were not devoid of politics of a personal character. As a matter of fact, Baron Kato was made a "victim" of domestic politics. He must have felt keenly the loss of the late Premier Hara, who would undoubtedly have saved him from such an embarrassment. Premier Takahashi was not the statesman to win over the members of the Privy Council or those of the Foreign Affairs Advisory

[2] K. K. Kawakami, *Japan's Pacific Policy,* pp. 36–37.

Council, the real authors of the instructions. Baron Kato intimated to the writer even the names of the men who were working against him. He knew the influence of these men. He knew that he must conciliate them regardless of the nature of their demands, otherwise the entire work of the conference might be wrecked. It may be added that the Privy Council ratifies treaties in Japan, or, strictly speaking, the Emperor upon the recommendation of that body.[3]

But to return to the conference, on January 9 Mr. Balfour called on Baron Kato for the purpose of obtaining the latter's consent to his new scheme of a parallelogram wherein the *status quo* was to be maintained. The proposed zone was bounded on the south by the Equator, on the north by the thirtieth degree of latitude, on the west by the one hundred tenth degree of longitude, and on the east by the one hundred eightieth degree of longitude. Mr. Balfour thought that this scheme would definitely describe the zone; but Baron Kato did not approve it, in view of the provisional agreement which embraced the whole of the Pacific region. He inquired if Mr. Balfour had any special motive for his proposal. Whereupon Mr. Balfour made it clear that the purpose of the scheme was to meet the demand of his Australian colleague, who desired to reserve the right to fortify Papuan Bay in British New Guinea. He added that actual fortification might not be undertaken. Baron Kato acceded to this desire and promised Mr. Balfour to support the British claim, but on the condition that the parallelogram be abandoned. Such an agreement was verbally entered into between the British and Japanese delegates.

[3] The Japanese Constitution, Articles XIII and LVI.

On January 10 the senior delegates of the five nations met to go over the first draft of the Naval Treaty, which was submitted to them by the Subcommittee of Naval and Legal Experts. When the fortification clause came up, Baron Kato expressed the desire to have that portion of the provisional agreement of December 15, pertaining to the subject, inserted in the proposed treaty. The reason he gave for the desire was simply to avoid any complications that might arise, should the statement of the agreement and the treaty provision fail to be harmonious. He assured his colleagues that Japan would maintain the *status quo* on Amami-Oshima, the Bonin Islands, the Pescadores, and Formosa, which were the islands included in the zone according to the understanding of the "Big Three." Only he did not desire to have these islands specifically designated in the treaty. Nevertheless, if his colleagues wished a specification of the islands, he would suggest that such might be done in the form of notes to be exchanged between the governments concerned.[4] Apparently Baron Kato thought that by such means he could meet the demand of his Government as well as that of his colleagues.

Mr. Hughes was not opposed to Baron Kato's suggestion, and said that since all would wish to make specifications this might be done by means of "notes," to make it clear and definite that the four islands in the case of Japan were included in the zone. He added, however, that such notes, as well as the treaty, must be made public. Baron Kato replied that such was his understanding.

[4] When the question as to the exact meaning of the expression "insular possessions and insular dominions" was raised by Baron Kato, Mr. Hughes suggested that a note giving the precise definition might be appended to the treaty.

But Mr. Balfour thought it absurd to re-publish the statement of the provisional agreement, in view of the definition of "Japan proper" given by the Japanese Government, which clearly conflicted with the understanding entered into between Mr. Hughes, Baron Kato, and himself. This fact, together with the imperfect character of the statement, would make it undesirable for him to accede to the proposal of Baron Kato. Should it be accepted, he feared that misunderstandings were bound to arise. He then suggested the following propositions: first, the *status quo* arrangement must apply only to insular possessions in the Pacific; second, it must not include either the islands off the coast of Canada or the islands in the neighborhood of Australia and New Zealand; third, his view would be adequately expressed by the formula, "The United States, the British Empire, and Japan agree that the following provisions shall apply to their respective possessions lying between the Equator and the parallel of 30 degrees north and between the meridians of 110 degrees east and 180 degrees east."

The proposal embodied exactly the same scheme which Mr. Balfour had presented to Baron Kato and had promised to withdraw because of the latter's assurance to support the British demand to have Papuan Bay excluded from the zone. Under the circumstances Baron Kato was naturally surprised and, indeed, chagrined to have that parallelogram again thrust in his face. He was too honest and too simple a "diplomat" to have believed in such a possibility. At any rate, this scheme of a parallelogram appeared satisfactory to Mr. Hughes. So Baron Kato was forced to say that he would do his best to secure the consent of his Government to agree to it, though he himself was opposed to the British scheme. That was the real beginning of trouble which saw no solution for nearly a month.

At this point, a word may be said as to Baron Kato's proposal of "notes." It is difficult to explain why such a proposal was made at all. It seemed evident from the beginning that Baron Kato had the intention of ignoring the instructions of his Government to have Amami-Oshima and the Bonin Islands excluded. He definitely stated to his colleagues that these islands would be included in the *status quo* zone. What particular merit he attached to "notes," which he suggested as means for specifications, was not clear to the writer at that time nor is it clear even now. He might have thought that the "notes" might be kept secret. If so, he could have saved the face of his Government, or those of the men behind the demand, or his own. Evidently he had consented to apply the *status quo* to the four groups of islands without authorization. But when Mr. Hughes reminded him that, regardless of the form, matters of binding character agreed upon must be made public, he said that he understood that. If so, what was the particular merit of "notes"? Thus viewed, Baron Kato's proposal was "flimsy and meaningless, because there was no difference between a treaty and a note as far as its binding force was concerned."[5] There was no logic in the proposal. Mr. Balfour was too keen a diplomat to have missed a chance like that. For him the right psychological moment had arrived to introduce his scheme of a parallelogram. It was a finished piece of diplomacy. He won Mr. Hughes' consent to the proposal even without the necessity of revealing the real motive behind it. Baron Kato stood isolated. He

[5] Kawakami, *op. cit.,* p. 37.

was forced to consider the parallelogram scheme which he had already disapproved. In reality he had to think out a counter-proposal which would prove so satisfactory to the American and British delegates as to cause them to drop the British plan. At the same time, he had to satisfy his own Government. Its demand must have appeared to him wholly unreasonable, as it surely did to all impartial observers. For the first time, one could see the lack of clearness in his expression. The writer called his attention to that fact more than once, and he gracefully admitted it. He said that it would be very easy for him to resign and thus save himself, but that that would not save the nation. Japan must not invite isolation. He knew who were behind the instructions, but he must not make them enemies, for that might make the work of the conference meaningless. At no other time was he so discouraged. Nevertheless, by tact and patience he was able to win both his opponents at home and his colleagues at the conference, and produced Article XIX of the Naval Treaty, which is as follows:

The United States, the British Empire, and Japan agree that the *status quo* at the time of the signing of the present treaty, with regard to fortifications and naval bases, shall be maintained in their respective territories and possessions specified hereunder:

1. The insular possessions which the United States now holds or may hereafter acquire in the Pacific Ocean, except (*a*) those adjacent to the coast of the United States, Alaska, and the Panama Canal Zone, not including the Aleutian Islands, and (*b*) the Hawaiian Islands;

2. Hongkong and the insular possessions which the British Empire now holds or may hereafter acquire in the Pacific Ocean, east of the meridian of 110 degrees east longitude, except (*a*) those adjacent to the coast of Canada, (*b*) the Commonwealth of Australia and its territories, and (*c*) New Zealand.

3. The following insular territories and possessions of Japan in the Pacific Ocean, to wit: the Kurile Islands, the Bonin Islands, Amami-Oshima, the Loochoo Islands, Formosa, and the Pescadores, and any insular territories or possessions in the Pacific Ocean which Japan may hereafter acquire.

The maintenance of the *status quo* under the foregoing provisions implies that no new fortifications or naval bases shall be established in the territories and possessions specified; that no measures shall be taken to increase the existing naval facilities for the repair and maintenance of naval forces; and that no increase shall be made in the coast defense of the territories and possessions above specified. This restriction, however, does not preclude such repair and replacement of worn-out weapons and equipment as is customary in naval and military establishments in time of peace.[6]

To sum up: a most scrutinizing reading of the original provisional agreement would not enable one to know exactly upon which of the islands of the three nations the *status quo* was to be maintained. But behind this written agreement there was a verbal understanding among the "Big Three," by which the *status quo* was to be applied to the Philippines, Guam, Hongkong, Amami-Oshima, the Bonins, Formosa, and the Pescadores. Apparently neither the agreement nor the understanding proved satisfactory to the British delegation. Mr. Balfour took the initiative for modification of the agreement and approached Baron Kato with a novel scheme of a parallelogram to indicate the zone wherein the *status quo* was to be maintained. Though a verbal agreement was entered into between Mr. Balfour and Baron Kato whereby the former promised to abandon the newly proposed scheme, he reintroduced it at the meeting of the senior delegates of the five nations. But before he did so, he reminded his colleagues that the *status*

[6] The Naval Treaty, Article XIX.

quo arrangement must apply only to insular possessions. What was the significance of the words, "insular possessions"? Did Mr. Balfour have in mind the case of Kowloon?[7] Possibly not, since his parallelogram embraced Kowloon within its zone and the words, "insular possessions," were not originally employed in this connection. Its chief aim was undoubtedly to exclude Papuan Bay.

If the writer understands it correctly, Article XIX binds the British Empire to maintain the *status quo* on the military and naval equipment of Hongkong, including Kowloon; otherwise, she is left free. She reserves the right to fortify Papuan Bay. Thus the position of the British Empire as regards the question of fortifications and naval bases has remained intact from the very beginning, unless she is better secured now under the treaty as to her right to fortify British New Guinea. But the United States is bound to maintain the *status quo* upon the fortifications and naval bases in the Philippines and Guam, as originally agreed upon, and also upon those in the Aleutian Islands. Japan's *status quo* zone includes not only the four groups of islands as originally proposed, but

---

[7] "The Military position at Hongkong had long been a subject of much concern to the British authorities. The harbor was bordered on much of its northern side by Chinese territory, and it was desired to secure such an extension of the colonial limits as would free the town and harbor from any danger of hostile attack. As direct compensation for the cession of Kwangchow-wan to France, the previous tentative negotiations for the extension were now pushed; and China, in her helpless search for support from one Western power or another, was ready to accede to the demand. A convention was accordingly signed at Peking on June 9th, 1898, by which England obtained on lease for ninety-nine years the whole of the Kowloon peninsula from Deep Bay to Mirs Bay, together with the waters of the two bays, and all the waters and islands north of 22° 39′ N. lat., and between 113° 52′ and 114° 30′ E. long."—H. B. Morse, *International Relations of the Chinese Empire* (London, 1918), III, 119–20.

the Kurile Islands and the Loochoo Islands as well. The inclusion of these additional islands within the *status quo* zone was the result of a compromise between the United States and Japan. The writer cannot judge the technical merit of this provision, so will accept it in the spirit in which it was agreed upon by the representatives of the three nations.

CHAPTER VIII

FRANCE REFUSES AUXILIARY LIMITATION

The French delegation gave its consent on December 28 to the ratio of capital ships proposed by the American plan, thus completing the settlement of the most important of the naval questions. But no amount of persuasion, argument, intimidation, or threat was able to bring about any alterations in the French demand for 90,000 tons of submarines, and consequently the desire to limit submarine tonnage had to be abandoned. Next in importance to the agreement on the ratio of capital ships was the question of a naval holiday, which according to the American plan was to extend over a period of ten years. In other words, the work of replacing old ships was not to begin before the year 1931. However, during the debate on the question of capital ships and submarines the French delegation expressed the desire that France be accorded the right to commence her replacement work as early as 1926, on the ground that she had actually begun her naval holiday in 1915. After a prolonged and tedious negotiation, a compromise was reached whereby France and therefore Italy also were conceded the right "to lay down new tonnage in the years 1927, 1929, and 1931,"[1] while the remaining powers were not to lay down ships before the last-mentioned date. Thus the duration of the holiday is only six years for France and Italy, and ten years for the United States, Great Britain, and Japan.

The conference then took up the question of limiting auxiliary-craft tonnage on the basis of the American plan. Here again, the French delegation reiterated that France could not reduce the tonnage of this class of vessels below 330,000 tons.[2] This French demand was naturally criti-

---

[1] See chapter ii of the Naval Treaty.   [2] See *Document,* p. 310.

cized in the same manner as had been her stand on submarine tonnage. The French position was thought to be contrary to the fundamental aim of the conference. What she had proposed meant an actual increase of the existing strength of her auxiliary craft. The nations at the conference were visibly distressed over the French stand. Their delegates did not conceal the fear of consequent danger of the French demand, which would open the door for rivalry in naval building and would, therefore, decrease the value of the agreement on capital-ship tonnage. However, neither by persuasion nor by argument were they able to effect modifications on the part of the French delegates. There was no possibility of reaching an agreement limiting auxiliary-craft tonnage. This was another failure.

How the French demand for 330,000 tons of auxiliary craft was regarded by the various foreign delegations may be gleaned from the following remarks.

Mr. Hughes confessed that he was disappointed with the French demand, but he did not wish to discuss details, in view of the existing situation. He only wished to say that an agreement for the expansion of armament was not under consideration.[3] Mr. Balfour concurred with the American delegate, and added that he was perfectly unable to conceive how that (the French demand) could be regarded as a defensive policy.[4] M. Schanzer expressed his deep regret that it was not possible to limit auxiliary boats and submarines, and remarked that in the absence of an agreement concerning the limitation of the latter naval forces it was but natural that each nation should retain full liberty of action.[5] The Japanese delegate thought it a misfortune if the conference failed to come to an agree-

[3] *Ibid.*, p. 311.   [4] *Ibid.*, p. 312.   [5] *Ibid.*, p. 313.

ment as regards the limitation of auxiliary combatant craft.[6]

The only agreement on auxiliary craft which the conference was able to bring about was limitation of their individual maximum size to 10,000 tons. Even on this question France had expressed her desire that she needed larger craft to defend her colonial possessions.

The question of aircraft carriers was then introduced, and Mr. Hughes stated that the American plan proposed to fix their total tonnage for the United States and Great Britain at 80,000 each, for Japan at 48,000, and, if the capital-ship ratio was adhered to, for France and Italy at 28,000. The plan also provided that no country possessing excess tonnage over the quota allotted was required to scrap such tonnage until replacements began. He now proposed, in addition, that the maximum size of individual aircraft carriers be limited to 27,000 tons, and that the guns carried by these vessels were not to exceed a caliber of eight inches. Of course, no new carrier was to be built during the ten-year holiday.[7]

In reply to the American proposals, Admiral Acton of Italy said that the tonnage allotted to his country would permit only one carrier of 27,000 tons. If this single ship were forced to go into dry dock or were to be sunk at sea, Italy would find herself, either temporarily or definitely, without any carrier whatsoever. He therefore asked that Italy be given 54,000 tons, which would allow her to have two standard carriers.[8]

Lord Lee sympathized with the Italian view, and said that the Italian claim was very difficult to resist. He thought that the proposals relative to the maximum size of individual carriers and of the caliber of guns were

[6] *Document*, p. 314.   [7] *Ibid.*, pp. 356–57.   [8] *Ibid.*, pp. 357–58.

necessary; likewise he thought that the ratio of capital ships already agreed to should be applied to carriers because these constituted an auxiliary to a modern fleet. Great Britain now possessed five carriers, but four of these were obsolete. He must, therefore, ask for the right to scrap the latter at any time and to replace them with new ships. Moreover, the allotment of tonnage made to his country being inadequate, he demanded a total of 135,000 tons, to enable Great Britain to have five standard carriers.[9]

Admiral de Bon said that France would be willing to fix the maximum size of individual carriers at 25,000 tons, but she needed two such vessels for European waters and a third for use in her colonial possessions. In other words, he would like to have a total of 75,000 tons, but he was willing to accept 60,000 tons.[10]

Baron Kato concurred with the general observation made by Lord Lee, and he too believed that the Italian demand was justifiable. But with the 48,000 tons allotted to his country, it could construct only two carriers, one standard and the other inferior, which would be inadequate for Japan because of her insular character. He desired to have three carriers of 27,000 tons each, or a total of 81,000 tons. He added that he was willing to agree to a proportionate increase on the part of the United States and Great Britain.[11]

Obviously these views did not harmonize with the proposals of the United States. Accordingly Mr. Hughes offered a new scheme by way of amendment to meet the demands of his colleagues. Great Britain desired five airplane carriers, at whatever the maximum for each individual ship might be taken to be; and if that were 27,000

[9] *Ibid.*, pp. 358–59.   [10] *Ibid.*, p. 359.   [11] *Ibid.*, pp. 359–60.

tons it would mean a maximum of 135,000 tons. France desired 60,000 tons, which, of course, could be divided in such a way as would be deemed best suited to the special needs of France. Italy desired two carriers, which at a maximum of 27,000 tons would make an allowance of 54,000. Japan desired three, which at the maximum of 27,000 tons would be 81,000 tons.

Now this appeared to be, with the single exception of a very slight difference between 54,000 in the case of Italy and 60,000 in the case of France, in the ratio of the capital ships. It was quite apparent, for the reasons that had been very cogently presented, that the original figures of the American proposal would not meet what was deemed to be the needs of the various governments. He also understood that there was agreement by all that the caliber of guns carried should be limited to eight inches, and the maximum tonnage of each ship to 27,000.

If that disposition was agreeable to the other powers, he saw no reason why the American delegation should not accept it, with the maximum allowance for the United States corresponding to that which Great Britain had asked; and he assumed also that there would be no objection if France had this slight excess over the exact amount allowed by the ratio, that is, 60,000 tons instead of 54,000 tons, and also if Italy were allowed a corresponding amount, on the basis of parity for which Italy had always contended. If that was agreeable he would put it to a vote, unless it was desirable to continue the discussion further.[12] The delegations being polled in turn, each voted in the affirmative.

In other words, an agreement was finally reached by which were allowed to the United States and Great Britain

[12] *Document,* pp. 360–61.

135,000 tons each; to Japan, 81,000; and to France and Italy, 60,000 each. The caliber of guns carried by aircraft carriers was limited to eight inches, and the maximum size of individual vessels to 27,000 tons. The new allotment, if reduced to ratio, would give 5-5-3-2.2-2.2; thus France and Italy gained slightly over the original ratio of 1.75.

The next subject of discussion was aircraft. This was one of the newly developed, important agencies of warfare, which demanded careful consideration by the conference. The subject, however, being of highly technical character, its study was entrusted to a Subcommittee of Aircraft Experts. That committee was instructed to consider the question of limiting this instrument of war as to number, character, and use. On January 7 it submitted a very comprehensive report, which concluded with the following recommendations:

> The committee is of the opinion that it is not practicable to impose any effective limitations upon the numbers or characteristics of aircraft, either commercial or military, excepting in the single case of lighter-than-air craft. The committee is of the opinion that the use of aircraft in war should be governed by the rules of warfare as adapted to aircraft by a further conference which should be held at a later date.[13]

In view of these conclusions of the subcommittee of experts, the conference deemed it inadvisable to proceed farther on the subject and decided to accept, for the present, the recommendations submitted.

It now remained for the conference to agree on the caliber and the number of guns that might be carried by each type of vessel and also to determine methods of "scrapping." Neither of these involved prolonged or

[13] *Ibid.*, pp. 407–8.

interesting debates. Furthermore, as technical matters they may be more conveniently treated in the next chapter, devoted to an analysis of the Naval Treaty.

From the survey above we see that the conference failed to effect any limitation on the total tonnage of submarines. The British must have felt chagrined at the failure, for they had fought for complete abolition of this class of vessels. If they earnestly entertained fears of submarines in French hands, these apprehensions were in no way allayed, for France could certainly continue to build these relatively inexpensive weapons. The conference also failed to limit auxiliary-craft tonnage. These failures were certainly serious matters, and may have left open the door to naval rivalry.

No comment is necessary on the modified limitation placed upon the total tonnage of aircraft carriers, except that it seems to be more logical than the limitation originally proposed by the American plan, even if it slightly violates the principle of the ratio. The agreement on the maximum size of individual light cruisers cuts off one of the important items on which rivalry might be continued. The limitation must also be considered as a distinct contribution to economy, and this was, after all, one of the chief aims of the Arms Conference.

A few words may now be said in respect to land-force limitation. In the early stage of the conference it became pretty well settled that there was no hope of effecting limitation of land armaments. At the third plenary session, on November 21, Mr. Hughes introduced the subject by commenting that so far as the army of the United States was concerned no question was presented. It had always been the policy of the United States—it was its traditional policy—to have the regular military establishment upon the smallest possible basis. At the time of the Armistice there had been in the field and in training approximately 4,000,000 men. At once upon the signing of the Armistice demobilization had begun, and it had been practically completed in the course of the following year; today the regular establishment numbered less than 160,000 men. Such was the fortunate situation in the United States; but he fully recognized the special difficulties relative to land armaments abroad, and, therefore, this subject should be discussed by the conference.[14]

M. Briand spoke at length on the land-armament situation in France. He reminded the conference that France had begun demobilization immediately after the Armistice, and was completing it as rapidly as possible. He explained that the existing military laws of France compelled three generations of young men to be under the flag, but the Government had reduced the three-year service to two years. It would continue to restrict it further in the future so that there would be actually serving one and one-half generations. This meant that the Metropolitan military force would be reduced to a half of the strength existing at the signing of the Armistice. Beyond this France was not prepared to go.[15]

Mr. Balfour commented on the declaration of M. Briand by saying that the speech to which he had just listened was not hopeful for any immediate solution of the great problem of land armaments.[16] M. Schanzer also spoke of the reduction of Italian land forces. He wished and hoped in spite of the difficulties set forth by M. Briand that the general limitation of land armaments might be-

[14] *Document*, pp. 76–77.   [15] *Ibid.*, pp. 77–78.   [16] *Ibid.*, p. 88.

come a reality.[17] Baron Kato gave his hearty approval to the principle aiming to relieve a people of heavy burdens by limiting land armaments, but he pointed out the difficulty of laying down a general scheme for this purpose.[18]

We learn from these expressions that the United States had no need of reduction so far as her army was concerned. France, the greatest military power, took the stand that she was not in a position to reduce her army. The British Empire concluded that there was no hope for limitation of land armaments, because of the French position. Japan expressed her willingness to reduce her army, but at the same time she recalled the difficulties involved in the task of effecting such limitation. Italy alone presented her positive desire for the consideration of the subject by the conference. Such being the case, Mr. Hughes was obliged to conclude that further consideration made it quite clear that no agreement for the limitation of land forces could be reached at this time.[19]

Criticizing the French stand on the question of armament limitations, an American author says,

The facts of record, which, on this point, are the essential part of the narrative of the Washington Conference, are: that the French delegates prevented the consideration of land armament; that the French delegates took a position about capital ships which would have made the Conference a complete failure, and only receded after Hughes "put it up" to the French premier that the action of that country would "determine the success or failure of this effort to reduce the heavy burden of naval armament"; that the French delegates made any limitation on the quantity of submarines impossible; and that the French delegates made any limitation on the quantity of auxiliary craft impossible. Those were the specific actions of the French delegates. One might say of all of them what Balfour said of the one action on

[17] *Document,* pp. 90–91. [18] *Ibid.,* pp. 91–92. [19] *Ibid.,* p. 794.

submarines, that they "constituted a singular contribution to a conference called to limit armament." The delegates of France never seemed to share the spirit of the Conference. In their self-centered intentness upon their *amour propre* they were cut off from the emotion of exaltation that gripped the Conference and the world. When the whole world was star-eyed in pursuit of the great adventure, the delegates of France were thinking of their place at the table.[20]

The last remark refers to an incident, if true, which is described by the same author as follows:

We noticed that when Briand sought his seat on the side that formed the top of the square, he did not find it there. The Americans and British filled all the top-side seats; and we thought we noticed something a little less than gratification on the countenance of the dark and heavy Frenchman when he found his seat around the corner, on the side. In all the later sessions [plenary] we observed there had been a new shuffling of the seats, and one of the British delegates, Ambassador Geddes, had been pushed around the corner to the left, so as to give France a seat at the head of the table. The incident was small, but it went to the heart of some of the things that happened about France during the subsequent weeks.[21]

It is gratifying, however, to add that the Japanese Government headed by Baron Kato decided on July 4, 1922, to reduce its army by 56,000 men, a cut of more than twenty per cent. It was estimated that the proposed reduction would save 250,000,000 yen in twelve years, and 25,000,000 yen annually thereafter.[22]

[20] Mark Sullivan, *The Great Adventure at Washington* (Garden City, 1922), pp. 200–1.

[21] *Ibid.*, pp. 6–7.

[22] See, for a critical estimate of the Japanese Army, M. D. Kennedy, *The Military Side of Japanese Life* (New York, 1924), pp. 305–14.

CHAPTER IX

THE NAVAL TREATY

The Naval Treaty consists of three chapters: the first containing the general principles or provisions relating to the limitation of naval armament; the second the rules for the execution of the agreement; and the third certain miscellaneous provisions.

First, then, let us consider the relative strength of the five navies measured in terms of their capital ships, as allotted by the original American plan, indicated below.[1]

Country	Number of Ships	Tonnage
United States	18	500,650
Great Britain	22	580,450
Japan	10	299,700
France	10	221,170
Italy	10	182,800

This allotment was slightly modified because of Japan's desire to retain the "Mutsu" and to scrap the "Settsu" instead. The substitution increased Japan's tonnage from 299,700 to 303,320. The "Mutsu" being a far more formidable ship than the "Settsu," it was found necessary to compensate the American and British navies in order that the relative strength of the three navies might be properly balanced. The United States is given by the treaty the right to complete two vessels of the "West Virginia" class. When these ships are completed, the "North Dakota" and the "Delaware" will be scrapped. That will give the nation eighteen capital ships with a total tonnage of 525,850. For the same purpose, Great Britain is accorded

---

[1] A capital ship, in the case of ships hereafter built, is defined as a vessel of war, not an aircraft carrier, whose displacement exceeds 10,000 tons (10,160 metric tons) standard displacement, or which carries a gun with a caliber exceeding eight inches (203 millimeters). Naval Treaty, chapter ii, Part 4.

the right to build two new ships of 35,000 tons, and when they are completed the "Thunderer," "King George V," "Ajax," and "Centurion" will be scrapped. That will give Great Britain twenty vessels with a total tonnage of 558,-950. The French and Italian capital ships remain unaffected by these changes. Now, the tonnage disparity between the American and British capital ships is accounted for by the factor of age. Though different in the tonnage, the capital ships of the American and British navies are considered of equal strength. Likewise, the disparity between the French and Italian tonnage is considered of no real value. In other words, it is thought that the ratio of strength indicated by the original American plan remains intact. The number and tonnage of capital ships retained under, and the maximum replacement tonnage[2] fixed by, the treaty are as follows:

Country	Number of Ships	Existing Tonnage	Maximum Replacement Tonnage
United States	18	525,850	525,000
Great Britain	20	558,950	525,000
Japan	10	303,320	315,000
France	10	221,170	175,000
Italy	10	182,800	175,000

The agreement on capital ships involves the scrapping[3] of an enormous tonnage, which astounded the world when

[2] The replacement tonnage may be properly considered as the real relative strength of the retained ships.

[3] I. A vessel to be scrapped must be placed in such condition that it cannot be put to combatant use.

II. This result must be finally effected in any one of the following ways:
    a) Permanent sinking of the vessel.
    b) Breaking the vessel up. This shall always involve the destruc-

it was first announced. Under the treaty the United States was to scrap thirteen vessels in process of construction and fifteen old ones, with a total tonnage of 845,740. In addition she would scrap two more old ships simultaneously with the completion of the two new ships already referred to. Great Britain was to abandon the construction of her four "Super-Hoods" and to scrap twenty old capital ships. She was to abandon and destroy about 583,000 tons.[4] Moreover, she was to scrap four more old ships when her two new "Hoods" were completed. Japan was to abandon her program of building four capital ships and four battle cruisers (not laid down). She was to scrap six vessels under construction and ten old ones. Japan was thus to destroy sixteen ships with a total tonnage of 435,328.[5] Neither France nor Italy was required to scrap a single vessel. Nevertheless, the treaty forced the three greatest naval powers to destroy in all sixty-six ships with an aggregate tonnage of 1,864,000.[6] This was

tion or removal of all machinery, boilers, and armor, and all deck, side, and bottom plating.

c) Converting the vessel to target use exclusively. In such case all the provisions of paragraph III of this part, except sub-paragraph (6), in so far as may be necessary to enable the ship to be used as a mobile target (7), must be previously complied with. Not more than one capital ship may be retained for this purpose at one time by any of the Contracting Powers, etc.—Naval Treaty, chapter ii, Part 2.

[4] The figure includes 172,000 tons which is estimated tonnage for the four "Super-Hoods," but excludes the tonnage of the four old vessels to be scrapped when the two new "Hoods" are completed.

[5] The figure considers the tonnage of the "Settsu" and not that of the "Mutsu."

[6] The figure excludes the tonnage of the four "Super-Hoods" and of the four old ships to be scrapped when the two new "Hoods" were completed, as well as of the two old ships to be scrapped by the United States when her two new vessels were completed. Perhaps it should be added that for sentimental reasons the United States was

surely a substantial reduction in the most essential element in naval armament.

The treaty limits the total tonnage of aircraft carriers as has been already mentioned. It also fixes the maximum size of three types of vessels so that at the time of replacement no capital ships of more than 35,000 tons, no aircraft carriers of more than 27,000 tons, and no light cruisers of more than 10,000 tons were to be built.[7] These restrictions had been agreed upon from both technical and financial points of view. Financially these limitations may be regarded as eliminating one of the important elements in competition. But technically it may be said that despite these limitations there still exists room for competition, namely in the technique of construction, internal arrangements, etc. In this respect, naval experts hold the opinion that technical advantages of any kind will not remain long a monopoly in the hands of any one navy.

The treaty had further provisions in the nature of limitation, namely, as regards the number and the caliber of guns to be carried by the various types of vessels. For instance, capital ships are not allowed by it to carry guns whose caliber exceeds sixteen inches.[8] If an aircraft carrier carries guns exceeding six inches, the total number carried by such vessel is limited to ten. It cannot carry a

---

allowed to retain the "Oregon" and the "Illinois," Great Britain the "Colossus" and the "Collingwood," and Japan the "Shikishima" and the "Asahi." These were for non-combatant purposes and were to be emasculated. Naval Treaty, chapter ii, Part 3, § II.

[7] "Tons" referred to here means tons standard displacement. Moreover, the treaty provides that the powers may build two aircraft carriers, the tonnage of which may be 33,000 tons each. This provision was made on behalf of the British, who desired to convert two of their capital ships into aircraft carriers.

[8] Art. VII.

gun whose caliber exceeds eight inches. It may carry, however, any number of five-inch guns and anti-aircraft guns.[9]

In the case of aircraft carriers of 33,000 tons, the total number of guns to be carried, in case any of such guns are of caliber exceeding 6 inches, except anti-aircraft guns and guns not exceeding 5 inches, can not number more than 8.[10]

In no case can light cruisers carry guns exceeding eight inches in caliber.[11] Such are the restrictions placed upon these naval weapons.

For its faithful execution, the treaty provides:

No ship designated in the present Treaty to be scrapped may be reconverted into a vessel of war.[12]

No preparations shall be made in merchant ships in time of peace for the installation of warlike armaments for the purpose of converting such ships into vessels of war, other than the necessary stiffening of decks for the mounting of guns not exceeding six-inch (152 millimeters) caliber.[13]

No vessel of war constructed within the jurisdiction of any of the contracting Powers for a non-contracting Power shall exceed the limitations as to displacement and armament prescribed by the present Treaty for vessels of a similar type which may be constructed by or for any of the contracting Powers; provided, however, that the displacement for aircraft carriers constructed for a non-contracting Power shall in no case exceed 27,000 tons (27,432 metric tons) standard displacement.[14]

If the construction of any vessel of war for a non-contracting Power is undertaken within the jurisdiction of any of the contracting Powers, such Power shall promptly inform the other contracting Powers of the date of the signing of the contract and the date on which the keel of the ship is laid; and shall also communicate to them the particulars relating to the ship prescribed in Chapter II, Part 3, Section I (b), (4) and (5).[15]

[9] Art. IX.   [10] Art. X.   [11] Art. XII.   [12] Art. XIII.
[13] Art. XIV.   [14] Art. XV.   [15] Art. XVI.

In the event of a contracting Power being engaged in war, such Power shall not use as a vessel of war any vessel of war which may be under construction within its jurisdiction for any other Power, or which may have been constructed within its jurisdiction for another Power and not delivered.[16]

Each of the contracting Powers undertakes not to dispose by gift, sale, or any mode of transfer of any vessel of war in such a manner that such vessel may become a vessel of war in the navy of any foreign Power.[17]

This last understanding is regarded as binding as a matter of honor upon the signatory Powers.

The question of the Pacific fortifications has already been amply discussed and need not be repeated. The term of the treaty is fifteen years.[18] It continues in force for five years after the expiration of the ten-year holiday. That sufficiently provides to meet all the possible complications which may arise after the naval holiday is over. Not only that, but it is provided in the treaty that its provisions may be reconsidered or even amended during the life of the treaty, should such action be deemed necessary:

If during the term of the present Treaty the requirements of the national security of any contracting Power in respect of naval defense are, in the opinion of that Power, materially affected by any change of circumstances, the contracting Powers will, at the request of such Power, meet in conference with a view to the reconsideration of the provisions of the Treaty and its amendment by mutual agreement.

In view of possible technical and scientific developments, the United States, after consultation with the other contracting Powers, shall arrange for a conference of all the contracting Powers, which shall convene as soon as possible after the expiration of eight years from the coming into force of the present Treaty to consider what changes, if any, in the Treaty may be necessary to meet such developments.[19]

[16] Art. XVII.   [17] Art. XVIII.   [18] Art. XXIII.   [19] Art. XXI.

With respect to the effect of an outbreak of war, the treaty provides:

> Whenever any contracting Power shall become engaged in a war which in its opinion affects the naval defense of its national security, such Power may, after notice to the other contracting Powers, suspend for the period of hostilities its obligations under the present Treaty other than those under Articles XIII and XVII, provided that such Power shall notify the other contracting Powers that the emergency is of such a character as to require such suspension.
>
> The remaining contracting Powers shall in such case consult together with a view of agreement as to what temporary modifications, if any, should be made in the Treaty as between themselves. Should such consultation not produce agreement, duly made in accordance with the constitutional methods of the respective Powers, any one of said contracting Powers may, by giving notice to the other contracting Powers, suspend for the period of hostilities its obligations under the present treaty, other than those under Articles XIII and XVII.
>
> On the cessation of hostilities the contracting Powers will meet in conference to consider what modifications, if any, should be made in the provisions of the present Treaty.[20]

Such is the nature and scope of the Naval Treaty, referring to which the American delegation in its report to the President observes:

> Probably no more significant treaty was ever made. Instead of discussing the desirability of diminishing the burdens of naval armament, the conference has succeeded in limiting them to an important degree.
>
> It is obvious that this agreement means ultimately an enormous saving of money and the lifting of a heavy and unnecessary burden. The Treaty absolutely stops the race in competition in naval armament. At the same time, it leaves the relative security of the great naval powers unimpaired. No national interest has

---

[20] Art. XXII.

been sacrificed; a wasteful production of unnecessary armament has been ended.

While it was desired that an agreement should be reached for the limitation of auxiliary craft and submarines, its importance should not be overestimated. Limitation has been effected where it was most needed, both with respect to the avoidance of the heaviest outlays and with reference to the promptings of war which may be found in excessive preparation. Moreover, it is far from probable that the absence of limitation, in the other field, will lead to production of either auxiliary craft or submarines in excess of their normal relation to capital ships. People are not in a mood for unnecessary naval expenditures. The limitation of capital ships, in itself, substantially meets the existing need, and its indirect effect will be to stop the inordinate production of any sort of naval craft.[21]

Mr. Balfour considered the Naval Treaty as "the crown and summit" of the achievements of the conference. He said:

Let no one think that this abandonment of rivalry in ship building, this diminution of fleets, this scrapping of great weapons of war carries with it anything in the nature of a diminution of security on the part of any nation. I do not think we need have feared that, no matter what supplementary arrangements had been made; but we have been fortunate enough to make a supplementary arrangement that puts the question beyond doubt or cavil. I do not think any clause in any treaty is more happily conceived to deal with the special peculiarities and difficulties of the Pacific situation than that which limits and fixes the places where the great naval Powers are permitted to extend and increase their naval bases. I do not say that is a necessary part of the policy. I do say it is a most happy and fortunate addition to it; that with this clause in the treaty, we can say with absolute assurance that this diminution of weapons of war has been accompanied by great augmentation in the sense of national security.[22]

[21] *Document*, p. 812.   [22] *Ibid.*, p. 216.

There was no opportunity for Baron Kato to present his views on the treaty at the plenary session. But his speeches at New York, San Francisco, and Tokyo embody such views:

> I think it is possible for me to say with reasonable certainty that the Conference on Disarmament has succeeded beyond the hopes of those who called it into being, and, in this connection, I have in mind your great President, who has done so much for the cause of international peace.
>
> As to the details of the Naval Agreement, it may be said that the limit on capital ships, although it does not totally destroy equipment for offensive war at sea, does effectually remove the distrust of the great naval powers on naval competition. This means not only relief from a staggering burden of taxation, but, what is of even greater importance, it brings spiritual relief to the world. Security will take the place of fear and a spirit of friendly competition will be substituted for distrust. This revival of confidence will be greatly strengthened by the action taken on submarines, which vessels are largely stripped of the offensive qualities which made them so odious during the recent war. To this feeling of security strength will be added by the decision to stay the development of Pacific bases and preserve the *status quo* of fortifications in the regions of the Pacific. At the risk of being classed among the Utopians, we further indulge the hope that the benefits of the naval agreement will not end with the naval holiday. After ten years of freedom from the burdens of armament and distrust, is it too much to expect that the nations will decide to indefinitely extend the blessings which are sure to come from the cessation of the ruinous course which the world has heretofore pursued?[23]

[23] From the speech made at the Japan Society's banquet in New York, January 14, 1922. Similar views are contained in his speech made at the Japan Society's dinner at San Francisco (see the *San Francisco Chronicle*, February 21, 1922), and in his speech delivered at the banquet tendered in his honor by Premier Takahashi (see the *Jiji* of Tokyo, March 13, 1922).

CHAPTER X

THE FOUR-POWER PACIFIC TREATY AND THE ANGLO-JAPANESE ALLIANCE

Chronologically the Four-Power Treaty was the first of the achievements of the conference. It was agreed upon on December 9, and when the agreement was announced at the fourth plenary session (on the 10th) the public was taken completely by surprise. The subject was nowhere suggested in the agenda, and naturally such a treaty was not expected. As a matter of fact, even the members of the various delegations were mostly unaware of the negotiations which resulted in the treaty, because they had been secretly carried out by a very few persons. The ever-alert newspapermen, too, were unable to divulge anything tangible about the negotiations, though of course they had been indulging in a general discussion of the possibility of such a treaty from the very beginning of the conference.[1]

[1] The first to get the clue on the subject was a Japanese reporter, who cabled to his paper in Tokyo on November 26, 1921, that negotiations were in progress concerning a tripartite agreement, and on the 30th he again cabled that the three-power pact was changed to a four-power agreement. The last-mentioned report soon reached London, whence it came to Washington on December 2. But America received it as a rumor so surprising as to be dubious. See S. Ito, *Kafu Kaigi to Sonogo* ("Washington Conference and After") pp. 292–93, and Sullivan, *op. cit.*, p. 204. Sullivan adds: "A few days later, the American newspaper men learned that on December 4th a British correspondent had sent to his paper in London a confident prediction and more or less detailed description of what was then expected to be a three-power treaty. So closely had the secret been guarded from the American newspapers, and so skeptical were they, that when, under an arrangement common during the Conference, a duplicate of the despatch to London was filed with one of the New York papers, the latter not only did not print it, but actually printed an article discounting the rumor" (*op. cit.*, pp. 204–5). See further a list of articles with their titles and authors on this subject, which appeared in various American papers between December 5 and 9, given on pages 135–37 at the end of this chapter.

Because of these circumstances, the proclamation of the pact produced a dramatic effect upon the audience. Mr. Hughes called upon one of his colleagues, saying with an unusual sign of enthusiasm:

> I shall now ask Senator Lodge to make a communication to the conference with respect to a matter which is not strictly within the agenda, but which should be made known to the conference at this first opportunity.[2]

Whereupon the learned Senator delivered the most flowery speech given during the entire conference, recalling the name of Robert Louis Stevenson, and borrowing the words of Browning to describe the Pacific isles:

> "Sprinkled isles,
> Lily on lily that o'erlace the sea."[3]

The prosaic pact was made a thing of poetic beauty, and indeed the audience drank deeply and became intoxicated. The pact fell from heaven like manna to cure the Pacific ills.

The origin of the Pacific Treaty like the origin of the conference itself is still in the dark. However, even if Great Britain was not the prime mover of the conference, certain it is that she paved the way for this treaty. The desirability of a tripartite treaty in place of the Anglo-Japanese Alliance was more than suggested by the Imperial Cabinet meeting of June–August, 1921. That meeting had seriously considered means for maintaining the peace in the Pacific and Far East, as well as methods of terminating the Anglo-Japanese Alliance. To that end, Great Britain had even consulted with the United States,

---

[2] *Document*, p. 102.   [3] See *ibid.*, pp. 102–6.

Japan, and China. These British activities were publicly known even before the American Government sent in "feelers" as regards the Washington Conference.[4]

Inasmuch as the Anglo-Japanese Alliance played such an important part in the formation of the Four-Power Treaty, it may not be amiss to discuss briefly this subject. The first alliance was signed in 1902.[5] Its object was to guard against the Russian aggressions upon China, which the allied nations considered as a serious menace. Nevertheless, it was a purely defensive alliance. This fact was soon proved beyond doubt. In 1904–1905 Japan was engaged in her life-and-death struggle against Russia, but Great Britain was in no way obliged to assist her ally. If Japan received any immediate benefit at all from the alliance, it was purely moral in character, though it must be admitted that Japan's elevation to the position of a world power was undoubtedly enhanced by the alliance. Great Britain also gained an advantage of no small value.

---

[4] Chapter i, pp. 7–9.

[5] "The preamble of this agreement affirmed that the contracting parties were solely actuated by a desire to preserve the *status quo* and the general peace of the Far East; that they were both specially interested in maintaining the independence and territorial integrity of the empires of China and Korea, and in securing equal opportunities in these countries for all nations; that they mutually recognized it as admissible for either of the contracting parties to take such measures as might be indispensable to safeguard these interests against a threat of aggressive action by any other power, or against disturbances in China or Korea, and that, if one of the contracting parties became involved in war in defense of these interests, the other should maintain strict neutrality and endeavor to prevent any third power from joining in hostilities against its ally. Finally, should a third power join in such hostilities, then the other contracting party promised to come to the assistance of its ally, to conduct the war in common, and to make peace by mutual agreement only."—F. Brinkley, *A History of the Japanese People*, p. 710.

British diplomacy assumed a new importance at Peking when backed by Japan, and, amongst other results, the Tibetan expedition was rendered possible. Since the beginning of the Russo-Japanese War, and the consequent revelation of Japan's power, the advantages to British diplomacy in Europe have been very considerable. In fact, British foreign policy all over the world has been influenced and strengthened by the alliance. The destruction of the Baltic Fleet enabled four British battleships to be sent home to play a very important part in the diplomatic crisis in Europe.[6]

The alliance was renewed, before its legal expiration, on August 12, 1905. This second treaty became enlarged in scope and was made both defensive and offensive in character. It became obligatory for the contracting parties to aid each other when one of them became involved in war. The alliance was to run for ten years.

England's main object in concluding the second alliance was to prepare against the rising tide of German influence which had begun to manifest itself both in Europe and in the Far East.[7]

[6] A. Stead, cited in K. K. Kawakami, *Japan in World Politics* (New York, 1917), pp. 244-45.

[7] K. K. Kawakami, *Japan in World Politics,* p. 249. In this connection it may be interesting to cite the views of Dr. Bau, a representative Chinese: "What is more, instead of being uncompromising and revengeful and relentless, as shown during the Boxer Uprising, she [Germany] manifested an attitude of friendliness and helpfulness, with a view of winning the friendship and good will of the Chinese and to extending German commerce and *kultur* in China. By the Tientsin-Pukow Railway loan of January 13, 1908, she gave the best terms for railway construction, which have since served as the model for other railway construction contracts. She inaugurated the project of systematic forestation, extending even into the hinterland of Kiaochow. She established high schools and professional schools for the spread of German *kultur,* to which Chinese students flocked from all parts of the country. As a result of this systematic and deliberate cultivation of Chinese friendship, her trade prospered by leaps and bounds, as evidenced by the following figures, which show that from

On the other hand, Japan regarded it as a safeguard against Russian revenge.

But before this alliance expired, it was again renewed in 1911. The important change in the new alliance was the provision:

> Should either high contracting party conclude a treaty of general arbitration with a third power, it is agreed that nothing in this agreement shall entail upon such contracting party an obligation to go to war with the power with whom such treaty of arbitration is in force.[8]

The purpose of this proviso was to allay the persistent criticism which the Americans directed against the alliance, that it was an alliance against the United States.[9]

It was because of the existence of the third Anglo-Japanese Alliance that Japan delivered her ultimatum to Germany, on August 15, 1914, that is, exactly eleven days after Great Britain had declared war against the Teutonic Powers.[10] That was the first and the last occasion when

---

1902 to 1911 the imports increased tenfold, and the exports about twenty."—M. J. Bau, *Foreign Relations of China* (New York, 1921), p. 128.

[8] Article IV of the Alliance.

[9] "Unhappily, the general arbitration treaty failed in the United States Senate. But in September, 1914, a 'peace commission' treaty was signed by Great Britain and the United States, and this was accepted, by Japan and Great Britain, as equivalent to a treaty of general arbitration."—P. J. Treat, *Japan and the United States, 1853–1921* (Revised and continued to 1928) (Stanford University, 1928), pp. 208–9.

[10] As to the cause of Japan's entrance into the Great War, writers differ in their opinion. Hornbeck says: "There is doubt as to how far the British Government asked for Japan's assistance. It has been affirmed on good authority that it endeavored at first to dissuade Japan from taking the offensive against Germany's possessions in the Far East" (in his *Contemporary Politics in the Far East,* first edition, p. 286). Willoughby indorses this opinion of Hornbeck, and adds:

the alliance was put into operation during its entire life of twenty years. Nevertheless, it "has been used by ignorant and designing people all over the world to arouse antagonism against the two signatories. Its purpose and its obligations have been grossly misinterpreted."[11] The critics here referred to are, or were, mostly Americans at home and abroad, British residents in the Far East, especially in China, and Chinese, and no amount of explanation could fully satisfy them.[12] Their criticism became most

---

"It is certain that Japan quickly saw that it would be to her interest to destroy German influence in the Far East and to lay the basis at least for a claim for herself of those interests or certain of them at the end of the war" (in his *Foreign Rights and Interests in China*, first edition, p. 380). But Reinsch is more explicit in his opinion: "On August 8, 1914, Japanese war vessels appeared near Tsingtau. Japan suggested on August 10th that the British Government might call for the co-operation of Japan under the terms of the Alliance. In view of possible consequences the British Government hesitated to make the call; the British in China considered it important that independent action by Japan in that country should be precluded. Acting on its own account on August 15th, the Japanese Government sent the Shantung ultimatum to Germany. The British Government was then informed of the action taken" (in his *An American Diplomat in China*, p. 123). On the other hand, Kawakami, on pages 3–4 of his *Japan and World Peace,* narrates in detail the British-Japanese negotiations which resulted in Japan's entrance into the war. Treat says: "The Anglo-Japanese Alliance was the reason which brought Japan promptly into the war" (in *op. cit.*, p. 212). The writer is in possession of the Japanese documents which Kawakami analyzes, and if these are read in conjunction with the correspondence by the British representatives at Tokyo to Sir Edward Grey (*British Documents on the Origins of the War*, XI, 256, 279, 292, and 305) it is evident beyond any doubt that it was the British pressure, based upon the Anglo-Japanese Alliance, which caused Japan's entrance into the war, and that the opinions of Hornbeck, Willoughby, and Reinsch are speculative and not historical.

[11] Treat, *op. cit.*, p. 209.

[12] See the articles which appeared under the title "The East and West" in *The London Times* for 1920–21.

boisterous in 1921 when the alliance was to expire if denounced by one of the contracting parties. By that time, some British at home as well as some Japanese public men began to favor the termination of their alliance on the ground that neither party would, any longer, derive benefits from such union or that benefits accruing from it were one-sided. In spite of all this, neither the British nor the Japanese Government would take the initiative of terminating the alliance. Such was the status of the alliance when the aforesaid Imperial Cabinet Conference took place at London. Naturally under the circumstances, the question of renewing the alliance was an acute issue at that conference.

The Prime Minister of Canada openly adhered to what may be called the American standpoint; while the Prime Ministers of Australia, New Zealand, and South Africa shared rather the British view that the Alliance might be renewed, in a modified form, if no larger and more acceptable substitute could be found.[13]

At this juncture,

the Lord Chancellor expressed the legal view that a decision was not immediately urgent, since the Alliance, not having been formally denounced, would automatically continue in force until it was denounced.[14]

This decision, at its best, could only be considered a temporary expediency. It was not a solution. Rumors became quite current that the question of the Anglo-Japanese Alliance would be referred to the Washington Conference for final solution. When the Japanese delegation arrived at Washington, the first question put to it by

[13] *The London Times,* July 10, 1921. See also *Journals of the Parliaments of the Empire,* II, 669, 721, 864–65.
[14] *Ibid.*

newspapermen was whether or not they would favor the abrogation of the Anglo-Japanese Alliance. Prince Tokugawa replied: "It would be highly beneficial to the maintenance of the world peace, if, for instance, America, Great Britain, and Japan could form an entente cordiale in one form or another."[15] On the same day, a report reached Washington saying that Mr. Harvey had declared it was "futile to hope any such agreement would be reached, however desirable such action might seem to be."[16] Whether the American Ambassador was authorized to make such a statement is not known. It is known that at that time Prince Tokugawa's reply was not to be interpreted as an official view either of the delegation or of the Government of Japan. It reflected, however, the opinion current in both Japan and Great Britain. A Japanese writer says: "On the eve of the Conference our thoughts naturally turn to the Anglo-Japanese Alliance, for the alliance is bound to be discussed and disposed of at this international gathering. There is no doubt that England and Japan stand at the parting of the ways."[17]

It is perhaps superfluous to add that American newspapers began to discuss freely the pros and the cons of an American-British-Japanese alliance. Yet, so far as the Japanese delegates were concerned, no action had been taken by them until very late in November. Because of the persistence of newspaper discussions they were led to a consultation among themselves; they concluded that it was wise for them to sound the opinion of the British delegates. To that end two of the Japanese delegates called on Mr. Balfour. The latter intimated to them at

[15] The *New York World*, November 4, 1921.
[16] The *Washington Post*, November 4, 1921.
[17] K. K. Kawakami, *Japan's Pacific Policy*, p. 43.

once that he was considering the desirability of a tripartite treaty to replace the Anglo-Japanese Alliance and was thus very happy to learn of the favorable view of the Japanese delegates on that proposition. He told the Japanese "incidentally" that he had given to Mr. Hughes a memorandum of his tentative suggestion for a triple or quadruple entente. This was the gentle breaking of the astounding news. The Japanese were dumbfounded. They little dreamed of such treatment at the hands of the British delegate. Negotiations for the proposed treaty were being conducted as early as December 1, when Mr. Balfour called on Baron Kato. The matter progressed very rapidly, and by December 7 the "Big Three" were able not only to compare their memoranda relative to the proposed text of the treaty but also to reach a practical agreement. France was then invited to join the group.[18] The pact was agreed upon on the night of the 9th and was announced on the 10th. The text of the treaty reads as follows:[19]

The United States of America, the British Empire, France, and Japan—

[18] Leon Archimbaud in his *La Conférence de Washington* tells us how France became a signatory of the Treaty as follows: A member of the French delegation, being warned of the intended exclusion of France from the treaty which Balfour, Hughes, and Kato were drawing up, requested the British and American delegates to include his country. After much pressure from the Americans, the British yielded to the French request. See *op. cit.*, pp. 50, 111, and 113–15. The writer knows that this French version is nothing more than pure fiction. True, the French delegates were not acquainted with the proposed treaty before December 7, but on that day the "Big Three" expressed the wisdom of asking France to join the Entente. There was neither the request from the French delegation nor the alleged pressure from the Americans upon the British. M. Archimbaud's story may be considered as another French slam against the British.

[19] *Document*, pp. 102–3.

With a view to the preservation of the general peace and the maintenance of their rights in relation to their insular possessions and insular dominions in the region of the Pacific Ocean—

Have determined to conclude a treaty to this effect and have appointed as their plenipotentiaries [here are enumerated the names of the delegates], who have agreed as follows:

I. The High Contracting Parties agree as between themselves to respect their rights in relation to their insular possessions and insular dominions in the region of the Pacific Ocean.

If there should develop between any of the High Contracting Parties a controversy arising out of any Pacific question and involving their said rights which is not satisfactorily settled by diplomacy and is likely to affect the harmonious accord now happily subsisting between them, they shall invite the other High Contracting Parties to a joint conference to which the whole subject will be referred for consideration and adjustment.

II. If the said rights are threatened by the aggressive action of any other Power, the High Contracting Parties shall communicate with one another fully and frankly in order to arrive at an understanding as to the most efficient measures to be taken, jointly or separately, to meet the exigencies of the particular situation.

III. This Treaty shall remain in force for ten years from the time it shall take effect, and after the expiration of said period shall continue to be in force subject to the right of any of the High Contracting Parties to terminate it upon twelve months' notice.

IV. This Treaty shall be ratified as soon as possible in accordance with the constitutional methods of the High Contracting Parties and shall take effect on the deposit of ratifications, which shall take place at Washington, and thereupon the agreement between Great Britain and Japan, which was concluded at London on July 13, 1911, shall terminate. The Government of the United States will transmit to all the Signatory Powers a certified copy of the procès-verbal of the deposit of ratifications.

The present Treaty, in French and in English, shall remain deposited in the Archives of the Government of the United States, and duly certified copies thereof will be transmitted by that Government to each of the Signatory Powers.

In faith whereof the above-named Plenipotentiaries have signed the present Treaty.

Done at the City of Washington, the thirteenth day of December, One Thousand Nine Hundred and Twenty-One.

The object of the treaty is plainly stated in its preamble. The contracting powers propose to maintain the general peace in their Pacific "insular possessions and insular dominions." Article I provides that should difficulties involving their interests in the Pacific region arise the parties will get together to solve them. Article II has been interpreted in two ways which do not harmonize, one group insisting that this clause makes the treaty an alliance involving military sanction, the other group denying such obligations. Article III provides that the Anglo-Japanese Alliance terminate with the ratification of the treaty. The pact will continue in force for ten years.

A curious incident which occurred soon after the announcement of the pact may be mentioned. President Harding expressed the opinion that the home-land of Japan did not come within the words "insular possessions and insular dominions."[20] The statement was surprising in view of the expression of Mr. Hughes a little before that Japan proper was included in the words quoted. Fortunately, however, Mr. Harding withdrew his opinion, issuing a new statement in which he said that he had learned from the United States delegates to the conference that they had agreed to the construction which included the home-land of Japan in the term "insular possessions and insular dominions," and had no objections to that construction.[21]

[20] The *New York World,* December 21, 1921.

[21] See the *New York World* and *New York Times,* December 21, 1921. The first statement was made in the afternoon, while the second was issued on the evening of the 20th.

But ever since the signing of the treaty this very question has created a good deal of discussion among the Japanese at Washington and at home. "The more serious-minded patriots from the Mikado's empire," as one Japanese writer stated, "are inclined to take it as an affront to Japan's dignity that the treaty should be interpreted as obligating the other contracting parties to extend even a moral assistance to the safeguarding of the territorial integrity of Japan proper. Quite properly they think that Japan can take care of herself as far as the protection of her main islands is concerned, and that no outsider need worry about it. Meanwhile, the Japanese delegation remain discreetly silent. Apparently they are in an embarrassing position."[22]

Evidently the Japanese delegates subscribed to the interpretation given by Mr. Hughes but without authorization of their Government. Later they were instructed by the Government to have the home-land excluded from the scope of the treaty. Certainly the Japanese delegates faced a humiliating situation and had to do much begging before they were able to bring about the so-called supplementary treaty to the Four-Power Pact by which the terms were clearly defined as follows:

The term "insular possessions and insular dominions" used in the aforesaid treaty shall, in its application to Japan, include only Karafuto [or the southern portion of the island of Sakhalin], Formosa and the Pescadores, and the islands under the mandate of Japan.[23]

Much has already been said about the authorship of the text of the treaty, and it has been intimated that two

[22] K. K. Kawakami, *Japan's Pacific Policy*, p. 66.

[23] This supplementary treaty was not announced until February 4. See *Document*, pp. 200–201.

persons claim this distinction.[24] As a matter of fact, it was not the work of any single person; it was composed on the basis of the three texts presented. Only the French delegates had small part in shaping the text. In any case, there is not much honor at stake in the question of authorship, for the text is cumbersome in places and shows evidence of hasty work. Such is the history of the Four-Power Pact, and such its nature and scope.

The official views on the treaty need not be analyzed, except to remark that they all express an unqualified satisfaction. Furthermore, they leave no doubt on the question of military sanction, for according to these views no such sanction is involved in the treaty. They declare that the strength and value of this international instrument is moral, and as such the signatory powers consider it a memorable achievement.[25]

But there now remain two points to be discussed: first, the official views on the termination of the Anglo-Japanese Alliance; and, secondly, the relation of the treaty to Portugal and the Netherlands.

In response to the enthusiasm which greeted the announcement of the Four-Power Pact, Mr. Balfour referred to the termination of the British-Japanese Treaty in the following words:

[24] Sullivan says, "it was Mr. Hughes who promptly took the initiative in making a concrete suggestion and drafting the treaty" (*The Great Adventure at Washington*, p. 233). This conclusion is based on a letter from Mr. Hughes to Senator Underwood, and is reproduced in Mr. Sullivan's book, pages 233-35. The letter, however, if carefully examined, does not claim the alleged authorship. Kawakami says (*Japan's Pacific Policy*, p. 61), "its final draft, which formed the basis of the treaty, was Baron Shidehara's work"; but he offers no evidence for this claim.

[25] See *Document*, pp. 103-14.

This treaty, remember, was not a treaty that had to be renewed. It was a treaty that ran until it was formally denounced by one of the two parties to it. It is true that the objects for which the treaty had been created no longer required international attention. But, after all, that treaty or its predecessors has been in existence within a few days of twenty years. It had served a great purpose in two great wars. It had stood the strain of common sacrifice, common anxieties, common effort, common triumphs.

When two nations have been united in that fiery ordeal, they cannot at the end of it take off their hats one to the other and politely part as two strangers part who travel together for a few hours in a railway train.[26]

Japan was naturally expected to make an important response. Prince Tokugawa dismissed the subject with the following brief remark:

The terms of the important pact assuring mutual security and friendship have just been made known. It is needless for me to say that all Japan will approve the consummation of this work. Japan will rejoice in this pledge of peace upon the Pacific Ocean.

As to the Anglo-Japanese agreement, which is soon to terminate, I desire to associate myself with the words of appreciation so ably expressed by our distinguished colleague, Mr. Balfour, with respect to the glorious service which that agreement has done for the preservation of peace and liberty.[27]

Finally, the American official view was given in these words:

It may be stated without reservation that one of the most important factors in the Far Eastern situation was the Anglo-Japanese Alliance. This Alliance has been viewed by the people of the United States with deep concern. . . . . It was, therefore, a matter of great gratification that the American delegation found that they were able to obtain an agreement by which the

[26] *Document*, p. 110.   [27] *Ibid.*, pp. 111–12.

Anglo-Japanese Alliance should be immediately terminated. No greater step could be taken to secure that unimpeded influence of liberal opinion in promoting peace in the Pacific region.[28]

In other words, the British view is that the objects of the Anglo-Japanese Alliance no longer required international attention; this view is indorsed unqualifiedly by Japan. Hence the termination of the entente is but a natural outcome. But the American opinion is that the alliance was a source of deep concern to its interests, and, therefore, its termination is a matter of great gratification. Senator Lodge went so far as to state that "the removal or the termination of the Anglo-Japanese Alliance was necessary to the successful conclusion of the naval treaty."[29]

Beyond these official views, there naturally occur differences of opinion among critics. While most Americans welcome the end of the Anglo-Japanese Alliance, some of them think that the price paid for it, the Four-Power Pact, is too great. In fact, these hold that America should never have become entangled in an alliance. Others defend the Pact because it ends the "dangerous" alliance; one writer says, "the four-power treaty is a device for terminating the Anglo-Japanese Alliance."[30] Furthermore, the same author presents his idea of the alliance in these words:

We came to feel that in our effort to check some of Japan's aggression in China we were baffled by the Anglo-Japanese Alliance. Under cover of it, Japan was doing things which she might have hesitated to do if Great Britain were free to unite

[28] *Ibid.*, pp. 821–22.

[29] *Congressional Record,* 67th Congress, 2nd Session, Vol. 62, Part 4, p. 3551.

[30] Mark Sullivan, *op. cit.*, p. 235.

with America in opposition. The alliance kept British sentiment silent.[31]

If the reader is interested in a more subtle indictment against the alliance, he will find one in a learned monograph written by Professor Dennis.[32]

In spite of these apparently overwhelming views of American officials, journalists, and academic men, the

[31] Sullivan, *op. cit.*, p. 230.

[32] "The Anglo-Japanese Alliance has had an unwholesome biography, and its disappearance will make for healthier relations between the United States, Great Britain, and Japan. The world is sick of the old diplomacy of which the alliance was such a marked example" (Note). The author premises his work on a novel theory of treaties. "Treaties are living things subject in interpretation and enforcement to inevitable alteration due to facts and events which are not necessarily embodied in any written document" (p. 3). The following are his reasons for indictment: (1) "the Alliance has served to cover and protect the annexation of Korea, the occupation of Manchuria, the push into Mongolia, the seizure of Vladivostok, the grabbing of Shantung, and much else of a less startling but equally objectionable kind" (quoted from the London *Nation*, Vol. XXX, No. 2, October 8, 1921, pp. 42–43); (2) "a second point against the alliance arises from the fact that both partners are members of the League of Nations"; (3) because of the decision of the Paris Conference in favor of Japan relative to Shantung; and, "if such settlements were possible under the aegis of the Anglo-Japanese agreement, or as an indirect and supplementary effect of that connection, the inclination [American] was strong to cry 'a plague on both your houses,' withdraw from participation in European affairs as far as possible and view the Asiatic situation with special attention and concern"; (4) "in the Far East the Anglo-Japanese Alliance has become anathema to intelligent and patriotic Chinese"; (5) "in the event of trouble she [Japan] felt she could count either on the active assistance of England or, at least, on a benevolent British neutrality; at all events England would not be against her in the Far East; such a feeling has acted as a stimulant to Japanese forward policies"; (6) "a sixth point comes from the attempted violations of the spirit of the agreement as suggested by its provisions"; and (7) "today the alliance is too old; it has served its purpose." Alfred L. P. Dennis, *The Anglo-Japanese Alliance* (Berkeley, 1923), pp. 94–97.

writer remains unconvinced as to the truth of the grounds upon which the opinions are premised. For instance, a careful perusal of the arguments presented by Professor Dennis convinces the writer that he has gathered together information for the purpose of proving his preconceived indictment against the alliance; he has not treated the subject from a historical standpoint. Hence, although he uses American, British, and Japanese sources, his selection is such as to establish a thesis apparently preconceived. He introduces the opinion of Lord Bryce, who says on this subject: "an attempt by Japan to dominate and exploit China—this is a possible eventuality on which Americans dwell—is, of course, an imaginable danger," but he refuses to accept this opinion of Bryce, although in his very next sentence he states that "Lord Bryce, in this analysis, is undoubtedly correct." Mr. Dennis then proceeds to insist on the view that the danger is not an imaginable one only and bases this claim on a number of extravagant assertions regarding Japan's policy, the truth of which he fails to prove (see *op. cit.*, p. 58). Again, Lord Wester-Wemyss, speaking of the alliance, says,

> the steadying effect which her alliance with one of the Great Powers has had on Japan is incalculable. Without her obligations to Great Britain she would, urged by her restless ambition, undoubtedly have gone much farther in China than she has done. .... Thus the Treaty has conferred great advantages on both Great Britain and Japan.[33]

This opinion seems to disturb the very foundation on which the American theory of the alliance is built up. A saner historical estimate of the entente is found in the

[33] Lord Wester-Wemyss, "And After Washington," in *The Nineteenth Century and After* (March 1922), pp. 414–15.

already quoted words of Professor Treat, which we repeat here:

> It [the alliance] has been used by ignorant and designing people all over the world to arouse antagonism against the two signatories. Its purpose and its obligations [it may be added, its application] have been grossly misinterpreted.

Moreover, it is incorrect to assume that the British official view was unanimous in favor of the abrogation of the alliance. At the Imperial Cabinet Meeting of 1921, Canada alone was opposed to its renewal. Likewise British public opinion was and still is divided. In 1925 the British Government and people found themselves in a difficult position in China, and soon after they launched a campaign to revive an alliance with Japan. In Japan public opinion was also divided on this subject, and, for that matter, it is still divided, but she accepted the termination of her alliance with England in the hope that its substitute would prove a better international instrument to maintain the general peace in the Far East. We may characterize the termination of the Anglo-Japanese Alliance as a happy incident, since the allies themselves were not particularly enthusiastic over its renewal and since the United States considered its termination as gratifying to herself.

Returning to the Four-Power Treaty, we note that it has been criticized because it is exclusive; Italy is one of the five Great Powers, but is kept out of the pact. The explanation is that Italy possesses no insular territory in the Pacific region. On the occasion of the announcement of the treaty, M. Schanzer said that any measure aiming at the creation of guaranties for the safeguard of peace in the world could not but meet with his fullest consent. The principles involved in the agreement were entirely in accordance with the main lines of policy inspired by the high aim of a peaceful elimination of conflicts between nations. He expressed his full confidence that this great agreement might represent the most firm and lasting guaranties for the safeguarding of peace in the Pacific region.[34]

The case of China was never considered by the men responsible for the pact, but just why the writer cannot tell. Possibly the observation made by her delegate, Dr. Sze, may explain. He said that the Chinese delegation anticipated, as indicated by the distinguished chairman, that this agreement would be supplemented by a further convention to which all the powers, including China, would be parties, which would adjust conditions in the Far East upon a basis satisfactory to all the powers and which it was hoped would provide for the amicable settlement of any future controversies.[35]

But both Holland and Portugal hold insular possessions in the Pacific region. Why then were they excluded? To speak very plainly, they are kept out of the pact because of their status as international powers. Nevertheless, their representatives were very graceful about it. Mr. Van Karnebeck of Holland remarked that he wanted to seize this opportunity to state that he felt that in his country this treaty would be received with great sympathy, because in that country it would be felt that it constituted and embodied an endeavor to promote peace and tranquillity in these far-off regions neighboring the Netherlands' possessions.[36] Viscount d'Alte of Portugal characterized the pact by saying that it was the spirit in which this memorable agreement had been conceived that would fill the whole civilized world with high hopes for the future. It would even seem as if the men who had

[34] *Document*, p. 112. [35] *Ibid.*, pp. 112–13. [36] *Ibid.*, p. 113.

drafted it had tried to signify that they had not placed their main reliance and the achievement of their aims in a long series of carefully worded clauses. Only four powers who reposed the most implicit trust in the honor and integrity of each other could sign a treaty such as this. And it was this fact that gave the agreement its tremendous binding power. The confidence so fully given, no nation would dare to betray.[37]

There is nothing indicative of dissatisfaction or disappointment in the remarks of the Dutch and Portuguese delegates. But they quietly approached the nations who had signed the pact and asked that their countries be given some recognition or guaranty in connection with it. The signatory powers gave an identical note to these two nations to that effect. Below is reproduced the note by the American Government to the Netherlands:

The United States of America has concluded on December 13, 1921, with the British Empire, France, and Japan, a treaty, with a view to the preservation of the general peace and the maintenance of their rights in relation to their insular possessions and insular dominions in the region of the Pacific Ocean. They have agreed thereby as between themselves to respect their rights in relation to these possessions and dominions.

The Netherlands not being signatory to the said treaty and the Netherlands possessions in the region of the Pacific Ocean therefore not being included in the agreement referred to, the Government of the United States of America, anxious to forestall any conclusion contrary to the spirit of the treaty, desires to declare that it is firmly resolved to respect the rights of the Netherlands in relation to their insular possessions in the region of the Pacific Ocean.[38]

[37] *Document*, pp. 113–14.

[38] *U.S. Senate Document No. 128*, 67th Congress, 2d Session, pp. 922–23.

In conclusion, we may present a summary statement of criticisms on the Four-Power Treaty. Mr. Sullivan's opinion that this treaty is a mere device to get rid of the Anglo-Japanese Alliance, which accords with the view of Senator Lodge, is an extreme one, for it attaches no value to the treaty itself. Dr. Buell criticizes the treaty in these words:

> The outstanding defect of the Treaty is that it provides no means by which acts of imperialism there [in Asia] can be called in question; yet it protects the consequences of those acts in case war should break out, ... As a result of the Four-Power Treaty, therefore, Japan has received the pledge of Great Britain and the United States that they will never undertake a joint military action against Japan, and Japan has also probably restricted the diplomatic pressure which the United States might otherwise bring to bear.[39]

Later he corrects himself by saying that he underestimated the moral forces resulting from the conference, which changed Japan's Oriental policy.[40] It is not clear whether or not this correction applies to the treaty in question. In either case, it should be recalled that the treaty has bearing only upon insular possessions and insular dominions. Lord Wester-Wemyss is pessimistic; he says, "whatever its advantages may be to others, to England, at any rate, it can never give that substantial guaranty which did her alliance with Japan."[41] M. Archimbaud laments the exclusion of French Indo-China from the pact, and he points out the uncertainty it allows in case of war between one of the signatories and a fifth power and the exclusion of

---

[39] Raymond L. Buell, *The Washington Conference* (New York, 1922), pp. 194–95.

[40] R. L. Buell, *Problems of the Pacific* (Boston, 1925), p. 33.

[41] Lord Wester-Wemyss, *op. cit.*, p. 415.

some powers interested in the Pacific and Far East.[42] Colonel Reboul sees no good whatever in the agreement.[43] To him the treaty is only a decoy destined to mask the lack of success of the negotiation of the conference; it is in effect neither an alliance nor a political entente, nor even a pact of mutual guaranties. Its only result was to permit England decently to denounce its alliance with Japan.[44] Thus we see that British, Americans, and Frenchmen are all pessimistic about the treaty. But Mr. Kawakami says,

the value of this four-power agreement is moral. Its importance lies not so much in what it says as in what it implies. . . . . The ultimate and real objective of this treaty is not the protection of the Pacific islands, but the moral effect which is certain to be produced upon the world by the proclamation, and the idea implied therein, that henceforward the four dominant powers are going to act in the spirit of perfect harmony and co-operation.[45]

This is one optimistic note we encounter which is in harmony with the official utterances made when the pact was announced to the world. Broadly surveying the international situation in the Pacific region, one is forced to conclude that while the instrument in question has not played any important positive rôle, yet, as Kawakami says, it has restrained the powers from becoming malevolently critical of each other. This is especially true of Japan and the United States.

There follows a list of articles with their titles and authors on the subject of the Anglo-Japanese Alliance, which appeared in various newspapers between December 5 and 9, showing a wide interest in journalistic circles.

[42] Archimbaud, *op. cit.,* pp. 324–25.

[43] Lieutenant-Colonel Reboul, *Le Conflit du Pacifique et notre marine de guerre* (Paris, 1922), p. 69.

[44] *Ibid.,* p. 87.   [45] Kawakami, *Japan's Pacific Policy,* p. 59.

THE FOUR-POWER PACIFIC TREATY 135

December 5, 1921

"U.S. Will Refuse to Turn Anglo-Japanese Alliance into Three-Power Treaty," by Louis Seibold in the *New York Herald*.

"Sees Anglo-Japanese Alliance as Dominant Problem," by Gabriel Hanotaux in the *Washington Post*.

"End of Treaty with Japanese Delights British," by Arthur S. Draper in the *New York Tribune*.

"France Favors Substitute for Anglo-Japanese Pact," by Henry Wales in the *Chicago Tribune*.

"Economic Council Urged to Replace Anglo-Japan Pact," by the Associated Press in the *Philadelphia Public Ledger*.

December 6, 1921

"Consider Four-Power Entente to Replace Alliance," by the Associated Press in the *Washington Post*.

"Pacific Agreement Near," by Edwin L. James in the *New York Times*.

"Triple Alliance Is Held Unlikely," by David Lawrence in the *Washington Star*.

"Four-Power Pact Welcomed by British Press," by London dispatch to the *New York Tribune*.

"Japanese Applaud Idea of Four-Power Alliance," by the Associated Press in the *New York Tribune*.

"Wickersham Favors Four-Power Treaty," the *New York Times*.

"See British Triumph in Far East Entente," by C. F. Bertelli in the *New York American*.

"Balfour Puts Idea of a Broader Pact to U.S. Spokesman," by Joseph W. Grigg in the *New York World*.

December 7, 1921

"Press Four-Power Entente Proposals," by the Associated Press in the *Washington Post*.

"America Proposes Four or Nine-Power Accord in Far East," by Henry Wales in the *Baltimore Sun*.

"Japan Is Prepared to Scrap Alliance, Says Noted Editor," by Adachi Kinnosuke in the *New York World*.

"No Treaty on Far East Likely," by Edwin L. James in the *New York Times*.

"Japanese Leader for Peace Entente," by the Associated Press in the *New York Herald*.
"Tokyo Approves Four-Party Pact," Tokyo dispatch to the *Washington Herald*.
"French Skeptical of Proposed Pact," by Pierre Marsac in the *Philadelphia Public Ledger*.
"Far East Entente Now Seems Likely," by Stephane Lauzanne in the *New York Times*.
"French for Four-Power Plan," by the Associated Press in the *New York Times*.

December 8, 1921

"Says Tokyo Approves Treaty," by the Associated Press in the *Washington Post*.
"Pacific Treaty Will Not Form an 'Alliance'," by Frederic William Wile in the *Philadelphia Public Ledger*.
"Triple Agreement over Sea Strength Will Be Separate," by Louis Seibold in the *New York Herald*.
"Treaty Rumors Stir Washington as Japan Is Reported Accepting," by Edwin L. James in the *New York Times*.
"Harding Ready to Give Senate Four-Power Plan," by Carter Field in the *New York Tribune*.
"Four Powers May Form Entente but No Treaty," the *New York Sun*.
"Japanese Look with Favor on Entente Plan," the *Baltimore Sun*.
"Hears Japan Favors Limit on Compact," by J. G. Hamilton in the *New York Times*.
"Think British Seek to Edge France Out," by Marcel Ray in the *New York Times*.
"Navy Base Parley Offered to Japan," the *New York Times*.
"5-5-3 Ratio and Four-Power Accord Are Accepted by Japan," by Lincoln Eyre in the *Baltimore Sun*.
"Secret Well Kept," the *Washington Herald*.

December 9, 1921

"Four-Power Treaty Pledges Consultation, Mediation, Arbitration; Ends the Anglo-Japanese Alliance," from the *New York Times*.

"Japan Said to Have Approved Four-Power Treaty," Associated Press in the *New York Times*.

"Delegates Silent on Four-Power Plan," by Edwin L. James in the *New York Times*.

"Old Anglo-Japanese Treaty Superseded," by Louis Seibold in the *New York Herald*.

"Harding Plan Included in Four-Power Draft," by the Associated Press in the *New York Tribune*.

"Japan Hesitates to Shelve Treaty," by Roderick O. Matheson in the *New York World*.

"New Pact Outline," the *Washington Herald*.

"Harding Gives Assurance on Pacific Accord," by J. F. Essary in the *Baltimore Sun*.

"Justifies Harding's View on Arms Session Success," by Wickham Steed in the *Washington Post*.

"Steed Sees U.S. Line-Up Behind Harding," by Wickham Steed in the *New York Herald*.

"Parley May Frame Arbitration Pact," by Frank W. Simonds in the *Washington Herald*.

"Nippon Backs Pacific Pact," by Robert J. Prew in the *New York American*.

"Pacific Agreement Favored by Britain," by Joseph W. Grigg in the *New York World*.

"Four-Power Entente Monroe Doctrine," by Henry W. Nevinson in the *New York World*.

CHAPTER XI

AN ESTIMATE OF THE WASHINGTON ARMS TREATIES, AND THE AFTERMATH AT GENEVA

We have now completed our story of the processes through which the Four-Power Pact, the Submarine and Poisonous Gas Treaty, and the Naval Treaty were achieved. We have analyzed these international agreements, and commented upon them in the hope that their meaning might be made clear. We are therefore ready to offer a brief critical estimate of these achievements of the Five-Power Washington Arms Conference.

As we have observed in the preceding pages, the Four-Power Pact, in conjunction with the Naval Treaty, has already produced the general effect of restraining foolish utterances against one another by the Pacific Powers, thus assisting in the maintenance of better international relations between them. But in order to understand the true significance of the contribution of the pact, one must recall the Pacific international situation prior to its enactment. The conclusion of the Russo-Japanese War of 1904–1905, with Japan as the victorious party, was followed by two general tendencies of international importance. One was a fear among Western nations that the defeat of Russia was but the first step in the expulsion of American and European interests from the Pacific region; the other was an elation among Asiatic peoples that the victory of Japan marked the beginning of Asia's emancipation from the Western yoke. Out of these tendencies there developed the "yellow peril" and the "white peril," which, in turn, bred suspicions and antagonisms hitherto unknown between the East and the West. War scares loomed large, and of course Japan was made the scapegoat and had to bear the brunt of Western hostility. For instance, the relations between the United States and Japan became so tense that their governments felt the need of a restraining measure, and the result was the Root-Takahira notes of 1908, the object of which was to inform the people of America and Japan that the governments were determined to continue to maintain their friendly relationship. But the war talk continued. The naval rivalry between these two powers was partly accounted for by this strained situation. Even after the United States had entered into the Great War and was fighting on the side of the Allies, one of which was Japan, American-Japanese relations showed no improvement. On November 2, 1917, the two governments renewed and extended the views embodied in the Root-Takahira notes, in what are known as the Lansing-Ishii notes. These notes also failed to produce the desired result between the two nations, and their antagonism and naval rivalry continued. In view of these circumstances, one cannot fail to appreciate the real significance of an amicable tendency effected by the Four-Power Pact and the Naval Treaty. War scares have been pushed to the background. Furthermore, so far as the writer can see, there has been no deterioration in the British-Japanese relationship in spite of the termination of the Anglo-Japanese Alliance; and there has been a decided improvement in the Franco-Japanese understanding, especially in regard to French Indo-China.

The Treaty on Submarines and Poisonous Gases does not propose to codify international rules relating to visit, search, or seizure of merchant vessels; it merely reiterates the important provisions in international law relative to the treatment of merchant ships by belligerent war vessels, declaring that submarines are not exempt from these rules for protecting the life of non-combatants. But it does undertake to declare that violation of these rules by submarines constitutes an act of piracy, and makes the offender liable to punishment as a pirate. It also denounces the use of poisonous gases and chemicals in war. Whether or not these rules will be adhered to in the stress of war is a question on which opinion is divided. But no effective counter-argument has yet been presented against the declaration of Mr. Root that "this treaty is an attempt to crystallize, in simple and unmistakable terms, the opinion of civilization that already exists." In fact, this opinion seems to have been accepted by all as a satisfactory estimate of the treaty.

On the Naval Treaty little or nothing has been heard from Italy, perhaps because she is not vitally involved in its stipulations. She secures a parity with France on capital ships and airplane carriers, and her general naval strength increases relatively because of the sweeping reduction of capital ships by the three great naval powers. From the position taken by the French delegation in the conference, it is obvious that no patriotic Frenchman would indorse the treaty. It seems no exaggeration to state that France unites in lamenting over the loss of her naval prestige, the sentiment eloquently voiced by Archimbaud, Reboul, and La Bruyère.[1] Archimbaud[2] says France was hurt at being relegated to a place below Japan and on a level with Italy, for before the war her naval force had nearly equaled that of the United States, had doubled that of Japan, and had been three times as strong as that of

[1] See L. Archimbaud, *op. cit.*, pp. 131–32; Reboul, *op. cit.*, pp. 65–88; and R. La Bruyère, "French Naval Ideas," in the *Atlantic Monthly* (June 1922), pp. 826–33.

[2] Archimbaud, *op. cit.*, p. 131.

Italy. The author is incorrect in his statement in regard to these relative naval strengths, for, according to M. de Kerguezec, Chairman of the Naval Committee of the French Senate, they stood on January 1, 1914, as follows: Great Britain, 2,189,000; the United States, 864,000; Japan, 570,000; France, 803,000; and Italy, 405,000 tons.[3] M. de Kerguezec is one Frenchman who admits:

> We [the French] realize that mistakes were made in Washington by the French Delegation. Its technical adviser was a General Officer who had evinced pronounced imperialistic views during the war and who had been, in consequence, relieved of his post as Chief of the General Staff. The same gentleman advertised his scorn for the will of Parliament and came home demanding 350,000 tons in battleships at a time when Parliament had expressly voted that it wanted none at all.[4]

In the British Empire, the United States, and Japan, vastly affected by the treaty, many and conflicting criticisms have been presented from various angles by different classes of writers. Neglecting the views of laymen for the moment, we may examine the representative estimates attempted by naval experts of the three nations.

Lord Wester-Wemyss, a British Admiral, laments the British voluntary resignation from the position of naval supremacy which was obtained as a result of a struggle for more than three hundred years, and was the foremost article of British political faith, as an act of renunciation unparalleled in history.

> Nor does Britannia rule the waves, or, if she does so, it is in partnership with the American eagle, on the principle of a limited liability company. It is difficult to know why America wants

---

[3] Gustave de Kerguezec, "French Naval Aims," in *Foreign Affairs* (April 1926), p. 372.

[4] *Ibid.*, p. 379.

a navy equal to that of Britain, and when the question was put to a distinguished American naval officer, his reply was, "Why shouldn't we?" Of late, the racial composition of American population has changed, and it is no longer Anglo-Saxon. It is hoped that it is not a vain lure of an eventual Anglo-American alliance which caused the British government to discard the Anglo-Japanese Alliance for the Four-Power Treaty. The conference has proven an unqualified success for the United States . . . . , but they never would have obtained so triumphant an issue without the whole-hearted co-operation of Great Britain.[5]

In reply, Admiral Sims of the United States criticizes the British Admiral's tone as one of pessimism, which is explained by the fact that the latter adopts a purely material criterion and neglects psychological factors; he goes to history to gain perspective but not far enough to gain a correct one, and he judges from a purely British point of view. Admiral Sims continues to say that the fundamental question is this:

whether the tangible Anglo-Japanese Alliance or a nebulous trust in Anglo-American friendship were the greater asset for Britain. Admiral Wemyss thought that the former promised more substantial returns to Great Britain. Perhaps, from his point of view, it did; but from the standpoint of the British Commonwealth of Nations, this judgment may be questioned. As to the value of American friendship, let us begin by putting aside cant, as one would any other poison, and, being perfectly candid, rely upon facts as the only secure basis for an enduring structure. We should begin by admitting freely that many Americans and Englishmen do not like each other and do not get along well together. . . . . But the same cannot be said of the relations between colonials and Americans. They like, admire, and understand each other.

[5] Lord Wester-Wemyss, "And After Washington," in *The Nineteenth Century and After*, March 1922, pp. 405–16.

In short, while he is willing to concede the magnificence of the British sacrifices, it is not apparent that the Anglo-Japanese Alliance was one of these sacrifices. Taking up the Naval Treaty, he says that while the United States is given a capital-ship strength equal with that of Great Britain, of the necessary auxiliaries the former has practically nothing but destroyers. To reach an equality, she must build, but the American people will not hear of a building program, and Congress dares not spend money. He continues:

> Our present policy makes us a bad third. Britannia not only still rules the waves but rules them more economically now; . . . . learned foreign naval experts are fond of pointing out that the Washington Conference was a shrewd Yankee move to gain naval supremacy because we were convinced that the battleship is doomed. But the irony of the situation is that our naval men are firmly convinced that it is not. Curiously enough, each country appears to be convinced that it made the heaviest sacrifices, and that the United States alone gained.[6]

But now comes a compatriot of Admiral Sims, who claims that the Washington Conference proved most beneficial to Japan.

> In all the diplomatic history of Japan there has been no victory quite so complete, so important, or one gained at so little cost, as her victory at the Washington Arms Conference. She has gained the position for which she has been struggling for fifty years, and accomplished it without bloodshed, and even without creating hard feelings.

This writer explains this to mean that Japan is the dominating military power of the East as she was before the conference, and is secure in that position, and no

[6] W. S. Sims, "Status of the United States Navy," in *Current History*, May 1922, pp. 185–94.

external military or naval alliances are necessary. He goes on:

> All other nations must now stand back, despite the fact that the naval treaty leaves Japan 40 per cent weaker than either the British Empire or the United States. The Anglo-Japanese Alliance has been terminated, and the Japanese Empire is no longer bound by agreements which it may be forced to keep .... Japan has absolutely a free hand in the Pacific and Asia today. We have given it to her in the Arms Conference treaties. I state these things not as arguments for or against the treaties. It would be useless to do so, for they have been ratified by our Senate, and nothing more is to be said. But of our own choosing, perhaps blundering, we must keep our hands off Asia in the future, if we are to have peace and retain our possessions.[7]

What then are the views of Japanese experts? Lieutenant-Commander Ishimaru says that no one can deny the fact that the Naval Treaty gives to the American and British navies a strength capable of offense while it fails to give to the remaining three navies a strength capable of even adequate defense. From the standpoint of her national defense, Japan suffers on account of the Naval Treaty: First, because of the unjust ratio of capital ships, she is forced to feel the insecurity of her position in the Pacific; secondly, she is placed in a disadvantageous position from the point of view of her fleet organization, for instance, in comparison with the United States, because of differences in the character of ships possessed by the two nations (Ishimaru holds the American ships to be distinctly superior to those of the Japanese Navy while Schornstheimer says the opposite to be true); and, thirdly, under the Four-Power Pact, Japan has sacrificed the

[7] G. Schornstheimer, "Japan's Naval Mastery in Asia," in *Current History*, August 1922, pp. 744–50.

Anglo-Japanese Alliance, and is made a co-partner to guarantee the security of Guam, the Philippines, etc.[8] In brief, this Japanese naval critic shares the view of Admiral Wester-Wemyss who says that the check to Japan's rising naval power is, after the surrender of Britain's naval supremacy, the most striking feature of the conference. Such are the lamentations of naval experts of America, Britain, and Japan over the Washington arms treaties. If these utterances can be taken as the representative opinions of experts in general, then it is unmistakably clear that the recent arms treaties are unhappy in the extreme. The British critic charges that the Americans have gained "the substance of all they desire" at the expense of the British and the Japanese; the American critic insists that Japan secured "the naval mastery in Asia"; and the Japanese critic laments that Japan's hand is tied and she is thus rendered helpless as a naval power.

If space were available, one might extend the ground of criticism by introducing new factors such as the questions of administration, dock-facility, ship-building resources, character of officers and men, etc., because these are factors of great importance. In addition, one might consider the question of politics and economics, since these constitute factors of potentiality, to say the least. Speaking of the economic resources of America and Japan, a British naval critic says:

> There is, of course, an enormous disparity between the economic resources of the United States and the Japanese Empire, so much so that no question exists as to which could endure for

[8] T. Ishimaru, "Why Not Insist upon a More Logical Plan for Limiting Naval Armament?" in the *Taiyo* (*The Sun*), January 1922, pp. 54–59; and "Public Opinion on the Imperial Navy after the Washington Conference," in the same magazine, February 1922, pp. 69–75.

longest the terrible burden of a great war. .... The United States, although a great maritime Power by virtue of its long coastline, its sea-borne trade, and its naval armaments, is not dependent on sea-communications for its existence. It is self-supporting in food and raw materials to a far greater extent than any other Power, with the possible exception of Russia. It could, for instance, raise, equip, and feed an army many millions strong without importing a ton of material from abroad. It has reserves of wealth which, if not boundless, are, at any rate, adequate to finance the longest and costliest war in which it is ever likely to be engaged. It has an industrial organization which is capable of producing war material of every description in unlimited quantities. .... Japan would therefore find herself opposed by a united people, outnumbering her two to one, and possessing resources tenfold greater than those which she commands. In spite of all her industry, Japan remains relatively poor.[9]

Japanese experts may say that this is another reason why Japan is worse off because of the Washington treaties. But in spite of all what do the laymen say?

The writer has examined extensively the writings of laymen of America, Britain, and Japan, and finds that these do not share the pessimistic views of the experts. On the contrary, they look upon the arms treaties as a distinct step toward progress, national and international. The Naval Treaty stops billions from being wasted on naval armaments and relieves the peoples from their staggering burdens. What treasure is thus saved can be diverted to productive enterprises, intellectual as well as material, and mankind will be better off. The prohibition of abusive uses of the submarine and of poisonous gases eliminates horrible barbarism from future wars. This is a positive step toward the making of the rules of war less savage.

[9] H. C. Bywater, *Sea Power in the Pacific* (Boston and New York, 1921), pp. 312-13.

Actuated by the same humane spirit, the nations have agreed to create a commission to revise international law of war. The Four-Power Pact brought into being an association of the four greatest powers with the maintenance of peace as its object. If naval experts stand askance on the arms treaties, mankind at large is overwhelmingly gratified by the Washington achievements. Let time prove which is right.

Although appreciative of the value of the Naval Treaty, the first of its kind in history, the writer cannot overlook the fact that this pact failed to effect any limitation on auxiliary craft. The seriousness of this failure becomes evident when one recalls the resumption of a race in building cruisers, destroyers, and submarines by the naval powers. To correct this situation, President Coolidge dispatched, on February 10, 1927, an identical note to the British, French, Italian, and Japanese governments and suggested that the principle of the Washington Naval Treaty be extended to the control of auxiliary craft. Despite the rejection of this proposal by France and Italy, the three greatest naval powers decided to hold a conference at Geneva.[10]

But since this tripartite conference failed absolutely, an elaborate or detailed discussion is not necessary. We may begin its story by presenting a summary statement of the auxiliary-craft situation at the time in order that we may follow more intelligently the true meaning of the proposals made at the conference. It was as follows:[11]

[10] Records of the Conference for the Limitation of Naval Armament held at Geneva, Switzerland, June 20 to August 4, 1927. *U.S. Senate Document No. 55,* 70th Congress, 1st Session, 1928.

[11] J. T. Gerould, "Disagreement at Conference on Naval Disarmament," in *Current History,* August 1927, p. 795. The figures are

Countries	Cruisers No.	Tons	Destroyers No.	Tons	Submarines No.	Tons
United States	18	155,000	276	329,153	59	59,479
Great Britain	54	332,290	171	197,115	45	49,605
Japan	25	156,205	92	105,880	63	68,577

On June 20, 1927, the conference held its first meeting, open to the public, at which each of the three nations presented its proposals.[12] The American plan called for the application of the ratios and principles of the Washington Treaty to auxiliary ships; namely, cruisers of from 3,000 to 10,000 tons, destroyers of 600 to 3,000 tons, with a speed greater than seventeen knots, and submarines designed to operate below the surface of the sea. The tonnage allocations by the American plan were as follows:[13]

Countries	Cruisers	Destroyers	Submarines
United States	250,000–300,000	200,000–250,000	60,000–90,000
Great Britain	250,000–300,000	200,000–250,000	60,000–90,000
Japan	150,000–180,000	120,000–150,000	36,000–54,000

The British plan was to extend the accepted (by the Washington Treaty) life of existing capital ships from twenty to twenty-six years; to fix the life of other vessels —eight-inch gun cruisers at twenty-four years, destroyers at twenty, and submarines at fifteen; to reduce the maximum size of individual capital ships to be built in replacement from 35,000 tons to something under 30,000 tons; to reduce the caliber of guns in capital ships from 16-inch to 13.5-inch; to reduce the size of aircraft carriers from 27,000 tons to 25,000 tons, and also the caliber of guns in these vessels from 8-inch to 6-inch; to accept the ratio

---

according to an American compilation. Note also that the eighteen American cruisers include those built and building.

[12] *Ibid.*, pp. 793-94.   [13] *Ibid.*, p. 793.

of 5-5-3 for cruisers of 10,000 tons carrying eight-inch guns, but to discuss the numbers of these cruisers required by each of the three countries; to limit the size of individual light cruisers to 7,500 tons and guns carried in these to six-inch; to limit the size of destroyer leaders to 1,750 tons and destroyers to 1,400 tons and guns carried in destroyers to five-inch; and to abolish submarines or to limit their size and number—1,600 tons for larger and 600 for smaller ones.[14]

Japan proposed a naval holiday on the basis of the existing auxiliary-craft strengths, which were clearly defined, but this holiday was not to apply to ships less than 700 tons each, ships carrying no gun exceeding three-inch in caliber, or carrying not more than four guns exceeding three-inch and not exceeding six-inch, with or without any number of guns not exceeding three-inch, provided the speed of such ships did not exceed twenty knots; aircraft carriers under 10,000 tons, etc.[15]

A glance at these proposals shows that the Japanese plan contained nothing radical but that there was a decided difference between the American and the British plans. The British proposals, if accepted, would nullify many of the important agreements embodied in the Washington Treaty, whereas the American proposals were based on that treaty. It was inevitable therefore that the attention of the conference should have centered about these two plans. The discussion lasted until August 4, but the conference broke up without any achievement. For this failure the Americans blame the British, and the British the Americans, while the Japanese hold both responsible. No matter who was to be blamed, the fact remains that the conference failed utterly. Let us summarize the more

[14] *Ibid.* [15] *Ibid.*, pp. 793-94.

important reasons which caused this failure purely from an objective point of view.

First, the British demand that the size of capital ships be reduced from 35,000 tons to 30,000 and the life of these vessels be prolonged from twenty years to twenty-six, if agreed to, would give the British an unmistakable advantage over the American navy because the former possess three "Hoods" of 42,000 and 37,000 tons, two of which were completed after the completion of the two newest American capital ships. America would have to wait six years longer than agreed at Washington, before she could replace her old capital ships. Moreover, the reduction in the size of replacement ships would mean to replace old ships by smaller ones; this, too, would give the British an advantage and would disturb the parity between the two navies.

Secondly, America proposed a limitation on the total tonnage of cruisers, but the British divided these vessels into two categories, those of 10,000 tons and those of 7,500 tons. The United States wanted to have larger cruisers because she has no naval bases and fuel stations such as are possessed by the British Empire. The American contention was that the British could convert their merchant ships into fighting craft in time of war.

Thirdly, perhaps the most important point in the American-British conflict was the question of the number of cruisers each desired to have. The British demanded fifteen 10,000-ton cruisers and sixty smaller ones, or a total of 600,000 tons. This demand was shocking to both the American and Japanese delegations in view of their own proposals. Then compromise after compromise was attempted, but all in vain.

Fourthly, Lord Cecil says,

she [America] wanted large guns in large cruisers, and on the question of large guns the final breakdown occurred. There were, of course, other difficulties regarding which criticism must be directed elsewhere, but without reopening recent controversies I must affirm my personal conviction that it was within America's power, not less than it was within Great Britain's power, to have carried away from Geneva an agreement entirely honorable and in no way disadvantageous to herself.[16]

Lastly, to the writer, the absence of France and Italy, in particular the former, from the conference, must be reckoned as another cause of its failure. The United States and Japan may well ignore the French navy, but Great Britain is a European power ambitious to dominate European affairs. France seems to be the only European power, at present, that can challenge the British ambition. Anglo-French rivalry was more than obvious during the Washington Conference, and their relationship has not altered since the gathering. Perhaps the recent Anglo-French naval agreement[17] may be taken to mean an attempt to improve their relations, and according to the press it "seems to settle the dispute between the two countries, which has lasted for the better part of a decade, as to the principle upon which limitation shall be approached."[18] If this is true, we may then assume that this instrument will help in future disarmament conferences, at least between France and Great Britain.

But what appears most disheartening to a lay observer is the fact that the Geneva Conference did not even pro-

[16] Viscount Cecil, "American Responsibilities for Peace," in *Foreign Affairs* (April 1928), pp. 364–65.

[17] The agreement was made known to the House of Commons on July 31, 1928. See *Revue Diplomatique* (*Gaiko Jiho*), August 15, 1928, pp. 149–50.

[18] *The Literary Digest*, August 18, 1928, p. 8.

pose to effect any reduction of naval armaments. Japan alone proposed the maintenance of the *status quo* of auxiliary craft on the basis of their existing strengths, but both the United States and the British Empire desired to increase their existing auxiliary strength. Thus, even if the conference might have emerged successful, it would only have been a conference for limitation and not reduction, and its collapse resembles the failure of the Washington Conference in respect to auxiliary craft, for which France was held solely responsible.

Such is the sad history of the Geneva Conference. But in many quarters it is said that many problems have been clarified in that gathering, and thus in spite of failure it paves the way for another disarmament conference. "The President [Coolidge] believed that the Conference at Geneva had failed only temporarily and that the failure must not be made the cause of naval competition."[19] This optimistic view is now enhanced by the signing of the Pact of Paris, August 27, 1928.[20] The nations do seem determined to outlaw war.

[19] J. T. Gerould, "The Failure of the Three-Power Naval Conference," in *Current History*, September 1927, p. 949.
[20] *The Literary Digest*, September 8, 1928, pp. 5–7.

PART II

THE PACIFIC AND FAR EASTERN CONFERENCE

CHAPTER XII

CHINA, THE PROBLEM OF THE PACIFIC

The Far East and Pacific Conference, if judged by its achievements, might justly be described as a "Conference on China." Two treaties were signed and ten resolutions were passed. In addition, though not as an act of the conference, the long-pending question of Shantung was settled by a treaty between Japan and China. A proper appreciation of the work of the conference is impossible without knowledge of the history not only of China's foreign relations but also of her domestic politics. But such an undertaking does not lie within the scope of the present work. The following summary observations, however, may help to clarify the approach to this subject.

Professor Treat says,

Contrary to the prevailing opinion, the history of China is replete with the narratives of wars and internal strife. The feudal struggles, the wars of conquest which brought the present domains within the Empire and still place China among the "imperialistic powers," the age-long struggle with the northerners, the invasions which at different times carried the Chinese arms into central Asia, into Burma, Annam, the frontiers of India, and some of the islands off the southern coast, and the frequently recurring rebellions, all testify that the profession of arms was by no means neglected in spite of the pacific teachings of Confucius and the Buddha. Even in comparatively recent times the punitive power of the Empire was felt, as when in 1790 the Gurkhas, of Nepal, were chastised by the army of Kienlung, while the suppression of the terrible Taiping rebellion, 1850–64, and the Yunnan, Kansu, and Kashgar revolts a few years later, involved vast armies and ruthless destruction of life.[1]

These facts and the frequent post-revolutionary civil wars

[1] P. J. Treat, *The Far East* (New York and London, 1928), pp. 20–21.

make it obvious that the Chinese have not been and are not a peaceable people.

Dr. Morse, another American authority on China, summarizes the history of China's modern relations with the Western nations in the following words:

> For three-fourths of a century there had been international, as distinguished from mercantile, relations between the Chinese Empire and the nations of the West. In 1834 Lord Napier had acted as an envoy of the British crown must have acted; the Chinese court and the viceroy of Canton had acted as must have been expected of them; and the result was the ignominious failure of Lord Napier's mission. In 1839 a conflict broke out in which all the foreign merchants in Canton were concerned, but the brunt of which was borne by England; to China and the Chinese people sole apparent cause of the conflict was the opium question; to the British Government and people its sole causes were the equal status of nations, and the right to protection for life and property for foreign traders commorant in the Chinese Empire. In the settlement effected by the treaties, 1842–44, the opium question was not settled, but the other questions were dealt with as far as Western opinion was then prepared to go. Chinese opinion did not accept this settlement, and friction continued between China and the West until, in 1856, cause was given to England and France to begin the second war. This was ended by the four treaties of 1858, which settled the relations between China and the West. A third war, that of 1860, was required to overcome the opposition of the war party. The settlement of 1860 consolidated that of 1858, and as the result of three wars the Chinese learned, and they accepted as their law, that whereas formerly it was China which dictated the conditions under which international relations were to be maintained, now it was the Western nations which imposed their will on China. This ended the Period of Conflict.
>
> Then followed the Period of Submission, in which China accepted the decision of war. Officials in the provinces may have taken the natural course of interpreting treaty stipulations in their favor; but the empire was exhausted by the great Taiping

rebellion, while its prestige was shaken by its foreign wars; and the central administration was unable to resist the demands of the foreign powers. For some years these demands were directed solely to the enforcement of the treaties, and the envoys at Peking were united in supporting the government; but gradually national ambitions asserted themselves. During these years China lost the control of nearly all her vassal states—the fringe of buffer states which had encircled the empire and protected it from direct contact with the outer world—Liuchiu, a fringe of Ili, Siam, Burma, Annam; and, in 1894, there remained only Tibet, Mongolia, and Korea. This was the period in which a wise and strong government, with a disorganized and exhausted empire, would have reformed and strengthened its administration and its finances; and in which any rulers, worthy to rule, would at least have looked to the defences of the empire. But this plain duty was neglected by the imperial government, and the period of submission—and of peace—was wasted.

Then followed the Period of Subjection. In 1895 the war with Japan brought to the empire deep humiliation, and the loss of Korea. In 1898 four powers seized for themselves naval stations and commercial ports on the coast of China, and the break-up of the empire seemed to be impending. Then came the mad outbreak of 1900, supported by the Manchus, but, of the Chinese, only by those in the provinces immediately around Peking; and, in punishment, China was reduced to a state of subjection so low that, if the empire was to survive, it was clear that radical reforms were essential. The period of submission had been wasted; of the period of subjection, the first part, 1901 to 1905, had been spent in futile reforms which should not touch the prestige and the emoluments of the ruling race; and in the last part the empire tried by belated and reluctant reform to stem the tide of the rising Chinese sense of nationality. All these belated efforts failed, and the Manchu empire fell, leaving to the republic, which was erected on its ruins, an inheritance of disorder and corrupt administration, and a status of subjection to the foreign powers.[2]

[2] H. B. Morse, *The International Relations of the Chinese Empire* (London, 1918), III, 444–46.

From the published accounts of post-revolutionary China one does not get much encouragement, for so far few if any real improvements have been effected.

Students of Far Eastern affairs consider the Sino-Japanese war as a turning point in Pacific history. The victory of Japan over her neighbor upset the old balance in the Far East, resulting in shifting of alignment and purpose. Japan became a real factor to be reckoned with in international affairs of the Pacific. Again, Dr. Morse says:

During the war her [China's] most energetic efforts were directed, not to defeating the enemy, but to invoking the intervention of foreign powers, which, her rulers hoped, might save her from the results of her own weakness, without the necessity of making any serious effort to remedy the causes of that weakness. It was the duty of foreign powers, and not any part of the duty of China, to save China from aggression and dismemberment.[3]

Peking diplomacy invited the European powers to interfere in its affairs. Russia, France, and Germany took advantage of this invitation and humiliated Japan.[4] Since then China has learned to utilize the jealousies of the Western powers to extricate herself from her own international difficulties by playing one foreign power against another. At the same time, the foreign powers interested in China found themselves in a situation of antagonism, and they, in turn, tried to shift the responsibility to the "other fellow." International rivalry, international jealousy, suspicion, and distrust became rampant among the

[3] H. B. Morse, *op. cit.*, p. 57.

[4] See *Die Grosse Politik der Europäischen Kabinette, 1871–1914* (edited by J. Lepsius, A. Mendelssohn Bartholdy, and F. Thimme), especially Vol. IX.

powers present in China. Such were the immediate important results of the war.

Later, inexperienced Japan committed a series of blunders in dealing with China, the most serious of which was undoubtedly her so-called twenty-one demands. The powers took advantage of this and, in conjunction with China, have held Japan responsible for every trouble that has befallen China since. She was blamed as a cause of the revolution of 1911, the counter-revolution, the corrupt and incompetent administration of the Peking government, all the warlike conduct of the provincial war-lords, and even of the floods and famines from which China periodically suffers. This state of affairs has naturally affected the larger relations between Japan and other powers. Indeed, strained Sino-Japanese relations have created a source of friction particularly between Japan and the United States. This fact is clearly reflected in the report of the American delegation to President Harding:

> When the Conference was called there existed with regard to the Far East causes of misunderstanding and sources of controversy which constituted a serious potential danger. These difficulties centered principally about China, where the developments of the past quarter of a century had produced a situation in which international rivalries, jealousies, distrust, and antagonism were fostered.[5]

In dealing with the problems of China, the first question the conference had to decide was that of principles, and when this matter was presented at the first meeting of the Committee of the Whole, on November 16, the Chinese delegate demanded that the following be adopted by the conference:

[5] *Document*, p. 819.

1. (*a*) The powers engage to respect and observe the territorial integrity and political and administrative independence of the Chinese republic. (*b*) China upon her part is prepared to give an undertaking not to alienate or lease any portion of her territory or littoral to any power.

2. China, being in full accord with the principle of the so-called open door or equal opportunity for the commerce and industry of all the nations having treaty relations with China, is prepared to accept and apply it in all parts of the Chinese republic without exception.

3. With a view to strengthening mutual confidence and maintaining peace in the Pacific and the Far East, the powers agree not to conclude between themselves any treaty or agreement directly affecting China or the general peace in these regions without previously notifying China and giving to her an opportunity to participate.

4. All special rights, privileges, immunities, or commitments, whatever their character or contractual basis, claimed by any of the powers in or relating to China are to be declared, and all such or future claims not so made known are to be deemed null and void. The rights, privileges, immunities, and commitments now known or to be declared are to be examined with a view to determining their scope and validity and, if valid, to harmonizing them with one another and with the principles declared by this conference.

5. Immediately, or as soon as circumstances will permit, existing limitations upon China's political, jurisdictional, and administrative freedom of action are to be removed.

6. Reasonable, definite terms of duration are to be attached to China's present commitments, which are without time limits.

7. In the interpretation of instruments granting special rights or privileges, the well-established principle of construction that such grants shall be strictly construed in favor of the grantors is to be observed.

8. China's rights as a neutral are to be fully respected in future wars to which she is not a party.

9. Provision is to be made for the peaceful settlement of international disputes in the Pacific and the Far East.

10. Provision is to be made for future conferences to be held from time to time for the discussion of international questions relative to the Pacific and the Far East, as a basis for determination of common policies of the signatory powers in relation thereto.[6]

No action was taken by the committee in respect to China's "Bill of Rights," as the foregoing demands came to be known among the journalists. The committee adjourned after it had appointed a subcommittee composed of the senior delegates of the nine nations for the purpose of arranging and classifying the topics for discussion by the conference. The Chinese demands were naturally referred to the newly organized body. The senior delegates met on the following day. What they had decided was communicated by Mr. Hughes to the Committee of the Whole on the 19th, viz.: the first eight points of the Chinese demand might be discussed by the committee in accordance with the order of the agenda. The last two points did not constitute matters particularly relative to China alone. However, if so desired, these might be discussed also. The matters upon which it was found difficult to reach agreement might be referred to special committees for detailed study. He then invited the delegates to a general discussion on the questions relative to China.

Baron Kato on behalf of Japan said that all that this conference could achieve was an adjustment of China's foreign relations, leaving her domestic situation to be worked out by the Chinese themselves. The Japanese delegation wished to assure the Chinese delegation and the whole conference that Japan had every desire to cultivate the happiest relations with China. Japan was eager to

[6] *Document*, p. 444.

make whatever contributions she was capable of toward China's realization of her just and legitimate aspirations. She was entirely uninfluenced by any policy of territorial aggrandizement in any part of China. She would adhere without condition or reservation to the principle of "the open door and equal opportunity" in China. Japan looked to China in particular for the supply of raw materials essential to her industrial life and for foodstuffs as well. In the purchase of such materials from China, as in all her trade relations with that country, the Japanese did not claim any special rights or privileges, and they welcomed fair and honest competition with all nations. With regard to the question of the abolition of extraterritoriality, which was perhaps one of the most important questions proposed by the Chinese delegation, it was Japan's intention to join with other delegations in the endeavor to come to an arrangement in a manner fair and satisfactory to all parties. Japan had come to this conference not to advance her own selfish interests, but to co-operate with all nations interested for the purpose of assuring peace in the Far East and friendship among nations.[7]

Mr. Balfour said that he had nothing to add to the frequent declarations of the government he had the honor to represent on all these questions, for example, the "open door" in China, the integrity of China, the desirability of leaving China to work out her own salvation and to maintain control over her own affairs, and that of substituting, when circumstances warranted, the normal processes of law for extraterritoriality. All these principles had been formulated over and over again in explicit terms by the government which he represented.[8]

[7] *Document*, p. 447.
[8] *Ibid.*, p. 449.

Baron de Cartier added that Belgium would take part willingly in all the measures that the conference might adopt to insure the territorial integrity of China and to furnish her with the means to overcome her present difficulties. She was convinced that support of the action of the government was the necessary condition of all progress and of the fruitful application of such rules as the conference might lay down in accord with the government of the Chinese republic. Belgium would unreservedly favor the policy of the "open door." She desired to see assured to the industry and commerce of all the nations the possibility of sharing on a footing of complete and genuine equality the development of the resources of China to the greatest benefit of the Chinese people and of all humanity.[9]

M. Schanzer remarked that he had the honor to state in the name of the Italian delegation that it fully subscribed to the noble sentiments that had been expressed by the orators who had preceded him. The Italian delegation was ready to examine, together with the other delegations, with the greatest care and in a spirit of sincere sympathy, the questions relating to China. It would give its support to the solutions that should appear to be best suited to assure the free development of China and to guarantee an equality in footing of the different nations in their efforts to promote the progress of China and of commerce with that country.[10]

M. Briand expressed the warm sympathy that France felt for China, with which she had a common frontier about 1,500 kilometers in length. The French delegation was disposed to consider in the most favorable light the Chinese claims in their entirety. But, in order to reach a

[9] *Ibid.*, p. 448.
[10] *Ibid.*, pp. 449–50.

practical result, it would be necessary to make a thorough examination of each claim.[11]

Jonkheer van Karnebeck (representing the Netherlands) remarked that in the present phase of the discussion there was not much for him to say of a general character and at the same time of material importance. He wished, however, to seize this occasion to say as the representative of one of China's neighbors that the Netherlands delegation would be happy to consider the principles which China had laid down and the problems themselves from the standpoint of the world's general welfare and to examine them in a spirit of sympathy and friendship toward China.[12]

Viscount d'Alte said that the Portuguese delegation saw with pleasure that the delegates of the other nations represented at the conference had expressed nearly identical views as to the desirability, in the interest of all, of a prosperous and united China. He gladly associated himself with his colleagues in the expression of this desire.[13]

Dr. Sze expressed on behalf of the Chinese delegation his sincere appreciation of the united sympathy and friendship of the delegations for China and her proposals. Of course, many of the proposals would be considered in connection with their applications. He would desire to reserve to the Chinese delegation the right of discussing them in detail. But he was sure that the friendly sentiments as expressed and the general spirit of accord thereby presented would be greatly conducive to the success of the conference.[14]

These expressions showed that there was an agreement among the delegates on certain principles. Therefore, Mr.

[11] *Document*, p. 448.   [12] *Ibid.*, p. 449.   [13] *Ibid.*, p. 450.
[14] *Ibid.*

Root was requested by the committee to formulate resolutions embodying those principles. Accordingly he presented to the committee on November 21 the following draft of resolutions:

> It is the firm intention of the powers attending this conference hereinafter mentioned, to wit: the United States of America, Belgium, the British Empire, France, Italy, Japan, the Netherlands, and Portugal:
>
> (1) To respect the sovereignty, the independence, and the territorial and administrative integrity of China.
>
> (2) To provide the fullest and most unembarrassed opportunity to China to develop and maintain for herself an effective and stable government, overcoming the difficulties incident to the change from the old and long-continued imperial form of government.
>
> (3) To safeguard for the world, so far as it is within our power, the principle of equal opportunity for the commerce and industry of all nations throughout the territory of China.
>
> (4) To refrain from taking advantage of the present conditions in order to seek special rights or privileges which would abridge the rights of the subjects or citizens of friendly states and from countenancing action inimical to the security of such states.[15]

After an exchange of views as to the meaning of certain words and phrases, the committee adopted the resolutions amended as follows:

> (1) To respect the sovereignty, the independence, and the territorial and administrative integrity of China.
>
> (2) To provide the fullest and most unembarrassed opportunity to China to develop and maintain for herself an effective and stable government.
>
> (3) To use their influence for the purpose of effectually establishing and maintaining the principle of equal opportunity for

[15] *Ibid.*, pp. 454–55.

the commerce and industry of all nations throughout the territory of China.

(4) To refrain from taking advantage of the present conditions in order to seek special rights or privileges which would abridge the rights of the subjects or citizens of friendly states and from countenancing action inimical to the security of such states.[16]

Speaking of the last of these amended resolutions, one of the foreign advisers to the Chinese delegation says its adoption "meant a decisive victory to China."[17] However, the resolutions as a whole failed to create enthusiasm in journalistic circles. As a matter of fact, the majority of journalists manifested skepticism, pointing out the inadequacy of "general principles"—that were little more than "four glowing but somewhat vague rules,"[18] "so general that they could be printed in a wreath and used as Christmas postcards."[19] "Everything is," they said, "in the air and is being held there with a view to compromise later on."[20] But naturally there were not lacking men who viewed the resolutions more favorably. One described these as "the first tangible results" of the conference.[21] Another wrote, "a way has been found to solve the riddle of the Pacific."[22] Such was the divided opinion of the American press.

[16] *Document*, pp. 459–60.

[17] W. W. Willoughby, *China at the Conference* (Baltimore, 1922), p. 43.

[18] J. W. Owens in the *Baltimore Sun*, November 22, 1921.

[19] Charles Merz in the *New York World*, November 22, 1921.

[20] Charles Michaelson in the *New York World*, November 22, 1921.

[21] A. W. Fox in the *Washington Post*, November 22, 1921.

[22] The *New York Herald*, November 22, 1921.

CHAPTER XIII

THE QUESTION OF TARIFF AUTONOMY

The conference was now ready for discussion of the application of the adopted principles, and it was suggested that China present such matters as she desired to have discussed by the committee. Whereupon Mr. Underwood called the attention of the committee to the financial condition of China, saying that a government could not be strong enough to meet its outside obligations unless it had an adequate revenue. China had grave difficulty, at the present time, in raising sufficient revenue; the main source of revenue was the customs dues, which were entirely inadequate; some understanding might be reached relative to this question and the source and amount of customs revenues in the future; an investigation to ascertain the facts in the case would be necessary; until the facts were available there was no foundation on which to base discussion. He would suggest therefore that the matter be referred in some way to a committee for adequate investigation and a report of facts and conclusions.[1]

After an exchange of views, it was agreed to appoint a subcommittee composed of one representative from each of the nine nations, for the purpose above suggested. But this did not preclude China from presenting her views to the Committee of the Whole on this or other matters if she so desired. Dr. Koo on behalf of the Chinese delegation made a statement of the origin and history of the Chinese treaty tariffs, at the conclusion of which he proposed to restore to China the right to fix and to differentiate the import tariff rates; but, as it appeared hardly possible to establish a new régime all at once, full autonomy should be restored to China after a certain period

[1] *Document*, p. 463.

to be agreed upon. In the meantime China would impose a maximum rate and would like to enjoy full freedom within a maximum, such as the right of differentiation among the different classes of commodities. But as the present financial condition of the Chinese Government was such as to require some immediate relief, it was proposed that on and after January 1, 1922, the Chinese import tariff be raised to 12½ per cent, as it was stipulated in the treaties of 1902–1903 with the United States, Great Britain, and Japan.[2]

A brief survey of the history of the Chinese tariffs may be given. The so-called Opium War which began in 1839 resulted in a British victory; and on August 29, 1842, was signed a peace treaty at Nanking concluding the war. The British wanted "to enforce reparations for past injuries and insults, and furthermore to compel the Chinese to abandon their policy of exclusion and attitude of superiority towards other civilized nations."[3] Under the treaty China was forced to open five ports: Canton, Amoy, Foochow, Ningpo, and Shanghai; to cede Hongkong; to pay an indemnity of twenty-one million dollars; to recognize the equal status of nations in diplomatic dealing, etc. Besides, China was compelled under Article X of the treaty to give up one of her sovereign rights, the right to regulate her own tariff. This last provision was amplified by a supplementary treaty signed on October 8, 1843, whereby "the duties under the tariff were partly specific but were based on the general idea of 5 per cent ad valorem both for imports and exports."[4] Not only that,

[2] *Document*, p. 471.

[3] A. J. Sargent, *Anglo-Chinese Commerce and Diplomacy* (Oxford, 1907), p. 83.

[4] *Ibid.*, p. 85.

THE QUESTION OF TARIFF AUTONOMY 169

but the right of extraterritoriality was also granted to Great Britain by China.[5]

Following the British, the Americans signed the Treaty of Commerce on July 3, 1844, and the French, on October 24, 1844. Belgium secured trade privileges by an Imperial rescript of July 25, 1845; Sweden and Norway signed, on March 20, 1847, a Treaty of Commerce, virtually the same as the American Treaty of 1844.[6]

Curiously enough, no allusion was made to opium in the Sino-British treaty which had concluded the opium war. Thus the vexed question was left untouched though it had so often threatened the amicable relations between the two countries. That was extremely unfortunate, for it was bound to form a stumbling-block in their intercourse. The Chinese

felt they were grossly wronged by the British who forced the opium traffic on them. They resented deeply the intrusion and compulsory intercourse of the unwelcome Western barbarians. They entertained the hope that, as soon as a chance should offer itself, they would expel all Western disturbers of their peace.[7]

But the British did not accept the interpretation that the opium question was the cause of the war; hence no allusion to it in the treaty. Mr. Sargent says that "opium, like spirits and tobacco, is an evil only in excess. Even from the point of view of our general commercial interests the trade was not an unmixed benefit."[8] "The British Government advocated legalization [of opium importation] at a higher rate than on merchandise, on the ground that prohibition was impossible."[9] There was no international solution for the problem.

[5] Ibid.
[6] Bau, Foreign Relations of China, p. 9.
[7] Ibid., p. 9.
[8] Sargent, op. cit., p. 89.
[9] Ibid., p. 87.

Perhaps more unfortunate was the fact that Great Britain, as well as the other treaty powers, soon discovered the difficulty of executing its newly acquired treaty rights because of the peculiar political conditions of the Chinese Empire at the time. "A state of peaceful trade at one port was quite consistent with open war at another."[10] At any rate, the incidents attendant upon the attempts of the powers to carry out their rights were often of a very grave character and resulted in another war in 1856 between China on the one hand and Britain and France on the other.[11] China was again defeated, and subsequently, in 1858, she concluded treaties with Great Britain, France, Russia, and the United States.[12] Among the important rights acquired by the Western powers under the treaties were the right to appoint their resident Ambassadors at Peking as well as their consular officers at the various treaty ports, and the full right of extraterritoriality. The troublesome question of *likin* (inland transit duties) was also settled; it was fixed at 2½ per cent ad valorem. A supplementary agreement was signed on November 8, 1858, with Great Britain and America, which fixed the tariff at 5 per cent ad valorem with a free list consisting of gold and silver bullion, foreign coins, flour, and the daily necessities of foreign residents in China. The 5 per cent tariff was to apply to both imports and exports.[13]

The British, French, and Russian treaties were to be

[10] Sargent, *op. cit.,* p. 92.

[11] See Bau, *op. cit.,* pp. 9–12, and Sargent, *op. cit.,* pp. 87–120.

[12] The British Treaty was signed June 26, 1858; the French, June 27; the Russian, June 13; and the American, June 18.

[13] Similar exactions were forced upon Japan; extraterritorial rights between 1854 and 1869, and the fixed tariff by the treaties of 1866.

ratified at Peking within a year, but such ratification was not actually effected until 1860 and after another armed conflict. "The period of 1859–1860 marked the initial stage of the opening of China," says a Chinese;[14] but, writes an American,

> as the result of three wars, the Chinese learned, and they accepted as their law, that whereas formerly it was China which dictated the conditions under which international relations were to be maintained, now it was the Western nations which imposed their will on China.[15]

More specifically of the tariff provisions in the treaties, a British writer says:

> Salt and munitions and implements of war are still contraband, but the restrictions as to opium, "cash," and grains are relaxed. The import of opium is allowed at a comparatively heavy rate of duty, though it is to be carried into the interior by Chinese only and as Chinese property; but special privileges as to transit duties are withheld and the Chinese Government may impose such dues as it thinks fit. British subjects may export copper "cash" and rice from one Chinese port to another under strict regulations, but export abroad is still prohibited. These concessions are important; and in a general tariff of imports staple British manufactures are treated with great moderation. In the case of imports, the idea of 5 per cent ad valorem is carried out in the specific duties; in other words, the tariff of 1843 is readjusted to correspond with the change in prices. The export duties on tea and silk are unchanged. The duty on silk is actually less than 5 per cent, but it cannot be raised owing to French interests being involved.[16]

On the other hand, a Chinese writer comments:

---

[14] Bau, *op. cit.*, p. 16.
[15] Already quoted; see page 156, above.
[16] Sargent, *op. cit.*, pp. 119–20.

The maximum rate [5 per cent] is so absurdly low that a reduction of it in favor of another State offers nothing attractive enough to make it reduce its imports on commodities of Chinese origin. In fact, when the tariff agreement of 1858 was concluded, there was no desire to give China anything by which she could bargain with other States. Stripped of all the characteristics of a conventional tariff, it can only be looked upon as a tariff imposed to produce revenues for the Chinese Government, and yet the rate is so low that its yield is much less than it would be if only a few articles were taxed which would produce the largest amount of revenue at a minimum cost of collection, the bulk of foreign goods being imported duty-free. An even greater anomaly is her duty on exports. While it is true that she is bound by no treaty to tax exports, she is nevertheless compelled to do it, and do it at the maximum rate permitted by the treaty [5 per cent], because she is faced with the urgent necessity of increasing her immediate revenue irrespective of the effects the taxation may produce on the foreign trade of the country or the productive capacity of the people.[17]

Under the circumstances, the Chinese naturally sought to effect revision of the treaties, which they were entitled to do at the end of ten years. On the other hand, it was easily seen that the Western powers would not give up provisions so advantageous to themselves. Even Japan, which effected every needed reform to conform to the Western standard, did not regain her sovereign rights until 1894, when her treaties were revised to provide for the abolition of extraterritoriality in 1899 and the restoration of tariff autonomy in 1911. If injustice was a ground upon which the revision of the Japanese treaties was agreed to by the powers, the same powers should be willing to accord a similar treatment to China, if she would effect needed reforms. But so far, China has failed in this respect to meet the demands of the treaty powers.

[17] S. G. Cheng, *Modern China* (Oxford, 1919), pp. 196–97.

THE QUESTION OF TARIFF AUTONOMY   173

Consequently her treaties of 1858 continued unrevised. Some adjustment was made in 1902 and 1903, when the Agreement of Shanghai was entered into between China and the United States, Great Britain, and Japan.[18] Under this convention the tariff was revised to make it an effective five per cent, but the value of the goods was calculated on the basis of the average prices in 1897, 1898, and 1899. The purpose was to enable China to meet the payment of an indemnity of 450,000,000 Haikwan taels imposed upon her in punishment for the Boxer Uprising.[19]

In 1902, Great Britain acting independently consented to the raising of import duties to twelve and one-half per cent and of export duties to seven and one-half per cent, provided China abolished *likin*.[20] A similar provision was made in the treaties signed in 1903 with the United States and Japan.[21] But since the consent was conditioned by the "most-favored-nation clause," this revision failed to materialize. Nothing was done as regards further revision until 1918, when it was agreed to bring the tariff to an effective five per cent. This revised tariff became effective in August 1919. The agreement was to continue for at least two years after the close of the war.[22] But the revision was based on the average prices at Shanghai during the years 1912 and 1916,[23] and consequently China did not obtain the full benefit of the revised five per cent effective. One writer estimates that the revised five per cent was no more than a four per cent effective tariff.[24] Dr. Koo said

[18] See J. V. A. MacMurray, *Treaties and Agreements with and concerning China* (New York, 1921), I, 339–40.

[19] *Ibid.*, pp. 278–85.   [20] *Ibid.*, pp. 342–53.   [21] *Ibid.*, pp. 411–52.

[22] *Ibid.*, pp. 1456–84.   [23] *China Year-Book, 1919*, p. 422.

[24] W. W. Willoughby, *Foreign Rights and Interests in China* (Baltimore, 1920), p. 119.

that it "yielded only 3½ per cent in comparison with the prices of commodities actually prevailing."[25] Such then were the origin, the history, and the actual status of Chinese tariffs.

To return to the conference, it created a special subcommittee to make a thorough investigation of the tariff question. After a prolonged discussion the subcommittee made its recommendations to the Committee of the Whole, which, in turn, formulated and agreed to a treaty.[26] It is presented in Appendix VI, page 398.

The object of the treaty as set forth in the preamble, is to enable China to secure increased revenues from customs duties. Article I makes the existing five per cent "effective" two months after the publication of the treaty without waiting for its ratification. The annex which accompanies this article provides for a Revision Commission composed of representatives of the signatory powers, to meet at Shanghai to complete the revision within four months. Article II creates a Special Conference to prepare the way for the speedy abolition of *likin* (transit duties), and for the fulfillment of the conditions laid down in the British, American, and Japanese treaties with China of 1902–1903, in order that the surtaxes provided therein may be levied. Article III provides that the same Special Conference is to fix the surtax at two and a half per cent on ordinary articles and up to five per cent on luxuries as an interim provision. Article IV makes it necessary to revise the tariff effective under Article I at the end of four years, and thereafter every seven years. Article V secures to the signatory powers equality of treatment and opportunity in all matters relating to customs duties. By Article

[25] *Document*, p. 470.
[26] *Ibid.*, pp. 899–901.

VI uniformity in duties at all the land and maritime frontiers of China is recognized, but the Special Conference is authorized to make equitable adjustments in cases where a customs privilege is granted in return for some local economic advantage. Article VII fixes the charge for transit passes at two and a half per cent until the arrangement is made according to Article II. Under Article VIII all non-signatory powers whose governments are recognized by the parties to the treaty, and who have treaties with China relative to the five per cent tariff, are to be invited to adhere to this treaty, and to take part in the proposed tariff conferences. By Article IX the treaty is made to override all other treaty stipulations between China and the signatory powers, which are inconsistent therewith. Article X is a usual provision for the ratification of the treaty. According to Senator Underwood, this Washington Treaty would materially increase China's customs revenue.[27]

The Revision Commission provided in the treaty met at Shanghai in March 1922, twelve powers and China attending. On September 25 the new schedule of the tariff was adopted, and on January 17, 1923, it was put in operation. But the Special Conference to deal with *likin* and surtaxes was delayed by the French refusal to ratify the tariff treaty because of the differences which arose over the proposed payment, by China, of the Boxer indemnity in paper francs. When this question was settled, France and Italy ratified the treaty on April 2, 1925. The conference was convened on October 26 at the invitation of the Peking government. Aside from the signatory powers, Denmark, Sweden, Norway, and Spain attended the gathering. Its sessions continued for nine months,

[27] *Ibid.*, pp. 590–91.

but resulted only in a resolution announced on November 19, 1925:

> The contracting powers other than China hereby recognize China's right to enjoy tariff autonomy; agree to remove the tariff restrictions which are contained in existing treaties between themselves, respectively, and China; and consent to the going into effect of the Chinese National Tariff law on January 1, 1929.
>
> The Government of the Republic of China declares that likin shall be abolished simultaneously with the enforcement of the Chinese National Tariff law; and further declares that the abolition of likin shall be effectively carried out by the first day of the first month of the eighteenth year of the Republic of China.[28]

But concerning this resolution, the *China Year-Book, 1928,* observes:

> The Tariff Conference reached no conclusion because of civil war conditions in China, the Chinese Delegates having left Peking and no new delegation having been appointed. No treaty was signed and therefore nothing that occurred at that Conference has any binding force. Certain discussions and resolutions in Committee, however, have been given such widespread publicity as to have led to the misapprehension that an agreement on these subjects had been reached. The two principal items under this head are:
>
> (1) That Tariff Autonomy should be granted China by January 1, 1929, and
>
> (2) That China would abolish likin by that date.[29]

In other words, the resolution had no validity until a treaty could be negotiated. China must be held responsible for the failure of the conference, for as the result of a civil war in the northern provinces, the chief executive of the Peking government fled from the capital in April

[28] *China Year-Book, 1926–27,* p. 1136.
[29] *China Year-Book, 1928,* p. 1065.

THE QUESTION OF TARIFF AUTONOMY

1926, and subsequently the Chinese delegates to the conference withdrew one by one from its meetings, causing its adjournment. On July 3, 1926, the foreign delegations notified the Chinese Government that they would resume their work when it appointed its new delegates. On the 14th the new delegates were designated by the Cabinet, but the conference decided on the 24th to postpone its meetings until the summer was over. Meanwhile the opposition parties to the Peking government declared their open hostility to any renewal of the conference activities, and consequently the conference was not revived. Yet in spite of the failure of this conference, the various factions assumed the right of levying and collecting a surtax conditionally made in the Washington Treaty, and other unauthorized duties, thus adding another series of diplomatic complications.[30] Furthermore, the American Government signed a treaty on July 25, 1928, whereby the Nationalist Government is given *de facto* recognition. It relates to tariff autonomy, stating that "the principle of complete national tariff autonomy shall apply." But it also provides for the most-favored-nation treatment, and therefore it may be presumed that the principle of tariff autonomy enunciated in the treaty will not be extended to China by the United States until all other powers have concluded similar treaties.[31]

[30] See P. J. Treat, *The Far East*, pp. 474–75, and J. H. Dolsen, "The Thorny Problems of China and the Powers," in *Current History*, November 1926, pp. 221–30.

[31] H. S. Quigley, "Recognition of Nationalist China by the United States," in *Current History*, September 1928, pp. 1060–64.

CHAPTER XIV

THE OPEN-DOOR POLICY

There is no international commitment which has proved more provocative of disputation among writers than the instrument which embodied the so-called principles of the open door as applied to China. In order to understand its exact meaning, one must know the circumstances which had led the American Government to address its original note on the open door to the several nations interested in China, as well as the exact character of the replies, which together formed the final authority on the subject until a restatement was effected at the Washington Conference.

In tracing these circumstances it is not necessary to go back beyond the Sino-Japanese war. At that time, there were five Western nations keenly interested in the outcome of the struggle between the two Asiatic powers. Russia had an eye on Manchuria, especially South Manchuria and Korea. France was her ally, but an enemy of Germany and England. These four European powers possessed, in contrast to the United States, more than commercial interests in the Far East, and were watching for opportunities to further them. The war gave them a chance. Russia and France started a campaign of winning China's friendship, and hence, according to Cordier, *"la France et la Russie n'hesitèrent pas un instant à prendre parti pour la Chine."*[1] Simultaneously the dominant influence of Great Britain at Peking began to wane. When the Bakan Treaty concluding the war was signed, Russia, France, and Germany intervened, and Japan was forced to retrocede the Liaotung Peninsula.[2] China was grateful

[1] H. Cordier, *Histoire générale de la Chine* (Paris, 1921–22), IV, 195.

[2] A. Gerard, *Ma Mission en Chine* (1893–97) (Paris, 1919), pp. 1–52.

to Russia, the leader of the intervention, and accepted her as her best friend. Russia, helped by France, forced China to borrow 400,000,000 francs on July 6, 1895, in order to pay her indemnity to Japan. This was another diplomatic defeat for England. However, the latter managed, in conjunction with Germany, to lend to China £32,000,000 in 1896 and 1898.[3] This was the commencement of "dollar diplomacy" in China.

In June 1896 Russia and China entered into a secret alliance

> to support each other by all the land and sea forces at their disposal against any aggression by Japan directed against Russian territory in eastern Asia, China, or Korea. During military operations all Chinese ports would be open to Russian vessels. And the right to build a railway across Manchuria would be granted to the Russo-Chinese Bank. The treaty would remain in force for fifteen years after the railway contract was confirmed.[4]

To make the railway clause more effective, a new convention was signed on September 8 of the same year.[5] Russia soon chartered the Russo-Chinese Bank, nominally a Russian corporation but one involving French financiers as well as the Chinese Government.[6] This bank chartered the Chinese Eastern Railway Company, which by 1904 had built the Russian railways in Manchuria from Manchuli to Pogranichnaya and from Harbin to Talien-wan and Port Arthur, a total of 1,596 miles.[7]

[3] See H. B. Morse, *op. cit.*, pp. 52-53.

[4] P. J. Treat, *The Far East*, pp. 324-25. See also P. H. Clyde, *International Rivalries in Manchuria, 1689-1922* (Columbus, 1928), second edition, pp. 44-62.

[5] See J. V. A. MacMurray, *op. cit.*, p. 81, and A. Gerard, *op. cit.*, pp. 146-49.

[6] H. B. Morse, *op. cit.*, p. 83.

[7] *Ibid.*, pp. 90-91.

On November 14, 1897, a German fleet occupied Tsingtao, the port at the mouth of Kiaochow Bay, because two German missionaries had been murdered at Kiachwang, Shantung (November 1). After prolonged negotiations, Germany forced China on March 6, 1898, to sign a treaty whereby Kiaochow Bay was leased for ninety-nine years, with the right to fortify and to maintain troops there as well as the right to build two railways and to exploit mines in Shantung Province.[8]

Soon after the German dash on Tsingtao, a Russian fleet entered Port Arthur and Talien-wan, and subsequently Russia forced China to sign a treaty on March 27, 1898, and an additional agreement on May 7, by which Russia was given the lease of territory on Liaotung Peninsula for twenty-five years, with rights similar to those accorded to Germany.[9] It is interesting to be told by Witte, in this connection, that

> he instructed his agent at Peking to pay Li Hung-chang 500,000 rubles, and Chang Yin-huan, 250,000. The former accepted 500,000 taels, and expressed his deep gratitude.[10]

France watched these movements, but the French foreign minister declared in February 1898 that his country had no intention to imitate the German seizure of a naval base in China. Yet on April 10 China was forced to agree to lease Kangchow Bay to France, and a treaty to that effect was signed on May 27.[11]

---

[8] See H. B. Morse, *op. cit.*, p. 107, and P. J. Treat, *The Far East*, pp. 326–29.

[9] See *ibid.*, respectively, pp. 111–12 and 329, and P. H. Clyde, *op. cit.*, pp. 63–101.

[10] P. J. Treat, *op. cit.*, p. 329.

[11] H. B. Morse, *op. cit.*, p. 118.

Great Britain, or at least her agent at Peking, apparently began to negotiate for the lease of Weihaiwei even while the Germans were pressing for Kiaochow. Japan was holding Weihaiwei pending the payment by China of her war indemnity. When this was paid Japan evacuated the Bay on May 5, and on the 24th the British flag was raised there. Great Britain was given the right to hold the place as long as Port Arthur remained in the possession of Russia.[12] In addition, she secured the lease of Kowloon opposite Hongkong for ninety-nine years by another convention signed on June 9.[13]

The territory leased to Germany amounted to about 200 square miles; to Russia, about 1,300; to France, 195; while to Great Britain, about 285 (Weihaiwei) and 376 (Kowloon); or in all a total of 2,356 square miles. Italy tried but failed to secure a lease.[14] Besides these territorial concessions, many other rights and privileges were obtained by the powers, among which mention may be made of railway concessions.

At the end of 1898, the British concessions amounted to 2,800 miles, including the Yünnan-Yangtse and the Hankau-Canton lines; Russian to 1,530, including the Manchurian section; German to 720; Belgian to 650; French to 420; and American to 300 (reckoning half interests at half the estimated length of the line).[15]

The methods employed by the Western powers in these negotiations for concessions were, as the Chinese unfailingly complain, those of "duress," or bribery, as to details of which, however, they remain discreetly silent.

[12] *Ibid.*
[13] *Ibid.*, pp. 119–20.
[14] *Ibid.*, pp. 124–25.
[15] A. J. Sargent, *op. cit.*, p. 243.

At any rate, even from this brief survey it may be seen that the dismemberment of China was threatened in the closing years of the last century. It was at this point that the United States commenced to play an important rôle. On September 6, 1899, Secretary Hay addressed a circular note to Great Britain, France, Germany, and Russia, and a little later to Japan (November 13) and Italy (November 17), to obtain from each a formal assurance, within its respective sphere of whatever influence,

(1) That it will in no wise interfere with any treaty port or any vested interest within any so-called "spheres of interest" or leased territory it may have in China.

(2) That the Chinese treaty tariff of the time being shall apply to all merchandise landed or shipped to all such ports within such "spheres of interest" (unless they be "free ports"), no matter to what nationality it may belong, and that duties so leviable shall be collected by the Chinese Government.

(3) That it will levy no higher harbor dues on vessels of another nationality frequenting any port in such "spheres" than shall be levied on vessels of its own nationality, and no higher railroad charges over lines built, controlled, or operated within its "sphere" on merchandise belonging to citizens or subjects of other nationalities transported through such "sphere" than shall be levied on similar merchandise belonging to its own nationals transported over equal distances.[16]

Accordingly, the American Government desired, in coöperation with these powers, to observe the principle of equal trade opportunity for all nations within the spheres of interest, first, by maintaining the Chinese treaty tariff, and, second, by applying uniform harbor dues and railroad charges. The replies given by the powers to the American note were favorable but not unconditional, ex-

[16] *United States Foreign Relations, 1899,* p. 129, and P. J. Treat, *The Far East,* p. 333.

cept that of Italy, which possessed no leased territory or sphere of interest. For instance, the British answer stated that

> Her Majesty's Government will be prepared to make a declaration in the sense desired by your Government in regard to the leased territory of Wei-hai Wei and all territory in China which may hereafter be acquired by Great Britain by lease or otherwise, and all spheres of interest now held or that may hereafter be held by her in China, provided that a similar declaration is made by the other Powers concerned.[17]

Kowloon was deliberately excluded, but Secretary Hay raised no objection to this.

> The final step was to inform each of the governments that, as the condition attached to its acceptance had been complied with, the United States considered its assent final and definitive.[18]

It is clear then that one must not depend on the original American note alone for an exact definition of the open door, but must also take into consideration whatsoever conditions were contained in the replies made by the several governments, for these notes, from March 20, 1900, until 1922, together constituted the complete substance of such international agreement as had been reached.

Secretary Hay, speaking on the subject of the open door in 1901, before the New York Chamber of Commerce, said, among other things,

> the vast development of our industries imperatively demands that we shall not only retain and confirm our hold on our present markets, but seek constantly by all honorable means to extend our commercial interests in every practical direction. .... We believe that "a fair field and no favor" is all we require; and

[17] J. V. A. MacMurray, *op. cit.*, I, 228.
[18] P. J. Treat, *The Far East,* p. 334.

with less than that we cannot be satisfied. If we accept the assurances we have received as honest and genuine, as I certainly do, that equality will not be denied us; and the result may safely be left to American genius and energy.[19]

The popular notion that the American policy was aimed against the maintenance or further establishment of spheres in China is nowhere evidenced in the notes declared to be final, nor is it even suggested in the remarks of Mr. Hay.

An American writer says,

the phrase "the open door" has a pleasing sound. There can be no doubt that the opening up of China's ports to commerce with all nations on equal terms would be of immediate advantage to us, and probably to China herself. Our interest in the matter, however, is frankly selfish.[20]

It does seem strange, if this open-door entente was intended for the benefit of China, as is frequently claimed in certain quarters, that China's pleasure in the matter was not consulted. Neither can it be justly said that the United States was entirely free from territorial ambitions in China. Secretary Hay sent, on December 7, 1900, the following telegram to Mr. Buck, American minister to Japan:

The Navy greatly desires a coaling station at Samshah Inlet north of Fuchow. Ascertain informally and discreetly whether Japanese Government would see any objection to our negotiating for this with China.[21]

---

[19] Quoted by S. Tomimas in his *Open-Door Policy and the Territorial Integrity of China* (New York, 1919), p. 45.

[20] W. E. Weyl, *American World Policies* (New York, 1917), p. 213.

[21] *United States Foreign Relations, 1915*, p. 113.

Japan replied, giving several reasons why it would be unfortunate if the United States should undertake such negotiations,[22] and the matter was dropped.

Another important point about the *modus vivendi* is its sanction, which was purely moral.

If any one offended in the future, it would be a violation of its plighted word. But no treaty obligations were incurred. The United States assumed no responsibility to compel one or all the other powers to keep the faith.[23]

But returning to China we find the powers confronted with a widespread anti-foreign movement known as the Boxer Uprising, which culminated in the general declaration of war by China on all the powers represented at Peking (June 20, 1900). An international expedition was dispatched to relieve the besieged foreigners in that city, and on September 7, 1901, the final protocol was signed to settle the difficulty. On July 3, 1900, more than a month before the relief expedition reached Peking (August 14), Secretary Hay sent a circular note to the eleven powers having treaty relations with China,[24] stating that the United States desired to maintain the peace with China and to

preserve Chinese territorial and administrative entity, protect all rights guaranteed to friendly powers by treaty and international law, and safeguard for the world the principle of equal and impartial trade with all parts of the Chinese Empire.[25]

This note has given rise to much misunderstanding in regard to the open-door policy. Many writers assume that

[22] *Ibid.*, pp. 114–15.

[23] P. J. Treat, *Japan and the United States, 1853–1921*, p. 175.

[24] Austria, Belgium, France, Germany, Great Britain, Italy, Japan, the Netherlands, Portugal, Spain, and Russia.

[25] *United States Foreign Relations, 1900*, p. 299.

this note was accepted by the parties to the original *modus vivendi,* but such was not clearly the case. It was technically a mere declaration of the attitude of the American Government, and cannot be considered as a part of the agreement.

Russia, which had taken a prominent part in the expedition against Peking, taking advantage of China's chaotic state, intrenched herself in Manchuria. Alarmed by this aggressive action of Russia, Germany and Great Britain formed an entente on October 16, 1900, which, among other things, stipulates,

It is a matter of joint and permanent international interest that the ports on the rivers and littoral of China should remain free and open to trade and to every other legitimate form of economic activity for the nationals of all countries without distinction; and the two governments agree on their part to uphold the same for all Chinese territory as far as they can exercise influence.[26]

This entente is often cited as another enunciation of the open-door policy, a point of view which fails to recognize that on March 15, 1901, Count von Bülow declared in the Reichstag that "the agreement had no reference to Manchuria."[27] Moreover, John Hay characterized the entente in the following words:

My heart is heavy about John Bull. Do you twig his attitude to Germany? When the Anglo-German pact came out, I took a day or two to find out what it meant. I soon learned from Berlin that it meant a horrible practical joke on England. From London I found out what I had suspected, but what it astounded me after all to be assured of—*that they did not know!* When Japan joined the pact, I asked them why. They said, "We don't know, only if

[26] *British Foreign and State Papers, 1900–1901,* XCIV, 897.
[27] P. H. Clyde, *op. cit.,* p. 91.

there is any fun going on, we want to be in." Cassini is furious—which may be because he has not been let into the joke.[28]

Such being the case, the agreement, either as an instrument of the open door or as a measure against the Russian aggression, was rendered meaningless, and the situation in North China was daily becoming dark.

On January 30, 1902, Great Britain and Japan formed an alliance the preamble of which reads:

The Governments of Great Britain and Japan, actuated solely by a desire to maintain the *status quo* and general peace in the extreme East, being moreover specially interested in maintaining the independence and territorial integrity of the Empire of China and the Empire of Korea, and in securing equal opportunities in those countries for the commerce and industry of all nations, etc.[29]

These words may be interpreted as a restatement of the open door so far as the two powers were concerned, or they may be interpreted as an indirect challenge to the Russian aggressions in China and Korea. On February 1, 1902, the American Government addressed another note, relative to the open door in Manchuria, to China, warning her not to grant a monopoly to a particular power.[30] Russia was trying to secure such a right. Although a copy of this memorandum was sent to the other powers having treaty relations with China, the note could not be considered as a part of the open-door agreement. At any rate, Russia replied to the newly formed Anglo-Japanese Al-

[28] W. R. Thayer, *Life and Letters of John Hay* (Boston and New York, 1915), II, 248.

[29] J. V. A. MacMurray, *op. cit.*, I, 324-25.

[30] *United States Foreign Relations, 1902*, pp. 275-76. The note was sent to Austria, Belgium, China, France, Germany, Great Britain, Italy, Japan, the Netherlands, Spain, and Russia.

liance by a new entente signed with France on March 3, 1902.

In 1903 the first real test of the practical value of the open-door agreement came, when Russia made, on April 18, her famous seven demands on China, which clearly violated the principle.[31] The United States, Great Britain, and Japan entered their protest against these demands. "America, however, could only exert a moral influence; England was not prepared to go beyond diplomatic pressure."[32] Thus Japan was left alone to fight out the issue with Russia, and a clash came between them in 1904–1905. Of course, Japan in her declaration of war against Russia was not actuated solely by her desire to uphold the open-door principle, but also by her desire to preserve her national existence, which was unmistakably threatened by the Russian aggressions on China and Korea. During the progress of the war, Mr. Hay dispatched (on January 13, 1905) another circular note to Austria, Belgium, France, Germany, Great Britain, Italy, and Portugal, stressing the American desire to perpetuate the broad policy of maintaining the *integrity* of China and the *"open door"* in the Orient.[33] Technically this was another American declaration. The fighting continued until the Russian Baltic fleet was annihilated near Tsushima on May 27–28, 1905. Then President Roosevelt mediated, and the war was brought to an end by the Portsmouth Treaty signed on September 5. Japan's victory over Russia awakened a new spirit of hope in the East, but it created a "yellow peril" in the West.

From the standpoint of the open door, the following

[31] K. Asakawa, *Russo-Japanese Conflict* (Boston, 1904), pp. 242–46.
[32] H. B. Morse, *op. cit.,* pp. 422–23.
[33] *United States Foreign Relations, 1905,* p. 1.

three items in the treaty are of special importance, namely, the Russian recognition of Japan's paramount interests in Korea, the Russian transfer to Japan of the lease of Liaotung, and her Manchurian railway south of Changchun. These enabled Japan to become a continental power. She proclaimed a protectorate over Korea on November 7, 1905, and annexed it on August 22, 1910. In Manchuria she faced great difficulties from the very beginning. She was unable to secure China's consent to the transfer of the lease and the railway until December 22, 1905. Moreover, she had no definite plan in regard to the transferred railway, as attested by Premier Katsura's memorandum to Mr. Harriman whereby a Japanese-American syndicate was to be formed to manage this railway.[34] This project, however, was changed shortly afterward, and the Japanese Government authorized, on June 7, 1906, the formation of the South Manchurian Railway Company.[35] This railway, together with the leased territory on the Liaotung Peninsula, made Japan a power in South Manchuria, while Russia was intrenched in North Manchuria. Moreover, the Japanese trade with Manchuria grew at a tremendous rate to the great discomfort of the resident American and British merchants, and at once Japan began to be accused of violating the open-door principle. These accusations were particularly vehement in 1906 and 1907, but naturally the Japanese Government protested against the charges. She formed an entente with France, and another with Russia, in 1907, and still another with the United States in 1908.[36] In 1905 the Anglo-Japanese

[34] See P. H. Clyde, *op. cit.*, pp. 150–52.

[35] Carnegie Endowment for International Peace, *Manchuria, Treaties and Agreements*, pp. 85–86.

[36] The Franco-Japanese entente was signed on June 10; the Russo-

Alliance had been renewed.[37] The ententes testify the desire on the part of the signatories to adhere to the open-door principle, but they failed to allay journalistic charges against Japan.

In this connection, it may be interesting to note the testimony of the American business men of Shanghai who visited Manchuria during 1906:

> After a most comprehensive inquiry it is most difficult, if not impossible, to offer any satisfactory evidence to substantiate the theory that the Japanese Government, through the instrumentality of either its military or civil authorities, is at present purposely interfering with or placing any obstacles in the path of other nations for the industrial exploitation of this important part of the Chinese Empire.[38]

Railway politics was another phase of international rivalries in Manchuria, the origin of which can be traced to the Harriman scheme of 1905. Actual rivalry, however, began with the British project of 1907, and this was followed in 1909 by an American scheme, which resulted in the well-known Knox neutralization proposal. By this proposal the United States, Great Britain, France, Germany, Russia, and Japan were to advance money jointly to China in order that she might buy the Russian and Japanese railways in Manchuria, or else they were to finance the construction of a railway from Chinchow to Aigun. The European powers did not favor either of these projects, while Russia and Japan saw no reason for changing the status of their railways. The scheme fell

---

Japanese pact, on July 30; and the Root-Takahira note, on November 30. See for the texts, MacMurray, *op. cit.*, I, 640, 657–58, and 769–71.

[37] MacMurray, *op. cit.*, pp. 516–18.

[38] *United States Foreign Relations, 1906*, p. 212.

through. On July 4, 1910, Russia and Japan agreed to maintain the *status quo* in Manchuria. The strained Japanese-American relations were made worse both by the proposal and by its failure. The alien land law of California (1913) intensified Japanese feelings against America, while the new policy of the South Manchurian Railway of offering a low rate on sea and rail shipments from Japan (1914) increased American indignation. In fact, the American Government protested against this policy on the ground that it violated the open-door principle. Professor Treat says:

> This [policy] applied to all goods originating there [Japan], but it was in principle a violation of the 1899 open-door definition, which forbade cheaper railway rates—although these rates might be enjoyed by non-Japanese exporters from Japan. It is safe to say that, aside from this violation in principle, the charges that Japan had failed to respect the open door in Manchuria fall to the ground.[39]

In the summer of 1914 the Great War broke out, and soon Japan joined the Allies because of the Anglo-Japanese Alliance. The Japanese dislodged the Germans from Kiaochow and occupied it on November 7, 1914. In 1915 Japan committed a serious diplomatic blunder by making her infamous twenty-one demands on China. It made the Chinese indignant, and gave Japan's hostile critics the chance to say, "Didn't we tell you so!" Many of the Japanese condemned their Government for these demands. But so far as the terms of the treaties which resulted from the demands are concerned, no specific protest was ever lodged with Japan by foreign governments save that of China.[40]

[39] P. J. Treat, *The Far East*, p. 402.
[40] See *ibid.*, pp. 464–65.

It seems proper to conclude these preliminary remarks with a statement of what the Chinese think of the open-door doctrine. Mr. Bau says:

> In subsequent history, when Great Britain put her mantle of influence over Tibet in 1906 and Russia over Outer Mongolia in 1913 and 1915, and when France secured the declaration from the Chinese Government for a preference in railroad and mining enterprises in Kwangsi in 1914, the United States Government was not reported to have lodged any protest, and in 1915 when Japan made Eastern Inner Mongolia her sphere of influence and South Manchuria virtually her exclusive preserve, the United States Government, while making a general declaration reaffirming the Open Door policy and reserving the right of exception to any agreements between China and Japan contrary to the principles of the Open Door or the treaty rights of the United States, did not make any specific representations of protest against the provisions regarding Eastern Inner Mongolia and South Manchuria.[41]

At the Washington Conference the question of the open door was introduced at the meeting of January 16 by Mr. Hughes with the following draft resolution:

> With a view to applying more effectually the principle of the open door or equality of opportunity for the trade and industry of all nations, the powers represented in this conference agree not to seek or support their nationals in asserting any arrangement which might purport to establish in favor of their interests any general superiority of rights with respect to commercial or economic development in any designated region of the territories of China, or which might seek to create any such monopoly or preference as would exclude other nationals from undertaking any legitimate trade or industry or from participating with the Chinese Government in any category of public enterprise, it being understood that this agreement is not to be so construed as to prohibit the acquisition of such properties or rights as may

[41] M. J. Bau, *op. cit.*, p. 153.

THE OPEN-DOOR POLICY 193

be necessary to the conduct of a particular commercial or industrial undertaking.[42]

Sir Auckland Geddes, commenting upon the last part of the resolution, said that unless some machinery were provided serious difficulty might arise in future out of such a proviso. It occurred to him that it might not be beyond the range of possibility to apply some quite simple machinery in the way of a court of reference to which such matters could be submitted. This was an important matter with regard to these proposals.[43]

On the 17th, Mr. Hughes submitted the following revised draft of the resolution:

1. With a view to applying more effectually the principle of the open door, or equality of opportunity, in China for the trade and industry of all nations, the powers other than China represented at this conference agree:

a) Not to seek or to support their nationals in seeking any arrangement which might purport to establish in favor of their interests any general superiority of rights with respect to commercial or economic development in any designated region of China.

b) Not to seek or to support their nationals in seeking any such monopoly or preference as would deprive other nationals of the right of undertaking any legitimate trade or industry in China or of participating with the Chinese Government or with any provincial government in any category of public enterprise, or which by reason of its scope, duration, or geographical extent is calculated to frustrate the practical application of the principle of equal opportunity.

It is understood that this agreement is not to be so construed as to prohibit the acquisition of such properties or rights as may be necessary to the conduct of a particular commercial, industrial, or financial undertaking or to the encouragement of invention and research.

[42] *Document*, pp. 613–14.   [43] *Ibid.*, p. 614.

2. The Chinese Government takes note of the above agreement and declares its intention of being guided by the same principles in dealing with applications for economic rights and privileges from governments and nationals of all foreign countries whether parties to that agreement or not.

3. The powers, including China, represented at this conference agree in principle to the establishment in China of a board of reference to which any question arising on the above agreement and declaration may be referred for investigation and report.

(A detailed scheme for the constitution of the board shall be framed by the special conference referred to in Article I of the convention on Chinese customs duties.)

4. The powers, including China, represented at this conference agree that any provisions of an existing concession which appear inconsistent with those of another concession or with the principles of the above agreement or declaration may be submitted by the parties concerned to the board of reference when established for the purpose of endeavoring to arrive at a satisfactory adjustment on equitable terms.[44]

In the general discussion of the amended proposal it soon developed that the chief interest of the delegates centered about Article 4. M. Sarraut said that this article might give rise to certain abuses. Any contract might be questioned by the mere fact that a new contract had been granted on the same subject, possibly in bad faith, with the sole object of having a ground for contest. Of course the present Government of China could not be suspected of taking any such steps; but the Government might change. Moreover, there was mention in the first article of concessions granted by several provincial governments which might be tempted to evade the central authority and which might purposely seek complications by questioning existing rights.[45]

[44] *Document*, p. 619. [45] *Ibid.*, p. 625.

Baron Shidehara said that the principles formulated in the draft resolution were of an entirely different scope from the policy of "the open door" as conceived in 1898–99; the draft resolution gave, in a certain sense, a new definition to that policy. It seemed natural, therefore, that this new definition should not have any retroactive force. According to Article 4 it appeared as if the concessions already granted by China would be subject to examination in the light of this new agreement. If that were the case, it seemed probable that this agreement would affect private parties unfairly. To meet this situation he offered a suggestion in regard to the wording of the article.[46]

Mr. Hughes then presented a résumé of international instruments bearing upon the open door, among which he mentioned the circular notes of Secretary Hay to the British, French, Japanese, and Italian governments, etc., the Anglo-German Agreement of October 16, 1900, and the Root-Takahira note of 1908.[47] In conclusion he said that in the light of these reiterated statements, which could hardly be regarded as ambiguous, he could not assume that the statement of principles recorded in the resolution before the committee was a new statement. He rather regarded it as a more definite and precise statement of the principle that had long been admitted, and to which the powers concerned had given their unqualified adherence for twenty years. In saying this he did not wish at all to detract from the force of the statement made by Baron Shidehara, as he understood it, that is, in the complete acceptance of the principle as it was here formulated.[48]

[46] *Ibid.*, pp. 630–31.
[47] See *ibid.*, pp. 631–35.
[48] *Ibid.*, p. 635.

Sir Robert Borden said that the principal difficulties in connection with this resolution appeared to have arisen over the fourth article. The powers concerned could act with equal effect if the fourth article were omitted altogether. Under that article there could be no effective action except with the consent of the parties concerned. If the fourth article were omitted, it would still be open to the powers, if they saw fit, to give the like consent and to utilize for the determination or investigation of any relevant question the board of reference to be established under Article 3.[49]

Dr. Sze argued for the retention of the debated article, but the chairman asked what was the pleasure of the committee as regards the Shidehara amendment of Article 4 and the Borden proposal to omit the same. The proposal of Sir Robert was adopted, and thus Article 4 was withdrawn. Otherwise, the Hughes resolution was adopted with one verbal change in Article 1 (*b*), from the word "provincial" to the word "local." On February 6 the so-called Nine-Power Open-Door Pact was signed. Its text is as follows:

The United States of America, Belgium, the British Empire, China, France, Italy, Japan, the Netherlands, and Portugal:

Desiring to adopt a policy designed to stabilize conditions in the Far East, to safeguard the rights and interests of China, and to promote intercourse between China and the other Powers upon the basis of equality of opportunity;

Have resolved to conclude a treaty for that purpose and to that end have appointed as their respective Plenipotentiaries;

[Here follows a list of delegates.]

Who, having communicated to each other their full powers, found to be in good and due form, have agreed as follows:

[49] *Document*, p. 635.

ARTICLE I

The Contracting Powers, other than China, agree:

(1) To respect the sovereignty, the independence, and the territorial and administrative integrity of China;

(2) To provide the fullest and most unembarrassed opportunity to China to develop and maintain for herself an effective and stable government;

(3) To use their influence for the purpose of effectually establishing and maintaining the principle of equal opportunity for the commerce and industry of all nations throughout the territory of China;

(4) To refrain from taking advantage of conditions in China in order to seek special rights or privileges which would abridge the rights of subjects or citizens of friendly States, and from countenancing action inimical to the security of such States.

ARTICLE II

The Contracting Powers agree not to enter into any treaty, agreement, arrangement, or understanding, either with one another, or, individually or collectively, with any Power or Powers, which would infringe or impair the principles stated in Article I.

ARTICLE III

With a view to applying more effectually the principles of the Open Door or equality of opportunity in China for the trade and industry of all nations, the Contracting Powers, other than China, agree that they will not seek, nor support their respective nationals in seeking:

(*a*) Any arrangement which might purport to establish in favor of their interests any general superiority of rights with respect to commercial or economic development in any designated region of China;

(*b*) Any such monopoly or preference as would deprive the nationals of any other Power of the right of undertaking any legitimate trade or industry in China, or of participating with the Chinese Government, or with any local authority, in any category of public enterprise, or which by reason of its scope, duration, or geographical extent is calculated to frustrate the practical application of the principle of equal opportunity.

It is understood that the foregoing stipulations of this Article are not to be so construed as to prohibit the acquisition of such properties or rights as may be necessary to the conduct of a particular commercial, industrial, or financial undertaking or to the encouragement of invention and research.

China undertakes to be guided by the principles stated in the foregoing stipulations of this Article in dealing with applications for economic rights and privileges from Governments and nationals of all foreign countries, whether parties to the present Treaty or not.

ARTICLE IV

The Contracting Powers agree not to support any agreements by their respective nationals with each other designed to create Spheres of Influence or to provide for the enjoyment of mutually exclusive opportunities in designated parts of Chinese territory.

ARTICLE V

China agrees that, throughout the whole of the railways in China, she will not exercise or permit unfair discrimination of any kind. In particular there shall be no discriminaton whatever, direct or indirect, in respect of charges or of facilities on the ground of the nationality of passengers or the countries from which or to which they are proceeding, or the origin or ownership of goods or the country from which they are consigned, or the nationality or ownership of the ship or other means of conveying such passengers or goods before or after their transport on the Chinese Railways.

The Contracting Powers, other than China, assume a corresponding obligation in respect of any of the aforesaid railways over which they or their nationals are in a position to exercise any control in virtue of any concessions, special agreement, or otherwise.

ARTICLE VI

The Contracting Powers, other than China, agree fully to respect China's rights as a neutral in time of war to which China is not a party; and China declares that when she is a neutral she will observe the obligations of neutrality.

ARTICLE VII

The Contracting Powers agree that, whenever a situation arises which in the opinion of any one of them involves the application of the stipulations of the present Treaty, and renders desirable discussion of such application, there shall be full and frank communication between the Contracting Powers concerned.

ARTICLE VIII

Powers not signatory to the present Treaty, which have Governments recognized by the Signatory Powers and which have treaty relations with China, shall be invited to adhere to the present Treaty. To this end the Government of the United States will make the necessary communications to non-signatory Powers and will inform the Contracting Powers of the replies received. Adherence by any Power shall become effective on receipt of notice thereof by the Government of the United States.

ARTICLE IX

The present Treaty shall be ratified by the Contracting Powers in accordance with their respective constitutional methods and shall take effect on the date of the deposit of all the ratifications, which shall take place at Washington as soon as possible. The Government of the United States will transmit to the other Contracting Powers a certified copy of the procès-verbal of the deposit of ratifications.

The present Treaty, of which the French and English texts are both authentic, shall remain deposited in the Archives of the Government of the United States, and duly certified copies thereof shall be transmitted by that Government to the other Contracting Powers.[50]

In pursuance of Article VII the following resolution was adopted by the conference:

Desiring to provide a procedure for dealing with questions that may arise in connection with the execution of the provisions of Articles III and V of the Treaty to be signed at Washington on February 6, 1922, with reference to their general policy de-

[50] *Document,* pp. 893–97.

signed to stabilize conditions in the Far East, to safeguard the rights and interests of China, and to promote intercourse between China and the other Powers upon the basis of equality of opportunity;

Resolve that there shall be established in China a Board of Reference to which any questions arising in connection with the execution of the aforesaid Articles may be referred for investigation and report.

The Special Conference provided for in Article II of the Treaty to be signed at Washington on February 6th, 1922, with reference to the Chinese Customs Tariff, shall formulate for the approval of the Powers concerned a detailed plan for the constitution of the Board.[51]

A comparison between the original American note of 1899 and the present treaty clearly shows that there is a vast difference in the meaning of the open door as defined by these two agreements. The meaning of the 1899 note was clear enough (see pages 182–83, above), but it had been misinterpreted by interested persons so persistently that there had come to prevail a general confusion in certain countries. Not only that, but because of the misinterpretation of the original entente, there followed a series of international vilifications. Japan, in particular, suffered from these unholy enterprises. But thanks to Article III of the Washington Treaty, we now have a new and careful definition of the open door. For the first time, too, China is made a party to the agreement. What the signatories intend to do in respect to China is clearly stated in Article I, that is, to respect her sovereignty, to enable her to develop and maintain a stable government, to maintain the principle of equal opportunity, and to refrain from taking advantage of chaotic conditions in China. Under Article II the powers agree not to impair the above

[51] *Document*, p. 775.

principles by entering into any agreement. By Article IV the powers agree not to support any agreement by their nationals designed to create spheres of influence or to provide for the enjoyment of mutually exclusive opportunities in designated parts of China. China pledges under Article V that she will not exercise or permit unfair discrimination on her railways, while the other powers assume a similar obligation in regard to their railways in China. By Article VI the powers agree to respect the rights of China as a neutral in time of war and she declares that she will observe the obligations of neutrality. Article VII provides for a full and frank communication between the signatory powers when any situation may arise involving the application of the present treaty; and to facilitate this provision a Board of Reference is created. Finally, other powers are to be invited to adhere to the agreement. Thus the treaty lays down the new, definite principles of diplomacy and commerce in China, and provides for the methods of their effective execution. Moreover, under the treaty, the former moral sanction of the open-door principle is made legal as well. The instrument marks a great forward step in the history of Far Eastern diplomacy.

CHAPTER XV

CHINA CHALLENGES EXTRATERRITORIALITY, FOREIGN TROOPS, AND FOREIGN POST OFFICES

Aside from the resolutions incorporated in the two treaties which we have already discussed, several other important ones were adopted by the conference, also with a view to improving China's relations with the powers. These resolutions concerned extraterritoriality, foreign post offices, foreign troops, radio stations, international commitments, the Chinese Eastern Railway, Chinese railways, and the Chinese land armament. The first three mentioned will be studied in this chapter.

In dealing with the subject of extraterritoriality in China, it is customary for Chinese writers to recall the Treaty of Nerchinsk of 1689, the first of Chinese treaties with a Western power, to show that this Sino-Russian convention recognized a reciprocal principle of extraterritoriality. However, a careful examination of the treaty will convince any one that the point in question is not definitive because of the ambiguity of its texts in six different languages. The term extraterritoriality as we understand it today was not clearly applied, or even implied, in the aforesaid treaty. What it crudely provided for was that fugitives and deserters and persons committing crimes would be turned over to the respective officials of the signatory powers. Moreover, the treaty was intended only to affect the subjects of the two empires on the frontier and not those in the interior.[1]

Speaking of extraterritoriality in China during the nineteenth century, a Chinese author says:

---

[1] See S. G. Cheng, *Modern China, a Political Study*, p. 178; P. J. Treat, *The Far East*, p. 119; P. H. Clyde, *op. cit.*, pp. 11–13; and H. B. Morse, *op. cit.*, I, 59–60.

In the few decades before the Opium War, foreign merchants and missionaries in China were nominally under her law, but the Chinese authorities, who were contemptuous of aliens, thought it derogatory from their dignity, if they were to interfere with disputes between "outside barbarians." They had no notion that the sovereign rights of a State included the rights of jurisdiction over foreigners within its dominion; and they deliberately refused to grant them any judicial redress. In consequence, the right of extraterritoriality was exercised by foreign Powers on sufferance.[2]

At the conference this subject was introduced by Dr. Wang, who said that extraterritoriality was clearly laid down in the treaty of 1844 between the United States and China and a similar provision had since been inserted in the treaties with other powers. Extraterritorial rights were granted at a time when there were only five treaty ports. Now, there were fifty such places and an equal number of places open to foreign trade on China's own initiative. This meant an ever increasing number of persons within China's territory over whom she was powerless. This anomalous condition had become a serious problem with which the local administration was confronted; and, if the impairment of the territorial and administrative integrity of China was not to be continued, the matter demanded immediate solution. The Chinese regarded the continuation of extraterritoriality as a national humiliation. It necessitated a multiplicity of courts, and the interrelation of such courts developed a perplexing legal situation. The location of consular courts often made it impossible to introduce the necessary witnesses or to produce other necessary evidence. Moreover, under cover of extraterritoriality, foreigners claimed immunity

[2] S. G. Cheng, *op. cit.*, pp. 178–79.

from local taxes and excises paid by the Chinese. Until the system was abolished or substantially modified, it was inexpedient for China to open her entire territory to foreign trade and commerce. The evils of the existing system had been so obvious that Great Britain in 1902, Japan and the United States in 1903, and Sweden in 1908 had agreed, subject to certain conditions, to relinquish their extraterritorial rights.

Twenty years had elapsed since the conclusion of these treaties, and, while it was a matter of opinion as to whether or not the state of China's laws had attained the standard to which she was expected to conform, it was impossible to deny that China had made great progress on the path of legal reform. A few facts suffice. Five codes had been prepared, some of which had already been put into force. These codes had been prepared with the assistance of foreign experts, and were based mainly on the principles of modern jurisprudence. The China of today was not what she had been twenty years before, when Great Britain had encouraged her to reform her judicial system. These observations were made not for the purpose of asking for an immediate and complete abolition of extraterritoriality, but for the purpose of inviting the powers to co-operate with China in taking initial steps toward improving and eventually abolishing the existing system. He asked that the powers now represented in this conference agree to relinquish their extraterritorial rights in China at the end of a definite period.[3]

The Chinese plea brought forth expression of sympathetic views from all the delegations. But they all held that the best way to proceed with the subject was to adopt the suggestion of Mr. Hughes to appoint a subcommittee

[3] *Document,* pp. 475–77.

to inquire into the facts of the case.[4] The subcommittee so appointed submitted on November 29 its recommendations, in the form of resolutions, which were adopted without discussion, namely:

> The representatives of the Powers hereinafter named, participating in the discussion of Pacific and Far Eastern questions in the Conference on the Limitation of Armament, to wit, the United States of America, Belgium, the British Empire, France, Italy, Japan, the Netherlands, and Portugal—
>
> Having taken note of the fact that in the Treaty between Great Britain and China dated September 5, 1902, in the Treaty between the United States of America and China dated October 8, 1903, and in the Treaty between Japan and China dated October 8, 1903, these several Powers have agreed to give every assistance towards the attainment by the Chinese Government of its expressed desire to reform its judicial system and to bring it into accord with that of Western nations, and have declared that they are also "prepared to relinquish extraterritorial rights when satisfied that the state of the Chinese laws, the arrangements for their administration, and other considerations warrant" them in so doing;
>
> Being sympathetically disposed towards furthering in this regard the aspiration to which the Chinese delegation gave an expression on November 16, 1921, to the effect that "immediately or as soon as circumstances will permit, existing limitations upon China's political, jurisdictional, and administrative freedom of action are to be removed";
>
> Considering that any determination in regard to such action as might be appropriate to this end must depend upon the ascertainment and appreciation of complicated states of fact in regard to the laws and the judicial system and the methods of judicial administration of China, which this Conference is not in a position to determine;
>
> Have resolved
>
> That the Governments of the Powers above named shall establish a Commission (to which each of such Governments shall

[4] *Ibid.*, pp. 477–79.

appoint one member) to inquire into the present practice of extraterritorial jurisdiction in China, and into the laws and the judicial system and the methods of judicial administration of China, with a view to reporting to the Governments of the several Powers above named their findings of fact in regard to these matters, and their recommendations as to such means as they may find suitable to improve the existing conditions of the administration of justice in China, and to assist and further the efforts of the Chinese Government to effect such legislation and judicial reforms as would warrant the several Powers in relinquishing, either progressively or otherwise, their respective rights of extraterritoriality;

That the Commission herein contemplated shall be constituted within three months after the adjournment of the Conference in accordance with detailed arrangements to be hereafter agreed upon by the Governments of the Powers above named, and shall be instructed to submit its report and recommendations within one year after the first meeting of the Commission;

That each of the Powers above named shall be deemed free to accept or reject all or any portion of the recommendations of the Commission herein contemplated, but that in no case shall any of the said Powers make its acceptance of all or any portion of such recommendations either directly or indirectly dependent on the granting by China of any special concession, favor, benefit, or immunity, whether political or economic;

That the non-signatory Powers, having by treaty extraterritorial rights in China, may accede to the resolution affecting extraterritoriality and the administration of justice in China by depositing within three months after the adjournment of the Conference a written notice of accession with the Government of the United States for communication by it to each of the signatory Powers;

That China, having taken note of the resolutions affecting the establishment of a Commission to investigate and report upon extraterritoriality and the administration of justice in China, expresses its satisfaction with the sympathetic disposition of the Powers hereinbefore named in regard to the aspiration of the Chinese Government to secure the abolition of extraterritoriality in China, and declares its intention to appoint a representative

CHINA CHALLENGES EXTRATERRITORIALITY 207

who shall have the right to sit as a member of the said Commission, it being understood that China shall be deemed free to accept or to reject any or all of the recommendations of the Commission. Furthermore, China is prepared to co-operate in the work of this Commission and to afford to it every possible facility for the successful accomplishment of its tasks.[5]

The question next taken up by the conference related to foreign post offices in China. The United States, Great Britain, France, and Japan were maintaining their own post offices in that country.[6] At the meeting of November 25, China demanded that all such postal services be abolished at once. Dr. Sze stated that China based her request upon the following propositions:

1. That China had organized and was now conducting a postal system covering the entire country, and maintaining relations with all foreign countries adequate to meet all requirements.

2. That the existence of these foreign post offices interfered with and made more difficult the development of this system, and deprived the system of revenue which legally and equitably should belong to it.

3. That the maintenance by foreign governments of post offices in China was in direct violation of the latter's territorial and administrative integrity, and rested upon no treaty or other legal rights.[7]

He concluded by pointing out that China, wholly apart from the financial loss suffered by her as a result of the existence of foreign post offices on her soil and the ob-

[5] *Document,* pp. 514–15.

[6] On postal development in China, see H. B. Morse, *The Trade and Administration of the Chinese Empire,* chap. xiii, or *The International Relations of the Chinese Empire,* Vol. III, chap. iii.

[7] *Document,* p. 480.

stacles thereby placed in the way of the development of her own postal system, considered the maintenance of such offices a direct violation of her territorial and administrative integrity. It was one, moreover, that was peculiarly objectionable, since it was a constant, visible reminder to the Chinese people that they were not accorded the consideration given to other peoples. This necessarily had a tendency to lower the prestige of the Chinese Government in the eyes of her people and to make more difficult the already difficult problem of maintaining a Government that would command the respect and ready obedience of her population. From whatever standpoint viewed, the continuance of the foreign post offices upon Chinese soil should, therefore, be disapproved.[8]

Mr. Root said that the foreign post offices in China were a growth from the diplomatic pouch and the special government messenger. According the evidence furnished to the committee, in place of the disturbed and irregular conditions which existed in China when the practice of having special messenger services arose and the system of pouches developed and enlarged until actual post offices were constituted, there was at present a regular and effective postal service. It was not a question of whether any nation should change its policy, but whether conditions which justified an enlarged messenger service twenty years ago still justified its maintenance. The same was true of extraterritoriality and the question of customs; he asked whether conditions had not so changed that foreign control in these matters was no longer justified. If so, it seemed that for the benefit of China, a change in a minor matter like the system of foreign post offices should be made.[9]

[8] *Document*, p. 485.   [9] *Ibid.*, pp. 488–89.

Mr. Balfour said that unlike some other exceptional provisions in China they were not based on treaties, but had grown up from the necessities of the foreign trading communities. There was one important consideration, however, in connection with the question of giving up the foreign post offices which the Chinese had failed to mention; while it was true that the postal system was under Chinese sovereignty and was in no way interfered with, it owed a great deal of its efficiency to the fact that there was a Frenchman at the head of it, a man accustomed to Western methods, and the present satisfactory condition of things was largely due to his influence. For the present, the aid and assistance of this co-director general of posts was almost essential to the proper working of the system; he did not know whether assurances were going to be given on this point. It was of the first importance that the Chinese postal service should not be allowed to deteriorate, as this would immediately bring about a resurgence of the demand for foreign post offices, and the best way to avoid that was some sort of assurance from the Chinese delegation that the presence of the present co-director general would be a permanent, though not an eternal, part of the postal system.[10]

M. Viviani said that France had several post offices in China; the desires of China could, however, be acceded to under three conditions, namely;

1. That all other foreign nations now maintaining post offices in China withdrew them.

2. That the Chinese postal system should function well enough to make return to the present system unnecessary.

3. That the present co-director general should be retained.

[10] *Ibid.,* pp. 489–90.

Should these conditions be fulfilled, France had no objection to withdrawing her post offices.[11]

Mr. Hanihara said that information received by the Japanese delegation had convinced it that safety of communication in China was not assured, and on this ground there was some reason why the foreign post offices should not be withdrawn; as a practical measure it would be difficult to withdraw at once. The plain fact was that there were more Japanese in China, either residents or travelers, than there were nationals of any other foreign power—possibly thirty or fifty times as many—and their activities were more varied; but Japan had no objection to the withdrawal of the foreign post offices under the guaranties suggested by Mr. Balfour and M. Viviani.[12]

Then a subcommittee was appointed to draft resolutions relative to the withdrawal of foreign post offices. Upon the basis of the recommendations made by the subcommittee, the conference adopted the following resolutions:

A. Recognizing the justice of the desire expressed by the Chinese Government to secure the abolition of foreign postal agencies in China, save or except in leased territories or as otherwise specifically provided by treaty, it is resolved:

1. The four Powers having such postal agencies agree to their abandonment subject to the following conditions:
   a) That an efficient Chinese postal service is maintained;
   b) That an assurance is given by the Chinese Government that they contemplate no change in the present postal administration so far as the status of the foreign Co-Director General is concerned.
2. To enable China and the Powers concerned to make the necessary dispositions, this arrangement shall come into force and effect not later than January 1, 1923.

[11] *Document*, p. 490.   [12] *Ibid.*

B. Pending the complete withdrawal of foreign postal agencies, the four Powers concerned severally undertake to afford full facilities to the Chinese customs authorities to examine in those agencies all postal matter (excepting ordinary letters, whether registered or not, which upon external examination appear plainly to contain only written matter) passing through them, with a view to ascertaining whether they contain articles which are dutiable or contraband or which otherwise contravene the customs regulations or laws of China.[13]

On November 28, Dr. Sze handed to the various delegations a written memorandum which read, in part, as follows:

It is the desire of the Chinese delegation to bring before you, for correction in accordance with the controlling principles which you have already affirmed, several other instances of subsisting violations of China's sovereignty and territorial and administrative integrity.

These relate to the maintenance upon the Chinese territory, without China's consent and against her protests, of foreign troops, railway guards, police boxes, and electrical wire and wireless communication installations.

In behalf of my government and the people whom I represent, I therefore ask that the conference give its approval to the following proposition:

Each of the powers attending this conference hereinafter mentioned, to wit, the United States of America, Belgium, the British Empire, France, Italy, Japan, the Netherlands, and Portugal, severally declare that, without the consent of the government of China, expressly and specifically given in each case, it will not station troops or railway guards, or establish and maintain police boxes, or erect or operate electrical communication installations, upon the soil of China; and that, if there now exist upon the soil of China such troops or railway guards or police boxes or electrical installations without China's express consent, they will be at once withdrawn.[14]

[13] *Ibid.*, pp. 496–97, 502, and 572.
[14] For the full statement see *Document*, pp. 499–501.

The immediate response of the various delegations to the foregoing proposal was the request that China present such matters as she desired to have discussed in a manner which would enable the delegates to do so more intelligently, that is, with preparation.[15]

At the following meeting Dr. Sze presented the data pertaining to Japanese troops, police boxes, and railway guards in China by saying that Japan maintained in Shantung four battalions, of an average strength of 525 men, stationed along the Tsingtao-Tsinan Railway, their respective headquarters being at Tsingtao, Kaomi, Fangtze, and Tsinanfu. There was also a force of gendarmerie. In Hankow one battalion was usually maintained, together with detachments of special troops. One full division was usually maintained in Manchuria. The Japanese troops which were withdrawn from Baikal were stationed along the Chinese Eastern Railway. Japan had also stationed sixteen independent battalions or guards along the line, each composed of 21 officers and 617 rank and file. Japan was said to maintain these railway guards in conformity with Article III of the Portsmouth Treaty of 1905, to which he claimed China had not given her consent. In March 1921 there were still several thousand Japanese soldiers in Hunchun.

In 1917, the number of police agencies in Manchuria, as reported by the local authorities of Fengtien and Kirin provinces, had reached twenty-seven. As a result of the Chengchiantun fracas and Hunchun affair, Japan established police stations in these places. According to *Mil-*

---

[15] The request came from the Japanese, French, and British delegates; see *Document,* p. 501. In the present discussion the question of electrical installations will be omitted. It will be treated separately elsewhere.

lard's Review (October 1, 1921), the Ministry of Foreign Affairs was in receipt of a telegram from the commissioner of Foreign Affairs at Swatow to the effect that the Japanese consul there was very active in increasing the Japanese police.

At Amoy a police station was established by Japan in December 1916. The Chinese Government lodged a strong protest against this illegal action on the part of Japan, but Japan had never withdrawn the police station.[16]

This was China's first direct challenge to Japan. A quick reply came from Mr. Hanihara. The Japanese delegation was persuaded that the withdrawal or abolition of the foregoing troops, railway guards, police stations, etc., would be inadvisable, if taken on the ground that China had not given her consent to them. There were specific reasons for the existence of such institutions in each special case. He was prepared to explain those specific reasons which had brought about the existing conditions in the cases in which Japan was concerned.[17] Later he submitted a statement in regard to the actual situation in Manchuria.[18]

At this point Mr. Hughes took occasion to clarify the Chinese proposal which related to the withdrawal of troops (*a*) where there was a difference of view upon the question whether they were there in accordance with a treaty stipulation, (*b*) where it was agreed that they were present without any treaty basis.[19]

Mr. Hanihara continuing said that at the outset he

[16] *Document*, pp. 504–5.

[17] *Ibid.*, p. 510.

[18] See "Japan's Statement on Existing Conditions in China" at the end of this chapter.

[19] *Document*, p. 511.

desired to disclaim most emphatically that Japan had ever entertained any aggressive purpose or any desire to encroach illegitimately upon Chinese sovereignty in establishing or maintaining these garrisons in China. Continuing, he dealt with four points:

1. Japanese railway guards were actually maintained along the South Manchuria Railway and the Shantung Railway. With regard to the Shantung Railway guards, Japan believed that she had, on more than one occasion, made her position sufficiently clear. She had declared and now reaffirmed her intention of withdrawing such guards as soon as China should have notified her that a Chinese police force had been duly organized and was ready to assume responsibility to protect the railway. The maintenance of troops along the South Manchuria Railway stood on a different footing. This was conceded and recognized by China under the treaty of Peking of 1905 (Additional Agreement, Art. II). It was a measure of absolute necessity under the existing state of affairs in Manchuria—a region which had been made notorious by the activity of mounted bandits.

2. Toward the end of 1911 the first revolution broke out in China, and there was complete disorder in the Hupeh district which formed the base of the revolutionary operations. As the lives and property of foreigners were exposed to danger, Japan, together with Great Britain, Russia, Germany, and other principal powers, dispatched troops to Hankow for the protection of her people. This was how a small number of troops had come to be stationed at Hankow. The region had since been the scene of frequent disturbances; there had recently been a clash between the North and South at Changsha, pillage by troops at Ichang, and a mutiny of soldiers at Hankow.

CHINA CHALLENGES EXTRATERRITORIALITY

Such conditions of unrest had naturally retarded the withdrawal of Japanese troops from Hankow. It had never been intended that these troops should remain there permanently, and the Japanese Government had been looking forward to an early opportunity of effecting complete withdrawal of this garrison.

3. The stationing of foreign garrisons in North China was recognized by the Chinese Government under the protocol relating to the Boxer Uprising of 1900. Provided there was no objection from the other countries concerned, Japan would be ready, acting in unison with them, to withdraw her garrison as soon as the actual conditions warranted.

4. The Japanese troops scattered along the lines of the Chinese Eastern Railway had been stationed in connection with an inter-Allied agreement concluded at Vladivostok in 1919. Their duties were to establish communication between the Japanese contingents in Siberia and South Manchuria. It would go without saying, therefore, that these troops would be withdrawn as soon as the evacuation of Siberia by the Japanese troops was effected.[20]

Dr. Sze expressed great pleasure at Mr. Hanihara's assurance that the Japanese troops now in China were not now and never had been intended for any aggressive purpose, and that they would eventually be withdrawn; and added that he would be glad to hear later from Mr. Hanihara as to the time when they would be withdrawn.[21]

In regard to the maintenance of Japanese police in Manchuria and the treaty ports of China, Mr. Hanihara said that two points must be taken into account. (1) Such police did not interfere with Chinese or other foreign nationals. Their functions were strictly confined to the

[20] *Document,* pp. 512–13.   [21] *Ibid.,* p. 513.

protection and control of Japanese subjects. And (2) the most important duties with which the Japanese police were charged were, first, to prevent the commission of crimes by Japanese, and, second, to find and prosecute Japanese criminals when crimes were committed.[22] Apart from the theoretical side of the question, it would thus be observed that the stationing of Japanese police in the interior of China had proved to be of much practical usefulness in the preventing of crimes among Japanese residents, without interfering with the daily life of Chinese or of other foreign nationals. The Japanese police provided a protection for the Chinese communities which at present their own organization failed to provide.[23]

Dr. Sze replied that he wished to point out that both of these matters were serious infringements of China's sovereignty and integrity, and that there was nothing in international law permitting one country to station troops or police upon the soil of another, especially over the protest of the latter. While expressing admiration for the efficiency of the Japanese police system and thanking Mr. Hanihara for his explanation of conditions, he could not accept that as justifying the presence of Japanese police.[24]

Thus the Sino-Japanese duel continued until the patience of the conferees was well-nigh exhausted. Mr. Hughes interposed and said that while listening to the replies and counter-replies of the Chinese and Japanese delegates he had realized that there were certain broad considerations of fact underlying the statements of both parties. Japan offered to withdraw her troops when China accorded adequate protection of life and property. China now offered that protection, and requested the immediate

[22] *Document*, pp. 515–16.   [23] *Ibid.*, p. 516.   [24] *Ibid.*

withdrawal of the troops. The question as to whether China was able to provide protection would involve a complicated and detailed investigation of facts regarding such matters as the number of police needed, etc., which could scarcely be undertaken in the committee itself. He therefore suggested the formation of a subcommittee to hear the presentation of facts by both sides and recommend a practical course of action to the committee.[25]

M. Viviani remarked that the number of subcommittees was multiplying until it threatened to get out of hand, and therefore he would suggest that the commission to investigate the question of extraterritoriality might examine facts relative to the question of withdrawing foreign troops, etc., from China. This Viviani plan was indorsed by the Italian and Japanese delegations, while it was opposed by the Chinese delegation. Mr. Balfour said that many of the questions now confronting the delegates could not be settled without a fair and authentic account of the existing conditions in China. In his very able statement Dr. Sze had used phrases which seemed to suggest that in all circumstances, and from all points of view, China must be regarded as a fully organized and stable State. He did not profess to be an expert on the subject, but he had made inquiries to the best of his ability and felt that it was impossible to say that China had arrived at the condition of a stable country. In this he might possibly be wrong; but if he were not mistaken it was evident that before the committee decided these questions the actual facts in regard to China must be ascertained. He felt that the question of extraterritoriality was closely connected with that of the security of foreign life and property; if this was so, M. Viviani was right,

[25] *Ibid.*, p. 632.

and the commission already decided upon was the fitting body to carry out the inquiry.[26]

Sir Robert Borden agreed with Mr. Balfour, but he suggested that the question might conveniently be turned over to the drafting committee. This last plan was finally adopted by the committee, despite Chinese opposition. On the recommendation of this drafting committee, the conference adopted on January 5 the following resolution:

WHEREAS

The Powers have from time to time stationed armed forces, including police and railway guards, in China to protect the lives and property of foreigners lawfully in China;

And WHEREAS

It appears that certain of these armed forces are maintained in China without the authority of any treaty or agreement;

And WHEREAS

The Powers have declared their intention to withdraw their armed forces now on duty in China without the authority of any treaty or agreement, whenever China shall assure the protection of the lives and property of foreigners in China;

And WHEREAS

China has declared her intention and capacity to assure the protection of the lives and property of foreigners in China;

Now

To the end that there may be clear understanding of the conditions upon which in each case the practical execution of those intentions must depend;

It is resolved:

That the Diplomatic Representatives in Peking of the Powers now in Conference at Washington, to wit, the United States of America, Belgium, the British Empire, France, Italy, Japan, the

[26] *Document,* p. 535.

Netherlands, and Portugal, will be instructed by their respective Governments, whenever China shall so request, to associate themselves with three representatives of the Chinese Government to conduct collectively a full and impartial inquiry into the issues raised by the foregoing declarations of intention made by the Powers and by China and shall thereafter prepare a full and comprehensive report setting out without reservation their findings of fact and their opinions with regard to the matter hereby referred for inquiry, and shall furnish a copy of their report to each of the nine Governments concerned which shall severally make public the report with such comment as each may deem appropriate. The representatives of any of the Powers may make or join in minority reports stating their differences, if any, from the majority report.

That each of the Powers above named shall be deemed free to accept or reject all or any of the findings of fact or opinions expressed in the report, but that in no case shall any of the said Powers make its acceptance of all or any of the findings of fact or opinions either directly or indirectly dependent on the granting by China of any special concession, favor, benefit, or immunity, whether political or economic.[27]

To summarize: The resolution on foreign troops in China made provision whereby China might request that diplomatic representatives of the signatories in conjunction with her own officials inquire into and report upon such issues which she might raise concerning the troops maintained on her territory without her express consent. It also provided that the powers having such troops might withdraw them of their own accord. In pursuance of this understanding, Japan promptly withdrew her battalion stationed at Hankow, and her troops placed at Tsingtao and along the Shantung railway. The resolution on foreign post offices provided for the abolition of these postal agencies in China, except those operating in leased terri-

[27] *Ibid.*, pp. 599–600.

tories or with China's consent, not later than January 1, 1923. Accordingly all such agencies in China proper were closed in November and December, 1922. The resolution on extraterritoriality provided for a commission of investigation which was to meet on May 3, 1922, but China asked for its postponement because of the existing internal disturbances.

However, she invited in December 1925 the commission to meet at Peking, and representatives of the signatories and four others—Denmark, Sweden, Norway, and Spain—held their first meeting on January 12, 1926. The commission remained at Peking until May 5, when its members began to visit a number of provinces for the purpose of studying the actual administration of the courts, prisons, and detention houses. More than a month was consumed in this tour of study. On September 16, 1926, the commission met for the last time to draft a report to be communicated to its respective governments. It is arranged in three parts.

In the first place, the report points out the general aspects in the practice of extraterritoriality, which the system involves, as follows:

1. Limitations upon the jurisdictional freedom of China;
2. Multiplicity of courts and diversity of laws;
3. Inaccessibility of courts, which results in burdensome delays, expenses, and other inconveniences;
4. Lack of legal and judicial training of consular judges, the conflicting nature of their administrative and judicial functions;
5. Difficulty in procedure in appeals, a situation which is obviously unfair to the Chinese litigants and sometimes inconvenient to foreigners;
6. Immunity of foreigners from the operation of Chinese Regulations;
7. Conflict of law relating to the nationality of persons of Chinese origin;

8. Irregular protection of Chinese;
9. Absence of extradition arrangements;
10. Inviolability of foreign premises;
11. Restriction upon trade, travel, and residence.[28]

Secondly, the report makes the following recommendations to the Chinese Government:

I. The administration of justice with respect to the civilian population in China must be entrusted to a judiciary which shall be effectively protected against any unwarranted interference by the executive or other branches of Government, whether civil or military.

II. (*a*) The Chinese should complete and put into force the following laws:
   (1) Civil code.
   (2) Commercial code (including negotiable instruments law, maritime law, and insurance law).
   (3) Revised criminal code.
   (4) Banking law.
   (5) Bankruptcy law.
   (6) Patent law.
   (7) Land expropriation law.
   (8) Law concerning notaries public.

b) The Chinese government should establish and maintain a uniform system for the regular enactment, promulgation, and rescission of laws, so that there may be no uncertainty as to the laws of China.

c) The Chinese government should extend the system of modern courts, modern prisons, and modern detention houses with a view to the elimination of the magistrates' courts and of the old-style prisons and detention houses.

d) The Chinese government should make adequate financial provision for the maintenance of courts, detention houses, and prisons, and their personnel.[29]

---

[28] Department of State (Washington, D.C.), *Report of the Commission on Extraterritoriality in China* (Peking, September 1926), p. 107.

[29] *Ibid.*, pp. 107–8.

Lastly, the report proposes to the various governments:

a) The powers concerned should administer, so far as practicable, in their extraterritorial or consular courts such laws and regulations of China as they may deem it proper to adopt.

b) The trial of mixed cases in the modern Chinese courts should be conducted without the presence of a foreign assessor to watch the proceedings. With regard to the existing mixed courts, their organization and procedure should, as far as the special conditions in the settlements and concessions warrant, be brought into accord with the organization and procedure of the modern Chinese judicial system.

c) The extraterritorial powers should correct certain abuses which have arisen through the extension of foreign protection to Chinese, as well as to business and shipping interests the actual ownership of which is wholly or mainly Chinese.

d) The extraterritorial powers which do not require compulsory periodical registration of their nationals in China should make provisions for such registration at definite intervals.

e) All agreements between foreigners and persons under Chinese jurisdiction which provide for the settlement of civil matters by arbitration should be recognized; and the awards made in pursuance thereof should be enforced, by the extraterritorial or consular courts in the case of persons under their jurisdiction, and by the Chinese courts in the case of persons under their jurisdiction, except when, in the opinion of the competent court, the decision is contrary to public order or good morals.

f) Satisfactory arrangements should be made between the Chinese government and the powers concerned for the prompt execution of judgments, summonses, and warrants of arrest or search, concerning persons under Chinese jurisdiction, duly issued by the Chinese courts and certified by the competent Chinese authorities, and vice versa.

g) Pending the abolition of extraterritoriality, the nationals of the powers should be required to pay such taxes as may be prescribed in laws and regulations duly promulgated by the competent authorities of the Chinese government and recognized by the powers concerned as applicable to their nationals.[30]

[30] *Report of Commission on Extraterritoriality in China,* pp. 108–9.

From the report above we learn definitely what are the difficulties involved in the existing system of extraterritoriality in China. Its recommendations to the Chinese Government make it clear also that the actual administration of justice in that country is far from being satisfactory; but the Chinese representatives could not acknowledge that such was the case, and made reservations to that effect. The commission, in recommending to the powers other than China certain modifications to minimize the difficulty attending the system, shows its sympathy and willingness to co-operate with China to prepare for the ultimate abolition of extraterritoriality. But China is not satisfied with these gradual processes, and the Chinese consider the work of the commission a complete failure.

Before leaving this subject, it may be noted that Germany and Austria-Hungary lost their extraterritorial rights in China when the latter declared war against the former in 1917. Russia also lost her rights in 1920, and agreed to renounce them in 1924. Bolivia and Peru have agreed not to claim them; the "mixed-court" at Shanghai was turned over to China in September 1926; and, finally, the Belgian Treaty was terminated by China on October 27, 1926, and the legal status of Belgian nationals in China was fixed by an interim *modus vivendi* of April 1, 1927.

JAPAN'S STATEMENT ON EXISTING CONDITIONS IN CHINA[31]

Regarding the present situation in Manchuria, even in and around the South Manchurian Railway zone, where peace and order are well maintained, the Chinese bandits have often made raids, having evaded the supervision of the Japanese railway guards.

[31] *Document,* pp. 554-57.

The facts above mentioned are clearly shown in the attached lists, Table A and Table C.

The condition of lawlessness and unrest prevailing in the interior of Manchuria far from the railway zone is beyond description. The attached list, Table B, shows the number of cases of attacks made on the Japanese by the Chinese bandits while the Japanese were traveling through those parts of Manchuria.

The actual cases of attacks made by them have been far more than we have shown here, because in the attached list we have mentioned only the ones which were reported to the Japanese authorities.

The number of cases of attacks made by them on the Koreans might be still greater. But most of the Koreans' cases are not reported to the Japanese authorities for fear of a retaliation by the bandits.

The condition is worse in North Manchuria.

TABLE A

CASES OF ATTACKS BY CHINESE BANDITS WITHIN THE SOUTH MANCHURIA RAILWAY ZONE BEYOND KWANGTUNG LEASED TERRITORY

Year	Number of Cases	Year	Number of Cases	Year	Number of Cases
1906	9	1912	33	1918	82
1907	32	1913	69	1919	106
1908	30	1914	64	1920	183
1909	46	1915	86		
1910	34	1916	71		
1911	57	1917	99	Total	1,001

In the region along the Chinese Eastern Railway, where they have the Chinese railway guards, we are informed that there were 50 cases of attacks made by the bandits during the months of April and May, 1921.

The forces of the bandits numbered from 50 to 400 men in each case, and they committed every kind of ravage.

The outrages committed by the Chinese bandits in Chien-Tao last year well demonstrate the fact that lawlessness and disorder are prevailing in that part of Manchuria.

TABLE B

CASES OF THE JAPANESE INJURED BY THE CHINESE BANDITS WHILE TRAVELING IN SOUTH MANCHURIA

Year	Number of Cases Within Railway Zone	Number of Cases Outside Railway Zone	Number of Victims Within Railway Zone	Number of Victims Outside Railway Zone	Dead Within Railway Zone	Dead Outside Railway Zone
1913.....	7	13	7	21	1	1
1914.....	11	13	14	19	3	..
1915.....	11	32	15	42	..	..
1916.....	15	43	16	53	3	3
1917.....	19	49	25	58	5	3
1918.....	17	35	18	41	2	4
1919.....	35	36	44	51	10	12
1920.....	32	24	41	30	3	3
Total....	147	245	180	315	27	26

Year	Seriously Wounded Within Railway Zone	Seriously Wounded Outside Railway Zone	Slightly Wounded Within Railway Zone	Slightly Wounded Outside Railway Zone
1913..........	..	3	..	3
1914..........	2	6	1	4
1915..........	6	2	4	1
1916..........	4	8	7	5
1917..........	5	9	11	2
1918..........	6	10	3	5
1919..........	9	8	5	6
1920..........	5	12	3	3
Total	37	58	34	29

In the worst case, the Chinese bandits made three attacks in the daytime on the city of Hungchung, near the Japanese border line, regardless of the fact that the Chinese troops were stationed in that city, and not only the Japanese consulate was burned but also a number of the Japanese were massacred by them.

The utterly unstable condition of China can be visioned at once from even a cursory review of the persistent and flagrant manner in which the bandits commit crimes everywhere in open

TABLE C

NUMBER OF THE CHINESE CRIMINALS ARRESTED WITHIN THE SOUTH MANCHURIA RAILWAY ZONE BY THE JAPANESE AUTHORITIES AND HANDED OVER TO THE CHINESE AUTHORITIES

Year	Thieves	Bandits	Burglars	Others	Total
1909	1,148	...	103	474	1,725
1910	1,093	15	70	534	1,712
1911	799	6	33	863	1,701
1912	959	16	39	678	1,692
1913	808	33	96	697	1,634
1914	1,033	55	64	729	1,881
1915	1,024	45	120	757	1,946
1916	1,003	54	111	510	1,678
1917	1,032	46	128	757	1,963
1918	1,328	63	116	917	2,424
1919	1,284	31	65	1,193	2,573
1920	1,671	14	134	1,211	3,030
Total	13,182	378	1,079	9,320	23,595

daylight and the incessant disorders caused by military elements there. A peculiar significance attaches to the incidents cited below because they have taken place in China proper, and they arose largely from the nonpayment of soldiers' wages and their hatred and grudge against the grafting officers, who too often fatten themselves at the expense of the privates. If the depredations and robbery committed by the defeated soldiers following the battle between the factions of the two Kuan Provinces (South China) and the uprising in Yunan and Kweichow and the battle of Shansi and in the uprisings in Manchuria and Mongolia and other border disturbances were taken into account, the number of such incidents would assume a tremendous scope. And it is no exaggeration at all to say that there scarcely passes a day when China is free from such political disorder. Even the major uprisings of this type which came to pass in the 11 months between October 1920 and August 1921 amounted to 33, as follows:

1. Chung-King, Szechuan Province (Oct. 14, 1920). Skirmishes took place between two factions of Chinese troops in urban districts. Pillage was committed and one Englishman was killed. The British warship in port had to fire.

2. Ho-Chien, Chihli Province (Oct. 31, 1920). Disturbances took place in the city, and 50 stores were attacked by soldiers.

3. Kao-Yang, Chihli Province (Nov. 17, 1920). Disturbances continued six days; troops pillaged 30 villages. More than 100 persons were injured.

4. Pao-Ting, Chihli Province (Nov. 23, 1920). Uprisings of soldiers.

5. Hsu-Chang, Honan Province (Nov. 10, 1920). As a result of disorder and pillage more than 40 persons were killed or injured, and more than 1,300 houses were attacked and pillaged. Damages amounted to several million taels.

6. Kui-Yang, Kui-Chao Province (Nov. 10, 1920). Massacre was committed by the troops. From 80 to 90 persons were slaughtered.

7. Ping-Yang, Hunan Province (Nov. 14, 1920). Disturbances between two different sections of Chinese Army took place, in which the commander of the army was murdered.

8. Huan-Chow, Hupeh Province (Nov. 18, 1920). Pillage threatened but barely prevented by a promise to distribute money among soldiers.

9. Chung-Hsian, Hupeh Province (Nov. 22, 1920). Chinese troops pillaged almost all the stores in the city.

10. Tien-Men, Hupeh Province (Nov. 24, 1920); Nau-Lin-Hshian, Hunan Province (Nov. 25, 1920). Uprising of troops during which houses and stores were looted.

11. Yang-Shin, Hupeh Province (Nov. 25, 1920); Fu-Chi-Kow (Nov. 25, 1920). Chinese troops mutinied and attacked the customs office and stores.

12. Yi-Chang, Hupeh Province (Nov. 29, 1920). Skirmishes took place in the city, causing fire; Chinese troops pillaged 14

Japanese stores. Other Japanese stores and storage of Japanese steamship company were burned down. The British American Co. and several other foreign firms were all burned down.

13. Ta-Yeh, Hupeh Province (Nov. 30, 1920). Disturbances were caused by troops, all the stores in the city sustaining heavy damages.

14. Hsian-Yang, Hupeh Province (Dec. 1, 1920). Insurrection of soldiers.

15. Sha-Shi, Hupeh Province (Dec. 10, 1920). Threatening situation reported on account of nonpayment of soldiers' salaries.

16. King-Chun, Hupeh Province (Dec. 10, 1920). Soldiers forced merchants' guilds to make contributions.

17. Chang-Sha, Hunan Province (Dec. 5, 1920). Uprising of Chinese troops during which the mint was looted, anarchic conditions continuing for three days.

18. Yueh-Chow, Hunan Province (Jan. 25, 1921). Wholesale pillage of stores in the city and railway traffic blocked for several days.

19. Hsin-Yii, Kiang-si (Jan. 20, 1921). Factional fights among soldiers accompanied by depredation of stores and houses.

20. Pao-ting, Chihli Province (Feb. 13, 1921). Mutiny of soldiers, 3,000 houses and stores spoliated.

21. Shen-Hsien, Chihli Province (Feb. 22, 1921). Soldiers mutinied and robbed stores.

22. Sha-shi, Hupeh Province (Feb. 23, 1921). Mutiny of troops, because of nonpayment of 10 months. They set fire to the stores and pillaged them. Damages amounted to more than 10,000,000 taels.

23. Chang-te, Honan Province (April 16, 1921). Serious disturbance caused by factional fights by troops.

24. Chou-Chia-Kow, Honan Province (Mar. 12, 1921). Soldiers caused trouble and disorder in the town.

25. Hsin-Yan, Honan Province (May 31, 1921). Insurrection occurred with mutiny and pillage.

26. Yi-Chang, Hupeh Province (June 8, 1921). Soldiers joined by local bandits, committed ravage and incendiarism, seven or eight hundred lives lost.

27. Wu-Chang, Hupeh Province (June 8, 1921). Troops pillaged stores and destroyed the mint. Banks and all the prin-

cipal firms and stores were burned down. The same soldiers, led by their commander, restored order in the town the following day.

28. Fu-Chi-Kow (June 20, 1921). Troops caused trouble. Many were injured and much damage done to property.

29. Wu-fu, An-Kui Province (June 2, 1921). Disturbances caused by troops, merchants' guilds forced to make pecuniary contribution.

30. Nan-Chang, Kiang-si Province (latter part of June, 1921). Chinese troops pillaged the village; an officer was murdered.

31. Hsiao-hsien, Hupeh Province (Aug. 24, 1921). Chinese troops damaged railroads, railroad trucks, cut telephone wires, and committed pillage.

32. Wu-Chue (Aug. 15, 1921). Pillage by soldiers lasted for 24 days in and around the town.

33. Wu-Chang (Aug. 24, 1921). Insurrection of troops.

CHAPTER XVI

THE POWERS MAKE CONCESSIONS TO CHINA

Five distinct questions relative to China had been disposed of, but she continued to occupy the attention of the conference. The matters now brought in for discussion pertained to foreign electrical installations, international commitments, and the Chinese Eastern Railway. China formally requested, on November 28, that the electrical stations maintained in China without her express consent be abolished or surrendered to her at once.[1]

The stations affected by the request were as follows:

Japan: at Peking, Chinwangtao, and Tientsin in Chihli; at Harbin, Manchouli, Kungchuling, Lungtsintsung, and Dalny in Manchuria; at Tsinan and Tsingtao in Shantung and at Hankow in Hupeh.[2]

France: at Shanghai in Kiangsu, Kwangchow-wan in Kwantung, Yunnanfu in Yunnan, and Tientsin in Chihli.

Great Britain: at Hongkong proper, and at Kowloon and Kashgar in Sinkiang.

United States: at Peking, Tientsin, and Tangshan in Chihli.[3]

Dr. Sze insisted that all the arguments that had been presented in favor of the immediate abolition of foreign postal stations applied with equal force to the abolition or surrender to the Chinese Government of these foreign electrical means of communication. Just as China had built up a highly efficient postal system capable of transporting with speed and safety written communications between China and foreign countries and between im-

---

[1] *Document*, p. 501.

[2] *Ibid.*, p. 523. Mr. Hanihara corrected the foregoing list by saying that the station at Harbin was not under the control of Japan, that there was no station at Manchouli and that the station at Lungtsintsung had been withdrawn.

[3] *Ibid.*, p. 501.

portant points within China so she had developed a system of telegraph stations adequate for the transmission of communications by wire between different parts of China, and had entered into contracts for the installation of high-powered wireless apparatus which would put her into communication with other countries. She already had a number of lower-powered wireless stations for wireless communication between points within China. There was thus no need for the maintenance in China by other countries of wire or wireless installations. Their operation not only seriously interfered with the continued development of the Chinese system by diverting from it business properly belonging to it, but represented an indefensible infringement of China's territorial and administrative integrity. Since certain of these represented the investment of considerable sums of money, China, though recognizing no legal obligation to do so, was willing to pay to the foreign governments owning them the fair value of such stations as were of such character or were so located that they could be made effective parts of her systems of electrical communications.[4]

Furthermore, Dr. Sze stated that a distinction should be made between the electrical installations established in the legations under the terms of the protocol of 1901 and the others which had not been based on treaty contractual basis. With regard to the legations' installations, the Chinese delegation were not asking for their withdrawal, but would consent to their maintenance upon two conditions: first, these wireless installations would be used only for official purposes, not for commercial ones; and, second, an arrangement should be reached with a view to preventing the wave lengths of the legations' installations from

[4] *Ibid.,* pp. 505–7.

interfering with the wave lengths of the Chinese wireless stations.[5]

China's request that the legations' installations should not be used for commercial purposes was complied with by all the powers except France. M. Viviani raised the question of whether it would be possible to do anything in this direction so long as a stable government had not been re-established in China. Should the powers consent not to use certain stations for the sending of commercial messages, what guaranty would they have that these messages could be sent by other means?[6] Moreover, the question of wave lengths proved troublesome. M. Viviani insisted that it would be necessary to know whether China had worked out any technical or financial plan.[7] The British delegate hoped that some arrangement would be made, but the question would involve work beyond the scope of the present conference and, therefore, it would not be wise to pursue it.[8] In view of the importance of the subject, Mr. Hughes hoped that some agreement might be arrived at between the governments operating the installations by referring the matter to a committee.[9] The Japanese concurred that a committee might be organized to look into the technical aspects of wireless.[10] Thereupon M. Viviani proposed to appoint a technical committee to tackle the problem.[11] But Mr. Balfour was not quite sure what kind of experts were required for the work.[12] The matter was finally referred to the drafting committee, and on December 7 it submitted its recommendations in the following resolution which was adopted by the Committee of the Whole:

[5] *Document*, p. 519. [6] *Ibid.*, p. 520. [7] *Ibid.* [8] *Ibid.*, p. 521.
[9] *Ibid.*, pp. 522–23. [10] *Ibid.*, p. 522. [11] *Ibid.*
[12] *Ibid.*, p. 525.

1. That all radio stations in China whether maintained under the provisions of the international protocol of September 7, 1901, or in fact maintained in the grounds of any of the foreign legations in China, shall be limited in their use to sending and receiving government messages and shall not receive or send commercial or personal or unofficial messages, including press matter: Provided, however, that in case all other telegraphic communication is interrupted, then, upon official notification accompanied by proof of such interruption to the Chinese Ministry of Communications, such stations may afford temporary facilities for commercial, personal, or unofficial messages, including press matter, until the Chinese Government has given notice of the termination of the interruption;

2. All radio stations operated within the territory of China by a foreign government or the citizens or subjects thereof under treaties or concessions of the Government of China shall limit the messages sent and received by the terms of the treaties or concessions under which the respective stations are maintained;

3. In case there be any radio station maintained in the territory of China by a foreign government or citizens or subjects thereof without the authority of the Chinese Government, such station and all the plant, apparatus, and material thereof shall be transferred to and taken over by the Government of China, to be operated under the direction of the Chinese Ministry of Communications upon fair and full compensation to the owners for the value of the installation, as soon as the Chinese Ministry of Communications is prepared to operate the same effectively for the general public benefit;

4. If any questions shall arise as to the radio stations in leased territories, in the South Manchurian Railway Zone or in the French Concession at Shanghai, they shall be regarded as matters for discussion between the Chinese Government and the Governments concerned.

5. The owners or managers of all radio stations maintained in the territory of China by foreign Powers or citizens or subjects thereof shall confer with the Chinese Ministry of Communications for the purpose of seeking a common arrangement to avoid interference in the use of wave lengths by wireless stations in China, subject to such general arrangements as may be made

by an international conference convened for the revision of the rules established by the International Radio Telegraph Convention signed at London, July 5, 1912.[13]

Concerning this resolution the conference agreed that the powers other than China declare that nothing in paragraphs three or four of the resolutions of December 7, 1921, was to be deemed to be an expression of opinion by the conference as to whether the stations referred to therein were or were not authorized by China. They further gave notice that the result of any discussion arising under paragraph four must, if it was not to be subject to objection by them, conform with the principles of the open door or equality of opportunity approved by the conference.[14]

In reply to this declaration the Chinese delegation stated that the Chinese Government did not recognize or concede the right of any foreign power or of the nationals thereof to install or operate, without its express consent, radio stations in legation grounds, settlements, concessions, leased territories, railway areas, or other similar areas.[15]

In a word, therefore, by this resolution the conference agreed that the signatory powers would not use their legation radio stations for commercial or personal or unofficial purposes, including press matter, unless all other telegraphic communication was interrupted. All the other foreign radio stations operating under treaties were to be governed by the terms of such treaties, while the stations operating without Chinese authority were to be sold to China. Questions relating to the stations in leased territories, in the South Manchurian Railway zone or in the French Shanghai concession, were to be settled by China

[13] *Document,* pp. 548–49.   [14] *Ibid.,* p. 907.   [15] *Ibid.*

and the powers directly involved. China and the powers operating radio stations were jointly to solve the problem of wave lengths. This resolution was accompanied by a statement by the powers other than China that the conference assumed no responsibility in deciding the status of the stations mentioned in paragraph three, but demanded that the stations in paragraph four must observe the principle of the open door. China declared on her part that she did not recognize any of these foreign stations unless they were being operated with her express consent.

Mr. Hughes introduced (January 19) the question of international commitments affecting China's interests, and said that it would be of great aid if it should be understood that the powers represented at the conference had full knowledge of all commitments which might thereafter exist, or be said to exist, and opportunity was now afforded for presentation of these commitments and for any discussion such presentation might suggest.[16]

Dr. Koo suggested that all the powers who had any claim or claims on China should make them known; it was desirable, in the opinion of the Chinese delegation, that the principle of publicity should be applied to international commitments with reference to China. The validity of these commitments should be determined, and after the validity of the existing commitments or claims was determined steps should be taken to harmonize them with one another and with the principles adopted by the committee.[17]

Mr. Hughes supposed that nothing they could do would promote to a greater degree friendly relations in the future, with respect to matters in which China and interests in China were involved, than a full disclosure of all the

[16] *Ibid.*, pp. 647–48. [17] *Ibid.*, p. 649.

commitments relied upon by the powers represented at the conference. He would suggest for their consideration that the powers represented prepare and file with the secretary-general of the conference lists of all the treaties and engagements with China upon which they relied.[18]

Sir Auckland Geddes said that the British Empire was fully prepared to publish all the commitments which it had with China, fully prepared to publish everything they relied on.[19]

Baron Shidehara said that it would not be difficult to give a full list of commitments and agreements to which the Japanese Government itself was a party. The question of Chinese obligations to individuals or firms, however, to which the Government itself was not a party, was an entirely different matter; it would be very difficult indeed for any government to ascertain the precise nature and terms of such contracts and to make a list of them. He assumed, therefore, that the chairman's statement referred only to those agreements and claims to which foreign governments themselves were parties.[20]

The chairman said that it was, of course, not supposed that governments would be under any obligation to list commitments in which they had no interest and of which they had no knowledge. In enterprises not wholly or strictly governmental, however, there were sometimes important features which involved government concessions. The question of degree was important. There were some matters which were not directly governmental engagements which were of a very serious character as affecting the interests of nations or their nationals. One illustration was that of the Chinese Eastern Railway.[21]

[18] *Document*, p. 650.
[19] *Ibid.*, p. 651.
[20] *Ibid.*, pp. 651–52.
[21] *Ibid.*, p. 652.

He presented a draft resolution, the salient points of which were as follows: First, the powers were to file with the conference, as soon as possible, a list of the official texts of all treaties, conventions, exchange of notes, or other international agreements, which they had with China or with other powers in relation to China, in case they were deemed to be still in force, upon which they might desire to rely. Similar commitments made in future were to be communicated to the conference powers within sixty days of their conclusion. Secondly, the powers were to file with the same body a list of the texts of all those contracts between their nationals and the Chinese Government or any of its administrative subdivisions, involving any concession, franchise, option, or preference with respect to railway construction, mining, forestry, navigation, river conservancy, harbor works, reclamation, electrical communications, or other public works or public service, or for the sale of arms or ammunition, or involving a lien upon any of the public revenues or properties of the Chinese Government or of the several provinces, or a financial obligation, on the Chinese Government or its subdivisions, of not less than $1,000,000 silver. Similar contracts made in future were to be communicated to the conference powers within sixty days of their conclusion.[22]

Baron Shidehara thought that the general idea of this resolution would no doubt be of great value to all concerned; but the practical side of the matter must also be considered. The texts of a great many treaties and other international agreements between Japan and China were in the Japanese and Chinese languages. They had been published from time to time in the *Official Gazette* of the Japanese Government, but no authentic translation had as

[22] *Ibid.*, pp. 658–59.

yet been made. Mr. J. V. A. MacMurray's book contained translations of most of these documents, but these could not be regarded as authoritative or official. So far as the Japanese delegation was concerned, therefore, they could only give citations from MacMurray or any other compilation in English or French on the understanding that these translations were in no way to be regarded as authoritative. The Japanese delegates had a general knowledge of the important contracts concluded between Japanese nationals and the Chinese Government, or local authorities, coming under the head of Article 2 of the draft resolution, but they had not at hand the full texts of these contracts, nor was there any legal means of compelling individual firms or corporations to produce the texts of these contracts; hence the practical execution of Article 2 seemed to require an action of legislation, so far as Japan was concerned, to compel each firm or corporation to notify the Japanese Government whenever such a contract was completed. Without such legal sanction it could not undertake that all contracts should be notified to the powers within sixty days of their conclusion.

Nevertheless, the Japanese Government would do everything in its power to supply such a list, but it could not guarantee that this would be complete. Baron Shidehara also wished to call attention to the fact that the first paragraph of Article 2 specified that the several powers were to file with the secretary-general of the conference, at their earliest convenience, for transmission to the participating powers, a list, as nearly complete as might be possible, of all those contracts between their nationals, etc., while the second paragraph of this same article did not contain such a limitation.[23]

[23] *Document,* pp. 659–61.

Mr. Balfour thought that the committee should explicitly throw upon China as well as upon the other powers the obligation of taking its fair share of this effort toward publicity, which would do so much in the future to purify the whole of these commercial or semi-commercial transactions. He might make one further observation on this second paragraph. It aimed at giving publicity to every transaction which was over a million dollars in amount. The ordinary practice of the British legation in Peking and of British subjects was that these last should notify the legation or the foreign office of all transactions of the kind they were dealing with. Although there was no written law upon the subject, he imagined that a British national who did not inform the British legation that he was making a contract would not expect that legation to give him any diplomatic support should any question on it arise thereafter. He would like to ask whether that wholesome rule ought to require that publicity be given to the terms of relatively small transactions. He suggested in addition that, as had been done in many previous cases, nations not represented around this table should be asked if they would agree to the final form in which this document might be embodied. He had no doubt that that was the intention of the American delegation. It should be put in black and white.[24]

After further discussion, the following resolution was adopted by the conference on January 21, 1922:

The Powers represented in this Conference, considering it desirable that there should hereafter be full publicity with respect to all matters affecting the political and other international obligations of China and of the several Powers in relation to China, are agreed as follows:

[24] *Ibid.*, pp. 661–62.

I. The several Powers other than China will at their earliest convenience file with the Secretariat-General of the Conference for transmission to the participating Powers a list of all treaties, conventions, exchange of notes, or other international agreements which they may have with China, or with any other Power or Powers in relation to China, which they deem to be still in force and upon which they may desire to rely. In each case, citations will be given to any official or other publication in which an authoritative text of the documents may be found. In any case in which the document may not have been published a copy of the text (in its original language or languages) will be filed with the Secretariat-General of the Conference.

Every Treaty or other international agreement of the character described which may be concluded hereafter shall be notified by the Governments concerned within sixty (60) days of its conclusion to the Powers who are signatories of or adherents to this agreement.

II. The several Powers other than China will file with the Secretariat-General of the Conference at their earliest convenience for transmission to the participating Powers a list, as nearly complete as may be possible, of all those contracts between their nationals, of the one part, and the Chinese Government or any of its administrative subdivisions or local authorities, of the other part, which involve any concession, franchise, option, or preference with respect to railway construction, mining, forestry, navigation, river conservancy, harbor works, reclamation, electrical communications, or other public works or public services, or for the sale of arms or ammunition, or which involve a lien upon any of the public revenues or properties of the Chinese Government or any of its administrative subdivisions. There shall be, in the case of each document so listed, either a citation to a published text or a copy of the text itself.

Every contract of the public character described which may be concluded hereafter shall be notified by the Governments concerned within sixty (60) days after the receipt of information of its conclusion to the Powers who are signatories of or adherents to this agreement.

III. The Chinese Government agrees to notify in the conditions laid down in this agreement every treaty agreement or contract of the character indicated herein which has been or may hereafter be concluded by that Government or by any local authority in China with any foreign Power or the nationals of any foreign Power whether party to this agreement or not, so far as the information is in its possession.

IV. The Governments of Powers having treaty relations with China which are not represented at the present Conference shall be invited to adhere to this agreement.

The United States Government, as convener of the Conference, undertakes to communicate this agreement to the Governments of the said Powers, with a view to obtaining their adherence thereto as soon as possible.[25]

Under this agreement the signatory powers bind themselves to make public all their public commitments as well as the private contracts entered into with the Chinese authorities. The Chinese Government is placed under the same obligation. Non-signatory nations having treaty relations with China are to be invited to adhere to this agreement. The resolution marks a new departure in Far Eastern diplomacy, for it makes it impossible to apply "secret diplomacy"; it is a step farther than the practice of the League of Nations, because it requires the publication of private contracts, while the League demands the publication of public instruments only.

The question of the Chinese Eastern Railway was introduced on January 18, 1922, by Mr. Hughes, who said that the problems of this railway concerned finance, the form of management, and efficiency of management. So far as the United States was concerned, there was but one interest, and that was that the railroad should be maintained as an artery of commerce, with free opportunity to all and unfair discrimination against none. It had no interest whatever in the ownership and had no

[25] *Document*, pp. 684–85.

desire to secure control. It wished merely to do anything within its power to promote the proper conduct of that road as one of the greatest instrumentalities of commerce in the East. But the subject was so difficult, there were so many different angles that had to be carefully considered, and the project and the relations of both Russia and China to it were such that he did not think, speaking for himself personally, that the matter could profitably be discussed in the committee at this time. Such discussion, by reason of the existing conditions in that part of the East, would almost necessarily involve a detailed consideration of history and of documents and interests, without dealing with the point of immediate requirements. He therefore suggested that a subcommittee of experts be appointed, drawn from technical advisers of the various delegations or from such representatives of the powers as might be deemed fitting by each, to consider at once whether there was anything that could be done at this conference which would aid in promoting the efficiency of that railroad and its proper management.[26]

This suggestion was adopted, and a subcommittee of experts was named. This subcommittee made its report on January 23, 1922, as follows:

The Chinese Eastern Railway being an indispensable factor in the economic development of Siberia, as well as Northern Manchuria, and constituting an essential link in a trans-continental railway system of international importance, the nations represented at this Conference are interested in its preservation, its efficient operation, and its maintenance as a free avenue of commerce, open to the citizens of all countries without favor or discrimination.

The status of the Chinese Eastern Railway is determined by the contract concluded in 1896 between China and the Russo-

[26] *Document*, pp. 640–41.

Chinese (Russo-Asiatic) Bank and the contract concluded in 1898 between China and the Chinese Eastern Railway Company, and subsequent contracts between China and that company. The necessary funds for its construction were furnished by the Russian Government and it was built under the direction and supervision of that Government, acting through the Chinese Eastern Railway Company. The railway is in effect the property of the Russian Government. China has certain ultimate reversionary rights which are provided for in the original contract of 1896.

The absence of the recognized Russian Government since 1917 has made imperative for some time past certain measures providing for the preservation and continued operation of the railway. Early in 1919—as a consequence of assistance which had been given to Russia, at her request, in the operation of the entire trans-Siberian system, including the Chinese Eastern Railway—certain Powers, which are represented at this Conference, undertook to continue this assistance upon definite terms. An agreement was concluded in January, 1919, between the United States and Japan, under the terms of which China, France, Great Britain, and Italy subsequently co-operated. The fundamental purpose of the arrangement thus brought about was explicitly declared to be the temporary operation of the railways in question, with a view to their ultimate return to those in interest without the impairing of any existing rights.

The trusteeship thus assumed continues in force. Changes which have intervened since 1919 render necessary readjustments in its mode of operation.

The three principal problems are:
1. Finance
2. Operation
3. Police

1. As to the first, it is to be observed that funds will be obtainable from bankers and other outside sources only if suitable conditions are established for the economical operation of the railway and if the funds provided are to be expended under adequate supervision. A suitable manner of providing such supervision, in the opinion of the committee, would be to establish at Harbin a Finance Committee, to consist of one representative each of the Powers represented at the Conference (so far as

they might care to participate). This Committee would replace the so-called Interallied Committee now established at Vladivostok and the so-called Technical Board at Harbin. It should exercise general financial control and be entrusted with the exercise of the trusteeship which was assumed in 1919 and which cannot be discharged until the general recognition by the Powers of a Russian Government.

2. As to operation, in order to disturb as little as possible the normal situation, this should, in the opinion of the committee, be left in the hands of the Chinese Eastern Railway Company, the Finance Committee not to interfere with the technical operation of the railway, except so far as may be necessary to meet the conditions stated in the first sentence of paragraph 1.

3. The protection of the railway property and the maintenance of public order within the railway zone are of fundamental importance. In order to assure these, it is necessary to provide a dependable and effective police force or gendarme. As the railway zone lies within Chinese territory, this could be made to consist, if China so desired, of Chinese; but it would be essential, in the opinion of the committee, that—as a temporary and exceptional measure, justified alike by existing conditions and the precedent of a Russian guard—this police or gendarme should be paid by and remain under the control of the Finance Committee, as this body would be responsible under the trusteeship for the preservation of the property of the railway and the maintenance of conditions suitable to unhampered operation.[27]

Dr. Yen, the Chinese representative on the subcommittee, observed that, of the three measures proposed in the report, he found it very difficult to agree to measures 1 and 3. With respect to measure 1, in view of the existing administrative organization and operation, it would be very difficult for China to agree to the general financial control and the exercise of trusteeship as stated in the report, and, with respect to measure 3, he doubted the propriety, not to say the advisability, of putting Chinese

[27] *Document,* pp. 689–91.

police or gendarmerie under a mixed committee as proposed, as the police or gendarmerie was a state force. In this connection, it might also be pointed out that the precedent of a Russian guard had no legal ground, as it was expressly stipulated in the Agreement of 1896 that it was the Chinese Government which was to take measures to assure the safety of the railway and of the persons in its service. Under such circumstances, he had to make reservations with respect to these two measures.

However, he did not wish it to be understood that he was not aware of the fact that there was room for improvement with respect to this railway. He was of the opinion that the Chinese Government would welcome friendly assistance of foreign powers and might be prepared to discuss matters regarding the technical and financial aspects of the railway in so far as not inconsistent with the recognition of its political rights.[28]

Mr. Hughes thought it inadvisable to discuss the report, in view of the disagreement between the subcommittee and the Chinese, and he suggested that a subcommittee of delegates might be appointed to consider and solve the points of difference, if possible.[29]

On February 2, Mr. Root reported on behalf of the Subcommittee of Delegates that it had before it both the report of the Technical Committee and many drafts of resolutions aimed at avoiding the impasse caused by the objection interposed by Dr. Yen to the conclusions of the Technical Committee. None of those drafts had seemed to the generality of the Committee of Delegates to make any improvement in the situation. They were all in the form of amendments to the inter-Allied agreement of 1919, which had been regarded by common consent and

[28] *Ibid.*, pp. 691–92. [29] *Ibid.*, p. 692.

general statement as being still in force and effect. The Committee of Delegates now wished to report unanimously the following resolution:

Resolved, That the preservation of the Chinese Eastern Railway for those in interest requires that better protection be given to the railway and the persons engaged in its operation and use, a more careful selection of personnel to secure efficiency of service, and a more economical use of funds to prevent waste of the property.

That the subject should immediately be dealt with through the proper Diplomatic channels.

The Powers other than China in agreeing to the resolution regarding the Chinese Eastern Railway reserve the right to insist hereafter upon the responsibility of China for performance or non-performance of the obligations toward the foreign stockholders, bondholders, and creditors of the Chinese Eastern Railway Company which the Powers deem to result from the contracts under which the railroad was built and the action of China thereunder and the obligations which they deem to be in the nature of a trust resulting from the exercise of power by the Chinese Government over the possession and administration of the railroad.[30]

Dr. Koo repeated China's position at length, but at the close of his remarks the resolution was adopted. Then the reservation was unanimously accepted, China not voting.[31]

To conclude our consideration of resolutions thus far examined: China carried her point in respect to the foreign radio stations maintained on her territory without her consent, but the proposed settlement of the remaining stations was so conditioned that it might be considered of no particular practical value to her. The merit of the agreement on international commitments is not to be doubted, for it will do away with one source of inter-

[30] *Document,* p. 751.   [31] *Ibid.,* pp. 753–54.

national irritation, but it is very much doubted that China will be an important beneficiary of this agreement; in fact, it is not inconceivable that she may even suffer because of this, for she can no longer secretly indulge in her customary diplomacy of playing one power against another. In respect to the Chinese Eastern Railway, China failed to command the confidence of the powers interested in the road. The conference passed, against her wish, a resolution making it very clear that she was responsible, as the trustee of the railway, for fulfilling her financial obligations to the powers.

CHAPTER XVII

PRINCIPLES VERSUS REALITIES

There still remain for discussion two resolutions, one relating to the Chinese army and the other to Chinese railways. These, together with the several other resolutions later incorporated in the Open-Door Treaty, touched upon the question of realities as well as principles and, therefore, caused the delegations to express their views in no uncertain terms. A study of these views will assist us further in understanding the real attitudes of the various powers in their relations with China.

The idea of advising China to reduce her vast army first arose in the subcommittee on the Chinese tariff, and on January 3 this body passed (the Chinese not voting) a resolution to that effect. This resolution was contained in the report of the subcommittee presented to the conference on the 5th. It was as follows:

> The members of the subcommittee in studying the question of increasing the customs tariff rates to meet the urgent needs of the Chinese Government have been deeply impressed with the severe drain on China's public revenue through the maintenance of excessive military forces in various parts of the country. Most of these forces are controlled by the military chiefs of the provinces, and their continued maintenance appears to be mainly responsible for China's present unsettled political conditions.
>
> It is felt that large and prompt reduction of these forces will not only advance the cause of China's political unity and economic development, but hasten her financial rehabilitation. Therefore, without any intention to interfere in the internal problems of China, but animated by the sincere desire to see China develop and maintain for herself an effective and stable Government, alike in her own interest and in the general interest of trade, and inspired by the spirit of this conference whose aim is to reduce, through the limitation of armament, "the enormous disbursements" which "manifestly constitute the greater part of

the encumbrance upon enterprise and national prosperity," the subcommittee ventures to suggest for the consideration of the committee the advisability of laying before the conference for its adoption a resolution expressing the earnest hope of the conference and embodying recommendation to China that immediate and effective steps be taken by the Chinese Government to reduce the aforesaid military forces and expenditure.[1]

On the 20th Mr. Underwood formally presented to the conference a resolution embodying the items mentioned above, and concluding with the words:

It is resolved, That this conference express to China the earnest hope that immediate and effective steps may be taken by the Chinese Government to reduce the aforesaid military forces and expenditures.[2]

Supporting the resolution, Sir Robert Borden remarked that the appointment of military governors for the Provinces, which was initiated shortly after the inception of the Republic by the then President, Yuan Shi-kai, had had an unfortunate effect and operation since his death. The power of these governors had increased to such an extent that the Central Government at Peking exercised very little control over a large part of the country. In fact the military governors had become military dictators within their respective provinces or spheres of influence; they recruited and maintained their own armies; they formed combinations among themselves and struggled for ascendancy, and at intervals they dictated the personnel and policy of the Central Government. That Government possessed very little authority in comparison with the power of the military governors and was only recognized by the latter in so far as it suited their inter-

[1] *Document,* pp. 593–94.   [2] *Ibid.,* p. 655.

ests. Up to the present there had been an unfortunate lack of such organizing capacity as would establish a strong and stable central government and bring the country once more under its effective direction and control. For such a purpose the provision of great revenues or the placing of large funds at the disposal of a weak administration was not of itself effective. So long as the military governors retained their present dominating authority and influence, such financial resources would probably be absorbed to a very great extent by these military chiefs instead of being employed to cut down their power. The forces enlisted under the various military chieftains were said to regard their military duties as entirely occupational, and it was believed that they would be quite ready to accept employment in the construction of railways, highways, and otherwise, provided the arrears in their pay were made good.[3]

The Chinese delegation did not have much to say on the proposal, but with respect to what Sir Robert had said, Dr. Koo wished to express his deep appreciation of the spirit animating his remarks.[4] In short, China was forced to submit to what she might have justly considered an interference in her domestic politics. The resolution was unanimously adopted by the conference.

On the previous day Mr. Hughes offered a resolution relating to Chinese railways which was adopted by the conference without discussion. It was as follows:

> The Powers represented in this Conference record their hope that, to the utmost degree consistent with legitimate existing rights, the future development of railways in China shall be so conducted as to enable the Chinese Government to effect the unification of railways into a railway system under Chinese con-

[3] *Document*, pp. 655–56. [4] *Ibid.*, p. 657.

trol, with such foreign financial and technical assistance as may prove necessary in the interest of that system.[5]

The Chinese delegation noted with sympathetic appreciation the expression of the hope of the powers that the existing and future railways of China might be unified under the control and operation of the Chinese Government, with such foreign financial and technical assistance as might be needed. It was their intention as speedily as possible to bring about this result. It was their purpose to develop existing and future railways in accordance with a general program that would meet the economic, industrial, and commercial requirements of China. It would be their policy to obtain such foreign financial and technical assistance as might be needed from the powers in accordance with the principles of the open door or equal opportunity; and the friendly support of these powers would be asked by the Chinese government in order to bring all the railways of China, now existing or to be built, under its effective and unified control and operation.[6]

Practically, the resolution was nothing more than a valueless diplomatic expression; and, of course, in spite of the enthusiastic reception given to it by the Chinese delegation, the railway situation in that country since then has shown no improvement; in fact, the roads have been allowed to deteriorate considerably. Moreover, questions involving vital interests of the powers have never been settled in this way.

We will now survey briefly those resolutions incorporated in the Open-Door Treaty, which have not yet been discussed. The first of these to be brought before the conference related to inter-power agreements on China.

[5] *Ibid.*, p. 647.   [6] *Ibid.*

On December 8 Dr. Koo presented China's case; he recalled the third of the Chinese Ten Points, namely,

with a view to strengthening mutual confidence and maintaining peace in the Pacific and the Far East, the powers agree not to conclude between themselves any treaty or agreement directly affecting China or the general peace in these regions without previously notifying China and giving to her an opportunity to participate.

He then stated that the essential principle laid down therein was that the Chinese Government should have had previous notification of the negotiation of any treaty or agreement which would affect Chinese interests. Agreements had in the past frequently been made, relating to the Far East or to China particularly, without participation on the part of China or previous notice to the Chinese Government. This type of agreement fell roughly into two divisions, one being in the nature of mutual engagements to abstain from certain action in special parts of China; the other being engagements for mutual assistance in support of the general interests of all foreign powers in China, or of the special interests claimed by the parties to the agreement.

The rights of China were involved because she must have wished that all the parts of her territory should be open on equal terms, or on such terms as she herself should determine, to foreign capitalists, merchants, and residents. As soon as such treaties as the foregoing were made, without consultation with China, her territory was divided into distinct spheres for foreign enterprise. To this she could by no means be indifferent. The other group of treaties dealt with the safeguarding and defending of territorial rights or special interests in the Far East, including or specially mentioning China. The assurance of peace and order in any part of Chinese territory was a matter of great concern to China herself. The maintenance of the independence and territorial integrity of China touched the supreme rights of China. As to the recognition of propinquity as creating special interests in China, it was equally obvious that such recognition could not be valid, because special interests on Chinese territory could not be created without the consent of China, and China had always contested the soundness of the doctrine of propinquity. The effect of all such treaties and agreements had been to maintain in China conditions which intimately affected the rights, prospects, and liberty of action of China herself. It appeared, therefore, that the Chinese Government had an equitable right to be consulted in all agreements which dealt with or pretended to deal with the general situation in the Far East, including China. Even if such treaties should have been animated by an entirely friendly spirit toward China, yet their bearing was such that they might involve consequences which would impart limitations on Chinese freedom of action, and they should, therefore, not be made without consultation with China.[7]

Mr. Balfour remarked that all that the conference would do was to see that no undue limitations, no limitations which were not necessitated by the facts in the situation, were placed on China's sovereign independence, and to give all the help in its power toward the creation of a pure and vigorous administration. He could not see that the position was helped by the principle proposed by the Chinese delegation, which went a good deal beyond any existing principle of international law. The term employed, namely, "the Pacific and the Far East," was as

[7] *Document,* pp. 561–62.

broad as the Pacific itself. He could not believe that the powers represented at this table would accept it, more especially as China was not in possession of material forces to enable her to carry out any policy outside her own frontier. He asked if it had occurred to Mr. Koo that his principle involved a limitation of the treaty-making rights of powers which could hardly be accepted. He then read the following extract:

> The powers agree not to conclude between themselves any treaty or agreement directly affecting China or the general peace in these regions without previously notifying China and giving her an opportunity to participate.

Translated into international language, this would prevent France and Belgium, he said, from entering into a defensive treaty of any kind without consulting Germany. Such a limitation could not be accepted. All agreed that treaties had been entered into in regard not only to China, but also to other nations, which reflected no credit on those who had concluded them. For this evil the great remedy was publicity. Most of the nations represented at this conference were members of the League of Nations and were bound under Article 18 of the covenant to register their treaties with the League, which was under an obligation to publish them. The United States of America was not a member of the League of Nations, but its Constitution necessitated wide publicity in regard to treaties. Hence, all the powers to which Mr. Koo referred were bound to make their treaties public and give them the widest notoriety. That was the real protection for China. The whole world would become the judge of future treaties. He would, therefore, ask his Chinese friends not to press the committee to adopt the resolution under discussion, but to deal with particular evils, as the conference was doing.[8]

Mr. Hughes at this point observed that there might be treaties affecting China not adverse to China, but it could be said that there would be no secret engagements. Mr. Balfour had quite properly said that the other governments here represented were bound not to make such engagements and that the Government of the United States could not. More than that could be done, however; there could be recorded an expression of a desire to be helpful to China in the preservation of the legitimate field of her administrative autonomy, and a reassertion, in connection with paragraph No. 1 of the "Root resolution," of the determination to do nothing in derogation of the sovereignty, independence, and territorial and administrative integrity of China. Therefore, if there were embodied, in the resolution relating to treaties, principles underlying the Chinese proposal and an expression of the intention to do nothing in derogation of these principles and to make no treaties or engagements in derogation of the sovereignty and administrative integrity of China, all that China desired would be attained without the committee being led into a discussion of the theoretical freedom of the treaty-making power.[9]

Mr. Hanihara said that the Japanese delegation believed that the sovereign nations had the right of concluding any treaty or agreement between themselves. At the same time, with the growing influence of public opinion and of international law, it was daily becoming evident that, should a treaty or agreement prove prejudicial to the peace of the world or derogatory to the rights of third powers, it was bound to fail by itself under strong pres-

[8] *Document*, p. 564.   [9] *Ibid.*, p. 565.

sure of popular condemnation, if not on account of action taken against it by aggrieved parties, either through diplomatic representation or through the instrumentality of the League of Nations, of which China was a member. But an engagement by the powers under the formula now proposed by China would operate as a serious limitation upon their sovereign right, and in the opinion of the Japanese delegation it was neither necessary nor desirable.[10]

Sir Auckland Geddes, as a means of surmounting the difficulty, ventured to suggest a resolution. After recalling the terms of the four resolutions adopted by the committee on November 21, he offered that to these should be added a fifth, namely,

> To enter into no treaty, agreement, arrangement, or understanding either with one another or, individually or collectively, with any other power or powers which would infringe or impair the principles which they have herein declared.[11]

Mr. Hanihara thought that the proposed addition was unnecessary in view of the contents of the Root Resolutions. Sir Robert Borden held similar opinion. But M. Viviani, M. Schanzer, and M. Van Karnebeck favored its incorporation.[12]

The Geddes resolution, with slight modifications, was then adopted. It reads:

> The powers attending this conference declare that it is their intention not to enter into any treaty, agreement, arrangement, or understanding, either with one another or, individually or collectively, with any power or powers which would infringe or impair the principles which have been declared by the resolution adopted November 21 by this committee.[13]

[10] *Document*, p. 566.   [11] *Ibid.*
[12] *Ibid.*, pp. 567–70.   [13] *Ibid.*, p. 570.

This resolution appears as Article II in the treaty.

The question of "spheres of influence" was introduced, and Dr. Wang said on behalf of China that the claims by the powers to spheres of interest had given rise to many misunderstandings and misgivings on the part of the Chinese people, and in view of the considerations which he had just advanced the Chinese delegation asked that the powers represented in this conference disavow all claims to a sphere or spheres of interest or influence or any special interests within the territory of China.[14]

Baron de Cartier explained that the Belgian policy in regard to the Hankow-Peking railway, in which Belgian and French capital was associated in a purely economic interest, was completely successful, owing to the attitude of the Chinese Government.[15] Whereupon Dr. Sze wished to testify to the correctness of the Belgian statement.[16] This exchange of irrelevant diplomatic courtesies was cut short by Mr. Root. He apprehended that little progress would be made unless rhetorical expressions were avoided. Spheres of influence presented questions in which he was not an expert; they appeared, however, to rest upon certain negative stipulations on the part of China. They were not a question of vested or affirmative rights, but grants of right arising from treaties entered into by the Chinese Government. If his own view was the correct one, China asked to be released from the effect of these restrictions and stipulations, which were collateral to certain grants. Thus practical progress depended upon exact specification. He therefore asked the Chinese delegation for specifications of these restrictions from which they wished to be released.[17] Mr. Balfour asked the Chinese when the specification would be furnished his delegation, and they re-

[14] *Ibid.*, pp. 580–81.   [15] *Ibid.*, p. 581.   [16] *Ibid.*   [17] *Ibid.*

plied the information would be forthcoming the next day (December 13), if possible. On the 14th the Chinese delegation furnished a list of so-called "restrictive stipulations," which included not only China's non-alienation agreements and the various agreements that had been entered into by the powers relating to China but to which she was not a party, but also the group of treaties and exchange notes of May 25, 1915, that had resulted from the twenty-one demands made by Japan on China.[18] Dr. Wang singled out the Sino-Japanese treaties and exchange of notes of 1915, and declared that, in the common interest of the powers as well as of China, and in conformity with the principles relating to China already adopted by

[18] The list was as follows:

1. Franco-Japanese Agreement, June 10, 1907.
2. Anglo-Japanese Treaty, July 13, 1911.
3. Russo-Japanese Convention, July 30, 1907.
4. Russo-Japanese Secret Convention, July 30, 1907.
5. Russo-Japanese Convention, July 4, 1910.
6. Russo-Japanese Secret Convention, July 4, 1910.
7. Russo-Japanese Secret Convention, July 8, 1912.
8. Russo-Japanese Convention, July 3, 1916.
9. Russo-Japanese Secret Treaty of Alliance, July 3, 1916.
10. American-Japanese Exchange of Notes, November 30, 1908.
11. American-Japanese Exchange of Notes, November 2, 1917.
12. Anglo-French Agreement, January 15, 1896.
13. Anglo-Russian Agreement, April 28, 1899.
14. Anglo-German Agreement, September 2, 1898.

Commitments and agreements which appear or have been alleged to create or recognize the existence of spheres of interest.

Non-alienation agreements:

1. Hainan.
2. Yangtse Valley.
3. Tong King Border.
4. Fukien.
5. Coast of China.

See *Document*, p. 584.

the committee, the Chinese delegation urged that the said treaties and exchange of notes be reconsidered and canceled.[19] Whereupon Mr. Hanihara desired to reply to the Chinese declaration after he had studied it carefully. He stated, however, that if there was a question of making the validity of the treaties or of the agreements of 1915, or the change or abrogation thereof, the subject of discussion at this conference, the Japanese delegation could not agree to such a course. He believed that this question was one to be taken up between Japan and China, if it were to be taken up at all, and not at this conference.[20] But no action was taken on the Chinese demand for the abrogation of spheres of influence, and thus this much-discussed question was allowed to rest without any solution.

Later (on January 21) the conference adopted the resolution incorporated in the Open-Door Treaty as Article 4. As we have already seen in our chapter on the open door, this article does not deal with the existing spheres of influence; it merely binds the powers not to create new spheres.

The question of Chinese railway tariffs was taken up, and on January 18 Sir Auckland Geddes offered a resolution from which the following declarations finally emerged:

That it is desirable that a provision to the following effect be in the convention on the Open Door in China:

The Chinese Government declares that, throughout the whole of the railways in China, it will not exercise or permit any unfair discrimination whatever, direct or indirect, in respect of charges or of facilities on the ground of the nationality of passengers or the countries from which or to which they are proceeding, or the origin or ownership of goods or the country from which or to

[19] *Ibid.*, p. 587. [20] *Ibid.*

which they are consigned, or the nationality or ownership of the ship or other means of conveying such passengers or goods before or after their transport on the Chinese railways.

The other powers represented at this conference take note of the above declaration and make a corresponding declaration in respect of any of the aforesaid railways over which they or their nationals are in a position to exercise any control in virtue of any concession, special agreement, or otherwise.

Any question arising under this declaration may be referred by any of the powers concerned to the board of reference, when established, for consideration and report.[21]

This resolution appears as Article 5 of the treaty; it binds China to assume the responsibility of applying uniform tariffs throughout her own railways, and the other powers to abide by such application. The item relative to the board of reference is embodied as Article 7 of the same treaty, with a slight modification in its wording.

It is hoped that the present survey together with the discussion of the Open-Door Treaty will clarify for the reader what China had attempted to secure, what were the views of the delegations, and to what degree the conference was actually willing to meet China's desires.

But the Chinese delegation presented two more claims to the conference, and, although no definite action was taken on these matters, a statement may be made of them to conclude this chapter. These related to the question of leased areas in China and to that of arms embargo, both of which, the Chinese claimed, embarrassed their administration.

The exportation of arms and ammunition to China had been a source of trouble for the Chinese Government, and when this subject was brought before the conference, Mr.

[21] *Document,* pp. 644–45.

Balfour proposed (January 24) a resolution to the effect that the powers refrain themselves and restrain their nationals from exporting to China arms and munitions of war until the establishment of a government whose authority was recognized throughout the whole country.[22] As a result of the conference discussion,[23] the resolution was amended (January 31) to read as follows:

I. The United States of America, Belgium, the British Empire, France, Italy, Japan, the Netherlands, and Portugal affirm their intention to refrain from exporting to China arms or munitions of war, whether complete or in parts, and to prohibit such exportation from their territories or territories under their control, until the establishment of a government whose authority is recognized throughout the whole of China.

II. Each of the above powers will forthwith take such additional steps as may be necessary to make the above restrictions immediately binding.

III. The scope of this resolution includes all concessions and settlements in China.

IV. The United States of America will invite the adherence to this resolution of the other powers in treaty relations with China.[24]

Another prolonged discussion ensued on this amended resolution, but because of the Italian stand the conference was forced to withdraw the resolution in entirety, and thus nothing was done on this subject of arms embargo.[25]

On the subject of foreign leaseholds in China, Dr. Koo stated that the existence of such leased territories had greatly prejudiced China's territorial and administrative integrity because they were all situated at strategical points. These foreign leaseholds had besides hampered her work of national defense by constituting in China "a

[22] *Ibid.*, p. 708. [23] *Ibid.*, pp. 709–12, and 733.
[24] *Ibid.*, p. 737. [25] See *ibid.*, pp. 737–46.

virtual *imperium in imperio,* i.e., an empire within the same empire." There was another reason which the Chinese delegation desired to point out: the shifting conflict of interests of the different lessee powers had involved China more than once in complications of their own. It would be sufficient to refer here to the Russo-Japanese war, which was caused by the Russian occupation of Port Arthur and Dalny. The Kiaochow leasehold brought upon the Far East the hostilities of the European war.

Furthermore, some of these territories were utilized with a view to economic domination over the vast adjoining regions as *points d'appui* for developing spheres of interest to the detriment of the principle of equal opportunity for the commerce and industry of all nations in China. In the interest not only of China but of all nations, especially for the peace of the Far East, the Chinese delegation asked for the annulment and early termination of these leases. But pending their termination these areas should be demilitarized—that is, their fortifications dismantled—and it was hoped that the lessee nations would undertake not to make use of their several leased areas for military purposes, either as naval bases or for military operations of any kind whatsoever. The Chinese delegation were, however, fully conscious of the obligations which would fall upon them after the termination of the leaseholds. The Chinese Government would be prepared to respect and safeguard the legitimately vested interests of the different powers within those territories.[26]

A diplomatic reply was made by M. Viviani that after having taken note of the request made by the Chinese delegation December 1, 1921, the French delegation stated that the government of the republic was ready to join in

[26] *Document,* pp. 539-40.

the collective restitution of territories leased to various powers in China, it being understood that, this principle being once admitted and all private rights being safeguarded, the conditions and time limits of the restitution should be determined by agreement between the Chinese Government and each of the governments concerned.[27]

But Mr. Hanihara made the following blunt refusal to accede to China's plea by saying that the leased territories held by Japan at present were Kiaochow, and Kwantung province, namely, Port Arthur and Dairen. It was characteristic of Japan's leased territories that she had obtained them, not directly from China, but as successor to other powers at considerable sacrifice in men and treasure. She had succeeded Russia in the leasehold of Kwantung province with the express consent of China, and she had succeeded Germany in the leasehold of Kiaochow under the Treaty of Versailles. As to Kiaochow, the Japanese Government had already declared, on several occasions, that they would restore that leased territory to China. Japan was prepared to come to an agreement with China on this basis. In fact, there were now going on conversations between representatives of Japan and China regarding this question initiated through the good offices of Mr. Hughes and Mr. Balfour, the result of which it was hoped would be a happy solution of the problem. Therefore, the question of the leased territory of Kiaochow was one which properly called for separate treatment. The only leased territory, therefore, which remained to be discussed at the conference, so far as Japan was concerned, was Kwantung province, namely, Port Arthur and Dairen. As to that territory, the Japanese delegates desired to make it clear that Japan had no intention at present to relinquish

[27] *Ibid.*, pp. 540–41.

the important rights she had acquired lawfully and at no small sacrifice.[28]

Mr. Balfour said that Great Britain had two different kinds of leases, and these, as he thought the Chinese delegation itself would admit, must be held to stand on a different footing one from the other. He referred first to the leased territory of Kowloon Extension. Why, he asked, was it considered necessary that the leased territory of Kowloon should come under the same administration as Hongkong? The reason was that without the leased territory Hongkong was perfectly indefensible and would be at the mercy of any enemy possessing modern artillery. He hoped that he would carry the conference with him when he asserted that the safeguarding of the position of Hongkong was not merely a British interest but one in which the whole world was concerned. He was informed that Hongkong was easily first among the ports of the world, exceeding in this respect Hamburg before the war, Antwerp, and New York. The motive of the British Government, on the other hand, in acquiring the lease of Weihaiwei had been connected with resistance to the economic domination of China by other powers; in fact, it had been based on a desire for the maintenance of the balance of power in the Far East, with a view to the maintenance of the policy of the open door, and had been intended as a check to the predatory action of Germany or Russia. The British Government would be perfectly ready to return Weihaiwei to China as part of a general arrangement intended to confirm the sovereignty of China and to give effect to the principle of the open door. This surrender, however, could only be undertaken as part of some such general arrangement, and he spoke with his

[28] *Document,* p. 541.

PRINCIPLES VERSUS REALITIES 265

Government behind him when he said that on these conditions he was prepared to give up the rights which Great Britain had acquired. The British Government's policy was to make use of the surrender of Weihaiwei to assist in securing a settlement of the question of Shantung. If agreement could be reached on this question, the British Government would not hesitate to do their best to promote a general settlement by restoring Weihaiwei to the Central Government of China.[29]

That was as far as the conference proceeded with the subject of leased territories in China; but a treaty was signed February 4, 1922, between China and Japan, whereby Japan handed back to China the lease of Kiaochow. (See chapter xviii.) When this treaty was announced in a plenary session (February 1), Mr. Balfour spoke eloquently on its significance, and then stated in very general terms that the British Empire was prepared to restore Weihaiwei, which, according to the speaker, had been used merely as a sanatorium or summer resort for ships of war coming up from the tropical or more southern portions of China.[30] In short, his speech left an impression with the audience and the press that Weihaiwei would be restored to China as Kiaochow had been.[31] Consequently the public and the press waxed enthusiastic over this British proposal; at the same time, the press again attacked France for her failure to make a promise similar to that of Great Britain. Thus wrote a journalist:

Since the French offer to release leaseholds was conditional on absolute withdrawal by all other powers, the voluntary action of the British Government had all the more significance today. Every Conference authority knew the French proposal was al-

[29] *Ibid.*, pp. 542–43. [30] *Ibid.*, p. 139.
[31] See *ibid.*, pp. 138–40.

Government behind him when he said that on these conditions he was prepared to give up the rights which Great Britain had acquired. The British Government's policy was to make use of the surrender of Weihaiwei to assist in securing a settlement of the question of Shantung. If agreement could be reached on this question, the British Government would not hesitate to do their best to promote a general settlement by restoring Weihaiwei to the Central Government of China.[29]

That was as far as the conference proceeded with the subject of leased territories in China; but a treaty was signed February 4, 1922, between China and Japan, whereby Japan handed back to China the lease of Kiaochow. (See chapter xviii.) When this treaty was announced in a plenary session (February 1), Mr. Balfour spoke eloquently on its significance, and then stated in very general terms that the British Empire was prepared to restore Weihaiwei, which, according to the speaker, had been used merely as a sanatorium or summer resort for ships of war coming up from the tropical or more southern portions of China.[30] In short, his speech left an impression with the audience and the press that Weihaiwei would be restored to China as Kiaochow had been.[31] Consequently the public and the press waxed enthusiastic over this British proposal; at the same time, the press again attacked France for her failure to make a promise similar to that of Great Britain. Thus wrote a journalist:

Since the French offer to release leaseholds was conditional on absolute withdrawal by all other powers, the voluntary action of the British Government had all the more significance today. Every Conference authority knew the French proposal was al-

[29] *Ibid.*, pp. 542–43.   [30] *Ibid.*, p. 139.
[31] See *ibid.*, pp. 138–40.

most impossible of fulfillment when René Viviani announced it. It was stage play of a wholly different sort from that of Mr. Balfour this afternoon, however useless Wei-hai Wei might have been to the British during the last few years.[32]

But such a characterization of the British and French stands on their leased territories is not quite fair. On February 3 Mr. Balfour addressed a letter to Dr. Sze, enumerating the conditions under which the British might retrocede Weihaiwei to China. It says:

There must be certain matters of detail to attend to and dispose of to the satisfaction of our two Governments before the transfer can be effected. I have in mind such matters as the making of arrangements which will permit His Majesty's ships to use Wei-hai Wei during the summer months as heretofore without restriction or harbor dues, to land, store, and ship without restriction or duty goods required for naval use, and to retain properties required for the above purposes. In addition, we shall wish to discuss certain points in connection with naval training, as well as matters affecting the due safeguarding of foreign property rights, and making suitable provision for the adequate representation of foreign interests in municipal affairs. It is also possible that my Government may desire some intimation of the willingness of the Chinese Government to grant facilities for the linking up of Wei-hai Wei with the hinterland by railway. These and other similar matters, such as the precise status of the port, will naturally have to be adjusted by mutual consent.[33]

In pursuance of the conditions thus laid down, an attempt has been made but without reaching any agreement, and Weihaiwei still remains with Great Britain.

[32] Robert Barry in the *Philadelphia Public Ledger*, February 2, 1922.

[33] *Great Britain, Accounts and Papers, State Papers*, Vol. XXIII, 1922, Miscellaneous. No. 1 (Cmd. 1627), p. 86.

CHAPTER XVIII

THE SHANTUNG TREATY

We now come to two subjects of special importance which involved primarily Japan and China, namely, the question of Shantung and that of the Twenty-One Demands. The first will be discussed in this chapter.

The Shantung issue loomed large after 1914, when the Japanese became the possessors of the German leased territory of Kiaochow Bay. Let us see how this happened. The assassination of Archduke Francis Ferdinand on June 28, 1914, precipitated the Great War. On August 4, Great Britain, Japan's ally, declared war against Germany. The day before, the British Ambassador at Tokyo informed the Japanese Minister of Foreign Affairs that his Government was compelled to open hostilities against Germany and desired to ascertain whether Japan would aid England should British interests in the Far East become jeopardized by German activities. On the following day the Japanese Minister replied that Japan would not evade the responsibilities of her alliance with Great Britain. On the 7th the British Ambassador told the Japanese Minister that the situation had developed in such a manner as would make Japan's immediate entrance upon the war most desirable.[1] On the 15th Japan delivered her ultimatum to Germany allowing her until the 23rd to reply, but no cognizance was taken of this by Germany. On November 7, the Japanese occupied Tsingtao and thus dislodged the Germans from their Asiatic base of operations. That was how Japan came into possession of the German rights in the province of Shantung.

In conducting her operations against Tsingtao, Japan followed the precedents of the Russo-Japanese War. The conditions

[1] See chapter x.

were fundamentally the same. Russia and Germany held fortified leaseholds on Chinese soil. To attack them, military operations had to be conducted within Chinese territory. In both cases China declared her neutrality, and, in 1904, Japan and Russia agreed to limit the war zone to South Manchuria. In 1914, Japan proposed to land troops at Lungkow, in Shantung, and advance across the peninsula, attacking Tsingtao from the rear. She advised China of this decision, and asserted that China gave her assent. The landing took place on September 2, and the next day China proclaimed a war zone, including the port of Lungkow. .... It was unfortunate that her neutrality should be disregarded, but it was a price she had to pay for having tolerated the presence of a fortified foreign leasehold on her shores.[2]

This conduct of the Japanese military authorities gave rise to severe condemnation of Japan by her hostile critics. Since the commencement of the Great War it had become customary with these critics to picture Japan as another Prussia. Of the violations of China's neutrality, the case of Japan had been singled out as the target of attack. While the writer will not defend Japan's violation, it should be borne in mind that such violation was not confined to Japan. The late Dr. Ariga, a former legal adviser to the Chinese President, recently published a study on the subject of China's neutrality during the Great War.[3] In this book the difficulty of enforcing the rights of China's neutrality is pointed out because of the existing extraterritorial system in China, a fact so often overlooked. For example China has no jurisdiction over foreigners residing or traveling in her territory. Should they violate the neutrality of China, they had to be punished by their own respective authorities. What did that mean during the Great War in which so many nations were involved?

[2] P. J. Treat, *Japan and the United States*, pp. 215–16.
[3] N. Ariga, *La Chine et la grande guerre européenne* (Paris, 1920).

Upon learning of the Japanese ultimatum to Germany, the Chinese civil and military governors jointly inquired of the Central Military Authority what they should do in case the neutral zone were violated, a development which might be expected if the fight took place around Tsingtao.

> How should we regard the zone of 50 kilometers around Kiaochow Bay in time of war? That point had not been determined by the treaty. Would you indicate to us the limitation of the theater of war?[4]

Naturally, the German garrison at Tsingtao did everything to defend themselves most effectively. They even captured neutral merchant vessels in Chinese waters, and despite China's neutrality they transported arms and ammunition across the hinterland of Tsingtao. The Chinese President ordered the Shantung governors to stop the transportation of war materials by the Tsinan-Kiaochow Railway, but in vain.[5] Despite her own violation of China's neutrality, the Berlin Government protested to the Chinese Government against possible transportation of the allied troops across China's neutral territory. In reply China said rightly that it was Germany which had first violated her neutrality.[6]

The Chinese Government called to the attention of the French Minister at Peking that those Frenchmen residing in China, who were unable to return to France to join her army, were organizing themselves in the French concession at Tientsin to attack Tsingtao. This was contrary to Article 4 of the Hague Convention. But in reply, the French Minister reminded the Chinese Government of the German military and naval activities in China's territory

[4] *Ibid.*, p. 30.   [5] *Ibid.*, pp. 31-35.   [6] *Ibid.*, pp. 37-40.

around Tsingtao. As to the troops, they were in Chihli by virtue of the protocol of 1901, and France was free to dispose them as she pleased.[7] Of course, such an interpretation of the protocol is far-fetched. Again, the French established an office for military enrollment at Tientsin and called upon every Frenchman residing in China to enroll.[8] Furthermore, it was reported that the French and English troops at Tientsin were ready to debark for Shantung and that three vessels were chartered for the purpose.[9] These are but a few of the facts which, together with the Japanese activities in Shantung, caused the Chinese Government to declare the war zone already referred to. As to Japan's specific case of violation, we may again quote what Professor Treat says:

> It was unfortunate that her [China's] neutrality should be disregarded, but it was a price she had to pay for having tolerated the presence of a fortified foreign leasehold on her shores.[10]

Much has been said as to the unwisdom of Great Britain in causing Japan's participation in the war.

> The mishandling of the Tsingtao question by the Allies—the British Government, for instance, could easily have induced Yuan Shi-kai to deliver a twenty-four hours' ultimatum on Germany to evacuate Chinese soil, since the President of China had 50,000 troops almost at Tsingtao's back doors—allowed Japan to make war as if by favor, using the belligerent conditions throughout the world to hasten on a policy which had nothing to do with the issues being so savagely fought out on European soil.[11]

---

[7] N. Ariga, *op. cit.*, pp. 40–42.   [8] *Ibid.*, p. 43.

[9] See further, *ibid.*, pp. 1–150, for this author's discussion of the entire question of neutrality.

[10] P. J. Treat, *Japan and the United States*, p. 216.

[11] B. L. P. Weale, *The Truth about China and Japan* (New York, 1919), p. 73.

The practicability of the suggested plan is much in doubt. The British could not have entrusted to the Chinese troops the task of driving out the Germans from Shantung for various reasons. Their number in no way indicated their fighting efficiency. Besides, at the time the Chinese were decidedly pro-German.

Had Japan delayed her action against Kiaochow, it was more than probable that the Germans would have raised a large army of Chinese in Shantung, captured the arsenal at Techow on the Tientsin-Nanking line, virtually seized the whole of that province, and thus compelled the Government at Peking to declare war upon the Entente Powers. In the state of disorganization in which China found herself at that time, it was obvious that such a German plan would have easily been put into practice. China would have had to accept the German yoke and been compelled to drive all British and French interests from that country. Only by Japan's prompt declaration of war upon Germany was such an eventuality prevented.[12]

Had she [Japan] declined to declare war upon Germany, Russia would have had to keep large forces in Siberia; France would have been compelled to garrison Indo-China with several army corps, while Great Britain would have been forced to maintain in the Indian and Pacific Oceans, for the protection of India, Australia, New Zealand, and Canada, a fleet equal to that of Japan. Had German cruisers and gunboats, with the splendid harbor of Kiaochow as their base of operations, marauded in the Pacific and Indian Oceans, the transportation of Australian and Indian forces to the scenes of war would have been well-nigh impossible, while British trade in those waters would have been completely paralyzed.[13]

Thus it seems inevitable that all the Chinophiles essay to belittle the value of the Japanese contribution to the war, while the Japanophiles are tempted to magnify the same.

[12] K. K. Kawakami, *Japan and World Peace*, p. 9.
[13] *Ibid.*, pp. 8–9.

Somewhere between these two extreme views lies the truth. M. Gerard, a distinguished French diplomat, points out the significance of the fall of Tsingtao in the following words:

> Le 11, les vainqueurs faisaient leur entrée solennelle dans Tsing-tao, à la date même où, sur le front d'Europe, les troupes françaises et britanniques arrêtaient dans les Flandres et sur l'Yser la ruée allemande qui avait espéré pénétrer jusqu'à Calais. Aux deux extrémités du monde et de l'infini theâtre de la guerre l'Allemagne voyait s'écrouler son rêve de domination et sentait le vent de la défaite.[14]

Since the British-Japanese military operations against the Germans had to be conducted in the territory of a neutral nation, a certain amount of friction between the Allies and China was inevitable. Some evidence of this has already been given. China's declaration of the "war zone," September 3, 1914, may be noted in this connection.

> Germany, Japan, and Great Britain being all on terms of amity with China, it is unfortunate to see that they should take such unexpected steps within the dominions of China, thus constituting extraordinary circumstances parallel to the war waged between Japan and Russia in the Liaotung Peninsula in 1904. Following this precedent, the Chinese Government can not but declare that at such points within Lungkow, Laichow, and the neighborhood of Kiaochow Bay adjoining thereto as are absolutely necessary for the passage and use of belligerent troops, it can not hold itself responsible for the obligations of strict neutrality.[15]

On September 27 China lodged a protest against the presence of Japanese troops at Weihsien and demanded of the Japanese Government the immediate withdrawal

[14] A. Gerard, *Ma Mission au Japon* (Paris, 1919), pp. 353–54.
[15] J. V. A. MacMurray, *op. cit.*, II, 1367.

of the troops therefrom, on the ground of China's being a neutral.[16] Again, a similar demand was made on the 30th against the Japanese occupation of the Kiaochow-Tsinan Railway which China claimed was private property.[17] On October 2 Japan replied:

Regarding the points misunderstood by Chinese Government, as shown in the two documents, [the notes of the 27th and 30th] we point out as follows:

1º. Whether the Shantung Railway is a German railway or a joint-interest railway can be determined substantially by the special permit given by Germany. As to the governmental nature of the said railway, there can be no doubt, in view of what has been said above.

2º. If the Shantung Railway can not be held as being the property of a neutral, how can it be said of our violating neutrality if it is transferred to our control? Now, China, in consequence of the delimitation of the war zone, suggests to change simultaneously the nature of the Shantung Railway. The Imperial Government cannot see the reason why China should do so. Furthermore, the question of delimiting the war zone and the question of the nature of the Shantung Railway, as well as its control and administration, are clearly separate questions which cannot be amalgamated into one.

3º. Although the Chinese Government holds that under the present condition the Shantung Railway cannot be utilized by the German troops in view of its severance with China, yet from the attacking troops' point of view, the Railway being immediately behind Tsingtao, and in view of the present situation, it is a serious danger to the military operations to leave a railway owned by the enemy perfectly free. We are, therefore, compelled to secure the railway by all means. Moreover, the Chinese Government has often failed to stop the assistance of the enemy on this railway, of which there are many examples.

4º. In the documents the Chinese Government emphatically declared its readiness to protect the railway between Weihsien

[16] *Ibid.*, pp. 1154–55.   [17] *Ibid.*, pp. 1156–57.

and Chinan [Tsinan], which declaration is said to have been agreed to by our Government. The Imperial Government would like to be informed as to what this refers to.[18]

But China was dissatisfied with the above note from Japan, and on the 9th she repeated her protest against the occupation of the Kiaochow-Tsinan Railway.[19] Thus the matter dragged along.

On January 7, 1915, China notified the British and Japanese governments of her cancellation of the war zone in the following words:

> Now, as the hostilities have ceased, and all military preparations have been entirely withdrawn, it is clear there will be no more occasion to use Lungkow or the places near Kiaochow for military actions. It is, therefore, hereby declared that the war zone shall be cancelled, and that the original status of the said area be restored.[20]

On the 9th Japan served China her refusal to recognize the cancellation of the war zone. By this time Japan was much irritated, and her irritation was still more intensified by China's second notification of the 16th.[21] "Japanese irritation reached such a point that they were forced to action."[22]

Then on January 18, 1915, Japan presented to China her famous twenty-one demands, with the object

> to provide for the readjustment of affairs consequent on the Japan-German War and for the purpose of ensuring a lasting peace in the Far East by strengthening the position of the Empire.

Of these demands we are concerned here with only the first four articles, which bear directly on the Shantung questions. These were as follows:

---

[18] J. V. A. MacMurray, *op. cit.*, II, 1156.   [19] *Ibid.*, pp. 1156–57.
[20] *Ibid.*, p. 1157.   [21] *Ibid.*, pp. 1158–59.   [22] Weale, *op. cit.*, p. 74.

The Japanese Government and the Chinese Government being desirous of maintaining the general peace in Eastern Asia and further strengthening the friendly relations and good neighborhood existing between the two nations agree to the following articles:

Article 1. The Chinese Government engages to give full assent to all matters upon which the Japanese Government may hereafter agree with the German Government relating to the disposition of all rights, interests, and concessions, which Germany by virtue of treaties or otherwise, possesses in relation to the Province of Shantung.

Article 2. The Chinese Government engages that within the Province of Shantung and along its coast, no territory or island will be ceded or leased to a third Power under any pretext.

Article 3. The Chinese Government consents to Japan's building a railway from Chefoo or Lungkou to join the Kiaochou-Tsinanfu Railway.

Article 4. The Chinese Government engages, in the interest of trade and for the residence of foreigners, to open by herself as soon as possible certain important cities and towns in the Province of Shantung as commercial ports. What places shall be opened are to be jointly decided upon in a separate agreement.[23]

The Shantung Treaty based on these demands was finally signed on May 25, 1915. Its terms were as follows:

Article I. The Chinese Government engage to recognize all matters that may be agreed upon between the Japanese Government and the German Government respecting the disposition of all the rights, interests, and concessions which, in virtue of Treaties or otherwise, Germany possesses vis-à-vis China in relation to the Province of Shantung.

Article II. The Chinese Government engage that, in case they undertake the construction of a railway connecting Chefoo or Lungkou with the Kiaochou-Tsinan Railway, they shall, in event of Germany's surrendering her right or providing capital for the

[23] *Japanese Official Documents concerning Shantung*, pp. 1–2.

Chefoo Weihsien railway line, enter into negotiations with Japanese capitalists for the purpose of financing the said undertaking.

Article III. The Chinese Government engage to open, of their own accord, as early as possible, suitable cities and towns in the province of Shantung for the residence and trade of foreigners.

Article IV. The present Treaty shall take effect on the day of its signature.[24]

The provisions contained in Article 3 of the original proposals appear in Article II of the Treaty with significant modifications; namely: The expression, "The Chinese Government consents to Japan building a railway from Chefoo or Lungkow to join the Kiaochow-Tsinanfu Railway," was changed to

The Chinese Government engages, that, in case they undertake the construction of a railway connecting Chefoo or Lungkow with the Kiaochow-Tsinan Railway, they shall, in the event of Germany's surrendering her right or providing capital for the Chefoo-Weihsien railway line, enter into negotiations with Japanese capitalists for the purpose of financing the said undertaking.

Article 2 of the original proposals is omitted from the Treaty, but on this subject of non-alienation notes were exchanged between the two Governments whereby China pledged non-alienation. Article 4 of the original proposals concerning the opening of certain cities and towns in Shantung province appears as Article III in the Treaty. But the clause, "what places shall be opened are to be jointly decided upon in a separate agreement," is omitted. On this point, notes were exchanged wherein China promises to consult Japan as to the selection of places to be opened. The most important provision in the Treaty is doubtless that which is contained in Article I by which

[24] *Japanese Official Documents concerning Shantung*, p. 4.

China gives Japan the right to dispose of the German rights in Shantung as the latter saw fit. However, Japan promised to return Kiaochow to China:

> If, upon the conclusion of the present war, the Japanese Government should be given an absolutely free disposal of the leased territory of Kiaochow Bay, they will return the said leased territory to China subject to the following conditions:
> 1. Opening of the whole of Kiaochow as a commercial port;
> 2. Establishment of a Japanese settlement in the locality to be designated by the Japanese Government;
> 3. Establishment, if desired by the Powers, of an international settlement;
> 4. Arrangements to be made, before the return of the said territory is effected, between the Japanese and Chinese Governments, with respect to the disposal of German public establishments and properties and with regard to the other conditions and procedures.[25]

Aside from the professed reasons of Japan in making the demands, she was doubtless actuated by her bitter experience of the past in dealing with China. When Russia transferred by the Portsmouth Treaty to Japan her leasehold in the Liaotung Peninsula and her rights and privileges, including her Manchurian Railway south of Changchun, Japan was forced to learn a lesson at the hand of China. As the transfer was conditioned by China's consent, Japan was confronted with the unexpected opposition of China to the transfer. Only after delay and difficulty was she able to effect the Treaty of Peking, which was not signed until December 22, 1905. By the treaty China recognized Japan's right to the Russian leasehold and other rights and privileges. It was natural for Japan, therefore, to avoid the necessity of repeating similar problems by settling the issues of Shantung in advance.

[25] *Ibid.*, pp. 8–9.

Having secured China's consent to the freedom of her action as regards the German rights in Shantung, Japan approached her allies to obtain their support to her claims over them at the time of settlement. The reply of Great Britain was that His Majesty's Government acceded with pleasure to the request of the Japanese Government for an assurance that they would support Japan's claims in regard to the disposal of Germany's rights in Shantung and possessions in the islands north of the Equator on the occasion of the Peace Conference, it being understood that the Japanese Government would, in eventual peace settlement, treat in the same spirit Great Britain's claims to German islands south of the Equator.[26] The document bears the date of February 16, 1917.

The French reply dated March 1, 1917, was that the Government of the Republic was disposed to give the Japanese Government its assistance in regulating, at the time of the peace negotiations, questions essential to Japan concerning Shantung and the German islands in the Pacific situated to the north of the Equator. It also agreed to support the demands of the Imperial Government for the surrender of the rights Germany possessed before the war in this Chinese province and the islands. M. Briand requested, on the other hand, that the Japanese Government give its support to obtain from China the rupture of its diplomatic relations with Germany, and that she push this act to a desirable extent. The consequences of this, according to him, would be: (1) The handing over of passports to the German diplomatic and consular agents. (2) The obligation of all German nationals to leave Chinese territory. (3) The internment of German ships having sought refuge in Chinese ports and the ulti-

[26] *Japanese Official Documents concerning Shantung*, pp. 11–12.

mate requisition of these ships in order to place them at the disposition of the Allies, following the example of Italy and Portugal. From the advices which reached the French Government, there were fifteen German ships in Chinese ports, totaling about 40,000 tons. (4) The sequestration of German commercial houses established in China. (5) The forfeiture of the rights of Germany in the concessions she possessed in certain ports.[27]

Finally, China entered into two agreements with Japan, on September 24 and 28, 1918, by which the Chinese Government reconfirmed all the rights and privileges granted to Japan in virtue of the Treaty of 1915.[28]

The Russian and Italian Governments gave Japan similar assurances of support.[29] Thus equipped Japan entered the Paris Conference. Her program consisted of three items: the principle of racial equality; the German islands north of the Equator; and the German rights in Shantung. Japan received a mandate over the islands in question and not a title of outright possession, but she lost her fight over the principle of racial equality by a very small minority opposition. Therefore she was in no humor to treat the Shantung issues generously. On the contrary, she was determined to carry her program as regards the Shantung matters.

On the other hand, China's program was made up of three groups of demands: the abrogation of the Japanese treaties of 1915, the direct restitution to China of the German leasehold and other rights in Shantung, and the abrogation of all treaty engagements impairing her sovereignty. It is obvious that with the exception of the

[27] *Ibid.*, pp. 15–16.
[28] J. V. A. MacMurray, *op. cit.*, pp. 1445–1452.
[29] *Japanese Official Documents concerning Shantung,* pp. 18 and 20.

second point none of these proposals had any bearing upon the treaty of peace which was to be formulated. Naturally they were not considered by the Peace Conference. So China was compelled to concentrate her effort upon the Shantung issues.

A clash followed between the two nations. Space is lacking for a review of the duel fought by Baron Makino of Japan and Dr. Koo of China. The latter proved to be a brilliant debater, but failed to attain his end.[30] The conference decided the issue in favor of Japan, as shown by Article 156 of the Treaty of Versailles, which states:

Germany renounces, in favor of Japan, all her rights, titles, and privileges—particularly those concerning the territory of Kiaochow, railways, mines, and submarine cables—which she acquired in virtue of the Treaty concluded by her with China on March 6, 1898, and all other arrangements relative to the Province of Shantung.

All German rights in the Tsingtao-Tsinanfu Railway, including its branch lines, together with its subsidiary property of all kinds, stations, shops, fixed and rolling stock, mines, plant, and material for the exploitation of the mines, are and remain acquired by Japan, together with all rights and privileges thereto.

The German State submarine cables from Tsingtao to Shanghai, and from Tsingtao to Chefoo, with all the rights, privileges, and properties attaching thereto, are similarly acquired by Japan free and clear of all charges and encumbrances.

Articles 157 and 158 add that,

The movable and immovable property owned by the German State in the territory of Kiaochow, as well as all the rights which Germany might claim in consequence of the works or improvements made or of the expenses incurred by her directly or indirectly in connection with this territory, are and remain acquired

[30] See Patrick Gallagher, *America's Aims and Asia's Aspirations* (New York, 1920), pp. 267-366.

by Japan, free and clear of all charges and encumbrances. Germany shall hand over to Japan within three months from the coming into force of the present Treaty, the archives, registers, plans, title-deeds, and documents of every kind, wherever they may be, relating to the administration, whether civil, military, financial, judicial, or other, of the territory of Kiaochow. Within the same period Germany shall give particulars to Japan of all treaties, arrangements, or agreements relating to the rights, titles, or privileges referred to in the two preceding Articles.[31]

As soon as the Treaty of Peace became effective in January 1920, the Japanese Government instructed its minister at Peking to open negotiations for the restoration of Kiaochow. The minister approached the Chinese Government on January 16 stating that the Japanese Government desired to open negotiations with the Chinese Government relative to the restoration of Kiaochow to China and the settlement of the details thereto, and hoped thus to effect a speedy solution of the entire question, and expressed the hope that the Chinese Government would make the necessary preparations to negotiate. It was the intention of the Japanese Government to withdraw the Japanese troops from the Shantung Railway as a matter of course upon an agreement between the two Governments with regard to disposition at Kiaochow.[32]

But China made no reply. So again, on April 26, the Japanese Minister approached and urged the Chinese Government to take the necessary steps. China remained silent until May 22, when she replied that China had not signed the Treaty of Peace and was not in a position to negotiate directly with Japan on the question of Tsingtao. Furthermore, the people throughout China had assumed an in-

---

[31] The Treaty of Versailles.
[32] *Japanese Official Documents concerning Shantung*, p. 31.

dignantly antagonistic attitude toward the question of Kiaochow. For these reasons, and also in consideration of the amity between Japan and China, the Chinese Government were not in a position to reply at this moment.[33]

The Japanese Government failed to understand the contention of the Chinese Government that they did not find it convenient to negotiate directly. It was a plain and positive fact that all the rights and interests which Germany formerly possessed in Shantung had been transferred to Japan in accordance with the Treaty of Peace. Since the Chinese Government had previously given her consent to the transfer, these rights and interests rightly came into the possession of Japan. It followed naturally, therefore, that these rights could not be affected in any way by the refusal of the Chinese Government to sign the Treaty of Peace. Thus the Tokyo authorities proceeded by stating that the Japanese Government, always considering the amity and good neighborhood between Japan and China, hereby reiterated their declaration that they would accept a proposal for negotiations at any time considered agreeable to the Chinese Government.[34] But no word came from China.

On September 7, 1921, Japan presented to China the following outline of the terms of settlement:

1. The leasehold of Kiaochow and the rights originally granted to Germany with regard to the fifty-kilometer zone around the Kiaochow Bay shall be restored to China.

2. The Japanese Government will abandon plans for the establishment of a Japanese exclusive settlement or of an international settlement in Tsingtao; provided that China engage to open of its own accord the entire leased territory of Kiaochow as a

[33] *Japanese Official Documents concerning Shantung*, p. 33.
[34] *Ibid.*, pp. 34–35.

port of trade, and to permit the nationals of all foreign countries freely to reside and to carry on commerce, industry, agriculture, or any other lawful pursuits within said territory, and that she further undertakes to respect the vested rights for all foreigners.

China shall likewise carry out forthwith the opening of suitable cities and towns within the Province of Shantung for residence and trade of the nationals of all foreign countries.

Regulations for the opening of places under the foregoing clauses shall be determined by the Chinese Government upon consultation with the Powers interested.

3. The Kiaochow-Tsinanfu Railway and all mines appurtenant thereto shall be worked as a joint Chino-Japanese enterprise.

4. Japan will renounce all preferential rights with regard to foreign assistance in persons, capital, and material, stipulated in the Sino-German Treaty of March 6, 1898.

5. Rights relating to the extension of the Kiaochow-Tsinanfu Railway, as well as options for the construction of the Tentai-Weishien Railway will be thrown open for the common activity of the international Financial Consortium in China.

6. The status of the Customs House at Tsingtao as forming an integral part of the general customs system of China shall be made clearer than under the German régime.

7. Public property used for administrative purpose within the leased territory of Kiaochow will, in general, be transferred to China; it being understood that the maintenance and operation of public works and establishments shall be previously arranged between the Japanese and Chinese Governments.

8. With a view to arranging detailed plans for carrying into effect the terms of settlement above indicated, and for the purpose of adjusting other matters not embodied therein, the Japanese and Chinese Governments shall appoint their respective commissioners as soon as possible.

9. The Japanese Government have on more than one occasion declared willingness to proceed to the recall of Japanese troops now stationed along the Kiaochow-Tsinanfu Railway upon organization by China of a police force to assume protection of the Railway. As soon as the Chinese Government shall have organized such a police force and shall have notified the Japanese Gov-

ernment to that effect, Japanese troops will be ordered to hand over to the Chinese police the charge of protecting the railway, and thereupon immediately to withdraw. It is, however, to be understood that the question of the organization of a special police guarding the Kiaochow-Tsinanfu Railway shall be reserved for future consideration between Japan and China.[35]

China replied on October 5 that after careful consideration the Chinese Government felt that much in Japan's new proposals was still incompatible with the repeated declaration of the Chinese Government, with the hopes and expectations of the entire Chinese people, and with the principles laid down in treaties between China and the foreign powers. If these proposals were to be considered the final concession on the part of Japan, they surely fell short of proving the sincerity of Japan's desire to settle the question.[36]

On the 19th Japan sent another note that, contrary to the expectation of the Japanese Government, the Chinese Government in their memorandum under consideration expressed their unwillingness to proceed for the time being with the negotiations in question, on the ground that the terms of settlement as proposed by the Japanese Government fell short of convincing them of the sincerity of Japan's desire to settle this question. Further, they used at the beginning of their memorandum an expression characterizing most of the Japanese declarations hitherto made as hollow and devoid of meaning. The Japanese Government keenly regretted for the sake of China that such a derogatory expression, contrary to the principles of international courtesy, should have been used by her.[37] Such were Japan's pre-Conference attempts.

[35] *Japanese Official Documents concerning Shantung*, pp. 41–43.
[36] *Ibid.*, p. 45.   [37] *Ibid.*, p. 51.

Then came the Washington Conference. It was persistently said that China would present the question of Shantung to the conference. But such a step would have proved disastrous for China. Seven of the nine nations were signatories of the Peace Treaty, and those nations could not and would not go back on their own words to satisfy China's pride. Needless to add, China was just as anxious to settle the Shantung question as was Japan, but the setlement had to be effected without hurting China's face. This delicate problem was solved by the good offices tendered by Mr. Balfour and Mr. Hughes.

The Sino-Japanese "conversations" ("negotiations" proved distasteful to the Chinese delegates) commenced on December 1, 1921, under the American and British referees. At the meeting of the Committee of the Whole on November 30, Baron Kato announced that, through the kind offices of the American and British delegates, a special meeting was to be held between the Japanese and Chinese representatives on the Shantung Question, on the following afternoon. Whereupon Dr. Sze said that the Chinese delegation had not solicited or asked for the meeting of the Chinese and Japanese delegations, as the Government and people of China had always hoped to be able to present this very important question to the consideration of the conference, not with any desire to add to the labors of the conference or to embarrass any delegation interested in this question, but merely in the hope of obtaining a fair and just settlement.[38]

The Japanese and Chinese had to face each other thirty-six times even without reckoning the meetings necessary for the drafting of the treaty, and produced a record of nearly four hundred closely printed pages, which the

[38] *Document*, pp. 526–27.

Japanese secretaries took the trouble of keeping day after day, both for the benefit of their own and for that of the Chinese delegation. Thus the long-pending issue of Shantung necessitated a long conversation before its settlement was effected. But it was settled by a treaty consisting of twenty-seven articles and an annex of six articles.[39] Under the treaty Japan restored to China the former German leased territory of Kiaochow, together with the documents bearing upon its administration, and transferred public properties in the same territory, within six months after the treaty became effective.[40] China was to compensate Japan only for the public properties purchased or constructed by the Japanese.[41] From this category such properties as were required for the Japanese consulate were to be retained by the Japanese Government while public schools, shrines, and cemeteries were to be left in the hands of the Japanese community.[42] The Japanese troops and gendarmes stationed along the Tsinan-Tsingtao Railway were to be withdrawn within six months.[43] But the Japanese garrison at Tsingtao was to be withdrawn within thirty days.[44] The Tsingtao customs house was to become a part of the Chinese Maritime Customs.[45] The Tsingtao-Tsinan Railway with its branches, including wharves, warehouses, and similar properties, was to be transferred to China; but for this China was to pay to Japan 53,401,-141 gold marks (the assessed value of the properties left behind by the Germans), within nine months.[46] The payment was to be made in Chinese treasury notes and the installment might spread over fifteen years, but China was

[39] See *Conversations between the Chinese and Japanese Representatives in regard to the Shantung Question,* pp. 384–93.

[40] Articles 1–4.   [41] Articles 5–6.   [42] Article 7.   [43] Articles 9–10.
[44] Article 11.   [45] Articles 12–13.   [46] Articles 14–17.

given an option to complete payment in five years. Pending the redemption of the treasury notes, a Japanese traffic manager and a Japanese auditor were to be sanctioned by China.[47] Mining in Shantung was to be made a Sino-Japanese joint enterprise.[48] The Japanese interests in the salt industry were to be sold to China.[49] The submarine cables, except that which connected Tsingtao and Sasebo, and the wireless stations in Shantung were to be restored to China.[50] Finally, Japan was not to seek an exclusive Japanese settlement in Shantung, but China was, of its own volition, to open the former leased territory to foreign trade in general.[51]

With such terms this treaty laid down general principles for the settlement of the Shantung question, but certain details had to be worked out before the final settlement was possible. On March 28 an agreement was signed at Peking, whereby the Japanese troops along the Tsingtao-Tsinanfu Railway were to be withdrawn. This withdrawal was completed on May 4.[52] The Sino-Japanese Commissions provided for in the treaty met at Peking and commenced their work on June 26 and completed it on December 5, thus effecting the final settlement of this long-standing question. The Kiaochow leasehold was transferred to China on December 10, and the Japanese troops stationed there were withdrawn on the 30th. For the public properties and the salt interests returned to China, she was to pay 16,000,000 yen; for the former German mines, 5,000,000 yen; and for the former German railway, 40,000,000 yen.

[47] Articles 18–20.   [48] Article 22.   [49] Article 25.
[50] Articles 26–27.   [51] Article 23.
[52] *Current History,* June 1922, p. 528.

An appropriate ceremony was to be held on the day when the formal transfer of the lease was to be made, but a foreign witness comments concerning the occasion,

hardly one prominent Chinese, other than the members of the Rendition Commission, was present to witness the consummation of what had been represented at Versailles and Washington as the passionate desire of the whole Chinese nation.[53]

"When the time came for the Japanese to withdraw their garrison, the bandits of the outlying region prepared to descend upon the city [Tsingtao]. The Chinese were forced to ask the Japanese to supply them with arms for their newly organized police, and these had to be sent from Japan."[54]

[53] H. G. W. Woodhead in *North China Herald*, December 23, 1922.
[54] P. J. Treat, *The Far East*, p. 474.

CHAPTER XIX

THE TWENTY-ONE DEMANDS

Early in 1915 the news leaked out that Japan had made her notorious twenty-one demands on China. These demands proved to be the most serious diplomatic blunder which she had ever committed, because they aroused the enmity of all intelligent Chinese and caused Japan to be a target for attack by foreign nations. Neither did the Japanese Government escape vehement denunciations by Japanese critics. Some tried to justify the demands by pointing out the circumstances which had brought them about, others by saying that Japan had merely imitated Western diplomacy; but the fair-minded Japanese could not accept such explanations as the true justification of Japan's bullying diplomacy. In the following pages we present a critical study of the history of these twenty-one demands and a discussion of the position taken by the Washington Conference.

We will begin with an analysis of the demands: The first four demands relating to Shantung have already been discussed. The next group was made up of seven demands relative to South Manchuria and Eastern Inner Mongolia, by which Japan demanded that the lease of Port Arthur and Dairen, the term of the South Manchurian Railway and of the Antung-Mukden Railway, should be extended to ninety-nine years; that the Japanese should be permitted to lease or own land in South Manchuria and Eastern Inner Mongolia for various economic enterprises; that they should have liberty to carry on business in the same regions; that they should be granted the right of mining; that China should obtain Japan's consent whenever China desired to grant to other foreigners the right of building railroads in the regions or whenever she desired to borrow money under security of the taxes of the regions; that Japan should first be consulted whenever China desired the expert service of foreign advisers or instructors; and that the control of the Kirin-Changchun Railway should be handed over to Japan for ninety-nine years.

The third group was composed of two articles relating to the Hanyehping Coal and Iron Company in the Yangtse region. Japan demanded that the company should be made a joint Sino-Japanese enterprise at an appropriate time; that the Chinese Government should not dispose of or permit the company to dispose of any right or property of the company; that no mines in the neighborhood should be worked without the consent of the company; and that China would adopt no measure which would affect the interests of the company.

The demand in the fourth group was that China should not cede or lease to other powers any harbor or bay on or any island along the coast of China.

The fifth and last group was composed of miscellaneous "requests," six in number, namely: China should engage Japanese political, financial, and military advisers; the Japanese hospitals, temples, and schools should be granted the right to own land in the interior; in certain localities the police should be placed under joint Sino-Japanese administration or China should employ Japanese in police offices in such localities; China should buy arms from Japan or should establish an arsenal under joint Sino-Japanese management, supplied with experts and materials from Japan; Japan should be granted the right to build a railway to connect Wuchang with the Kiukiang-Nanchang line and another between Nanchang and Hangchow and Nanchang and Chaochow; Japan should first be consulted whenever China desired foreign capital in connection with railways, mines, and harbor works in the Province of Fukien; and, finally, the Japanese should be granted freedom of religious propaganda in China.[1]

The circumstances which led Japan to make these demands have already been touched upon. Sino-Japanese friction after the dislodgment of the Germans from China's territory increased steadily. The attitude of China toward Japan had daily been becoming more and more irritating. But when on January 7, 1915, China revoked, without any apparently valid reason, the war zone, Japan's indignation reached its climax. She retaliated by presenting the foregoing demands. And the purpose of the demands according to Japan's official statement was

to provide for the readjustment of affairs consequent on the Japan-German War and for the purpose of ensuring a lasting peace in the Far East by strengthening the position of the Empire.[2]

Accepting this statement, it appears to an impartial observer that the actual demands were far in excess of the purposes for which they were sought. One can easily understand Japan's anxiety to obtain security for her vast economic interests in South Manchuria and the Liaotung Peninsula. Her desire for extension of the lease of Port Arthur and Dairen and the term of her railways and other related rights and interests was quite natural. But what justification was there for Japan to demand the right of owning land, of residing and carrying on business outside of the regions specified by treaty, in a country where extraterritoriality operates? Japan should have known better because of her own experience with consular juris-

[1] J. V. A. MacMurray, *op. cit.*, II, 1231–34.
[2] *Ibid.*, p. 1231.

diction until very recent years. Her demand that Japanese should be employed in the service of China was nothing short of being preposterous. If Japanese experts should prove superior or more suitable to China's needs, they would be so employed by China of her own accord. The demand for a veto on economic development of South Manchuria and Eastern Inner Mongolia and the demand for mining operations in the Yangtse region were clearly at variance with the spirit of the open door which, until this time, Japan had so honorably upheld. To demand a share in police work of a sovereign nation was in direct violation of the sovereignty of that country. So also was the demand that China should buy arms from Japan. Military matters are considered secret by every nation. Japan had no right to make such a demand. Even the attempt to impose alien religions has always met with the "none-of-your-business attitude." Of course the demand for the right of preaching only provokes a smile. What do the Japanese think of the customary demand of Christian nations for such a right in making treaties with non-Christian nations?

An American scholar sees the demands from another angle and says:

These demands contained many very valuable concessions which China was asked to yield to Japan. For them no *quid pro quo* of any kind was offered. In this, and in many other respects, Japanese diplomacy was following the sinister precedents of European diplomacy in China in the past. What equivalents had been given China for the great concessions extorted by the powers since treaty-making began in 1842? For most of the Japanese demands a precedent, in the record of Russia or other European powers, might be found. But Japan relied too much upon these precedents. They were bad in themselves, and they should never have been imitated. The Chinese, an Asiatic people, naturally resented bitterly this imitation, on a large scale, by Japan of the worst of European examples. And whereas in the old days few Chinese knew or cared about the concessions forced from China at Nanking or Tientsin or Peking, in the twentieth century the spread of modern education, and the rapid development of a Chinese press, caused the evil tidings to be diffused from one border of the land to the other. The Chinese were aroused by the Japanese demands as they had never been in the past.[3]

Again,

In presenting the demands directly to President Yuan, instead of through the Minister of Foreign Affairs, an unusual procedure was adopted. The request that secrecy be observed was not unusual, for even today open covenants are not openly arrived at. The publication by Japan, on February 14, of a summary of the demands, omitting the fifth group and certain other details, while lacking in frankness, was not exceptional. It was far more than Russia divulged when she was trying to establish her protectorate over Manchuria in 1900.[4]

Moreover, because the Chinese Government was slow to meet the demands of the Japanese Government, the latter delivered an ultimatum on May 7, 1915. China accepted the first four groups considerably modified and the items relative to Fukien in the last group, and signed two treaties and exchanged several notes with Japan on May 25, 1915. The treaty and exchange of notes relating to Shantung have already been discussed, and the treaty relating to South Manchuria and Eastern Inner Mongolia merits treatment here. Under this pact the Japanese may lease but not own land necessary for trade, manufacture, or agriculture in the regions. They are free to travel or reside or engage in business, and joint Sino-Japanese

[3] P. J. Treat, *Japan and the United States, 1853–1921*, pp. 219–20.
[4] *Ibid.*, pp. 221–22; and see also P. H. Clyde, *op. cit.*, pp. 229–44.

enterprises may be permitted by the Chinese Government. But the Japanese who avail themselves of these privileges are to be placed under the Chinese police laws and ordinances and are subject to Chinese taxation. Mixed civil cases are to be tried by a mixed court but in accordance with Chinese laws and local usage.

> When, in future, the judicial system in the said region is completely reformed, all civil and criminal cases concerning Japanese subjects shall be tried and adjudicated entirely by Chinese law courts.[5]

The provision as to the completion of the Kirin-Changchun Railway requires China to borrow the necessary capital from Japan. China, of her own accord, will open suitable places in Eastern Inner Mongolia. The lease of Port Arthur and Dairen and the term of the Manchurian railways are extended for ninety-nine years.[6]

Several notes were exchanged between the two nations covering many points. Nine mining districts in Manchuria, mostly coal mines, are to be open to Japanese enterprises.[7] For railroad building in South Manchuria and Eastern Inner Mongolia Japanese capitalists are to be given the first preference in supplying foreign capital, and in case China desires to borrow money on the security of the taxes of these regions, Japanese capitalists are to be first consulted.[8] When China desires to employ experts on political, financial, military, and police matters in South Manchuria, Japanese are to be employed first.[9] Land leases in South Manchuria are not to run more than thirty years, but are to be unconditionally renewable.[10]

---

[5] J. V. A. MacMurray, *op. cit.*, II, 1220–21.
[6] *Ibid.* [7] *Ibid.*, pp. 1224–25. [8] *Ibid.*, p. 1225.
[9] *Ibid.*, p. 1226. [10] *Ibid.*, pp. 1226–27.

As regards the police laws and ordinances and the taxation to which Japanese subjects are to submit in South Manchuria and Eastern Inner Mongolia, China is to consult with the Japanese Consul before their enforcement.[11]

China permits co-operation between the Hanyehping Company and Japanese capitalists and agrees not to confiscate the company, not to convert it into a state enterprise without the consent of the Japanese capitalists, and not to cause it to borrow and use foreign capital other than Japanese.[12] Lastly, China concedes that she will not permit any foreign nation to build any dockyards or naval or military establishments on the Fukien coast, and also promises not to borrow foreign capital for similar purposes.[13] For these concessions Japan promises to restore to China the former German lease of Kiaochow Bay.[14]

The concessions actually made by China fell far short of the original Japanese demands. Yet,

their effect was to isolate Japan, to bring down upon her the bitter enmity of all thoughtful Chinese, and to confirm the suspicions which had arisen in Europe and America of the aggressive policies of Japan in China. No advantage which the concessions could bring her could recompense Japan for the hostility aroused from one end of China to the other.[15]

The Chinese demands at the Paris Peace Conference of 1919 covered the readjustment by the conference of all the treaties, including the Sino-Japanese treaties and notes of 1915, on the grounds that these had been secured under duress and that they impaired China's sovereignty, but this demand was ruled out.[16] Her demand for the direct

---

[11] *Ibid.*, pp. 1227–28. [12] *Ibid.*, pp. 1229–30. [13] *Ibid.*, p. 1230.
[14] *Ibid.*, pp. 1218 f. [15] Treat, *Japan and the United States*, p. 225.
[16] See P. Gallagher, *America's Aims and Asia's Aspirations*, especially pp. 267–375.

restitution of Shantung and the conference decision on this demand have already been discussed in chapter xviii.

At the Washington Conference the question of the Sino-Japanese agreements of 1915 was introduced on December 14. A Chinese delegate presented to his colleagues a list of Chinese non-alienation agreements and other inter-power engagements affecting China's interests. As has been noted before in our discussion of foreign spheres of influence in China, Dr. Wang singled out the foregoing Sino-Japanese engagements and demanded that the conference reconsider and cancel these agreements. But Mr. Hanihara objected to Dr. Wang's proposal. The conference dropped the whole question of these Sino-Japanese engagements in view of the progress of the negotiations between China and Japan, relating to the Shantung issues. However, on February 2, 1922, Baron Shidehara made a comprehensive statement on the subject of the twenty-one demands.

He reiterated at the outset that Japan could not accede to the Chinese demand for the cancellation of the treaties and the exchange notes in question, and, moreover, he presumed that the Chinese delegation had no intention of questioning the validity of these compacts since they had been formally signed by the two sovereign states. Whatever Japan enjoyed under these engagements could not be canceled in the manner suggested by the Chinese, without creating a dangerous precedent upon the stability of existing international relations in Asia, Europe, and elsewhere. In reply to the Chinese assertion that these agreements were derogatory to the principles adopted by the conference relative to China's sovereignty and independence, he reminded the Chinese delegation that these principles could not affect concessions made by China *ex contractu,* on the ground of inconsistency with her sovereignty and independence. The term "Twenty-One Demands," often used to denote the compacts, was inaccurate and misleading, and might give rise to an erroneous impression that the whole original proposals of Japan had been accepted *in toto* by China. In fact, "Group V" and several other matters contained in the demands were eliminated entirely or modified considerably according to the wishes of China. In respect to Japan's ultimatum, he called attention to the fact that official records of the negotiations showed that the most important terms of the agreements had already been agreed to by the Chinese representatives before the delivery of the said ultimatum which seemed to the Japanese Government the only way of bringing the negotiations to a speedy close. He stated once more that no useful purpose would be served by re-examining, by the conference, old grievances held by one power against another. The conference should look forward to the future with hope and confidence.

But in view of the changes which had occurred since the signing of the agreements of 1915, the Japanese delegation was happy to make the following declaration:

1. Japan is ready to throw open to the joint activity of the international Financial Consortium recently organized the right of option granted exclusively in favor of Japanese capital, with regard, first, to loans for the construction of railways in South Manchuria and Eastern Inner Mongolia, and, second, to loans to be secured on taxes in that region; it being understood that nothing in the present declaration shall be held to imply any modification or annulment of the understanding recorded in the officially announced notes and memoranda which were exchanged among the Governments of the countries represented in the Consortium and also among the national financial groups composing the Con-

sortium, in relation to the scope of the joint activity of that organization.

2. Japan has no intention of insisting on her preferential right under the Sino-Japanese arrangements in question concerning the engagement by China of Japanese advisers or instructors on political, financial, military, or police matters in South Manchuria.

3. Japan is further ready to withdraw the reservation which she made, in proceeding to the signature of the Sino-Japanese Treaties and Notes of 1915, to the effect that Group V of the original proposals of the Japanese Government would be postponed for future negotiations.

It would be needless to add that all matters relating to Shantung contained in those Treaties and Notes have now been definitely adjusted and disposed of.

In coming to this decision, which I have had the honor to announce, Japan has been guided by a spirit of fairness and moderation, having always in view China's sovereign rights and the principle of equal opportunity.[17]

In reply Dr. Wang said that the Chinese delegation learned with satisfaction Japan's new proposals, but it greatly regretted that that nation should not renounce the other claims predicated upon the agreements. He recited that if a strong power could obtain from a weak nation valuable concessions for which no *quid pro quo* was offered, that would establish a dangerous precedent. Because of the exceptional conditions under which the agreements of 1915 were negotiated, the American Government had seen fit to send, on May 11, 1915, an identical note to the Chinese and Japanese Governments, which was as follows:

In view of the circumstances which have taken place and which are now pending between the Government of China and

[17] *Document,* pp. 754–55.

the Government of Japan and of the agreements which have been reached as the result thereof, the Government of the United States has the honor to notify the Government of the Chinese Republic [Japan] that it can not recognize any agreement or undertaking which has been entered into between Governments of China and Japan impairing the treaty rights of the United States and its citizens in China, the political or territorial integrity of the Republic of China, or the international policy relative to China commonly known as the open-door policy.

Dr. Wang continued, saying that, conscious of its obligations to the other powers, the Chinese Government, after the signing of the agreements, had published a formal protest against these engagements, disclaiming responsibility for consequent violations of treaty rights of the other powers. Because of the injustice of these compacts, the Chinese delegation had felt itself in duty bound to present to the conference the question as to the equity and justice of these agreements and therefore as to their fundamental validity. The Chinese were of the opinion that these engagements should be considered by the conference with a view to their abrogation, for the following reasons:

1. In exchange for the concessions demanded of China, Japan offered no *quid pro quo*. The benefits derived from the agreements were wholly unilateral.

2. The agreements, in important respects, are in violation of treaties between China and the other powers.

3. The agreements are inconsistent with the principles relating to China which have been adopted by the conference.

4. The agreements have engendered constant misunderstandings between China and Japan, and, if not abrogated, will necessarily tend, in the future, to disturb friendly relations between the two countries, and will thus constitute an obstacle in the way of realizing the purpose for the attainment of which this conference was convened. As to this, the Chinese Delegation, by

way of conclusion, can, perhaps, do no better than quote from a resolution introduced in the Japanese Parliament, in June 1915, by Mr. Hara, later Premier of Japan, a resolution which received the support of some one hundred and thirty of the members of the Parliament. The resolution reads:

"*Resolved,* That the negotiations carried on with China by the present Government have been inappropriate in every respect; that they are detrimental to the amicable relationship between the two countries, and provocative of suspicions on the part of the Powers; that they have the effect of lowering the prestige of the Japanese Empire, and that, while far from capable of establishing the foundation of peace in the Far East, they will form the source of future trouble."[18]

Mr. Hughes followed Dr. Wang, and read the American note referred to previously and remarked that the note was in accord with the historic policy of the United States in its relation to China, which had been and still was maintained. He was gratified to learn that the matters embodied in "Group I" of the Japanese original demands had now been settled. He was also gratified to be advised by Baron Shidehara that Japan was now ready to withdraw her reservation relating to "Group V," which had been an occasion for considerable apprehension on the part of China and foreign nations because the renewal of this group would prejudice the principles of the integrity of China and the open door; that Japan would not insist upon her preferential rights in South Manchuria and Eastern Inner Mongolia; but that she would throw open financial arrangements to the joint activity of the international financial consortium. Thus the principles of the open door were assured to the citizens of all nations. Mr. Hughes concluded his remarks with the following statement:

[18] *Document,* pp. 776–78.

I may pause here to remark that the question of the validity of treaties as between Japan and China is distinct from the question of the treaty rights of the United States under its treaties with China; these rights have been emphasized and consistently asserted by the United States.

In this, as in all matters similarly affecting the general right of its citizens to engage in commercial and industrial enterprises in China, it has been the traditional policy of the American Government to insist upon the doctrine of equality for the nationals of all countries, and this policy, together with the other policies mentioned in the note of May 11, 1915, which I have quoted, are consistently maintained by this Government. I may say that it is with especial pleasure that the Government of the United States finds itself now engaged in the act of reaffirming and defining, and I hope that I may add, revitalizing, by the proposed Nine-Power Treaty, these policies with respect to China.[19]

To recapitulate: The "Twenty-One Demands," like all other important events in diplomatic annals, have caused a wide range of speculation, resulting in a general confusion as to its true meaning, because each speculator has read the history of Far Eastern international relations from his peculiar point of view or his particular interest. Much has been said, for instance, on the precise origin of these famous demands; but on this point the writer must satisfy himself with a statement that he is unable to go beyond the date of the Japanese occupation of the German leasehold of Kiaochow Bay, namely, November 7, 1914. Even this date may be doubtful, for it was on December 3 that the Japanese minister at Peking received from his Foreign Minister the first instructions relating to the demands. On January 7, 1915, China withdrew her war-zone proclamation, which was designed to concentrate the Japanese troops within the German leasehold. Japan pro-

[19] *Ibid.*, pp. 778–80.

tested against this action but in vain, and naturally the Japanese Government interpreted this act as one of hostility, perhaps giving Japan an excuse to present her demands. On January 18 President Yuan Shi-kai was approached on this subject by Minister Hioki—but these demands need not be specified again as they have been minutely dealt with in the preceding pages.

There are, however, certain matters which should be touched upon here in order that we may further clarify our story. The first of these is the political situation in Japan during the progress of the Sino-Japanese negotiations concerning the demands. Premier Okuma, facing a strong opposition, dissolved the House of Representatives on December 24, 1914, and the new election was to take place on March 24, 1915. During these intervening days the Okuma Cabinet had undoubtedly used its strong policy toward China as a political measure because as soon as the victory of the government party was assured in the election, Japan relaxed her pressure on China. Nevertheless, the negotiations continued, and, although China had agreed to the most important terms of the agreements pending, Japan presented her ultimatum on May 7. On May 25 two treaties and several exchange notes were signed, settling the issues. But these agreements brought about an international situation for Japan that did not bespeak the wisdom of Japanese statesmanship. In short the demands proved to be the most serious diplomatic blunder yet committed by Japan.

It is incorrect, on the other hand, to assume as is so frequently done that China had been wholly an innocent, abused party in this connection. Besides what has been already said, it is to be remembered that the Revolution of 1911 had created a nominal republic in China, but at the time of the Sino-Japanese negotiations, Yuan Shi-kai, a true disciple of Li Hung Chang politics and diplomacy, notorious for corruption and unscrupulousness, was the practical dictator of China. Yuan, well known to the Japanese from the time of his Residency-General in Korea (1894), now was on very friendly terms with the Japanese Government. It is intimated in Japan that Yuan himself had suggested to Japan that she ignore the customary diplomatic practice and present her demands directly to him. The writer can not verify this point. However, there is no question as to the intimate relationship that existed between Yuan and the Japanese officials. Of course, Yuan, like Okuma, was involved in domestic politics as well. At any rate, when the Yuan-Japanese relationship is understood, the extraordinary diplomatic method employed by Japan does not seem so unusual after all.

Lastly, it must be remembered that in spite of the Chinese note disclaiming responsibility for the agreements in regard to the treaty rights of the other powers, the Chinese Government, for instance, reconfirmed the Sino-Japanese engagements relative to Shantung by the two new agreements signed on September 24 and 28, 1918. Under Article 9 of the later of these, China accepted an advance of 20,000,000 yen.[20] If the 1915 agreements were signed by China under duress, this 1918 agreement was clearly effected by mutual consent. This latter agreement was one of the chief reasons for the decision of the Paris Peace Conference.

With these additional facts in mind let us summarize the views expressed at the Washington Conference. On December 14 China demanded the abrogation of the 1915 engagements on the grounds that these vitally affected the

[20] J. V. A. MacMurray, *op. cit.*, p. 1446.

very existence, independence, and integrity of China, and also violated the principles relative to China adopted by the conference. In reply, Japan made it plain that she would not accede to the Chinese proposal. The question was dropped, and was not revived until February 2, 1922, when Baron Shidehara made a comprehensive statement on the whole subject. He expressed his appreciation of the difficult position of the Chinese delegation, but he could not favor their proposal. He presumed that the Chinese did not question the validity of the agreements in question. In respect to the principles adopted by the conference, he called attention to the fact that these were not retroactive. After he had specified the stipulations embodied in the agreements, Baron Shidehara informed the conference that Japan was ready to give up her reservation made on "Group V," and all the other preferential rights possessed by Japan under the agreements, in South Manchuria and Eastern Inner Mongolia.

Dr. Wang disagreed with Baron Shidehara on the question of validity, and said that these engagements were "a *de facto* situation without any legal recognition on the part of China."[21] On the following day he replied at length to the Japanese declaration, and in conclusion he again demanded the abrogation of the agreements on the grounds that these were unilateral, inconsistent with the principles adopted by the conference, provocative of misunderstandings between China and Japan, and in violation of Chinese treaties with the other powers.

On the same day Mr. Hughes presented the American view on the subject. He drew a clear distinction between the question of the validity of the agreements and the question of the treaty rights of the United States,

[21] *Document*, p. 756.

and insisted upon these rights under the doctrine of equality.

Aside from the agreement to have the Japanese, Chinese, and American statements repeated at a plenary session (February 4), the conference did nothing more. Its position on these agreements was precisely the same as that of the Paris Peace Conference. China was defeated again, and thus the Japanese *status quo* in South Manchuria and Eastern Inner Mongolia, as far as China was concerned, was maintained by the Washington Conference. However, in 1923 the original Russian lease of Liaotung expired; China notified Japan of this fact, but the latter ignored it. Since the establishment of the Nationalist Government in the summer of 1928, the Chinese have started the same agitation; but it appears to the student of Far Eastern politics that China is not likely to obtain any substantial gains from Japan.

CHAPTER XX

THE SIBERIAN EXPEDITION

One of the tasks of the Washington Conference was to settle certain problems which had arisen in connection with the ill-fated inter-Allied expedition to Siberia (1918–1920). The facts relating to this expedition have remained, generally speaking, confused, and it seems appropriate that we should begin this chapter with a brief survey of its history.

It was the Great War that gave Russian liberals their opportunity to overthrow the Romanoff dynasty and to establish the short-lived provisional government of March 7, 1917. The fall of this government was brought about by the Bolsheviki. These new rulers gained control over European Russia by the end of 1917, and by the beginning of the following year they became dominant in important places in Asiatic Russia. On December 15, 1917, the new régime declared an armistice with Germany and Austria; on February 9, 1918, Ukraine (South Russia) signed a separate treaty with Germany; and the next day the Bolsheviki published a statement that Russia's war with Germany was at an end. On March 3, 1918, Germany forced the Soviet to sign the infamous treaty of Brest-Litovsk whereby Russia not only formally ended her co-operation with the Allies, but also practically put herself under German control as it was then understood by the Allies. The Allied statesmen became apprehensive of this newly developed situation and its possibilities.[1] They feared, in particular, possible developments in Siberia, such as the spread of Bolshevism and German penetration. It happened that there were some 120,000 Czecho-Slovaks in Russia, who had been originally con-

[1] See *The Times History of the War,* London, XVI, 1–10.

scripted by Austria-Hungary to fight against Russia but who had deserted to the Russians. When these Czecho-Slovaks had found their way into Siberia, they allied themselves with the anti-Bolshevist Russians. Early in June 1918 some 15,000 of these men arrived at Vladivostok and took possession of the military supplies stored there, because they feared that these supplies might fall into the hands of Germans, Austrians, or Bolsheviki.

It was now recognized that in Siberia there were developing three distinct problems for Allied statesmen to solve: to check the Bolshevist advance eastward; to prevent possible German control of Siberia; and to rescue the stranded pro-Ally Czecho-Slovak troops. Japan was particularly concerned with this situation because of her geographical propinquity, but no action was taken by her until April 5, 1918, when a small marine force was landed at Vladivostok after one Japanese had been murdered and two more had been wounded by Russians. British and American marines followed the Japanese example. The Allies now began to discuss seriously the need of intervention. However, no definite step was adopted until August 3, when the American Government issued a statement which in part reads as follows:

> As the Government of the United States sees the present circumstances, military action is admissible in Russia now only to render such protection and help as is possible to the Czecho-Slovaks against the armed Austrian and German prisoners who are attacking them, and to steady any efforts at self-government or self-defense in which the Russians themselves may be willing to accept assistance. Whether from Vladivostok or from Murmansk and Archangel, the only present object for which American troops will be employed will be to guard military stores which may subsequently be needed by Russian forces, and to render

such aid as may be acceptable to the Russians in the organization of their own self-defense.

With such objects in view, the Government of the United States is now co-operating with the Governments of France and Great Britain in the neighborhood of Murmansk and Archangel. The United States and Japan are the only powers which are just now in a position to act in Siberia in sufficient force to accomplish even such modest objects as those that have been outlined. The Government of the United States has therefore proposed to the Government of Japan that each of the two Governments send a force of a few thousand men to Vladivostok, with the purpose of co-operating as a single force in the occupation of Vladivostok, and in safeguarding, so far as it may, the country to the rear of the westward-moving Czecho-Slovaks, and the Japanese Government has consented.

In taking this action, the Government of the United States wishes to announce to the people of Russia in the most public and solemn manner that it contemplates no intervention in her internal affairs—not even in the local affairs of the limited areas which her military force may be obliged to occupy—and no impairment of her territorial integrity, either now or hereafter, but that what we are about to do has as its single and only object the rendering of such aid as shall be acceptable to the Russian people themselves in their own endeavors to regain control of their own affairs, their own territory, and their own destiny. The Japanese Government, it is understood, will issue a similar assurance.[2]

Accordingly an international expeditionary force was organized with American, British, Canadian, French, Italian, and Japanese troops, which soon landed at Vladivostok, and accomplished at once one of its prime objects, the safety of the war supplies stored at the port. The next problem was to rescue the Czecho-Slovaks who were still stranded west of Lake Baikal. This task too was completed without much difficulty, and the last detachment of

[2] *New York Times,* August 4, 1918.

these stranded Czechs sailed from Vladivostok in September 1920. In other words, two of the three objects of the expedition were now a *fait accompli*.

But meanwhile there had arisen new complications in chaotic Siberia; numerous dictatorships, directorates, and other mushroom governments sprang up in 1918 and 1919 —"Horvath in Harbin, Orloff in Pogranichnaya, Semenoff at large, and conspicuously, Kolchak in Omsk, all of whom were reactionaries under an anti-Bolshevist disguise to deceive the Allies."[3] Admiral Kolchak, supported by the Allies, overthrew the Bolsheviki on November 18, 1918, and established his government, which was allowed to assume control over Siberia. But his rule came to an abrupt end in the closing days of 1919 when he was captured and executed by the Bolsheviki. "To the Kolchak fiasco and the support given to it by the Allies may be traced all the evils that subsequently developed."[4] This case perhaps illustrates what might have been the hidden meaning of the third object of the expedition, which was couched in ambiguous language—"to steady any effort at self-government or self-defense in which the Russians themselves may be willing to accept assistance .... to render such aid as shall be acceptable to the Russian people themselves in their endeavors to regain control of their own affairs, their own territory, and their own destiny."

At any rate, soon after the fall of Kolchak, the Japanese Government sounded the American Government as to its future policy.[5] The latter made a categorical reply,

[3] C. H. Smith, "What Happened in Siberia," in *Asia*, May 1922, p. 374.

[4] *Ibid.*, p. 375.

[5] C. K. Cumming and W. W. Pettit, *Russian-American Relations* (New York, 1920), p. 355 (Document 154).

which was made public on January 16, 1920, and read in part as follows:[6]

> The Government of the United States has decided to begin at once arrangements for the concentration of the American forces at Vladivostok with a view to their embarkation and departure immediately .... about February 1. Arrangements will be made for withdrawal of American railway experts under same conditions and simultaneously with the departure of American military forces.

By March 1920 all the American soldiers had been withdrawn, and this example had been followed by all other Allies except Japan. The Allies who withdrew had apparently washed their hands of the whole affair. But Japan, blinded by her fear of Bolshevism, was unable to realize the wisdom of the Allies. Instead, she now stupidly launched an anti-Bolshevist campaign single-handed. She withdrew, for this purpose, her troops from Transbaikal and Amur provinces, concentrated them within a radius of about 150 miles from Vladivostok, and continued her futile efforts against the Bolsheviki until the spring of 1921. On March 13, 1920, had occurred at Nikolaievsk a terrible massacre of some seven hundred Japanese, including the Japanese Consul. This tragedy caused public opinion in Japan to demand the instant withdrawal of the troops from Siberia, but in vain. In the summer of 1921 the Japanese authorities changed their campaign against the "Reds" when they began to approach the "Pink" government at Chita with a view to effecting an understanding concerning Siberian-Japanese relations. In August a conference was arranged for this purpose between the Japanese and Chita governments at Dairen,

[6] Cumming and Pettit, *op. cit.*, pp. 355–57.

South Manchuria, but it resulted in failure.[7] The Japanese troops continued to remain in Siberia in spite of public opinion both at home and abroad until the convocation of the conference at Washington in November 1921.

At the Washington Conference, Baron Shidehara made a declaration (January 23, 1922) on the position of the Japanese Government in regard to the Siberian question. He reviewed the history of the expedition and its tasks, and then explained that for Japan the question of the withdrawal of troops from Siberia was not quite as simple as it had been for other Allied Powers. In the first place, there were a considerable number of Japanese residents who had lawfully and under guarantees of treaty established themselves in Siberia long before the Bolshevist eruption, and had been entirely welcome. In 1917, prior to the joint American-Japanese military enterprise, the number of such residents had been no less than 9,717. In the actual situation prevailing there, those Japanese residents could hardly be expected to look for the protection of their lives and property to any other authority than that of Japanese troops. Whatever districts those troops had evacuated in the past had fallen into disorder, and practically all Japanese residents had had precipitately to withdraw for personal safety. In so withdrawing, they had been obliged to leave behind large portions of their property, abandoned and unprotected, and their homes and places of business had been destroyed. While the hardships and losses already suffered by the Japanese in the Trans-Baikal and the Amur provinces had been serious enough, more extensive damage was likely to follow from the evacuation of Vladivostok, in which a

[7] See K. K. Kawakami, *Japan's Pacific Policy*, pp. 239–41.

larger number of Japanese had always been resident and a greater amount of Japanese capital invested.

There was another difficulty which Japan faced in proceeding to the recall of her troops from the Maritime Province. Owing to geographical propinquity, the general situation in the districts around Vladivostok and Nikolsk was bound to affect the security of the Korean frontier. In particular, it was known that these districts had long been the base of Korean conspiracies against Japan. Those hostile Koreans, joining hands with lawless elements in Russia, had attempted in 1920 to invade Korea through the Chinese territory in Chientao. They had set fire to the Japanese consulate at Hunchun and committed indiscriminate acts of murder and pillage. At the present time they were under the effective control of Japanese troops stationed in the Maritime Province, but they would no doubt renew the attempt to penetrate into Korea at the first favorable opportunity that might present itself.

Having had regard to these considerations, the Japanese Government had felt bound to exercise precaution in carrying out the contemplated evacuation of the Maritime Province. Should it have taken hasty action without adequate provision for the future, it would have been delinquent in its duty of affording protection to a large number of its nationals resident in the districts in question and of maintaining order and security in Korea.

It should be made clear that no part of the Maritime Province was under Japan's military occupation. Japanese troops were still stationed in the southern portion of the province, but they had not set up any civil or military administration to displace local authorities. Their activity was confined to measures of self-protection against the menace to their own safety and to the safety of their country and nationals. They were not in occupation of those districts any more than American or other Allied troops could be said to have been in occupation of the places in which they had been formerly stationed.

The Japanese Government was anxious to see an orderly and stable authority speedily re-established in the Far Eastern possessions of Russia. It was in this spirit that it had manifested a keen interest in the patriotic but ill-fated struggle of Admiral Kolchak. It had shown readiness to lend its good offices in prompting the reconciliation of various political groups in Eastern Siberia. But it had carefully refrained from supporting one faction against another. It would be recalled, for instance, that it had withheld all assistance from General Rozanov against the revolutionary movements which had led to his overthrow in January 1920. It had maintained an attitude of strict neutrality, and had refused to interfere in these movements, which it would have been quite easy for it to suppress if it had so desired.

In relation to this policy of non-intervention, it might be useful to refer briefly to the past relations between the Japanese authorities and Ataman Semenoff, which seemed to have been a source of popular misgiving and speculation. It will be remembered that the growing rapprochement between the Germans and the Bolshevik Government in Russia in the early part of 1918 naturally had given rise to apprehension in the Allied countries that a considerable quantity of munitions supplied by those countries and stored in Vladivostok might have been removed by the Bolsheviki to European Russia, for the use of the Germans. Ataman Semenoff was then in Siberia and had been organizing a movement to check such Bolshevist activities and to preserve order and stability in that region. It was in this situation that Japan, as well as some of the Allies, had begun to give support to the Cossack chief. After a few months, such support by the other powers had been discontinued. But the Japanese were reluctant to abandon their friend, whose efforts in the Allied cause they had originally encouraged; and they maintained for some time their connection with him. They had had, however, no intention whatever of interfering in the domestic affairs of Russia, and when it was found that the assistance rendered to Semenoff was likely to complicate the internal situation in Siberia, Japan had terminated all relations with him, and no support of any kind had since been extended to him by the Japanese authorities.

The Japanese Government was now seriously considering plans which would justify it in carrying out a decision for the complete withdrawal of Japanese troops from the Maritime Province, with reasonable precaution for the security of Japanese residents and of the Korean frontier regions. It was for this purpose that negotiations had been opened some time ago at Dairen between the Japanese representatives and the agents of the Chita Government.

The occupation of certain points in the Russian Province of Sakhalin was wholly different, both in nature and in origin, from the stationing of troops in the Maritime Province. History afforded few instances similar to the incident of 1920 at Nikolaievsk, where more than seven hundred Japanese, including women and children, as well as the duly recognized Japanese Consul and his family and his official staff, had been cruelly tortured and massacred. No nation worthy of respect could forbear taking action under such a strain of provocation. Nor had it been possible for the Japanese Government to disregard the just popular indignation aroused in Japan by the incident. Under the actual condition of things, Japan had found no alternative but to occupy, as a measure of reprisal, certain points in the Russian Province of Sakhalin in which the outrage had been committed, pending the establishment in Russia of a responsible authority with whom she could communicate in order to obtain due satisfaction.

Nothing was farther from the thought of the Japanese Government than to take advantage of the present helpless condition of Russia for prosecuting selfish designs. Japan recalled with deep gratitude and appreciation the brilliant rôle which Russia had played in the interest of civilization during the earlier stage of the war. The Japanese people had shown and would continue to show every sympathetic interest in the efforts of patriotic Russians aspiring to the unity and rehabilitation of their country. The military occupation of the Russian Province of Sakhalin was only a temporary measure, and would naturally come to an end as soon as a satisfactory settlement of the question should have been arranged with an orderly Russian government.

In conclusion, the Japanese delegation was authorized to declare that it was the fixed and settled policy of Japan to respect the territorial integrity of Russia, and to observe the principle of non-intervention in the internal affairs of that country, as well as the principle of equal opportunity for the commerce and industry of all nations in every part of the Russian possessions.[8]

[8] *Document,* pp. 698–701.

This statement of the Japanese representative is astonishingly candid, almost undiplomatically so. The position of the Japanese Government was made unmistakably clear. But equally candid was the statement which Mr. Hughes made in behalf of the American Government. He said that the American Government had opposed the idea of military intervention, but had regarded military action as admissible at the time solely for the purpose of helping the Czecho-Slovaks consolidate their forces and get into successful co-operation with their Slavic kinsmen, and to steady any efforts at self-government or self-defense in which the Russians themselves might be willing to accept assistance. It had been stated that the American Government had proposed to ask all associated in this course of action to unite in assuring the people of Russia in the most public and solemn manner that none of the governments uniting in action either in Siberia or in Northern Russia had contemplated any interference of any kind with the political sovereignty of Russia, any intervention in her internal affairs, or any impairment of her territorial integrity, either now or thereafter, but that each of the associated powers had had the single object of affording such aid as should have been acceptable, and only such aid as should have been acceptable, to the Russian people in their endeavor to regain control of their affairs, their own territory, and their own destiny. Japan had agreed to these fundamental desires of America.

The United States had withdrawn, he continued, its troops from Siberia in the spring of 1920, because it had considered that the original purpose of the expedition had either been accomplished or would no longer have been subserved by continued military activity in Siberia. The American Government then had ceased to be a party to the expedition, but it had remained a close observer of events in Eastern Siberia, and had had an extended diplomatic correspondence upon this subject with the Government of Japan.

It must be frankly avowed that this correspondence had not always disclosed an identity of views between the two governments. The United States had not been unmindful of the direct exposure of Japan to Bolshevism in Siberia, and the special problems which the conditions existing there had created for the Japanese Government, but it had been strongly disposed to the belief that the public assurances given by the two governments at the inception of the joint expedition nevertheless had required the complete withdrawal of Japanese troops from all Russian territory—if not immediately after the departure of the Czecho-Slovak troops, then within a reasonable time.

As to the occupation of Sakhalin in reprisal for the massacre of the Japanese at Nikolaievsk, the United States had not been unimpressed by the serious character of that catastrophe; but, having in mind the conditions accepted by both governments at the outset of the joint expedition, of which the Nikolaievsk massacre must have been considered an incident, it had regretted that Japan should have deemed necessary the occupation of Russian territory as a means of assuring a suitable adjustment with a future Russian government.

The Government of Japan would appreciate that in expressing its views the Government of the United States had no desire to impute to the Government of Japan motives or purposes other than those which had heretofore been so frankly avowed. The purpose of this Government was to inform the Japanese Government of its own conviction that, in the present time of disorder in Russia, it was more than ever the duty of those who looked forward to the tranquilization of the Russian people, and a restoration of normal conditions among them, to avoid action which might have kept alive their antagonism and distrust toward outside political agencies. Now, especially, it was incumbent upon the friends of Russia to hold aloof from the domestic contentions of the Russian people, to be scrupulous to avoid inflicting what might have appeared to them a vicarious penalty for sporadic acts of lawlessness, and, above all, to abstain from even the temporary and conditional impairment by any foreign power of the territorial status which, for them as for other peoples, was a matter of deep and sensitive national feeling, transcending perhaps even the issues at stake among themselves.

To that American note the Japanese Government had replied in July 1921, setting forth in substance what Baron Shidehara had now stated to this committee, pointing out the condition under which Japan had taken the action to which reference was made, and giving the assurances which had here been reiterated with respect to its intention and policy.

While the discussion of these matters had been attended with the friendliest feeling, it had naturally been the constant and earnest hope of the American Government—and of Japan as well, he was sure—that this occasion for divergence of views between the two governments might be removed with the least possible delay. It had been with a feeling of special gratification, therefore, that the American delegation had listened to the assurances given by their Japanese colleague, and it was with the greatest friendliness that they reiterated the hope that Japan would find it possible to carry out within the near future her expressed intention of terminating finally the

Siberian expedition and of restoring Sakhalin to the Russian people.[9]

This American official declaration seems to imply that Japan was responsible for the Siberian debacle or at least for the intensification of the already tragic developments there, but such implications are not supported by the facts. As early as 1919 an American officer in the expeditionary force wrote:

> I consider the Siberian campaign a failure..... We went to Siberia with armed forces to help Russia, and did little but talk, nurse the railroad, distribute pamphlets, and show pictures to prove to the Russians what a great nation we were—at home. Among the pamphlets we distributed was one in Russian, entitled: "If you want a republic we will show you how to build one".... How, they asked, are you showing us the way to build a republic if every time we submit a problem, you throw up your hands and say: "We cannot advise you, for that would be interfering. This is something you must settle for yourselves." There was no reason why, when the Siberian situation developed its own peculiar problem after the armistice, the Siberian expedition could not have been increased to a strength which would make it possible to protect itself, and carried out a definite policy in regard to Russia. If we could formulate no policy for Siberia which seemed to fit our national aims toward Russia and Siberia, our expedition should have been withdrawn.[10]

C. H. Smith, another American occupying a far more important position than Moore in the Allied work in Siberia, wrote in 1922:

> To the Kolchak fiasco and the support given it by the Allies may be traced all the evils that subsequently developed. This is not wisdom after the fact. I may say that the majority of those who knew Siberian conditions most intimately and had been

[9] *Document*, pp. 703–6.
[10] F. Moore, *Siberia Today* (New York, 1919), pp. 327–28.

longest on the scene and were without preconceived prejudices felt at the time that a mistake was being made, and those of us who were in official position said so. As American representatives on an inter-Allied organization I did say so repeatedly in my official dispatches. The arrival of the Allied troops was the signal for the reactionaries to mass and prepare to act. I have always supposed they knew they would get foreign support. On November 18, 1918, at any rate, they did act. They overthrew the democratic Directorate at Omsk, and Kolchak was proclaimed supreme ruler..... So long as the Japanese are in Siberia, there must be trouble. Until they leave, a real Siberian government cannot possibly be established. Trumped-up revolutions will be unceasing, and each will bring its loss of life and property. This is the real crime of the Japanese occupation. But I would not seem to lay the crime at Japanese doors exclusively. I have tried to point out that the European Allies and America must share in the guilt. That is the real tragedy of Siberia.[11]

These views appear to the writer a fairer estimate of the expedition. It must be emphatically stated also that the people of Japan had never looked with favor upon Japan's venture in Siberia. As a matter of fact, they were greatly distressed at the American proposal to dispatch a joint Allied expedition, although they did not at that time clearly understand the actual state of affairs that existed. However, they were gradually led to believe with the rest of the world that they would be exposed to the danger of German control of Siberia and of Bolshevist conquest. As soon as they discovered that the danger so pictured had been much exaggerated, they questioned the wisdom of Japan's military co-operation with the Allies. The people had been less confident of their government since its application of a drastic policy toward China in 1915. Just as they had anticipated, Japan's military enterprise became

[11] C. H. Smith, "What Happened in Siberia," in *Asia*, May 1922, pp. 375 and 403.

a source of foreign criticism, while she herself gained nothing from it. In fact, it is estimated that the unfortunate undertaking had cost Japan nearly 1,500,000,000 yen. Moreover, the soldiers sent to Siberia suffered from the frigid climate and indignities at the hands of ignorant Siberians, whether white or otherwise. These Asiatic Russians looked upon the Japanese soldiers and civilians as their former enemy. Mr. Moore gives us a pathetic picture of the situation of the Japanese soldiers, and expresses his astonishment at their marvelous display of discipline, despite the fact that they did not know why they were there, subjected to severe tasks and to insults by the Russian peasants. Many of these soldiers it is said returned home converts to Bolshevism.

At the time of the withdrawal of American soldiers, the public sentiment of Japan, as has been indicated already, favored the withdrawal of its own soldiers. Why, then, it might be asked, did not that public opinion force the Japanese Government to carry out its will? The truth is, at that time the military element in the Government was more powerful in shaping Japan's foreign policy than public opinion. Nevertheless, the public agitation continued, and it would be well if Western readers could acquaint themselves with the public opinion of Japan as expressed in her newspapers and periodicals.

Perhaps it is not superfluous to say that no student should fail to realize the peculiarly difficult position of Japan in regard to the Siberian issue or other matters pertaining to the Far East. The question of Bolshevism in the Far East was and is a matter of reality to Japan and not a question of academic interest. The chaotic state of affairs, whether in Siberia, China, or Korea, was and is of immediate consequence to Japan.

Reference has been made to the Dairen Conference of 1921, but nothing came of it; nothing should have been expected. The Changchun Conference of 1922 proved equally fruitless. The Russians, under the pretense of a commercial entente, sought Japan's recognition of the Soviet Government, and thus Japan faced an impossible situation. There was no hope of peace between Asiatic Russia and Japan until the latter recognized the Bolshevist régime. That, Japan could not do safely until Soviet Russia abandoned her unscrupulous diplomacy.

In view of these trying circumstances, it was indeed gratifying to learn that Japan withdrew (October 26, 1922) her troops from the Russian mainland,[12] and reestablished her diplomatic relations with Russia by signing a new treaty on January 21, 1925.[13] Subsequently the last contingent of her troops occupying northern Sakhalin was withdrawn, on May 15, 1925. Since then Japan and Russia, relatively speaking, have been enjoying amity and peace.

[12] See Leo Pasvolsky, "Russia Takes Over Vladivostok," in *Current History*, December 1922, pp. 499–501.

[13] See A. L. P. Dennis, "The New Russo-Japanese Treaty Explained," in *Current History*, May 1925, pp. 240–44.

CHAPTER XXI

THE YAP SETTLEMENT

In the autumn of 1920 public opinion throughout the world was surprised to discover that there was in progress an American-Japanese controversy over the Island of Yap, an unheard-of spot in the Pacific Ocean. It later developed that these governments and also the League of Nations were seriously involved in this apparently insignificant question. The negotiations were prolonged, and it was not until December 1921 that a final agreement was reached, which was later embodied in a treaty signed on February 11, 1922. In view of the diplomatic complications which were involved before a solution was obtained and in view of a certain international significance which we must attach to the treaty, a historical study of the subject may be in order.

The tiny island of Yap is the westernmost of the Caroline group, and lies about nine degrees north of the Equator in longitude 138° E. The distance from the island to Yokohama is about 1,660 miles and to Manila about 1,150 miles. The Caroline Archipelago including Yap was discovered by Portuguese navigators in 1527, but some one hundred and fifty years later these islands were annexed by Spain and were named in honor of Carolus II.[1] At the close of the Spanish-American war in 1898, the whole group was sold by Spain to Germany for $3,300,000.

Soon after the outbreak of the Great War, Japanese naval forces occupied the German Pacific islands north of the Equator including Yap, while the Australian forces took the islands south of the line. In 1917 Japan secured the consent of the Allies to support her claim to the out-

[1] See Wm. H. Furness, *The Island of Stone Money* (Philadelphia, 1910), p. 16.

right possession of these islands. However, the Peace Conference conferred upon Japan only mandatory administration over these islands, by a decision of the Supreme Council on May 7, 1919. More than a year later, on November 12, 1920, the Japanese Foreign Office received a note from the American Government, stating, among other things, that it was the clear understanding of the United States that for reasons vitally affecting international communications the Supreme Council of the Peace Conference at the request of President Wilson had reserved for future consideration the final disposition of the Island of Yap in the hope that some agreement might be reached by the Allied and Associated Governments to place the island under international control and thus render it available as an international cable station. For this reason it was the understanding of the Government of the United States that the Island of Yap had not been included in the action of the Supreme Council on May 7, 1919.[2]

On the 19th the Japanese Government replied to the note by stating that according to the definite understanding of the Japanese Government the Supreme Council on May 7, 1919, came to a final decision to place under the mandate of Japan the whole of the German islands north of the Equator. The decision involved no reservation whatever in regard to the Island of Yap. For the above-mentioned reason the Department of Foreign Affairs informed the United States Embassy that the Japanese Government would not be able to consent to any proposition which, reversing the decision of the Supreme Coun-

[2] *The Asian Review,* May–June, 1921, p. 329, and the *New York Times,* April 19, 1921.

cil, would exclude the Island of Yap from the territory committed to its charge.[3]

On December 10 another American note followed, in which the alleged Wilson-Lansing reservations (not found in the official records) relative to Yap are reiterated at length, and in which it was stated that five meetings had been held between April 21 and May 6 in which the said reservations were said to have been made. According to the note, at the meeting held on May 6 mentioned above, Mr. Lloyd George expressed his understanding that the Japanese should receive a mandate for certain islands north of the Equator. According to the record, President Wilson consented in principle to this, with an explanatory statement that, with respect to mandates, the policy of the "open door" would have to be applied, and that there must be equal opportunity for the trade and commerce of other members of the League. The note continued to the effect that the Island of Yap, having been previously cited as a special case for particular further consideration, was not intended to be included among the "certain islands" designated as available to Japan under mandate. The decision relative to mandates had been made at the meeting on May 7, but the note says that the President recollected no proposal offered in this meeting to change the decision of May 6, and it was certain he had agreed to no variants of the original proposition. It then cited the statement of Mr. Wilson relative to Yap before the Senate Committee of Foreign Affairs on August 19, 1919, which was as follows:

[3] *Ibid.* Note that on November 20 the American Government addressed a protest to the British Government relative to her mandatory over Mesopotamia, stating that the said mandate was invalid without American agreement. See League of Nations, *Official Journal,* March–April, 1921, p. 137.

It is one of the bases and centres of cable and radio communication of the Pacific, and I made the point that the disposition, or rather the control, of that island should be reserved for the general conference which is to be held in regard to the ownership and operation of the cables. That subject is mentioned and disposed of in this treaty, and that general cable conference is to be held.

The note pointed out further that this statement evidenced the understanding of the President, and it was interesting that, though wide publicity had been given to the President's declaration at the time, no comments had been received by the Government from any nation indicating a contrary opinion. The Government of the United States could not agree that the Island of Yap had been included in the decision of May 7 or in any other agreement of the Supreme Council; and, in addition, as the Island of Yap must form an indispensable part of international communications, it was essential that its free and unhampered use for such purpose should not be limited or controlled by any one power. Even on the assumption that the Island of Yap should be included among the islands held by mandate by Japan, it was not conceivable that other powers should not have free and unhampered access and use of the islands for the landing and operation of cables. This was a right which the United States would be disposed to grant upon any of its unfortified islands which might be essential for such purposes.[4]

This note was not answered by the Japanese Government until February 26, 1921. Meanwhile the cable conference referred to by Mr. Wilson was in progress at Washington to settle the controversy over the two former German cables connecting Emden and New York, and a third connecting San Francisco and the Far East via Yap.

[4] *The Asian Review,* May–June, 1921, pp. 393–94.

The former were held by France and Great Britain, and the latter by Japan. It was clear by December 14, 1920, that the conference was unable to reach any agreement on these cable lines.[5] Moreover, at this juncture (December 17) the Supreme Council of the League of Nations made public its approval of the Japanese mandate in question, and defined it as "all the former German islands situated in the Pacific Ocean and lying north of the Equator."[6] This act of the League unmistakably put Yap in the hands of Japan, and it naturally created a furor in the United States. Little Yap loomed large.

On February 21, 1921, the American Government submitted a note on the whole subject of mandates to the Supreme Council of the League of Nations. We are concerned only with that which relates specifically to Yap:

> This Government is also in receipt of information that the Council of the League of Nations, at its meeting at Geneva on December 17 last, approved, among other mandates, a mandate to Japan embracing "all the former German islands situated in the Pacific Ocean and lying north of the Equator." The text of this mandate to Japan, which was received by this Government, and which, according to available information, was approved by the Council, contains the following statement: "Whereas the Principal Allied and Associated Powers agreed that, in accordance with Article XXII, Part I (Covenant of the League of Nations), of the said Treaty, a mandate should be conferred upon His Majesty the Emperor of Japan to administer the said islands, and have proposed that the mandate should be formulated in the following terms, ..."
>
> The Government of the United States takes this opportunity respectfully and in the most friendly spirit to submit to the President and Members of the Council of the League that the statement above quoted is incorrect and is not an accurate recital

---

[5] See *Current History*, April 1921, pp. 108–10.

[6] League of Nations, *Official Journal*, (Second Year) No. 1, p. 87.

of the facts. On the contrary, the United States, which is distinctly included in the very definite and constantly used descriptive phrase "the Principal Allied and Associated Powers," has not agreed to the terms or provisions of the mandate which is embodied in this text, nor has it agreed that a mandate should be conferred upon Japan covering all the former German islands situated in the Pacific Ocean and lying north of the Equator.

The United States has never given its consent to the inclusion of the Island of Yap in any proposed mandate to Japan, but, on the other hand, at the time of a discussion of a mandate covering the former German islands in the Pacific Ocean north of the Equator, and in the course of the said discussion, President Wilson, acting on behalf of the Government, was particular to stipulate that the question of the disposition of the Island of Yap should be reserved for future consideration. Subsequently this Government was informed that certain of "the Principal Allied and Associated Powers" were under the impression that the reported decision of the Supreme Council, sometimes described as the Council of Four, taken at its meeting of May 7, 1919, included or inserted the Island of Yap in the proposed mandate to Japan.

As one of the Principal Allied and Associated Powers, the United States has an equal concern and an inseparable interest with the other Principal Allied and Associated Powers in the overseas possessions of Germany, and concededly an equal voice in their disposition, which it is respectfully submitted cannot be undertaken or effected without its assent. The Government of the United States therefore respectfully states that it cannot regard itself as bound by the terms and provisions of the said mandate, and desires to record its protest against the reported decision of December 17 last of the Council of the League of Nations in relation thereto, and at the same time to request that the Council, having obviously acted under a misapprehension of the facts, should reopen the question for the further consideration which the proper settlement of it clearly requires.[7]

The Supreme Council made its reply on March 26, 1921. In regard to the American contention that the con-

[7] *The London Times,* February 26, 1921.

sent of the United States was essential to the validity of any determination which might be reached on mandates, the note stated that the rights acquired by the United States by the part she had played during the war and in making the peace were not likely to be challenged in any quarter. But the note added that the American Government would itself recognize that the situation was complicated by the fact that the United States, for reasons which the Council would be the last to question, had so far abstained from ratifying the Peace Treaty and had not taken her seat on the Council of the League of Nations. As regards the protest about Yap, it simply stated that the American complaint did not lie against the Council of the League but rather against the Principal Allied Powers.[8] America was thus left to negotiate with these powers.

On February 26, 1921, Japan replied to the American note of December 10. She pointed out to the American Government that the Japanese delegates had not been present at three of the meetings mentioned by the American note, namely, those held on April 21, May 6 and 7, and, therefore, the Japanese Government was without any information as to what had taken place at those meetings. To show that Yap was excluded from the mandate, the American Government must prove, not merely the fact that this particular line of views had been stated at the meetings, but also that the meeting had decided in favor of those views. Japan considered the decision of May 7 as final, according to which Yap was included in the mandate.

It must also be remembered that if a decision in favor of the exclusion of the Island of Yap—a question of grave concern to Japan, and one on which the Japanese

[8] League of Nations, *Official Journal*, March–April, 1921, p. 142.

delegation invariably had maintained a firm attitude—had really been made, as had been implied by the argument of the United States Government, at the meeting of May 7, at which Japan had not been represented, it could not but have been regarded as an act of entirely bad faith. It was, therefore, inconceivable to the Imperial Government that such a decision could have been reached at a meeting at which no Japanese delegation had been present. Since the decision under consideration said on the one hand "German islands" and on the other, did not make any exception of Yap, the Imperial Government regarded it as perfectly clear that the ex-German Pacific islands north of the Equator, with no exception whatever, all belonged to the mandatory territory allocated to Japan. Nor was the Imperial Government alone and unsupported in its interpretation of the decision, for it was in receipt of authentic information that the Governments of Great Britain and France, being of the same opinion as Japan on the matter, made statements to that effect in their replies to the American Note in November 1920.

The note concluded that the Imperial Government could not agree in giving an extraordinary and unusual interpretation to the decision on a vague ground that certain thoughts or intentions not expressed in the text thereof had existed in the mind of the delegate of one power only. The decision of May 7 had been made public on the following day. If the American Government had found it erroneous, it should have entered an immediate protest. No such step had been taken, however, at the time, and the Imperial Government failed to understand the reasons why the American Government should have allowed more than a year and a half to pass by before electing to question the decision. Japan considered the

President's statement before the Senate Committee of Foreign Relations as "a pure domestic affair," and no third power was called upon to make any refutation or correction. It was observed, however, that even on the assumption that the Island of Yap should be included among the islands held under the mandate by Japan it was conceivable that other powers should have free and unhampered access to and use of the Island, for the landing and operation of cables. If this observation was put forth irrespective of the fact that the Island was within the mandatory territory, then the question seemed to be one which should be freely settled by the nation which had charge of the place, namely, Japan. If the meaning was, however, that owing to the nature of the mandate the island should have its doors kept open, the Imperial Government would draw attention to the fact that at the meeting of the Commission on Mandates held on July 8, 1919, Colonel House had opposed Count (then Viscount) Chinda's claim that the same equal opportunities for commerce and trade should be guaranteed in territories belonging to the C class as in those belonging to the B class. In view of the position thus taken by the American delegate the Imperial Government felt obliged to state that in its opinion the American Government could not with justice contend for the open door in the C class territories, at least as against Japan, and to inform the United States Government at the same time that it could not consider itself bound in any way to recognize the freedom of other nations, in the manner insisted upon by the American Government, in regard to the landing and the operation of cables, even in places where the principle of the open door was to be guaranteed.[9]

[9] *The Asian Review,* May–June, 1921, pp. 394–98.

Thus the Yap controversy dragged on. In the spring of 1921 the American administration changed, and Mr. Hughes became Secretary of State. On April 5 the new Secretary addressed an identical note on the subject of Yap to the British, French, Italian, and Japanese Governments, in which were reiterated at length the arguments and regrets presented in the various notes already examined. However, the note contained a new statement by Mr. Wilson which was as follows:

I never abandoned or modified this position in respect to the Island of Yap and I did not agree on May 7, 1919, or any other time that the Island of Yap should be included in the assignment of mandates to Japan.

The note concluded that, in particular as no treaty had ever been concluded with the United States relating to the Island of Yap and as no one had ever been authorized to cede or surrender the right or interest of the United States in the Island, the Government must insist that it did not lose its right or interest, as it had existed prior to any action of the Supreme Council or of the League of Nations and could not recognize the allocation of the Island or the validity of the mandate to Japan.[10]

To sum up the development thus far, it may be pointed out that at the Paris Peace Conference Japan claimed the former German Pacific islands north of the Equator on the basis of her occupation and her agreements with the Allies, and was given a mandate over these islands by a decision of the Supreme Council on May 7, 1919. The Treaty of Versailles was signed on June 28. Under Article 119 of the Treaty Germany renounced all her rights and titles to her oversea possessions. The aforesaid man-

[10] *Ibid.*, pp. 398–401.

date was put into effect in accordance with Article 22 of the Covenant of the League of Nations. On November 12, 1920, the American Government sent a note to the Japanese Government that relative to the decision of May 7, 1919, Mr. Wilson had made a reservation to have the Island of Yap excluded from the Japanese mandate. To this note of protest, Japan replied that she could not accede to the American proposition. On December 10 the American Government reiterated its position with a new note, in which it was also stated that Yap was one of the cable centers of the Pacific the control of which was to be decided by a conference of the Allied and Associated Powers. Such a conference was held in the fall of 1920 at Washington to reach a settlement of the former German cable lines, but it broke up without any agreement. On December 17, the Supreme Council declared that the Japanese mandate included the Island of Yap, and this was followed by an American note of protest on the whole subject of mandates to the Supreme Council. In reply to this American note the League suggested that the differences relative to mandates might be settled between the United States and the individual mandatory powers. On February 26, 1921, Japan replied to the American note of December 10, 1920, stating that the decision of May 7, 1919, could not be altered but that the United States might enjoy whatever rights and privileges were granted to the members of the League in such mandated countries. On April 5 the American Government wrote to the Japanese Government suggesting that this question be settled between the two nations by a treaty. As far as the writer has been able to find out, this note was the last step in the negotiations to settle the question before the convocation of the Washington Conference.

We may pause here for a moment to comment upon the unusual diplomatic procedure adopted by the various authorities involved in the controversy. The notes exchanged were published as soon as they were received by the League and the individual governments. The writer does not wish to claim that the notes in question were made public *in toto,* although our examination of the notes above seems to indicate that such was the case. Public interest was naturally aroused as it easily is over any controversial matter between nations. From the point of view of American-Japanese relations, the wisdom of this open diplomacy might have been questioned, for it led to unrestrained utterances by the press in both America and Japan. "The general attitude of the American press was that it would be intolerable for us [Americans] to have to submit our cable dispatches to the Philippines and the Far East to the official censorship of the Japanese Government."[11] It gave "the Yellow Peril advocates a chance to say something."[12] In fact, all the old-time animosity against Japan was revived.[13] Part of the Japanese press was equally unrestrained.[14] An American humorist, however, wrote an article under the title of "Yap for Yappers," ridiculing the size and the conditions of the island, but stating the American desire to have this pin-point isle from "a naval point of view." Accordingly he suggested a song:

"Give us Yap! Give us Yap!
The Yanks have put it

[11] See *Current History,* April 1921, pp. 108–10.
[12] See *Current Opinion,* April 1921, pp. 443–46.
[13] See *Literary Digest,* March 12, 1921, pp. 16–17.
[14] See *ibid.,* April 30, 1921, pp. 17–18.

The Yanks have put it
The Yanks have put it
On the map."[15]

But to return to the negotiations: In the agenda for the Washington Conference we find "mandated islands" as one of the questions to be discussed. For some reason this subject was not taken up by the conference, but negotiations on it were carried on between the American and Japanese delegates. On December 12, Mr. Hughes announced at a meeting of the conference that the subject of the status of Yap and the mandated islands north of the Equator was now settled.[16] The general public did not learn of this until the following day when the *New York Times* published an article on the subject, giving with it the text of the treaty. But the final signing of this treaty was not effected until February 11, 1922.[17]

The preamble states clearly the four specific considerations upon which the present treaty is based, namely:

1. By Article 119 of the Treaty of Versailles, signed on June 28, 1919, Germany renounced in favor of the Principal Allied and Associated Powers (the United States, British Empire, France, Italy, and Japan) all her rights and titles over her oversea possessions;

2. The benefits accruing to the United States under the aforesaid article were confirmed by the American-German treaty signed on August 25, 1921;

3. The British Empire, France, Italy, and Japan conferred upon Japan a mandate, pursuant to the Versailles treaty, over the former German Pacific islands north of

[15] See *The Nation*, September 6, 1919, p. 328.
[16] *Document*, p. 582.
[17] *The Statutes at Large of the United States of America*, Vol. XLII, Part 2, p. 2149.

the Equator, in accordance with the principle of mandates of the League of Nations, as follows:

Article 1.—The islands over which a mandate is conferred upon his Majesty, the Emperor of Japan, (hereinafter called the Mandatory) comprise all the former German islands situated in the Pacific Ocean and lying north of the Equator.

Article 2.—The Mandatory shall have full power of administration and legislation over the territory subject to the present Mandate as an integral portion of the Empire of Japan, and may apply the laws of the Empire of Japan to the territory, subject to such local modifications as circumstances may require. The Mandatory shall promote to the utmost the material and moral well-being and the social progress of the inhabitants of the territory subject to the present Mandate.

Article 3.—The Mandatory shall see that the slave trade is prohibited and that no forced labor is permitted, except for essential public works and services, and then only for adequate remuneration.

The Mandatory shall also see that the traffic in arms and ammunition is controlled in accordance with principles analogous to those laid down in the Convention relating to the control of the arms traffic, signed on September 10, 1919, or in any convention amending same.

The supply of intoxicating spirits and beverages to the natives shall be prohibited.

Article 4.—The military training of the natives, otherwise than for purposes of internal police and the local defense of the territory, shall be prohibited. Furthermore, no military or naval bases shall be established, or fortifications erected in the territory.

Article 5.—Subject to the provisions of any local law for the maintenance of public order and public morals, the Mandatory shall insure in the territory freedom of conscience and the free exercise of all forms of worship, and shall allow all missionaries, nationals of any State Member of the League of Nations, to enter into, travel, and reside in the territory for the purpose of prosecuting their calling.

Article 6.—The Mandatory shall make to the Council of the League of Nations an annual report to the satisfaction of the

Council, containing full information with regard to the territory, and indicating the measures taken to carry out the obligations assumed under Articles 2, 3, 4, and 5.

Article 7.—The consent of the Council of the League of Nations is required for any modification of the terms of the present Mandate.

The Mandatory agrees that, if any dispute whatever should arise between the Mandatory and another member of the League of Nations relating to the interpretation or the application of the provisions of the Mandate, such dispute, if it cannot be settled by negotiation, shall be submitted to the Permanent Court of International Justice provided for by Article 14 of the Covenant of the League of Nations.

4. The United States did not ratify the Versailles treaty and did not participate in the agreement respecting the aforesaid mandate.

These considerations led the American and Japanese governments to reach a definite understanding as regards the rights of the two governments and their nationals in the mandated islands, including Yap. Under Article I of this treaty the United States consents to the Japanese mandate as it is defined in Section 3 of the preamble, thereby recognizing the principle of mandates of the League of Nations. By Article II the United States secured all the rights and privileges granted to members of the League as defined by the mandatory provisions 3, 4, and 5 above stated, although it is not a member of the League. In addition, Japan insures, in her mandated islands, religious freedom, and grants the right to American missionaries to "acquire and possess property, erect religious buildings, and open schools throughout the islands," subject to such control by the Japanese Government as may be necessary to maintain public order and good government. Japan pledges to send to the United

States a duplicate copy of the annual report on the administration of the mandate to be made by her to the Council of the League of Nations, and in addition to apply all the existing treaties between the two nations to the mandated islands.

Article III secures to American citizens free access to the Island of Yap, on equal footing with Japanese subjects or any other nationals "in all that relates to the landing and operation of the existing Yap-Guam cable, or of any cable which may hereafter be laid or operated by the United States or by its nationals connecting with the Island of Yap." The same rights and privileges are secured with respect to radio-telegraphic communication, but with the proviso that so long as Japan maintains an adequate station the foregoing rights and privileges will be suspended. Article IV secures to American citizens unrestricted right to enter, reside in, and leave the Island of Yap, and the right to acquire and hold therein, on equal footing with all other nationals, all kinds of property and interests, personal and real—including "lands, buildings, residences, offices, works, and appurtenances." Nationals of the United States shall not be obliged to obtain any permit or license to land or to operate cables on the Island or to establish radio-telegraphic service. They are also exempt from censorship or supervision over cable or radio messages, and from taxes for landing and operating cables or radio stations as well as taxes on property, persons, or vessels connected with the foregoing, and from discriminatory police regulations. Finally, "the Government of Japan will exercise its power of expropriation in the Island to secure to the United States or its nationals needed property and facilities for the purpose of electrical communications if such property or facilities cannot otherwise be obtained."

Such is the nature and scope of the American-Japanese treaty on Yap by which the long-outstanding question was finally settled. As one now reflects upon the issues raised by the United States during the negotiations and upon the stipulations embodied in the treaty, he is impressed with the fact that it was a case of much ado about nothing. From the beginning it was logical enough that the Island of Yap had to be included in the Japanese mandate; surely the United States was neither desirous of, nor would the Senate countenance, a mandate over the Island. Who else was there that could assume this mandate? Yet the American Government had insisted upon the exclusion of Yap from the Japanese mandate in spite of Japan's firm stand to the contrary, supported by the League of Nations. The alleged reservation of Mr. Wilson was made the sole cause of the American demand, and, granting the truth of the reservation, it would be interesting to speculate just how Mr. Wilson would have settled the status of Yap. Aside from the question of inclusion of the Island in, or of exclusion from, the Japanese mandate, there were no real issues, for it was early indicated by Japan that she was willing to extend to the United States such rights and privileges as were granted to members of the League. The treaty as we have analyzed it shows that, while the United States secures these rights and privileges, the Island of Yap remains in the hands of Japan. From a broad international point of view, the most significant phase of this instrument is the fact that under it the United States recognizes the mandatory regulations as formulated by the League of Nations, and thus becomes a beneficiary of that international body. In respect to American-Japanese relations another sore spot was healed by this pact.

CHAPTER XXII

THE PACIFIC CONFERENCE AND AFTER—CONCLUSIONS

The survey in the preceding pages makes it clear now, it is hoped, that the Far Eastern and Pacific Conference concerned itself primarily with the problems of China, involving international interests and therefore calling for their solution by international agreements. We have traced the causes internal and external which brought these problems into existence; we have sketched briefly the history of Chinese foreign relations, which is divided by Dr. Morse into three periods: He calls the first period, embracing the years between 1834 and 1858, the "Period of Conflict"; the second, between 1858 and 1895, the "Period of Submission"; and the last, between 1895 and 1911, the "Period of Subjection." The writer added that the years following the downfall of the Manchu Dynasty constituted a continuation of the last period. We saw in the beginning of this third period the rise of a new power; Japan became a factor to be reckoned with in Far Eastern international affairs. This fact tended to complicate the already complicated inter-relations of the Western nations interested in China. These circumstances produced a situation in which international rivalries, jealousies, distrust, and antagonism ran rampant. These dangerous tendencies were rendered more so by Chinese officials, many of whom were willing to sacrifice their national interests for their personal profit. What happened during the Sino-Japanese war of 1894-95 and immediately after will elucidate this fact for anyone who is not very familiar with the history of Chinese diplomacy. China tried to win the war by involving the Western nations interested in her. A triple intervention resulted, which forced Japan to retrocede some of the fruits secured by the Bakan Treaty. But China did not escape paying the price of this diplomatic victory over the Japanese; in fact, she was subjected to aggression upon aggression by the Western powers, and even her very existence was threatened. These Western aggrandizements are in no way to be justified, but for them the Chinese officials must be held, in part, responsible.

Japan watched these developments with a keen interest, and she soon decided to imitate the conduct of Western powers in her relations with China. She joined the international expedition against the Boxers; she formed an alliance with Great Britain; she fought and defeated Russia; she was now a full-fledged Great Power. But the West began to apprehend this aggressive Asiatic nation, and, when she proved herself so successful in her economic enterprises in South Manchuria, Europe and America became hostile to her. Japan was severely criticized by her Western colleagues for doing what they were doing; she was vehemently charged with violating the sacred open-door principle. In short, she was made the scapegoat for all the ills of the Sick Man of the Far East. Her blunder in 1915 proved conclusively to the West that she was the devil incarnate.

Be that as it may, when the Washington Conference was convoked "there existed with regard to the Far East causes of misunderstandings and sources of controversy which constituted a serious potential danger." These difficulties centered about China. At the conference the interested powers faced China's problems sympathetically with a view to helping her, but the delegates were forced to realize that their Chinese colleagues often became too eloquent over their "Bill of Rights." The foreign delegations preferred to see China seeking and not demanding; nevertheless, they granted many and unparalleled concessions to her. The most important of these concessions related to the tariff. The treaty signed at Washington by the nine powers became operative two months later without ratification. It provided for revision of the tariff into an effective 5 per cent, which would enable China to secure an extra revenue of $17,000,000 silver on the basis of the 1920 customs revenue. It also provided for a surtax of 2½ per cent ad valorem, which would enable her to collect about $27,000,000 silver extra. Furthermore, it provided for a special surtax on luxuries at 5 per cent ad valorem, which would enable her to gain $2,000,000 more, or a total additional revenue of about $46,000,000 silver; on this basis, the new tariff would yield about $110,000,000 silver, or an increase by 70 per cent.[1] The treaty further provided for future revisions of the tariff in order that China might enjoy the fruit of effective rates. According to a stipulation of the treaty, the Revision Commission met at Shanghai in March 1922 and put the revised tariff in force on January 17, 1923. The proposed conference on likin and surtax, however, was delayed by France because of her Boxer indemnity controversy with China. When this difficulty was settled, she and Italy ratified the treaty on April 2, 1925, and the conference was summoned on October 26, but it failed because of the Chinese attitude. Despite this fact, the various factions in China levied and collected the surtax, causing some diplomatic complications. Nevertheless, the powers affected by these high-handed acts seem to have taken rather a tolerant attitude, and it is hoped that a proper solution can be found when a stable government is established in that chaotic country.

[1] *Document,* pp. 590–91.

Equally important was the open-door treaty. By it the famous open-door principle was re-defined and given a legal sanction. It guaranteed the maintenance of the principle in future international dealings in China because under it the signatory powers pledge themselves to abide by that principle. It further provided against the future creation of spheres of influence. It also provided against the violation of China's rights as a neutral nation. But China was made responsible to abide by the open-door principle also; she was not to make unfair discrimination as regards her railroad charges. Finally, the treaty created an international board "with special reference to their [signatory powers'] general policy, designed to stabilize conditions in the Far East, to safeguard the rights and interests of China, and to promote intercourse between China and other Powers upon the basis of equality of opportunity." These stipulations constitute a contribution toward emancipation of China from further foreign encroachments; the treaty undoubtedly marks a great progressive step toward improving Far Eastern diplomacy.

The question of Shantung and the Twenty-one Demands involved Japan and China alone, but were not without interest to the conference. The Shantung issue was settled by a treaty signed at Washington, though not as a part of the conference. Under it Japan restored all the rights and privileges formerly held by the German Government and later transferred to Japan by the Treaty of Versailles. On the other hand, China acknowledged the validity of the Sino-Japanese treaty of 1915, the Sino-Japanese agreement of 1918, and the Treaty of Versailles. In other words, the technicality with which China had been fighting Japan since the Peace Conference at Paris was thrown into the junk-pile once for all by the Washington Treaty. On the Twenty-one Demands Japan offered several modifications, but China wanted a complete renouncement. The conference, the majority of whose participants were signatories of the Treaty of Versailles, could not do more than accept the offers of Japan. China was defeated once more as she had been in Paris. But when the original Russian lease of the Liaotung Peninsula expired in 1923, the Chinese Government undertook to notify Japan of that fact, but the latter paid no attention to it. Japan is likely to remain in that region for many years to come.

Aside from these treaties, several resolutions were adopted by the conference whereby the powers pledged themselves to discontinue to exercise rights and privileges which they had assumed to enjoy. The United States, Great Britain, France, and Japan maintained their post offices in China, but these were completely withdrawn by January 1, 1923. The powers agreed to withdraw their armed forces stationed in China "without the authority of any treaty or agreement whenever China shall assure the protection of the lives and property of foreigners in China." Accordingly Japan withdrew her troops of this category from China. The powers acceded to China her request that the use of their radio stations authorized in China would be confined to official messages, while their unauthorized ones would be transferred to her. They pledged themselves to make public their treaties, conventions, exchange of notes, or other international instruments, made in the past concerning China. They further agreed to notify each other of their future treaties, conventions, and so forth, with China. In this connection, it should be mentioned that China demanded that "the Powers agree not to conclude between themselves any treaty or agreement directly affecting China or the general peace in the Pacific and the Far East without previously notifying China and giving her an opportunity to participate." The British delegate reminded the Chinese that their demand "went a good deal beyond any existing practice of international law." The Japanese delegate recalled that "the sovereign nations had the right of concluding any treaty or agreement between themselves." But a resolution was adopted whereby the powers would refrain from concluding treaties that would infringe the open-door principle.

The settlement of the Chinese Eastern Railway was left to diplomatic channels; meanwhile the powers reserved "the right to insist hereafter upon the responsibilities of China for performance or non-performance of the obligations toward the foreign stockholders, bondholders, and creditors of the Chinese Eastern Railway." For the future of China's railways, the powers expressed their hope for the ultimate "unification of railways into a railway system under Chinese control with foreign financial and technical co-operation." Such were the altruistic contributions of the conference toward helping China, but the conference reminded China of her own responsibilities. For instance, it gave China concrete advice that she should reduce her army because it had been causing severe drain upon her notoriously bankrupt treasury. This advice was given when the powers agreed to raise China's tariff, and was later put in the form of a resolution, but this was not to be interpreted as an interference with Chinese domestic affairs.

Of course, China demanded that the powers relinquish their extraterritorial rights in China "at the end of a definite period." In response, the conference created an international commission to look into the actual state of affairs, to advise the powers what they might do with regard to their extraterritorial rights. Obviously one could not draw an optimistic conclusion as to their abrogation; the actual conditions in China did not warrant such a conclusion.[2] At any rate, China was obliged to ask the powers to postpone the proposed investigation into the actual state of administration of justice. The Commission was finally convened on January 12, 1926; it continued its session until May 5, when the Commissioners started a tour of inspection through several provinces. Its report was far from encouraging; it recommended certain modifications to minimize difficulties arising from the system of extraterritoriality; it advised the Chinese Government to effect certain reforms in its laws and legal institutions, and it did not favor the relinquishment of the system.

Finally, the Chinese demanded that the leased areas and spheres of influence in their country be abrogated, and that arms and ammunition be not imported into their territory. The conference was unable to agree on any of these demands. Thus, aside from the leasehold of Kiaochow, all the leased areas remain intact. The powers agreed not to create new spheres of influence, but the existing ones remain untouched. Italy prevented any agreement on arms embargo. So much then for what the conference succeeded or failed to achieve on behalf of China.

The Siberian question loomed large at Washington, but its main issue was whether Japan would withdraw her troops from Siberia. The Japanese delegate declared that Japan would withdraw as soon as she could, and this pledge the Japanese Government fulfilled. Likewise the

[2] See G. B. Rea, "Facing the Facts," in the *Far Eastern Review,* September, 1922, pp. 565–68.

question of Yap was settled by a treaty between the United States and Japan.

We have traced the circumstances leading up to the summoning of the Washington Conference; we have examined the matters discussed by the gathering; and we have analyzed the achievements made by the participating nations. We are now ready for a critical estimate of this international conference, and will begin by presenting the official estimates of its accomplishments. President Harding in closing the gathering said, among other things:

> This Conference has wrought a truly great achievement. It is hazardous sometimes to speak in superlatives, and I will be restrained. But I will say, with every confidence, that the faith plighted here today, kept in national honor, will mark the beginning of a new and better epoch in human progress.[3]

Similar sentiments were expressed by the various representatives of the other participating nations.[4] Later the American delegation made its report to the President in which we find the following estimate:

> The sum total of the action taken by the Conference regarding China, together with the return of Shantung by direct agreement between China and Japan, the withdrawal of the most unsatisfactory of the so-called "Twenty-One Demands," and the explicit declaration of Japan regarding the closely connected territory of Eastern Siberia, justify the relation of confidence and good will expressed in the Four-Power Treaty and upon which the reduction of armament provided in the Naval Treaty may be contemplated with a sense of security.[5]

[3] *Document*, p. 867.

[4] See the speeches made, on February 4, by Balfour, Sarraut, Schanzer, Shidehara, Cartier, Sze, Van Blokland, and d'Alte, *Document*, pp. 212–28.

[5] *Document*, pp. 866–67.

Contemporary press views were no less enthusiastic over the conference achievements; an editorial of the *Washington Post,* February 5, 1922, epitomizes these sentiments in the following words:

> One nation could have blocked the conference. No nation did so, but on the contrary each nation strived to adapt its plans and interests to the general plan for limitation. The outcome is success instead of disappointment. The world has moved forward a distinct step, not merely in the limitation of armament, but in the knowledge that a conference of nations can be held and agreements reached by the voluntary co-operation of sovereign wills.
>
> It is this latter fact which encourages lovers of peace throughout the world, and which will give an impetus to the splendid project for a permanent world association of nations. There is more reason today, February 5, 1922, for confidence in the successful formation of such an organization than there was yesterday, February 4, before the greatest nations had solemnly pledged themselves to safeguard the integrity of China. They took this pledge voluntarily, as sovereigns, mutually co-operating for the world's welfare. They sacrificed selfish interest to make this pledge. That fact speaks volumes for the betterment of human conditions.[6]

Nearly eight years have elapsed since the memorable November 12, 1921, and we have an opportunity to evaluate the conference in a better perspective, especially in view of the crowded events which have followed its close. On the Washington arms treaties we have already presented our view that, in spite of the general lamentation of naval experts of the various signatory powers, these agreements have already contributed toward a betterment of the world. On the post-conference armament development, and, in particular, the failure of the three-power naval

---

[6] The *Washington Post,* February 5, 1922.

conference at Geneva, we have stated that our position is one of optimism. The nations are being educated as to the fallacy of upholding their dignity by arming themselves to the teeth.

But in China chaos has continued to prevail, and the powers have been forced to face difficulties just as before the conference. Patient, watchful waiting seems to be the only way out of the situation. It has been perhaps fortunate for China that the powers have no longer approached her with a united front as in the past; she has had and has an opportunity to deal with each nation separately. If she proceeds patiently and wisely, there is no reason why she should not be able to free herself from the disabilities imposed on her by foreign powers, but, in order to do so successfully, she must develop and maintain a unified, stable government. Opinion is divided on the recently established Nationalist Government; it may hold its own or it may collapse; nobody can prophesy its outcome one way or the other. Nevertheless, this Government secured the recognition of the American Government and a number of others, and if China succeeds in this respect with all the other nations vitally interested in her, we may justly hope for the better. Yet optimism is not warranted, and pessimism seems prejudicial to Chinese interests; it is for China to prove her case.

Aside from the very gloomy state of affairs in China, the general situation in Pacific international affairs shows a considerable improvement. Consider Japan's relations with America, the British Empire, France, and Russia. The only sore spot still left unhealed in friendly relations between America and Japan is the discriminatory exclusion of Japanese from the United States. The deep resentment of the Japanese against this treatment is not fully appreciated in this country; it is a question which has to be tackled sooner or later. The British and the Japanese have been getting along with no deterioration in their international relationship despite the termination of the Anglo-Japanese Alliance; Australia, once very suspicious of Japan, is now friendly.[7] Likewise Japan enjoys amicable relationships with France and Russia. Of late much has been said on Anglo-American antagonism, and on European hostility against America, but when their relationships are surveyed from the Pacific standpoint, there is no substantial ground for any real danger. Perhaps the recent Pact of Paris will facilitate in the maintaining of general peace in the Pacific region. The Washington Conference ushered in an era of peace; it is for the nations to continue it. The peoples of all the nations bordering the Pacific are anxious to maintain peace, as is clearly attested by their organized international efforts to learn to cooperate in solving their problems, the most conspicuous example being the Institute of Pacific Relations.

[7] See E. L. Piesse, "Japan and Australia," in *Foreign Affairs*, April 1926, pp. 475–88.

APPENDIX

DOCUMENTS AND BIBLIOGRAPHY

APPENDIX I

THE PROPOSAL OF THE UNITED STATES FOR A LIMITATION OF NAVAL ARMAMENTS[1]

The United States proposes the following plan for a limitation of the naval armaments of the conferring nations. The United States believes that this plan safely guards the interests of all concerned.

In working out this proposal the United States has been guided by four general principles:

A. The elimination of all capital-ship building programs, either actual or projected.
B. Further reduction through the scrapping of certain of the older ships.
C. That regard should be had to the existing naval strength of the conferring powers.
D. The use of capital-ship tonnage as the measurement of strength for navies and a proportionate allowance of auxiliary combatant craft prescribed.

CAPITAL SHIPS

UNITED STATES

1. The United States to scrap all new capital ships now under construction and on their way to completion. This includes 6 battle cruisers and 7 battleships on the ways and building and 2 battleships launched.

Note.—Paragraph 1 involves a reduction of 15 new capital ships under construction, with a total tonnage when completed of 618,000 tons. Total amount of money already spent on 15 capital ships, $332,000,000.

2. The United States to scrap all battleships up to, but not including, the *Delaware* and *North Dakota*.

Note.—The number of old battleships scrapped under paragraph 2 is 15; their total tonnage is 227,740 tons. The grand total of capital ships to be scrapped is 30, aggregating 845,740 tons.

[1] *Document,* pp. 56–63.

Great Britain

3. Great Britain to stop further construction of the 4 new *Hoods*.

Note.—Paragraph 3 involves a reduction of 4 new capital ships not yet laid down, but upon which money has been spent, with a total tonnage when completed of 172,000 tons.

4. In addition to the 4 *Hoods,* Great Britain to scrap her pre-dreadnoughts, second-line battleships and first-line battleships up to, but not including, the *King George V* class.

Note.—Paragraph 4 involves the disposition of 19 capital ships (certain of which have already been scrapped) with a tonnage reduction of 411,375 tons. The grand total tonnage of ships scrapped under this agreement will be 583,375 tons.

Japan

5. Japan to abandon her program of ships not yet laid down, viz., the *Kii, Owari, No. 7, No. 8,* battleships, and *Nos. 5, 6, 7,* and *8,* battle cruisers.

Note.—Paragraph 5 does not involve the stopping of construction on any ship upon which construction has begun.

6. Japan to scrap 3 battleships: the *Mutsu* launched, the *Tosa* and *Kaga* building; and 4 battle cruisers: the *Amagi* and *Akagi* building, and the *Atago* and *Takao* not yet laid down but for which certain material has been assembled.

Note.—Paragraph 6 involves a reduction of 7 new capital ships under construction, with a total tonnage when completed of 288,100 tons.

7. Japan to scrap all pre-dreadnoughts and capital ships of the second line. This to include the scrapping of all ships up to but not including the *Settsu*.

Note.—Paragraph 7 involves the scrapping of 10 older ships with a total tonnage of 159,928 tons. The grand total reduction of tonnage on vessels existing, laid down, or for which material has been assembled, is 448,928 tons.

France and Italy

8. In view of certain extraordinary conditions due to the World War affecting existing strengths of the navies of France

PROPOSAL FOR LIMITATION OF ARMAMENTS 355

and Italy, the United States does not consider necessary the discussion at this stage of the proceedings of the tonnage allowance of these nations, but proposes it be reserved for the later consideration of the Conference.

Other New Construction

9. No other capital ships shall be constructed during the period of this agreement except replacement tonnage as provided hereinafter.

10. If the terms of this proposal are agreed to then the United States, Great Britain, and Japan agree that their navies, three months after the making of this agreement, shall consist of the following capital ships:

LIST OF CAPITAL SHIPS

United States	Great Britain	Japan
Maryland	Royal Sovereign	Negato
California	Royal Oak	Hiuga
Tennessee	Resolution	Ise
Idaho	Ramillies	Yamashiro
Mississippi	Revenge	Fuso
New Mexico	Queen Elizabeth	Settsu
Arizona	Warspite	Kirishima
Pennsylvania	Valiant	Haruna
Oklahoma	Barham	Hiyei
Nevada	Malaya	Kongo
Texas	Benbow	Total 10
New York	Emperor of India	
Arkansas	Iron Duke	Total tonnage 299,700
Wyoming	Marlborough	
Utah	Erin	
Florida	King George V	
North Dakota	Centurion	
Delaware	Ajax	
Total 18	Hood	
	Renown	
Total tonnage 500,650	Repulse	
	Tiger	
	Total 22	
	Total tonnage 604,450	

DISPOSITION OF OLD AND NEW CONSTRUCTION

11. Capital ships shall be disposed of in accordance with methods to be agreed upon.

Replacements

12. (*a*) The tonnage basis for capital ship replacement under this proposal to be as follows:

    United States .... 500,000 tons
    Great Britain .... 500,000 tons
    Japan .... 300,000 tons

b) Capital ships twenty years from date of completion may be replaced by new capital ship construction, but the keels of such new construction shall not be laid until the tonnage which it is to replace is 17 years of age from date of completion. Provided, however, that the first replacement tonnage shall not be laid down until 10 years from the date of the signing of this agreement.

c) The scrapping of capital ships replaced by new construction shall be undertaken not later than the date of completion of the new construction and shall be completed within three months of the date of completion of new construction; or if the date of completion of new construction be delayed, then within four years of the laying of the keels of such new construction.

d) No capital ships shall be laid down during the term of this agreement whose tonnage displacement exceeds 35,000 tons.

e) The same rules for determining tonnage of capital ships shall apply to the ships of each of the Powers party to this agreement.

f) Each of the Powers party to this agreement agrees to inform promptly all of the other Powers party to this agreement concerning:

(1) The names of the capital ships to be replaced by new construction;
(2) The date of authorization of replacement tonnage;
(3) The dates of laying the keels of replacement tonnage;
(4) The displacement tonnage of each new ship to be laid down;

(5) The actual date of completion of each new ship;
(6) The fact and date of the scrapping of ships replaced.

g) No fabricated parts of capital ships, including parts of hulls, engines and ordnance, shall be constructed previous to the date of authorization of replacement tonnage. A list of such parts will be furnished all Powers party to this agreement.

h) In case of the loss or accidental destruction of capital ships, they may be replaced by new capital ship construction in conformity with the foregoing rules.

AUXILIARY COMBATANT CRAFT

13. In treating this subject auxiliary combatant craft have been divided into three classes:

a) Auxiliary surface combatant craft.
b) Submarines.
c) Airplane carriers and aircraft.

a) AUXILIARY SURFACE COMBATANT CRAFT

14. The term auxiliary surface combatant craft includes cruisers (exclusive of battle cruisers), flotilla leaders, destroyers, and all other surface types except those specifically exempted in the following paragraph.

15. Existing monitors, unarmored surface craft as specified in paragraph 16, under 3,000 tons, fuel ships, supply ships, tenders, repair ships, tugs, mine sweepers, and vessels readily convertible from merchant vessels are exempt from the terms of this agreement.

16. No new auxiliary combatant craft may be built exempt from this agreement regarding limitation of naval armaments that exceed 3,000 tons displacement and 15 knots speed, and carry more than four 5-inch guns.

17. It is proposed that the total tonnage of cruisers, flotilla leaders, and destroyers allowed each Power shall be as follows:

For the United States............	450,000 tons
For Great Britain..............	450,000 tons
For Japan	270,000 tons

Provided, however, that no Power party to this agreement whose total tonnage in auxiliary surface combatant craft on November 11, 1921, exceeds the prescribed tonnage shall be required to scrap such excess tonnage until replacements begin, at which time the total tonnage of auxiliary craft for each nation shall be reduced to the prescribed allowance as herein stated.

Limitation of New Construction

18. (*a*) All auxiliary surface combatant craft whose keels have been laid down by November 11, 1921, may be carried to completion.

b) No new construction in auxiliary surface combatant craft except replacement tonnage as provided hereinafter shall be laid down during the period of this agreement, provided, however, that such nations as have not reached the auxiliary surface combatant craft tonnage allowances hereinbefore stated may construct tonnage up to the limit of their allowance.

Scrapping of Old Construction

19. Auxiliary surface combatant craft shall be scrapped in accordance with methods to be agreed upon.

b) SUBMARINES

20. It is proposed that the total tonnage of submarines allowed each Power shall be as follows:

>   For the United States............ 90,000 tons
>   For Great Britain............... 90,000 tons
>   For Japan .... 54,000 tons

Provided, however, that no Power party to this agreement whose total tonnage in submarines on November 11, 1921, exceeds the prescribed tonnage shall be required to scrap such excess tonnage until replacements begin, at which time the total tonnage of submarines for each nation shall be reduced to the prescribed allowance as herein stated.

Limitation of New Construction

21. (*a*) All submarines whose keels have been laid down by November 11, 1921, may be carried to completion.

b) No new submarine tonnage except replacement tonnage as provided hereinafter shall be laid down during the period of this agreement; provided, however, that such nations as have not reached the submarine tonnage allowance hereinbefore stated may construct tonnage up to the limit of their allowance.

Scrapping of Old Construction

22. Submarines shall be scrapped in accordance with methods to be agreed upon.

c) AIRPLANE CARRIERS AND AIRCRAFT

Airplane Carriers

23. It is proposed that the total tonnage of airplane carriers allowed each Power shall be as follows:

United States	80,000 tons
Great Britain	80,000 tons
Japan	48,000 tons

Provided, however, that no Power party to this agreement whose total tonnage in airplane carriers on November 11, 1921, exceeds the prescribed tonnage shall be required to scrap such excess tonnage until replacements begin, at which time the total tonnage of airplane carriers for each nation shall be reduced to the prescribed allowance as herein stated.

Limitation of New Construction

24. (*a*) All airplane carriers whose keels have been laid down by November 11, 1921, may be carried to completion.

b) No new airplane carrier tonnage except replacement tonnage as provided herein shall be laid down during the period of this agreement; provided, however, that such nations as have not reached the airplane carrier tonnage hereinbefore stated may construct tonnage up to the limit of their allowance.

Scrapping of Old Construction

25. Airplane carriers shall be scrapped in accordance with methods to be agreed upon.

AUXILIARY COMBATANT CRAFT

Replacements

26. (*a*) Cruisers 17 years of age from date of completion may be replaced by new construction. The keels for such new construction shall not be laid until the tonnage it is intended to replace is 15 years of age from date of completion.

b) Destroyers and flotilla leaders 12 years of age from date of completion may be replaced by new construction. The keels of such new construction shall not be laid until the tonnage it is intended to replace is 11 years of age from date of completion.

c) Submarines 12 years of age from date of completion may be replaced by new submarine construction, but the keels of such new construction shall not be laid until the tonnage which the new tonnage is to replace is 11 years of age from date of completion.

d) Airplane carriers 20 years of age from date of completion may be replaced by new airplane carrier construction, but the keels of such new construction shall not be laid until the tonnage which it is to replace is 17 years of age from date of completion.

e) No surface vessel carrying guns of caliber greater than 8 inches shall be laid down as replacement tonnage for auxiliary combatant surface craft.

f) The same rules for determining tonnage of auxiliary combatant craft shall apply to the ships of each of the Powers party to this agreement.

g) The scrapping of ships replaced by new construction shall be undertaken not later than the date of completion of the new construction and shall be completed within three months of the date of completion of the new construction, or, if the completion of new tonnage is delayed, then within 4 years of the laying of the keels of such new construction.

h) Each of the Powers party to this agreement agrees to inform all other Powers party to this agreement concerning:
  (1) The names or numbers of the ships to be replaced by new construction;
  (2) The date of authorization of replacement tonnage;
  (3) The dates of laying the keels of replacement tonnage;

(4) The displacement tonnage of each new ship to be laid down;
(5) The actual date of completion of each new ship;
(6) The fact and date of the scrapping of ships replaced.

i) No fabricated parts of auxiliary combatant craft, including parts of hulls, engines, and ordnance, will be constructed previous to the date of authorization of replacement tonnage. A list of such parts will be furnished all Powers party to this agreement.

j) In case of the loss or accidental destruction of ships of this class they may be replaced by new construction in conformity with the foregoing rules.

AIRCRAFT

27. The limitation of naval aircraft is not proposed.

Note.—Owing to the fact that naval aircraft may be readily adapted from special types of commercial aircraft, it is not considered practicable to prescribe limits for naval aircraft.

GENERAL RESTRICTION ON TRANSFER OF COMBATANT VESSELS OF ALL CLASSES

28. The Powers party to this agreement bind themselves not to dispose of combatant vessels of any class in such a manner that they later may become combatant vessels in another navy. They bind themselves further not to acquire combatant vessels from any foreign source.

29. No capital-ship tonnage nor auxiliary combatant craft tonnage for foreign account shall be constructed within the jurisdiction of any one of the Powers party to this agreement during the term of this agreement.

MERCHANT MARINE

30. As the importance of the merchant marine is in inverse ratio to the size of naval armaments, regulations must be provided to govern its conversion features for war purposes.

APPENDIX II

PROVISIONAL AGREEMENT BETWEEN THE UNITED STATES, BRITISH EMPIRE, AND JAPAN

The following are the points of agreement that have been reached in the course of the negotiations between the United States of America, Great Britain, and Japan with respect to their capital fighting ships:

An agreement has been reached between the three powers—the United States of America, the British Empire, and Japan—on the subject of naval ratio. The proposal of the American Government that the ratio should be 5-5-3 is accepted. It is agreed that with respect to fortifications and naval bases in the Pacific region, including Hongkong, the *status quo* shall be maintained, that is, that there shall be no increase in these fortifications and naval bases except that this restriction shall not apply to the Hawaiian Islands, Australia, New Zealand, and the islands composing Japan proper, or, of course, to the coasts of the United States and Canada, as to which the respective powers retain their entire freedom.

The Japanese Government had found special difficulty with respect to the "Mutsu," as that is their newest ship. In order to retain the "Mutsu," Japan has proposed to scrap the "Settsu," one of her older ships, which, under the American proposal, was to have been retained. This would leave the number of Japan's capital ships the same, that is, 10, as under the American proposal. The retention of the "Mutsu" by Japan in place of the "Settsu" makes a difference in net tonnage of 13,600 tons, making the total tonnage of Japan's capital ships 313,300 tons, as against 299,700 tons under the original American proposal.

While the difference in tonnage is small, there would be considerable difference in efficiency, as the retention of the "Mutsu" would give to Japan 2 post-Jutland ships of the latest design.

In order to meet this situation and to preserve the relative strength on the basis of the agreed ratio, it is agreed that the United States shall complete two of the ships in course of construction, that is, the "Colorado" and the "Washington," which are now about 90 per cent completed, and scrap two older ships, that is, the "North Dakota" and the "Delaware," which under the original proposal were to be retained.

This would leave the United States with the same number of capital ships, that is, 18, as under the original proposal, with a tonnage of 525,850 tons, as against 500,650 tons as originally proposed. Three of the ships would be post-Jutland ships of the "Maryland" type.

As the British have no post-Jutland ships, except one "Hood," the construction of which is only partly post-Jutland, it is agreed that in order to maintain proper relative strength the British Government may construct two new ships not to exceed 35,000 legend tons each, that is, calculating the tonnage according to British standards of measurement, or, according to American calculations, the equivalent of 37,000 tons each.

It is agreed that the British Government shall, on the completion of these two new ships, scrap four of their ships of the "King George V" type, that is the "Erin," the "King George V," the "Centurion," and the "Ajax," which were to have been retained under the original American proposal. This would leave the British capital ships in number 20, as against 22 under the American proposal. Taking the tonnage of the two new ships, according to American calculation, it would amount to 74,000, and the four ships scrapped having a tonnage of 96,400 tons, there would be a reduction in net tonnage of 22,400 tons, leaving the British tonnage of capital ships 582,050 instead of 604,450.

This would give the British as against the United States an excess of 56,200 tons, which is deemed to be fair, in view of the age of the ships of the "Royal Sovereign" and the "Queen Elizabeth" types.

The maximum limitation for the tonnage of ships to be constructed in replacement is to be fixed at 35,000 legend tons, that is, according to British standards of measurement, or, according to American calculations, the equivalent of 37,000 tons, in order to give accommodation to these changes. The maximum tonnage of capital ships is fixed, for the purpose of replacement, on the basis of American standards of calculations, as follows:

United States...................... 525,000 tons
Great Britain..................... 525,000 tons
Japan .... 315,000 tons

Comparing this arrangement with the original American proposal, it will be observed that the United States is to scrap 30 ships as proposed, save that there will be scrapped 13 of the 15 ships under construction and 17 instead of 15 of the older ships.

The total tonnage of the American capital ships to be scrapped under the original proposal, including the tonnage of ships in construction, if completed, was stated to be 845,740 tons. Under the present arrangement the tonnage of the 30 ships to be scrapped, taking that of the ships in construction if completed, will be 820,540 tons.

The number of the Japanese ships to be retained remains the same as under the original proposal. The total tonnage of the ships to be scrapped by Japan under the original American proposal, taking the tonnage of new ships when completed, was stated to be 448,923 tons. The total tonnage of the ships to be scrapped under the present arrangement is 435,326 tons.

Under the original proposal Great Britain was to scrap 19 capital ships (including certain pre-dreadnoughts already scrapped), whereas under the present arrangement she will scrap four more, or a total of 23. The total tonnage of ships to be scrapped by Great Britain, including the tonnage of the four "Hoods," to which the proposal referred as laid down, if completed, was stated to be 583,375 tons. The corresponding total of scrapped ships under the new arrangement will be 22,600 tons more, or 605,975 tons.

Under the American proposal there were to be scrapped 66 capital fighting ships built and building, with a total tonnage (taking ships laid down as completed), of 1,878,043 tons. Under the present arrangement, on the same basis of calculations, there are to be scrapped 68 capital fighting ships, with a tonnage of 1,861,643 tons.

The naval holiday of ten years with respect to capital ships, as originally proposed by the American Government, is to be maintained except for the permission to construct ships as above stated. This arrangement between the United States, Great Britain, and Japan is, so far as the number of ships to be retained and scrapped is concerned, dependent upon a suitable agreement with France and Italy as to their capital ships, a matter which is now in course of negotiations.

APPENDIX III

A TREATY BETWEEN THE UNITED STATES OF AMERICA, THE BRITISH EMPIRE, FRANCE, ITALY, AND JAPAN, LIMITING NAVAL ARMAMENT[1]

The United States of America, the British Empire, France, Italy, and Japan;

Desiring to contribute to the maintenance of the general peace, and to reduce the burdens of competition in armament;

Have resolved, with a view to accomplishing these purposes, to conclude a treaty to limit their respective naval armament, and to that end have appointed as their Plenipotentiaries;

(Here follows a list of delegates.)

Who, having communicated to each other their respective full powers, found to be in good and due form, have agreed as follows:

CHAPTER I

GENERAL PROVISIONS RELATING TO THE LIMITATION OF NAVAL ARMAMENT

Article I.—The Contracting Powers agree to limit their respective naval armament as provided in the present Treaty.

Article II.—The Contracting Powers may retain respectively the capital ships which are specified in chapter ii, Part 1. On the coming into force of the present Treaty, but subject to the following provisions of this Article, all other capital ships, built or building, of the United States, the British Empire and Japan shall be disposed of as prescribed in chapter ii, Part 2.

In addition to the capital ships specified in chapter ii, Part 1, the United States may complete and retain two ships of the *West Virginia* class now under construction. On the completion of these two ships the *North Dakota* and *Delaware* shall be disposed of as prescribed in chapter ii, Part 2.

The British Empire may, in accordance with the replacement table in chapter ii, Part 3, construct two new capital ships not exceeding 35,000 tons (35,560 metric tons) standard displacement

[1] *Document*, pp. 871–85.

each. On the completion of the said two ships the *Thunderer, King George V, Ajax,* and *Centurion* shall be disposed of as prescribed in chapter ii, Part 2.

Article III.—Subject to the provisions of Article II, the Contracting Powers shall abandon their respective capital-ship building programs, and no new capital ships shall be constructed or acquired by any of the Contracting Powers except replacement tonnage which may be constructed or acquired as specified in chapter ii, Part 3.

Ships which are replaced in accordance with chapter ii, Part 3, shall be disposed of as prescribed in Part 2 of that chapter.

Article IV.—The total capital-ship replacement tonnage of each of the Contracting Powers shall not exceed in standard displacement, for the United States 525,000 tons (533,400 metric tons); for the British Empire 525,000 tons (533,400 metric tons); for France 175,000 tons (177,800 metric tons); for Italy 175,000 tons (177,800 metric tons); for Japan 315,000 tons (320,040 metric tons).

Article V.—No capital ship exceeding 35,000 tons (35,560 metric tons) standard displacement shall be acquired by, or constructed by, for, or within the jurisdiction of, any of the Contracting Powers.

Article VI.—No capital ship of any of the Contracting Powers shall carry a gun with a caliber in excess of 16 inches (406 millimeters).

Article VII.—The total tonnage for aircraft carriers of each of the Contracting Powers shall not exceed in standard displacement, for the United States 135,000 tons (137,160 metric tons); for the British Empire 135,000 tons (137,160 metric tons); for France 60,000 tons (60,960 metric tons); for Italy 60,000 tons (60,960 metric tons); for Japan 81,000 tons (82,296 metric tons).

Article VIII.—The replacement of aircraft carriers shall be effected only as prescribed in chapter ii, Part 3, provided, however, that all aircraft carrier tonnage in existence or building on November 12, 1921, shall be considered experimental, and may be replaced, within the total tonnage limit prescribed in Article VII, without regard to its age.

Article IX.—No aircraft carrier exceeding 27,000 tons (27,432 metric tons) standard displacement shall be acquired by, or constructed by, for, or within the jurisdiction of, any of the Contracting Powers.

However, any of the Contracting Powers may, provided that its total tonnage allowance of aircraft carriers is not thereby exceeded, build not more than two aircraft carriers, each of a tonnage of not more than 33,000 tons (33,528 metric tons) standard displacement, and in order to effect economy any of the Contracting Powers may use for this purpose any two of their ships, whether constructed or in course of construction, which would otherwise be scrapped under the provisions of Article II. The armament of any aircraft carriers exceeding 27,000 tons (27,432 metric tons) standard displacement shall be in accordance with the requirements of Article X, except that the total number of guns to be carried in case any of such guns be of a calibre exceeding 6 inches (152 millimeters), except anti-aircraft guns and guns not exceeding 5 inches (127 millimeters), shall not exceed eight.

Article X.—No aircraft carrier of any of the Contracting Powers shall carry a gun with a caliber in excess of 8 inches (203 millimeters). Without prejudice to the provisions of Article IX, if the armament carried includes guns exceeding 6 inches (152 millimeters) in caliber the total number of guns carried, except anti-aircraft guns and guns not exceeding 5 inches (127 millimeters), shall not exceed ten. If alternatively the armament contains no guns exceeding 6 inches (152 millimeters) in caliber, the number of guns is not limited. In either case the number of anti-aircraft guns and of guns not exceeding 5 inches (127 millimeters) is not limited.

Article XI.—No vessel of war exceeding 10,000 tons (10,160 metric tons) standard displacement, other than a capital ship or aircraft carrier, shall be acquired by, or constructed by, for, or within the jurisdiction of, any of the Contracting Powers. Vessels not specifically built as fighting ships nor taken in time of peace under government control for fighting purposes, which are employed on fleet duties or as troop transports or in some other way for the purpose of assisting in the prosecution of hostilities otherwise than as fighting ships, shall not be within the limitations of this Article.

Article XII.—No vessel of war of any of the Contracting Powers, hereafter laid down, other than a capital ship, shall carry a gun with a caliber in excess of 8 inches (203 millimeters).

Article XIII.—Except as provided in Article IX, no ship designated in the present Treaty to be scrapped may be reconverted into a vessel of war.

Article XIV.—No preparations shall be made in merchant ships in time of peace for the installation of warlike armaments for the purpose of converting such ships into vessels of war, other than the necessary stiffening of decks for the mounting of guns not exceeding 6-inch (152 millimeters) caliber.

Article XV.—No vessel of war constructed within the jurisdiction of any of the Contracting Powers for a non-Contracting Power shall exceed the limitations as to displacement and armament prescribed by the present Treaty for vessels of a similar type which may be constructed by or for any of the Contracting Powers; provided, however, that the displacement for aircraft carriers constructed for a non-Contracting Power shall in no case exceed 27,000 tons (27,432 metric tons) standard displacement.

Article XVI.—If the construction of any vessel of war for a non-Contracting Power is undertaken within the jurisdiction of any of the Contracting Powers, such Power shall promptly inform the other Contracting Powers of the date of the signing of the contract and the date on which the keel of the ship is laid; and shall also communicate to them the particulars relating to the ship prescribed in chapter ii, Part 3, Section I (*b*), (4) and (5).

Article XVII.—In the event of a Contracting Power being engaged in war, such Power shall not use as a vessel of war any vessel of war which may be under construction within its jurisdiction for any other Power, or which may have been constructed within its jurisdiction for another Power and not delivered.

Article XVIII.—Each of the Contracting Powers undertakes not to dispose by gift, sale or any mode of transfer of any vessel of war in such a manner that such vessel may become a vessel of war in the Navy of any foreign Power.

Article XIX.—The United States, the British Empire and Japan agree that the *status quo* at the time of the signing of the present Treaty, with regard to fortifications and naval bases, shall be maintained in their respective territories and possessions specified hereunder:

1. The insular possessions which the United States now holds or may hereafter acquire in the Pacific Ocean, except (*a*) those adjacent to the coast of the United States, Alaska and the Panama Canal Zone, not including the Aleutian Islands, and (*b*) the Hawaiian Islands;

2. Hongkong and the insular possessions which the British Empire now holds or may hereafter acquire in the Pacific Ocean, east of the meridian of 110° east longitude, except (*a*) those adjacent to the coast of Canada, (*b*) the Commonwealth of Australia and its Territories, and (*c*) New Zealand.

3. The following insular territories and possessions of Japan in the Pacific Ocean, to wit: the Kurile Islands, the Bonin Islands, Amami-Oshima, the Loochoo Islands, Formosa and the Pescadores, and any insular territories or possessions in the Pacific Ocean which Japan may hereafter acquire.

The maintenance of the *status quo* under the foregoing provisions implies that no new fortifications or naval bases shall be established in the territories and possessions specified; that no measures shall be taken to increase the existing naval facilities for the repair and maintenance of naval forces, and that no increase shall be made in the coast defences of the territories and possessions above specified. This restriction, however, does not preclude such repair and replacement of worn-out weapons and equipment as is customary in naval and military establishments in time of peace.

Article XX.—The rules for determining tonnage displacement prescribed in chapter ii, Part 4, shall apply to the ships of each of the Contracting Powers.

CHAPTER II

RULES RELATING TO THE EXECUTION OF THE TREATY—DEFINITION OF TERMS

PART 1. CAPITAL SHIPS WHICH MAY BE RETAINED BY THE CONTRACTING POWERS

In accordance with Article II ships may be retained by each of the Contracting Powers as specified in this Part.

Ships which may be retained by the United States:

Name	Tonnage
Maryland	32,600
California	32,300
Tennessee	32,300
Idaho	32,000
New Mexico	32,000
Mississippi	32,000
Arizona	31,400
Pennsylvania	31,400
Oklahoma	27,500
Nevada	27,500
New York	27,000
Texas	27,000
Arkansas	26,000
Wyoming	26,000
Florida	21,825
Utah	21,825
North Dakota	20,000
Delaware	20,000
Total tonnage	500,650

On the completion of the two ships of the *West Virginia* class and the scrapping of the *North Dakota* and *Delaware,* as provided in Article II, the total tonnage to be retained by the United States will be 525,850 tons.

Ships which may be retained by the British Empire:

Name	Tonnage
Royal Sovereign	25,750
Royal Oak	25,750
Revenge	25,750
Resolution	25,750
Ramillies	25,750
Malaya	27,500
Valiant	27,500
Barham	27,500
Queen Elizabeth	27,500
Warspite	27,500
Benbow	25,000
Emperor of India	25,000
Iron Duke	25,000
Marlborough	25,000

THE NAVAL TREATY

Name	Tonnage
Hood	41,200
Renown	26,500
Repulse	26,500
Tiger	28,500
Thunderer	22,500
King George V	23,000
Ajax	23,000
Centurion	23,000
Total tonnage	580,450

On the completion of the two new ships to be constructed and the scrapping of the *Thunderer, King George V, Ajax,* and *Centurion,* as provided in Article II, the total tonnage to be retained by the British Empire will be 558,950 tons.

Ships which may be retained by France:

Name	Tonnage (metric tons)
Bretagne	23,500
Lorraine	23,500
Provence	23,500
Paris	23,500
France	23,500
Jean Bart	23,500
Courbet	23,500
Condorcet	18,890
Diderot	18,890
Voltaire	18,890
Total tonnage	221,170

France may lay down new tonnage in the years 1927, 1929, and 1931, as provided in Part 3, Section II.

Ships which may be retained by Italy:

Name	Tonnage (metric tons)
Andrea Doria	22,700
Caio Duilio	22,700
Conte Di Cavour	22,500
Giulio Cesare	22,500
Leonardo Da Vinci	22,500
Dante Alighieri	19,500
Roma	12,600
Napoli	12,600

Name	Tonnage (metric tons)
Vittorio Emanuele	12,600
Regina Elena	12,600
Total tonnage	182,800

Italy may lay down new tonnage in the years 1927, 1929, and 1931, as provided in Part 3, Section II.

Ships which may be retained by Japan:

Name	Tonnage
Mutsu	33,800
Nagato	33,800
Hiuga	31,260
Ise	31,260
Yamashiro	30,600
Fuso	30,600
Kirishima	27,500
Haruna	27,500
Hiyei	27,500
Kongo	27,500
Total tonnage	301,320

PART 2. RULES FOR SCRAPPING VESSELS OF WAR

The following rules shall be observed for the scrapping of vessels of war which are to be disposed of in accordance with Articles II and III.

I. A vessel to be scrapped must be placed in such condition that it cannot be put to combatant use.

II. This result must be finally effected in any of the following ways:

a) Permanent sinking of the vessel;

b) Breaking the vessel up. This shall always involve the destruction or removal of all machinery, boilers and armour, and all deck, side and bottom plating;

c) Converting the vessel to target use exclusively. In such case all the provisions of paragraph III of this Part, except sub-paragraph (6), in so far as may be necessary to enable the ship to be used as a mobile target, and except sub-paragraph (7), must be previously complied with. Not more than one capital ship may be retained for this purpose at one time by any of the Contracting Powers.

d) Of the capital ships which would otherwise be scrapped under the present Treaty in or after the year 1931, France and Italy may each retain two seagoing vessels for training purposes exclusively, that is, as gunnery or torpedo schools. The two vessels retained by France shall be of the *Jean Bart* class, and of those retained by Italy one shall be the *Dante Alighieri* and the other of the *Giulio Cesare* class. On retaining these ships for the purpose above stated, France and Italy respectively undertake to remove and destroy their conning-towers, and not to use the said ships as vessels of war.

III. (*a*) Subject to the special exceptions contained in Article IX, when a vessel is due for scrapping, the first stage of scrapping, which consists in rendering a ship incapable of further warlike service, shall be immediately undertaken.

b) A vessel shall be considered incapable of further warlike service when there shall have been removed and landed, or else destroyed in the ship:

(1) All guns and essential portions of guns, fire-control tops and revolving parts of all barbettes and turrets;

(2) All machinery for working hydraulic or electric mountings;

(3) All fire-control instruments and range-finders;

(4) All ammunition, explosives and mines;

(5) All torpedoes, war-heads and torpedo tubes;

(6) All wireless telegraphy installations;

(7) The conning tower and all side armour, or alternatively all main propelling machinery; and

(8) All landing and flying-off platforms and all other aviation accessories.

IV. The periods in which scrapping of vessels is to be effected are as follows:

a) In the case of vessels to be scrapped under the first paragraph of Article II, the work of rendering the vessels incapable of further warlike service, in accordance with paragraph III of this Part, shall be completed within six months from the coming into force of the present Treaty, and the scrapping shall be finally effected within eighteen months from such coming into force.

b) In the case of vessels to be scrapped under the second and third paragraphs of Article II, or under Article III, the work of rendering the vessel incapable of further warlike service in accordance with paragraph III of this Part shall be commenced not later than the date of completion of its successor, and shall be finished within six months from the date of such completion. The vessel shall be finally scrapped, in accordance with paragraph II of this Part, within eighteen months from the date of completion of its successor. If, however, the completion of the new vessel be delayed, then the work of rendering the old vessel incapable of further warlike service in accordance with paragraph III of this Part shall be commenced within four years from the laying of the keel of the new vessel, and shall be finished within six months from the date on which such work was commenced, and the old vessel shall be finally scrapped in accordance with paragraph II of this Part within eighteen months from the date when the work of rendering it incapable of further warlike service was commenced.

PART 3. REPLACEMENT

The replacement of capital ships and aircraft carriers shall take place according to the rules in Section I and the tables in Section II of this Part.

Section I

Rules for Replacement

a) Capital ships and aircraft carriers twenty years after the date of their completion may, except as otherwise provided in Article VIII and in the tables in Section II of this Part, be replaced by new construction, but within the limits prescribed in Article IV and Article VII. The keels of such new construction may, except as otherwise provided in Article VIII and in the tables in Section II of this Part, be laid down not earlier than seventeen years from the date of completion of the tonnage to be replaced, provided, however, that no capital-ship tonnage, with the exception of the ships referred to in the third paragraph of Article II, and the replacement tonnage specifically mentioned in

Section II of this Part, shall be laid down until ten years from November 12, 1921.

b) Each of the Contracting Powers shall communicate promptly to each of the other Contracting Powers the following information:

(1) The names of the capital ships and aircraft carriers to be replaced by new construction;

(2) The date of governmental authorization of replacement tonnage;

(3) The date of laying the keels of replacement tonnage;

(4) The standard displacement in tons and metric tons of each new ship to be laid down, and the principal dimensions, namely, length at waterline, extreme beam at or below waterline, mean draft at standard displacement;

(5) The date of completion of each new ship and its standard displacement in tons and metric tons, and the principal dimensions, namely, length at waterline, extreme beam at or below waterline, mean draft at standard displacement, at time of completion.

c) In case of loss or accidental destruction of capital ships or aircraft carriers, they may immediately be replaced by new construction subject to the tonnage limits prescribed in Articles IV and VII and in conformity with the other provisions of the present Treaty, the regular replacement program being deemed to be advanced to that extent.

d) No retained capital ships or aircraft carriers shall be reconstructed except for the purpose of providing means of defense against air and submarine attack, and subject to the following rules: The Contracting Powers may, for that purpose, equip existing tonnage with bulge or blister or anti-air attack deck protection, providing the increase of displacement thus effected does not exceed 3,000 tons (3,048 metric tons) displacement for each ship. No alterations in side armour, in caliber, number or general type of mounting of main armament shall be permitted except:

(1) In the case of France and Italy, which countries within the limits allowed for bulge may increase their armour protection and the caliber of the guns now carried on their existing capital ships so as not to exceed 16 inches (406 millimeters) and

(2) The British Empire shall be permitted to complete, in the case of the *Renown,* the alterations to armour that have already been commenced but temporarily suspended.

Section II

REPLACEMENT AND SCRAPPING OF CAPITAL SHIPS—UNITED STATES

Year	Ships Laid Down	Ships Completed	Ships Scrapped (Age in Parentheses)	Pre-Jutland	Post-Jutland
			Maine (20), Missouri (20), Virginia (17), Nebraska (17), Georgia (17), New Jersey (17), Rhode Island (17), Connecticut (17), Louisiana (17), Vermont (16), Kansas (16), Minnesota (16), New Hampshire (15), South Carolina (13), Michigan (13), Washington (0), South Dakota (0), Indiana (0), Montana (0), North Carolina (0), Iowa (0), Massachusetts (0), Lexington (0), Constitution (0), Constellation (0), Saratoga (0), Ranger (0), United States (0),* Delaware	17	1
1922..	....	A, B†	(12), North Dakota (12).	15	3
1923..	....	....	....	15	3
1924..	....	....	....	15	3
1925..	....	....	....	15	3
1926..	....	....	....	15	3
1927..	....	....	....	15	3
1928..	....	....	....	15	3
1929..	....	....	....	15	3
1930..	....	....	....	15	3

* The United States may retain the *Oregon* and *Illinois,* for non-combatant purposes, after complying with the provisions of Part 2, III, (*b*).
† Two *West Virginia* class.

NOTE.—A, B, C, D, etc., represent individual capital ships of 35,000 tons standard displacement, laid down and completed in the years specified.

REPLACEMENT AND SCRAPPING OF CAPITAL SHIPS—UNITED STATES (*Continued*)

Year	Ships Laid Down	Ships Completed	Ships Scrapped (Ages in Parentheses)	Pre-Jutland	Post-Jutland
1931..	C, D	....	....	15	3
1932..	E, F	....	....	15	3
1933..	G	....	....	15	3
1934..	H, I	C, D	Florida (23), Utah (23), Wyoming (22)	12	5
1935..	J	E, F	Arkansas (23), Texas (21), New York (21)	9	7
1936..	K, L	G	Nevada (20), Oklahoma (20)	7	8
1937..	M	H, I	Arizona (21), Pennsylvania (21)	5	10
1938..	N, O	J	Mississippi (21)	4	11
1939..	P, Q	K, L	New Mexico (21), Idaho (20)	2	13
1940..	....	M	Tennessee (20)	1	14
1941..	....	N, O	California (20), Maryland (20)	0	15
1942..	....	P, Q	2 ships of West Virginia class	0	15

REPLACEMENT AND SCRAPPING OF CAPITAL SHIPS—BRITISH EMPIRE

Year	Ships Laid Down	Ships Completed	Ships Scrapped (Age in Parentheses)	Pre-Jutland	Post-Jutland
			Commonwealth (16), Agamemnon (13), Dreadnought (15), Bellerophon (12), St. Vincent (11), Inflexible (13), Superb (12), Neptune (10), Hercules (10), Indomitable (13), Temeraire (12), New Zealand (9), Lion (9), Princess Royal (9),	21	1

REPLACEMENT AND SCRAPPING OF CAPITAL SHIPS—BRITISH EMPIRE (*Continued*)

Year	Ships Laid Down	Ships Completed	Ships Scrapped (Age in Parentheses)	Pre-Jutland	Post-Jutland
1922..	A, B†	....	Conqueror (9), Monarch (9), Orion (9), Australia (8), Agincourt (7), Erin (7), 4 building or projected.*	21	1
1923..	....	....	....	21	1
1924..	....	....	....	21	1
1925..	....	A, B	King George V (13), Ajax (12), Centurion (12), Thunderer (13)	17	3
1926..	....	....	....	17	3
1927..	....	....	....	17	3
1928..	....	....	....	17	3
1929..	....	....	....	17	3
1930..	....	....	....	17	3
1931..	C, D	....	....	17	3
1932..	E, F	....	....	17	3
1933..	G	....	....	17	3
1934..	H, I	C, D	Iron Duke (20), Marlborough (20), Emperor of India (20), Benbow (20).	13	5
1935..	J	E, F	Tiger (21), Queen Elizabeth (20), Warspite (20), Barham (20)	9	7
1936..	K, L	G	Malaya (20), Royal Sovereign (20)	7	8
1937..	M	H, I	Revenge (21), Resolution (21)	5	10
1938..	N, O	J	Royal Oak (22)	4	11
1939..	P, Q	K, L	Valiant (23), Repulse (23).	2	13
1940..	....	M	Renown (24)	1	14
1941..	....	N, O	Ramillies (24), Hood (21).	0	15
1942..	....	P, Q	A (17), B (17)	0	15

* The British Empire may retain the *Colossus* and *Collingwood* for non-combatant purposes, after complying with the provisions of Part 2, III, (*b*).
† Two 35,000-ton ships, standard displacement.

NOTE.—A, B, C, D, etc., represent individual capital ships of 35,000 tons standard displacement laid down and completed in the years specified.

REPLACEMENT AND SCRAPPING OF CAPITAL SHIPS—FRANCE

Year	Ships Laid Down	Ships Completed	Ships Scrapped (Age in Parentheses)	Summary of Ships Retained Pre-Jutland	Summary of Ships Retained Post-Jutland
1922..	....	....	....	7	0
1923..	....	....	....	7	0
1924..	....	....	....	7	0
1925..	....	....	....	7	0
1926..	....	....	....	7	0
1927..	35,000 tons	....	....	7	0
1928..	....	....	....	7	0
1929..	35,000 tons	....	....	7	0
1930..	....	35,000 tons	Jean Bart (17), Courbet (17)	5	(*)
1931..	35,000 tons	....	....	5	(*)
1932..	35,000 tons	35,000 tons	France (18)	4	(*)
1933..	35,000 tons	....	....	4	(*)
1934..	....	35,000 tons	Paris (20), Bretagne (20)	2	(*)
1935..	....	35,000 tons	Provence (20)	1	(*)
1936..	....	35,000 tons	Lorraine (20)	0	(*)
1937..	....	....	....	0	(*)
1938..	....	....	....	0	(*)
1939..	....	....	....	0	(*)
1940..	....	....	....	0	(*)
1941..	....	....	....	0	(*)
1942..	....	....	....	0	(*)

* Within tonnage limitations; number not fixed.

NOTE.—France expressly reserves the right of employing the capital-ship tonnage allotment as she may consider advisable, subject solely to the limitations that the displacement of individual ships should not surpass 35,000 tons, and that the total capital-ship tonnage should keep within the limits imposed by the present treaty.

REPLACEMENT AND SCRAPPING OF CAPITAL SHIPS—ITALY

Year	Ships Laid Down	Ships Completed	Ships Scrapped (Age in Parentheses)	Pre-Jutland	Post-Jutland
1922				6	0
1923				6	0
1924				6	0
1925				6	0
1926				6	0
1927	35,000 tons			6	0
1928				6	0
1929	35,000 tons			6	0
1930				6	0
1931	35,000 tons	35,000 tons	Dante Alighieri (19)	5	(*)
1932	45,000 tons			5	(*)
1933	25,000 tons	35,000 tons	Leonardo da Vinci (19)	4	(*)
1934				4	(*)
1935		35,000 tons	Giulio Cesare (21)	3	(*)
1936		45,000 tons	Conte di Cavour (21) Duilio (21)	1	(*)
1937		25,000 tons	Andrea Doria (21)	0	(*)

Summary of Ships Retained

* Within tonnage limitations; number not fixed.

NOTE.—Italy expressly reserves the right of employing the capital-ship tonnage allotment as she may consider advisable, subject to the limitations that the displacement of individual ships should not surpass 35,000 tons, and the total capital-ship tonnage should keep within the limits imposed by the present treaty.

REPLACEMENT AND SCRAPPING OF CAPITAL SHIPS—JAPAN

Year	Ships Laid Down	Ships Completed	Ships Scrapped (Age in Parentheses)	Summary of Ships Retained Pre-Jutland	Summary of Ships Retained Post-Jutland
			Hizen (20), Mikasa (20), Kashima (16), Katori (16) Satsuma (12), Aki (11), Settsu (10), Ikoma (14), Ibuki (12), Kurama (11), Amagi (0), Akagi (0), Kaga (0), Tosa (0), Takao (0), Atago (0). Projected program 8 ships not laid down.*	8	
1922..	....	....	....	8	2
1923..	....	....	....	8	2
1924..	....	....	....	8	2
1925..	....	....	....	8	2
1926..	....	....	....	8	2
1927..	....	....	....	8	2
1928..	....	....	....	8	2
1929..	....	....	....	8	2
1930..	....	....	....	8	2
1931..	A	....	....	8	2
1932..	B	....	....	8	2
1933..	C	....	....	8	2
1934..	D	A	Kongo (21)	7	3
1935..	E	B	Hiyei (21), Haruna (20)..	5	4
1936..	F	C	Kirishima (21)	4	5
1937..	G	D	Fuso (22)	3	6
1938..	H	E	Yamashiro (21)	2	7
1939..	I	F	Ise (22)	1	8
1940..	....	G	Hiuga (22)	0	9
1941..	....	H	Nagato (21)	0	9
1942..	....	I	Mutsu (21)	0	9

* Japan may retain the *Shikishima* and *Asahi* for non-combatant purposes, after complying with the provisions of Part 2, III, (b).

NOTE.—A, B, C, D, etc., represent individual capital ships of 35,000 tons standard displacement, laid down and completed in the years specified.

NOTE APPLICABLE TO ALL THE TABLES IN SECTION II

The order above prescribed in which ships are to be scrapped is in accordance with their age. It is understood that when replacement begins according to the foregoing tables the order of scrapping in the case of the ships of each of the Contracting Powers may be varied at its option; provided, however, that such Power shall scrap in each year the number of ships above stated.

Part 4. Definitions

For the purposes of the present Treaty, the following expressions are to be understood in the sense defined in this part.

Capital Ship

A capital ship, in the case of ships hereafter built, is defined as a vessel of war, not an aircraft carrier, whose displacement exceeds 10,000 tons (10,160 metric tons) standard displacement, or which carries a gun with a caliber exceeding 8 inches (203 millimeters).

Aircraft Carrier

An aircraft carrier is defined as a vessel of war with a displacement in excess of 10,000 tons (10,160 metric tons) standard displacement designed for the specific and exclusive purpose of carrying aircraft. It must be so constructed that aircraft can be launched therefrom and landed thereon, and not designed and constructed for carrying a more powerful armament than that allowed to it under Article IX or Article X as the case may be.

Standard Displacement

The standard displacement of a ship is the displacement of the ship complete, fully manned, engined and equipped ready for sea, including all armament and ammunition, equipment, outfit, provisions and fresh water for crew, miscellaneous stores and implements of every description that are intended to be carried in war, but without fuel or reserve feed water on board.

The word "ton" in the present Treaty, except in the expression "metric tons," shall be understood to mean the ton of 2,240 pounds (1,016 kilos).

Vessels now completed shall retain their present ratings of displacement tonnage in accordance with their national system of measurement. However, a Power expressing displacement in metric tons shall be considered for the application of the present Treaty as owning only the equivalent displacement in tons of 2,240 pounds.

A vessel completed hereafter shall be rated at its displacement tonnage when in the standard condition defined herein.

CHAPTER III

MISCELLANEOUS PROVISIONS

Article XXI.—If during the term of the present Treaty the requirements of national security of any of the Contracting Powers in respect to naval defense are, in the opinion of that Power, materially affected by any change of circumstances, the Contracting Powers will, at the request of such Power, meet in conference with a view to the reconsideration of the provisions of the Treaty and its amendment by mutual agreement.

In view of possible technical and scientific developments, the United States, after consultation with the other Contracting Powers, shall arrange for a conference of all the Contracting Powers, which shall convene as soon as possible after the expiration of eight years from the coming into force of the present Treaty to consider what changes, if any, in the Treaty may be necessary to meet such developments.

Article XXII.—Whenever any Contracting Power shall become engaged in a war which in its opinion affects the naval defense of its national security, such Power may after notice to the other Contracting Powers suspend for the period of hostilities its obligations under the present Treaty other than those under Articles XIII and XVII, provided that such Power shall notify the other Contracting Powers that the emergency is of such a character as to require such suspension.

The remaining Contracting Powers shall in such case consult together with a view to agreement as to what temporary modifications if any should be made in the Treaty as between themselves. Should such consultation not produce agreement, duly made in accordance with the constitutional methods of the respective Powers, any one of the said Contracting Powers may, by giving notice to the other Contracting Powers, suspend for the period of hostilities its obligations under the present Treaty, other than those under Articles XIII and XVII.

On the cessation of hostilities the Contracting Powers will meet in conference to consider what modifications, if any, should be made in the provisions of the present Treaty.

Article XXIII.—The present Treaty shall remain in force until December 31st, 1926 and in case none of the Contracting Powers shall have given notice two years before that date of its intention to terminate the Treaty, it shall continue in force until the expiration of two years from the date on which notice of termination shall be given by one of the Contracting Powers, whereupon the Treaty shall terminate as regards all the Contracting Powers. Such notice shall be communicated in writing to the Government of the United States, which shall immediately transmit a certified copy of the notification to the other Powers and inform them of the date on which it was received. The notice shall be deemed to have been given and shall take effect on that date. In the event of notice of termination being given by the Government of the United States, such notice shall be given to the diplomatic representatives at Washington of the other Contracting Powers, and the notice shall be deemed to have been given and shall take effect on the date of the communication made to the said diplomatic representatives.

Within one year of the date on which a notice of termination by any Power has taken effect, all the Contracting Powers shall meet in conference.

Article XXIV.—The present Treaty shall be ratified by the Contracting Powers in accordance with their respective constitutional methods and shall take effect on the date of the deposit of all the ratifications, which shall take place at Washington as soon as possible. The Government of the United States will transmit to the other Contracting Powers a certified copy of the *procès-verbal* of the deposit of ratifications.

The present Treaty, of which the French and English texts are both authentic, shall remain deposited in the archives of the Government of the United States, and duly certified copies thereof shall be transmitted by that Government to the other Contracting Powers.

In faith whereof the above-named Plenipotentiaries have signed the present Treaty.

Done at the City of Washington the sixth day of February, One Thousand Nine Hundred and Twenty-Two.

APPENDIX IV

A TREATY IN RELATION TO THE USE OF SUBMARINES AND NOXIOUS GASES IN WARFARE[1]

The United States of America, the British Empire, France, Italy, and Japan, hereinafter referred to as the Signatory Powers, desiring to make more effective the rules adopted by civilized nations for the protection of the lives of neutrals and noncombatants at sea in time of war, and to prevent the use in war of noxious gases and chemicals, have determined to conclude a Treaty to this effect, and have appointed as their plenipotentiaries:

(Here follows a list of delegates.)

Who, having communicated their full powers, found in good and due form, have agreed as follows:

Article I.—The Signatory Powers declare that among the rules adopted by civilized nations for the protection of the lives of neutrals and non-combatants at sea in time of war, the following are to be deemed an established part of international law:

1. A merchant vessel must be ordered to submit to visit and search to determine its character before it can be seized.

A merchant vessel must not be attacked unless it refuse to submit to visit and search after warning, or to proceed as directed after seizure.

A merchant vessel must not be destroyed unless the crew and passengers have been first placed in safety.

2. Belligerent submarines are not under any circumstances exempt from the universal rules above stated; and if a submarine cannot capture a merchant vessel in conformity with these rules the existing law of nations requires it to desist from attack and from seizure and to permit the merchant vessel to proceed unmolested.

Article II.—The Signatory Powers invite all other civilized Powers to express their assent to the foregoing statement of es-

---

[1] *Document*, pp. 886–89.

tablished law so that there may be a clear public understanding throughout the world of the standards of conduct by which the public opinion of the world is to pass judgment upon future belligerents.

Article III.—The Signatory Powers, desiring to insure the enforcement of the humane rules of existing law declared by them with respect to attacks upon and the seizure and destruction of merchant ships, further declare that any person in the service of any Power who shall violate any of those rules, whether or not such person is under orders of a governmental superior, shall be deemed to have violated the laws of war and shall be liable to trial and punishment as if for an act of piracy and may be brought to trial before the civil or military authorities of any Power within the jurisdiction of which he may be found.

Article IV.—The Signatory Powers recognize the practical impossibility of using submarines as commerce destroyers without violating, as they were violated in the recent war of 1914–1918, the requirements universally accepted by civilized nations for the protection of the lives of neutrals and noncombatants, and to the end that the prohibition of the use of submarines as commerce destroyers shall be universally accepted as a part of the law of nations they now accept that prohibition as henceforth binding as between themselves and they invite all other nations to adhere thereto.

Article V.—The use in war of asphyxiating, poisonous, or other gases, and all analogous liquids, materials, or devices having been justly condemned by the general opinion of the civilized world and a prohibition of such use having been declared in treaties to which a majority of the civilized Powers are parties;

The Signatory Powers, to the end that this prohibition shall be universally accepted as a part of international law binding alike the conscience and practice of nations, declare their assent to such prohibition, agree to be bound thereby as between themselves, and invite all other civilized nations to adhere thereto.

Article VI.—The present Treaty shall be ratified as soon as possible in accordance with the constitutional methods of the Signatory Powers and shall take effect on the deposit of all ratifications, which shall take place at Washington.

The Government of the United States will transmit to all the Signatory Powers a certified copy of the *procès-verbal* of the deposit of ratifications.

The present Treaty, of which the French and English texts are both authentic, shall remain deposited in the archives of the Government of the United States, and duly certified copies thereof will be transmitted by that Government to each of the Signatory Powers.

Article VII.—The Government of the United States will further transmit to each of the Non-Signatory Powers a duly certified copy of the present Treaty and invite its adherence thereto.

Any Non-Signatory Power may adhere to the present Treaty by communicating an Instrument of Adherence to the Government of the United States, which will thereupon transmit to each of the Signatory and Adhering Powers a certified copy of each Instrument of Adherence.

In faith whereof, the above-named plenipotentiaries have signed the present Treaty.

Done at the City of Washington, the sixth day of February, one thousand nine hundred and twenty-two.

APPENDIX V

TREATY FOR THE SETTLEMENT OF OUTSTANDING QUESTIONS RELATIVE TO SHANTUNG[1]

Japan and China, being equally animated by a sincere desire to settle amicably and in accordance with their common interest outstanding questions relative to Shantung, have resolved to conclude a treaty for the settlement of such questions, and have to that end named as their plenipotentiaries, that is to say:

(Here follows a list of delegates.)

Who, having communicated to each other their respective full powers, found to be in good and due form, have agreed upon the following Articles:

SECTION I

RESTORATION OF THE FORMER GERMAN LEASED TERRITORY OF KIAOCHOW

Article I.—Japan shall restore to China the former German Leased Territory of Kiaochow.

Article II.—The Government of Japan and the Government of the Chinese Republic shall each appoint three Commissioners to form a Joint Commission, with powers to make and carry out detailed arrangements relating to the transfer of the administration of the former German Leased Territory of Kiaochow and to the transfer of public properties in the said territory and to settle other matters likewise requiring adjustment.

For such purposes, the Joint Commission shall meet immediately upon the coming into force of the present treaty.

Article III.—The transfer of the administration of the former German Leased Territory of Kiaochow and the transfer of public properties in the said territory, as well as the adjustment of other matters under the preceding article, shall be completed as

[1] *Conversations between the Chinese and Japanese Representatives in Regard to the Shantung Question, Prepared by the Japanese Delegation* (Washington, 1922), pp. 384–91.

soon as possible, and, in any case, not later than six months from the date of the coming into force of the present treaty.

Article IV.—The Government of Japan undertakes to hand over to the Government of the Chinese Republic, upon the transfer to China of the administration of the former German Leased Territory of Kiaochow, such archives, registers, plans, title-deeds and other documents in the possession of Japan, or certified copies thereof, as may be necessary for the transfer of the administration, as well as those that may be useful for the subsequent administration by China of the said territory and of the Fifty-Kilometer Zone around Kiaochow Bay.

SECTION II
TRANSFER OF PUBLIC PROPERTIES

Article V.—The Government of Japan undertakes to transfer to the Government of the Chinese Republic all public properties including land, buildings, works, or establishments in the former German Leased Territory of Kiaochow, whether formerly possessed by the German authorities, or purchased or constructed by the Japanese authorities during the period of the Japanese administration of the said territory, except those indicated in Article VII of the present treaty.

Article VI.—In the transfer of public properties under the preceding article, no compensation will be claimed from the Government of the Chinese Republic: *Provided,* however, that for those purchased or constructed by the Japanese authorities, and also for the improvements on or additions to those formerly possessed by the German authorities, the Government of the Chinese Republic shall refund a fair and equitable proportion of the expenses actually incurred by the Government of Japan, having regard to the principle of depreciation and continuing value.

Article VII.—Such public properties in the former German Leased Territory of Kiaochow as are required for the Japanese Consulate to be established at Tsingtao shall be retained by the Government of Japan, and those required more especially for the benefit of the Japanese community, including public schools, shrines, and cemeteries, shall be left in the hands of the said community.

Article VIII.—Details of the matters referred to in the preceding three articles shall be arranged by the Joint Commission provided for in Article II of the present treaty.

SECTION III

WITHDRAWAL OF JAPANESE TROOPS

Article IX.—The Japanese troops, including gendarmes, now stationed along the Tsingtao-Tsinanfu Railway and its branches, shall be withdrawn as soon as the Chinese police or military force shall have been sent to take over the protection of the railway.

Article X.—The disposition of the Chinese police or military force and the withdrawal of the Japanese troops under the preceding article may be effected in sections.

The date of the completion of such process for each section shall be arranged in advance between the competent authorities of Japan and China.

The entire withdrawal of such Japanese troops shall be effected within three months, if possible, and, in any case, not later than six months, from the date of the signatures of the present treaty.

Article XI.—The Japanese garrison at Tsingtao shall be completely withdrawn simultaneously, if possible, with the transfer to China of the administration of the former German Leased Territory of Kiaochow, and, in any case, not later than thirty days from the date of such transfer.

SECTION IV

MARITIME CUSTOMS AT TSINGTAO

Article XII.—The Custom House of Tsingtao shall be made an integral part of the Chinese Maritime Customs upon the coming into force of the present treaty.

Article XIII.—The Provisional Agreement of August 6, 1915, between Japan and China, relating to the reopening of the office of the Chinese Maritime Customs at Tsingtao shall cease to be effective upon the coming into force of the present treaty.

SECTION V

TSINGTAO-TSINANFU RAILWAY

Article XIV.—Japan shall transfer to China the Tsingtao-Tsinanfu Railway and its branches, together with all other properties appurtenant thereto, including wharves, warehouses, and other similar properties.

Article XV.—China undertakes to reimburse to Japan the actual value of all the railway properties mentioned in the preceding article.

The actual value to be so reimbursed shall consist of the sum of fifty-three million four hundred and six thousand, one hundred and forty-one (53,406,141) gold marks (which is the assessed value of such portion of the said properties as was left behind by the Germans), or its equivalent, plus the amount which Japan, during her administration of the railway, has actually expended for permanent improvements on or additions to the said properties, less a suitable allowance for depreciation.

It is understood that no charge will be made with respect to the wharves, warehouses, and other similar properties mentioned in the preceding article, except for such permanent improvements on or additions to them as may have been made by Japan, during her administration of the railway, less a suitable allowance for depreciation.

Article XVI.—The Government of Japan and the Government of the Chinese Republic shall each appoint three commissioners to form a Joint Railway Commission, with powers to appraise the actual value of the railway properties on the basis defined in the preceding article, and to arrange for the transfer of the said properties.

Article XVII.—The transfer of all the railway properties under Article XIV of the present treaty shall be completed as soon as possible, and, in any case, not later than nine months from the date of the coming into force of the present treaty.

Article XVIII.—To effect the reimbursement under Article XV of the present treaty, China shall deliver to Japan simultaneously with the completion of the transfer of the railway properties Chinese Government treasury notes, secured on the properties and revenues of the railway, and running for a period of fifteen years, but redeemable, whether in whole or in part, at the option of China, at the end of five years from the date of delivery of the said treasury notes, or at any time thereafter upon six months' previous notice.

Article XIX.—Pending the redemption of the said treasury notes under the preceding article, the Government of the Chinese Republic will select and appoint, for so long a period as any part of the said treasury notes shall remain unredeemed, a Japanese subject to be Traffic Manager, and another Japanese subject to be Chief Accountant jointly with the Chinese Chief Accountant and with co-ordinate functions.

These officials shall all be under the direction, control, and supervision of the Chinese Managing Director, and removable for cause.

Article XX.—Financial details of a technical character relating to the said treasury notes, not provided for in this section shall be determined in common accord between the Japanese and Chinese authorities as soon as possible, and, in any case, not later than six months from the date of the coming into force of the present treaty.

SECTION VI

EXTENSIONS OF THE TSINGTAO-TSINANFU RAILWAY

Article XXI.—The concessions relating to the two extensions of the Tsingtao-Tsinanfu Railway, namely, the Tsinanfu-Shunteh and the Kaomi-Hsuchowfu lines, shall be made open to the common activity of an international financial group, on terms to be arranged between the Government of the Chinese Republic and the said group.

SECTION VII

MINES

Article XXII.—The mines of Tsechwan, Fangtze, and Chinlingchen, for which the mining rights were formerly granted by China to Germany, shall be handed over to a company to be formed under a special charter of the Government of the Chinese Republic, in which the amount of Japanese capital shall not exceed that of Chinese capital.

The mode and terms of such arrangement shall be determined by the Joint Commission provided for in Article II of the present treaty.

SECTION VIII

OPENING OF THE FORMER GERMAN LEASED TERRITORY OF KIAOCHOW

Article XXIII.—The Government of Japan declares that it will not seek the establishment of an exclusive Japanese settlement, or of an international settlement, in the former German Leased Territory of Kiaochow.

The Government of the Chinese Republic, on its part declares that the entire area of the former German Leased Territory of Kiaochow will be open to foreign trade, and that foreign nationals will be permitted freely to reside and carry on commerce, industry, and other lawful pursuits within such area.

Article XXIV.—The Government of the Chinese Republic further declares that vested rights lawfully and equitably acquired by foreign nationals in the former German Leased Territory of Kiaochow, whether under the German régime or during the period of the Japanese administration, will be respected.

All questions relating to the status or validity of such vested rights acquired by Japanese subjects or Japanese companies shall be adjusted by the Joint Commission provided for in Article II of the present treaty.

SECTION IX

SALT INDUSTRY

Article XXV.—Whereas the salt industry is a Government monopoly in China, it is agreed that the interests of Japanese subjects or Japanese companies actually engaged in the said industry along the coast of Kiaochow Bay shall be purchased by the Government of the Chinese Republic for fair compensation, and that the exportation to Japan of a quantity of salt produced by such industry along the said coast is to be permitted on reasonable terms.

Arrangements for the above purposes, including the transfer of the said interests to the Government of the Chinese Republic, shall be made by the Joint Commission provided for in Article II of the present treaty. They shall be completed as soon as possible, and, in any case, not later than six months from the date of the coming into force of the present treaty.

SECTION X

SUBMARINE CABLES

Article XXVI.—The Government of Japan declares that all the rights, title, and privileges concerning the former German submarine cables between Tsingtao and Chefoo and between Tsingtao and Shanghai are vested in China, with the exception of those portions of the said two cables which have been utilized by the Government of Japan for the laying of cable between Tsingtao and Sasebo; it being understood that the question relating to the landing and operation at Tsingtao of the said Tsingtao-Sasebo cable shall be adjusted by the Joint Commission provided for in Article II of the present treaty, subject to the terms of the existing contracts to which China is a party.

SECTION XI

WIRELESS STATIONS

Article XXVII.—The Government of Japan undertakes to transfer to the Government of the Chinese Republic the Japanese wireless stations at Tsingtao and Tsinanfu, for fair compensation for the value of these stations, upon the withdrawal of the Japanese troops at the said two places, respectively.

Details of such transfer and compensation shall be arranged by the Joint Commission provided for in Article II of the present treaty.

Article XXVIII.—The present treaty (including the Annex thereto) shall be ratified, and the ratifications thereof shall be exchanged at Peking as soon as possible, and not later than four months from the date of its signature.

It shall come into force from the date of the exchange of ratifications.

In witness whereof, the respective plenipotentiaries have

signed the present treaty in duplicate, in the English language and have affixed thereto their seals.

Done at the City of Washington this fourth day of February, one thousand nine hundred and twenty-two.

ANNEX

I. RENUNCIATION OF PREFERENTIAL RIGHTS

The Government of Japan declares that it renounces all preferential rights with respect to foreign assistance in persons, capital, and material stipulated in the Treaty of March 6, 1898, between China and Germany.

II. TRANSFER OF PUBLIC PROPERTIES

It is understood that public properties to be transferred to the Government of the Chinese Republic under Article V of the present treaty include (1) all public works, such as roads, water-works, parks, drainage, and sanitary equipment, and (2) all public enterprises such as those relating to telephone, electric light, stockyard, and laundry.

The Government of the Chinese Republic declares that in the management and maintenance of public works to be so transferred to the Government of the Chinese Republic, the foreign community in the former German Leased Territory of Kiaochow shall have fair representation.

The Government of the Chinese Republic further declares that, upon taking over the telephone enterprise in the former German Leased Territory of Kiaochow, it will give due consideration to the requests from the foreign community in the said territory for such extensions and improvements in the telephone enterprise as may be reasonably required by the general interests of the public.

With respect to public enterprises relating to electric light, stockyard, and laundry, the Government of the Chinese Republic, upon taking them over, shall retransfer them to the Chinese municipal authorities of Tsingtao, which shall, in turn, cause commercial companies to be formed under Chinese laws for the management and working of the said enterprises, subject to municipal regulation and supervision.

III. MARITIME CUSTOMS AT TSINGTAO

The Government of the Chinese Republic declares that it will instruct the Inspector-General of the Chinese Maritime Customs (1) to permit Japanese traders in the former German Leased Territory of Kiaochow to communicate in the Japanese language with the Custom House of Tsingtao; and (2) to give consideration, within the limits of the established service regulations of the Chinese Maritime Customs, to the diverse needs of the trade of Tsingtao, in the selection of a suitable staff for the said Custom House.

IV. TSINGTAO-TSINANFU RAILWAY

Should the Joint Railway Commission provided for in Article XVI of the present treaty fail to reach an agreement on any matter within its competence, the point or points at issue shall be taken up by the Government of Japan and the Government of the Chinese Republic for discussion and adjustment by means of diplomacy.

In the determination of such point or points, the Government of Japan and the Government of the Chinese Republic shall, if necessary, obtain recommendations of experts of a third power or powers who shall be designated in common accord between the two governments.

V. CHEFOO-WEIHSIEN RAILWAY

The Government of Japan will not claim that the option for financing the Chefoo-Weihsien Railway should be made open to the common activity of the International Financial Consortium, provided that the said railway is to be constructed with Chinese capital.

VI. OPENING OF THE FORMER GERMAN LEASED TERRITORY OF KIAOCHOW

The Government of the Chinese Republic declares that, pending the enactment and general application of laws regulating the system of local self-government in China, the Chinese local authorities will ascertain the views of the foreign residents in the former German Leased Territory of Kiaochow in such municipal matters as may directly affect their welfare and interests.

APPENDIX VI

THE CHINESE TARIFF TREATY

The United States of America, Belgium, the British Empire, China, France, Italy, Japan, The Netherlands, and Portugal:

With a view to increasing the revenues of the Chinese Government, have resolved to conclude a Treaty relating to the revision of the Chinese customs tariff and cognate matters, and to that end have appointed as their Plenipotentiaries:

[Here follows a list of delegates.]

Who, having communicated to each other their full powers, found to be in good and due form, have agreed as follows:

ARTICLE I

The representatives of the Contracting Powers having adopted, on the fourth day of February, 1922, in the City of Washington, a Resolution, which is appended as an Annex to this Article, with respect to the revision of Chinese Customs duties, for the purpose of making such duties equivalent to an effective 5 per centum ad valorem, in accordance with existing treaties concluded by China with other nations, the Contracting Powers hereby confirm the said Resolution and undertake to accept the tariff rates fixed as a result of such revision. The said tariff rates shall become effective as soon as possible but not earlier than two months after publication thereof.

Annex

With a view to providing additional revenue to meet the needs of the Chinese Government, the Powers represented at this Conference, namely, the United States of America, Belgium, the British Empire, China, France, Italy, Japan, The Netherlands, and Portugal, agree:

That the customs schedule of duties on imports into China adopted by the Tariff Revision Commission at Shanghai on December 19, 1918, shall forthwith be revised so that the rates of duty shall be equivalent to 5 per cent effective, as provided for in the several commercial treaties to which China is a party.

A Revision Commission shall meet at Shanghai, at the earliest practicable date, to effect this revision forthwith and on the general lines of the last revision.

This Commission shall be composed of representatives of the Powers above named and of the representatives of any additional Powers having Governments at present recognized by the Powers represented at this Conference and who have treaties with China providing for a tariff on imports and exports not to exceed 5 per cent. ad valorem and who desire to participate therein.

The revision shall proceed as rapidly as possible with a view to its completion within four months from the date of the adoption of this Resolution by the Conference on the Limitation of Armament and Pacific and Far Eastern Questions.

The revised tariff shall become effective as soon as possible but not earlier than two months after its publication by the Revision Commission.

The Government of the United States, as convener of the present Conference, is requested forthwith to communicate the terms of this Resolution to the Governments of Powers not represented at this Conference, but who participated in the Revision of 1918, aforesaid.

Article II

Immediate steps shall be taken, through a Special Conference, to prepare the way for the speedy abolition of likin and for the fulfillment of the other conditions laid down in Article VIII of the Treaty of September 5th, 1902, between Great Britain and China, in Articles IV and V of the Treaty of October 8th, 1903, between the United States and China, and in Article I of the Supplementary Treaty of October 8th, 1903, between Japan and China, with a view to levying the surtaxes provided for in those articles.

The Special Conference shall be composed of representatives of the Signatory Powers, and of such other Powers as may desire to participate and may adhere to the present Treaty, in accordance with the provisions of Article VIII, in sufficient time to allow their representatives to take part. It shall meet in China within three months after the coming into force of the present Treaty, on a day and at a place to be designated by the Chinese Government.

Article III

The Special Conference provided for in Article II shall consider the interim provisions to be applied prior to the abolition of likin and the fulfillment of the other conditions laid down in the articles of the treaties mentioned in Article II; and it shall authorize the levying of a surtax on dutiable imports as from such date, for such purposes, and subject to such conditions as it may determine.

The surtax shall be at a uniform rate of 2½ per centum ad valorem, provided, that in the case of certain articles of luxury which, in the opinion of the Special Conference, can bear a greater increase without unduly impeding trade, the total surtax may be increased, but may not exceed 5 per centum ad valorem.

Article IV

Following the immediate revision of the customs schedule of duties on imports into China, mentioned in Article I, there shall be a further revision thereof to take effect at the expiration of four years following the completion of the aforesaid immediate revision, in order to ensure that the customs duties shall correspond to the ad valorem rates fixed by the Special Conference provided for in Article II.

Following this further revision there shall be, for the same purpose, periodical revisions of the customs schedule of duties on imports into China every seven years, in lieu of the decennial revision authorized by existing treaties with China.

In order to prevent delay, any revision made in pursuance of this Article shall be effected in accordance with rules to be prescribed by the Special Conference provided for in Article II.

Article V

In all matters relating to customs duties there shall be effective equality of treatment and opportunity for all the Contracting Powers.

Article VI

The principle of uniformity in the rates of customs duties levied at all the land and maritime frontiers of China is hereby recognized. The Special Conference provided for in Article II shall make arrangements to give practical effect to this principle; and it is authorized to make equitable adjustments in those cases in which a customs privilege to be abolished was granted in return for some local economic advantage.

In the meantime, any increase in the rates of customs duties resulting from tariff revision, or any surtax hereafter imposed in pursuance of the present Treaty, shall be levied at a uniform rate ad valorem at all land and maritime frontiers of China.

Article VII

The charge for transit passes shall be at the rate of 2½ per centum ad valorem until the arrangements provided for by Article II come into force.

Article VIII

Powers not signatory to the present Treaty whose Governments are at present recognized by the Signatory Powers, and whose present treaties with China provide for a tariff on imports and exports not to exceed 5 per centum ad valorem, shall be invited to adhere to the present Treaty.

The Government of the United States undertakes to make the necessary communications for this purpose and to inform the Governments of the Contracting Powers of the replies received. Adherence by any Power shall become effective on receipt of notice thereof by the Government of the United States.

Article IX

The provisions of the present Treaty shall override all stipulations of treaties between China and the respective Contracting Powers which are inconsistent therewith, other than stipulations according most-favored-nation treatment.

Article X

The present Treaty shall be ratified by the Contracting Powers in accordance with their respective constitutional methods and shall take effect on the date of the deposit of all the ratifications, which shall take place at Washington as soon as possible. The Government of the United States will transmit to the other

Contracting Powers a certified copy of the procès-verbal of the deposit of ratifications.

The present Treaty, of which the English and French texts are both authentic, shall remain deposited in the Archives of the Government of the United States, and duly certified copies thereof shall be transmitted by that Government to the other Contracting Powers.

In faith whereof the above-named Plenipotentiaries have signed the present Treaty.

Done at the City of Washington on the sixth day of February, One Thousand Nine Hundred and Twenty-Two.

BIBLIOGRAPHY

The reader is entitled to a brief statement, characterizing in general terms the scope of the following bibliography. The classifications selected by the author are:

1. Official publications
2. Collections of treaties
3. Books
4. Periodical articles
5. Periodical materials in Japanese

The aim has been to select such primary sources only as deal directly with the subject-matter of this study. So far as the third classification of books is concerned, it may be stated that general works dealing primarily with domestic history and politics of the countries involved have been omitted. The selection is confined to a limited number of books dealing specifically with international problems closely related to the work of the Washington Conference.

In respect to periodical literature the aim has been to present a picture of representative current opinion, and in this connection the writer has listed a number of leading Japanese magazines but without specifying particular articles. It should also be observed that the titles listed as periodical literature represent only a small fraction of an immense amount of such material which the author has felt obliged to consult.

Finally, it may be added that certain dailies have been used in the study, such as *The London Times* and the *New York Times,* the *Jiji* and the *Asahi* of Tokyo, and *Le Temps* and *Le Matin* of Paris.

OFFICIAL PUBLICATIONS

Canada

Conference on the Limitation of Armament Held at Washington, Report of the Canadian delegate, including treaties and resolutions. Ottawa, 1922.

China

History of the Peace Negotiations between China and Japan, March–April, 1895. Tientsin, 1895.

The Sino-Japanese Negotiations. Chinese official statement with documents and treaties with annexures. Peking, 1915.

France

La Conférence de Washington (12 Novembre 1921—6 Février 1922), *Archives de la Paix*—la documentation internationale sous la direction de A. de Lapradelle. Tome II, *Limitation des Armements, Règlementation de la Guerre.* Tome III, *Question du Pacifique, Question de l'Extrême-Orient.* Paris, 1922.

Germany

Die Grosse Politik der Europäischen Kabinette, 1871–1914. Sammlung der diplomatischen Akten des Auswärtigen Amtes im Auftrage des Auswärtigen Amtes, herausgegeben von Johannes Lepsius, A. M. Bartholdy, Friedrich Thimme. Deutsche Verlagsgesellschaft für Politik und Geschichte. Berlin, 1925.

Great Britain

Accounts and Papers, Vol. XXIII, Cmd. 1627, 1922, pp. 1–89 (Conference on the Limitation of Armament, Washington, 1921–1922); Vol. XV, 1923, pp. 1–109 (Fleets of the British Empire and foreign countries); Vol. XIII, Cmd. 1867, 1923, pp. 1–9 (Memorandum on present and pre-war expenditure with particulars of government staffs at certain dates). London, 1922–1923.

British Documents on the Origins of the War, Vols. I–III and XI, 1898–1914 (edited by G. P. Gooch and H. Temperley). London, 1926–1927.

Journals of the Parliaments of the Empire, issued under the authority of the Empire parliamentary association (United Kingdom branch), Vols. 1–7. London, 1920–1927.

Japan

Conversations between the Chinese and Japanese Representatives in regard to the Shantung Question by the Japanese Delegation. Washington, 1922.

Correspondence Regarding the Negotiations between Japan and Russia, 1903–1904. Washington, 1904.

Japanese Official Documents concerning Shantung. Washington, 1921.

Recueil des Traités et Conventions conclus entre l'Empire du Japon et les Puissances Etrangères. Tokyo, 1918.

Traités et Conventions entre l'Empire du Japon et les Puissances Etrangères, 2 vols. Tokyo, 1908.

United States

Congressional Record, 65th Congress, 2d Session, Vol. 56, Part 1, 1918; 66th Congress, 2d Session, Vol. 59, Part 5, 1920; 66th Congress, 3d Session, Vol. 60, Part 3, 1921; 67th Congress, 1st Session, Vol. 61, Part 9, 1921; 67th Congress, 2d Session, Vol. 62, Parts 3, 4, 5, and 13, 1922. Washington, 1918–1922.

Foreign Relations, 1899–1917. Washington, 1901–1926.

Navy Department. American Naval Policy as Outlined in Messages of the Presidents of the United States from 1790 to 1924. Washington, 1924.

Report of the Commission on Extraterritoriality in China. Washington, 1926.

Senate Documents. No. 3, 64th Congress, 1st Session, Vol. 3, 1915; No. 555, 64th Congress, 2d Session, Vol. 2, 1916; No. 418, 65th Congress, 3d Session, Vol. 7, 1919; No. 428, 66th Congress, 3d Session, Vol. 14, 1922; Nos. 125 and 126, 67th Congress, 2d Session, Vols. 9 and 10 (*Conference on the Limitation of Armament,* 1922), and No. 55, 70th Congress, 1st Session, Vol. 7 (*Records of the Conference for the Limitation of Naval Armament held at Geneva, Switzerland, from June 20 to August 4, 1927*). Washington, 1915–1928.

Statistical Abstracts, 1915–1924. Washington, 1916–1925.

Statutes at Large, 67th Congress, Section 9, 1922, Treaty Series, No. 671. Washington, 1923.

Washington Conference

Conference on the Limitation of Armament, Washington, November 12, 1921— February 6, 1922; Conférence de la Limitation des Armements, Washington, 12 Novembre 1921—6 Février 1922. Washington, 1922.

Conference on the Limitation of Armament, Subcommittee, Washington, November 12, 1921—February 6, 1922; Conférence de la Limitation des Armements, Sous-Commission, Washington, 12 Novembre 1921—6 Février 1922. Washington, 1922.

COLLECTIONS OF TREATIES

Carnegie Endowment for International Peace, Division of International Law.
Korea. Treaties and Agreements. Washington, 1921.
Manchuria. Treaties and Agreements. Washington, 1921.
Outer Mongolia. Treaties and Agreements. Washington, 1921.
Sino-Japanese Negotiations, Japanese and Chinese Documents and Chinese Official Statement. Washington, 1921.

Chung, H. *Korean Treaties.* New York, 1919.

Hertslet's *China Treaties.* Treaties, etc., between Great Britain and China; and between China and Foreign Powers; and Orders in Council, Rules, Regulations, Acts of Parliament, Decrees, etc., affecting British Interests in China. In force on January 1, 1908. Third edition, 2 vols. London, 1908.

MacMurray, J. V. A. *Treaties and Agreements with and concerning China, 1894–1919,* 2 vols. New York, 1921.

Malloy, W. M. *Treaties, Conventions, International Acts, Protocols and Agreements between the United States of America and other Powers.* 3 vols. Washington, 1909–1923.

Mayers, W. F. *Treaties between the Empire of China and Foreign Powers,* etc. Third edition. Shanghai, 1901.

Rockhill, W. W. *Treaties and Conventions with or concerning China and Korea, 1894–1904.* Washington, 1904.

BOOKS

Abbott, J. F. *Japanese Expansion and American Policies.* New York, 1916.

Adachi, K. *Manchuria, a Survey.* New York, 1925.

Archimbaud, L. *La Conférence de Washington.* Paris, 1923.

Ariga, N. *La Chine et la Grande Guerre Européenne.* Paris, 1920.

———. *La Guerre Sino-Japonaise.* Paris, 1896.

———. *La Guerre Russo-Japonaise.* Paris, 1908.

Asakawa, K. *The Russo-Japanese Conflict*. Boston, 1904.
Aubert, L. *Paix Japonaise*. Paris, 1906.
Baker, P. J. N. *Disarmament*. Second edition. London, 1927.
Baker, R. S. *Woodrow Wilson and World Settlement*. 3 vols. Garden City, 1922.
Balet, J. C. *Le Japon militaire*. Yokohama et Paris, 1910.
Ballard, G. A. *The Influence of the Sea on the Political History of Japan*. London, 1921.
Bau, M. J. *The Foreign Relations of China: a History and a Survey*. New York, 1921.
———. *The Open Door Doctrine in Relation to China*. New York, 1923.
Bernstein, H. *The Willy-Nicky Correspondence, being the Secret and Intimate Telegrams between the Kaiser and the Tsar*. New York, 1918.
Blakeslee, G. H. *The Recent Foreign Policy of the United States*. New York, 1925.
Bland, J. O. P. *Li Hung Chang*. New York, 1917.
Brandt, M. von. *Dreiunddreissig Jahre in Ost-Asien*. 3 vols. Leipzig, 1901.
Brown, A. J. *The Mastery of the Far East*. London, 1919.
Bryce, J. *International Relations*. New York, 1922.
Buell, R. L. *The Washington Conference*. New York, 1922.
Bullard, A. *The A.B.C.'s of Disarmament and the Pacific Problems*. New York, 1921.
Bülow, Prince B. von. *Imperial Germany* (translated by M. A. Lewenz). New York, 1917.
Bywater, H. C. *Sea-Power in the Pacific*. Boston and New York, 1921.
Cambridge History of British Foreign Policy, Vol. III, 1866–1919. Cambridge, 1923.
Castex, Capitaine de Frégate. *Synthèse de la Guerre Sous-Marine*. Paris, 1920.
Cheng, S. G. *Modern China: A Political Study*. Oxford, 1919.
China Year-Book, 1916–1927 (edited by H. G. W. Woodhead). Peking, Tientsin, and London.
Chirol, V. *The Far Eastern Question*. London, 1896.
Chung, H. *The Case of Korea*. New York, 1921.

Clyde, P. H. *International Rivalries in Manchuria, 1689–1922.* Second edition. Columbus, 1928.
Cordier, H. *Histoire des relations de la Chine avec les puissances occidentales.* 3 vols. Paris, 1901–1902.
———. *Histoire générale de la Chine et ses relations avec les pays etrangers.* 4 vols. Paris, 1920–1921.
Croly, H. *Willard Straight.* New York, 1924.
Curzon, G. N. *Problems of the Far East.* Westminster, 1896.
Das Problem Japans (von einem ehemaligen Gesandtschaftsrat im Fernen Osten). Leipzig, 1920.
Dennett, T. *Americans in Eastern Asia.* New York, 1922.
———. *Roosevelt and the Russo-Japanese War.* Garden City, 1925.
Dennis, A. L. P. *Adventures in American Diplomacy, 1896–1906.* New York, 1928.
———. *The Anglo-Japanese Alliance.* Berkeley, 1923.
———. *The Foreign Policies of Soviet Russia.* New York, 1924.
Dillon, E. J. *The Eclipse of Russia.* New York, 1918.
Draves, J. W. *The Renaissance of Korea.* Philadelphia, 1920.
Du Boulay, N. W. H. *An Epitome of the Chino-Japanese War, 1894–1895.* London, 1896.
Dutcher, G. M. *The Political Awakening of the East.* New York, 1925.
Eckardstein, Baron von. *Ten Years at the Court of St. James, 1895–1905* (translated and edited by G. Young). London, 1921.
Enoch, A. G. *The Problem of Armaments.* New York, 1923.
Fish, C. R. *American Diplomacy.* Third edition. New York, 1919.
Foster, J. W. *American Diplomacy in the Orient.* Boston, 1903.
———. *Diplomatic Memoirs.* 2 vols. Boston, 1909.
Francke, V. *Die Grossmächte in Ostasien von 1894 bis 1914.* Brunswick and Hamburg, 1923.
Fujisawa, R. *The Recent Aims and Political Development of Japan.* New Haven, 1923.
Furness, W. H. *The Island of Stone Money.* Philadelphia, 1910.
Gallagher, P. *America's Aims and Asia's Aspirations.* New York, 1920.

Gerard, A. *L'Extrême Orient et la paix.* Paris, 1919.
———. *Ma Mission en Chine, 1893–1897.* Paris, 1918.
———. *Ma Mission au Japon, 1907–1914.* Paris, 1919.
Goodnow, F. J. *China, an Analysis.* Baltimore, 1926.
Grey, Sir E. *Twenty-five Years, 1892–1916.* 2 vols. New York, 1925.
Harris, N. D. *Europe and the East.* Boston, 1926.
Hayashi, Count T. *The Secret Memoirs of Count Tadasu Hayashi* (edited by A. M. Pooley). New York, 1915.
Hershey, A. S. *The International Law and Diplomacy of the Russo-Japanese War.* New York, 1906.
Hishida, S. G. *The International Position of Japan as a Great Power.* New York, 1905.
Hornbeck, S. K. *Contemporary Politics in the Far East.* New York, 1916.
Hoshino, T. *Economic History of Chosen.* Seoul, 1921.
———. *Economic History of Manchuria.* Seoul, 1921.
Howland, C. P. *American Foreign Relations, 1928.* New Haven, 1928.
Hsu, M. C. *Railway Problems in China.* New York, 1915.
Hsü, S. *China and Her Political Entity.* New York and London, 1926.
Ireland, A. *The New Korea.* New York, 1926.
Iswolsky, A. *Recollections of a Foreign Minister* (translated by L. Seeger). Garden City, 1921.
Ito, S. *Kafu Kaigi to Sonogo (The Washington Conference and After).* Tokyo, 1922.
Japan Year-Book, 1905–1927. Tokyo.
Jones, J. *The Fall of Tsingtau.* Boston and New York, 1915.
Kawakami, K. K. *American-Japanese Relations.* New York and Chicago, 1912.
———. *Japan and World Peace.* New York, 1919.
———. *Japan in World Politics.* New York, 1917.
———. *Japan's Pacific Policy.* New York, 1922
Kennan, G. *E. H. Harriman, a Biography.* 2 vols. Boston and New York, 1922.
Kennedy, M. D. *The Military Side of Japanese Life.* New York, 1924.

Korff, S. A. *Russia's Foreign Relations During the Last Half-Century.* New York, 1922.
Kotenev, A. M. *Shanghai, Its Mixed Court and Council.* Shanghai, 1925.
Labroue, H. *L'Impérialisme japonais.* Paris, 1911.
La Mazeliere, A. R. Marquis de. *Le Japon, histoire et civilisation.* 8 vols. Paris, 1907–1923.
Lawton, L. *Empires of the Far East.* 2 vols. London, 1912.
Legendre, A. F. *Tour d'Horizon Mondial, Quo Vadis Europa atque America?* Paris, 1920.
Le Roux, Hughes. *L'Heure du Japon.* Paris, 1918.
Liu, S. S. *Extraterritoriality: Its Rise and Decline.* New York, 1925.
Lyautey, P. *Le drame oriental et le rôle de la France.* Second edition. Paris, 1924.
McLaren, W. W. *Japan's Foreign Relations Prior to 1911.* Washington, 1922.
McNair, H. F. *China's International Relations and Other Essays.* Shanghai, 1926.
Mahan, A. T. *The Problem of Asia and Its Effects upon International Politics.* Boston, 1900.
Miliukov, P. N. *Russia Today and Tomorrow.* New York, 1922.
Millard, T. F. *A.B.C.'s of the Hay Doctrine.* Shanghai, 1921.
———. *America and the Far Eastern Question.* New York, 1909.
———. *The Conflict of Policies in Asia.* New York and London, 1924.
Mirrors of Downing Street, The (Begbie, H.). New York and London, 1921.
Mirrors of Washington, The (Gilbert, C. W.). New York and London, 1921.
Moore, F. F. *Siberia Today.* New York, 1919.
Morse, H. B. *The International Relations of the Chinese Empire.* 3 vols. New York and London, 1910–18.
———. *The Trade and Administration of the Chinese Empire.* New York and London, 1908.
National Institute of Social Science. *Results of the Conference on Limitation of Armament.* New York, 1922.

Norton, H. K. *The Far Eastern Republic of Siberia.* London, 1923.
———. *China and the Powers.* New York, 1927.
Overlach, T. W. *Foreign Financial Control in China.* New York, 1919.
Pasvolsky, L. *Russia in the Far East.* New York, 1922.
Player, C. A. *Arms and the Men.* Detroit, 1922.
Poleman, F. Q. *Japan or Germany.* New York, 1918.
Pooley, A. M. *Japan at the Cross Roads.* New York, 1917.
———. *Japan's Foreign Policies.* London, 1920.
Reboul, Lieut.-Col. *Le Conflit du Pacifique et notre marine de guerre.* Paris, 1922.
Reinsch, P. S. *An American Diplomat in China.* Garden City and Toronto, 1922.
Révész, A. *La conferencia de Wáshington y el problema del Pacífico.* Madrid, 1922.
Rosen, W. W., Baron de. *Forty Years of Diplomacy.* 2 vols. New York, 1922.
Russian-American Relations, March, 1917–March, 1920 (documents and papers compiled and edited by Cumming, C. K., and Pettit, W. W., under direction of Ryan, J. N., Scattergood, J. H., and White, W. A.). New York, 1920.
Sargent, A. J. *Anglo-Chinese Commerce and Diplomacy.* Oxford, 1907.
Satow, Sir E. M. *A Diplomat in Japan.* Philadelphia, 1922.
Sauter, J. A. *Die Isolierung Japans.* Charlottenburg, 1919.
Sears, L. M. *A History of American Foreign Relations.* New York, 1927.
Shinobu, J. *Taisho Gaiko Jugonen Shi* (A Diplomatic History of the Fifteen Years of Taisho, 1912–1926). Tokyo, 1927.
Smidt, H. *Japan in Weltkriege und das China Problem.* Bremen, 1915.
Soyeshima, M., and Kuo, P. M. *Oriental Interpretations of the Far Eastern Problem.* Chicago, 1926.
Sullivan, M. *The Great Adventure at Washington.* Garden City, 1922.
Sunderland, J. T. *Rising Japan: Is She a Menace or a Comrade in the Fraternity of Nations?* New York and London, 1918.

Tatsumi, R. *Kiokuto Kinji Gaiko Shi* (A History of Recent Far Eastern Diplomacy). Second edition. Tokyo, 1914.

Tchen, H. *Les relations diplomatiques entre la Chine at le Japon de 1871 à nos jours.* Paris, 1921.

Thayer, W. R. *The Life and Letters of John Hay.* 2 vols. Boston and New York, 1915.

Times History of the War, The. 22 vols. London, 1921.

Tomimas, S. *The Open-Door Policy and the Territorial Integrity of China.* New York, 1919.

Transcript, Boston Evening. Review of the Conference on Limitation of Armament in Connection with the Far Eastern and Pacific Questions. Boston, 1922.

Treat, P. J. *The Far East, A Political and Diplomatic History.* New York and London, 1928.

———. *Japan and the United States, 1853–1921.* Revised and Continued to 1928. Stanford University, 1928.

Vladimir (Volpicelli, Z.). *The Chino-Japanese War.* London, 1896.

———. *Russia on the Pacific and the Siberian Railway,* London, 1899.

Weale, B. L. P. (Simpson, B. L.). *Indiscreet Chronicle from the Pacific.* New York, 1922.

———. *The Truth about China and Japan.* New York, 1919.

Wehberg, H. *Die International Beschränkung der Rüstungen.* Stuttgart and Berlin, 1919.

———. *The Limitation of Armaments.* Washington, 1921.

Wells, H. G. *Washington and the Riddle of Peace.* New York, 1922.

Weyl, W. E. *American World Policies.* New York, 1917.

Wheeler, W. R. *China and the World War.* New York, 1919.

Wheeler-Bennett, J. W. *Information on the Reduction of Armaments.* London, 1925.

Willoughby, W. W. *China at the Conference.* Baltimore, 1922.

———. *The Constitutional Government in China.* Washington, 1922.

———. *Foreign Rights and Interests in China.* Baltimore, 1920.

Witte, Count S. *The Memoirs of Count Witte* (translated and edited by H. Yarmolinsky). Garden City and Toronto, 1921.

Wood, Ge-Zay. *The Chino-Japanese Treaties of May 25th, 1915.* New York, 1921.
——. *The Shantung Question, a Study in Diplomacy and World Politics.* New York, 1922.
——. *The Twenty-One Demands.* New York, 1921.
Woodhead, H. G. W. *The Truth about the Chinese Republic.* London, 1926.
Woodhead, H. G. W., Arnold, J., and Norton, H. K. *Occidental Interpretations of the Eastern Problem.* Chicago, 1926.
Yen, E. T. *The Open Door Policy.* Boston, 1923.

PERIODICAL ARTICLES

Abbott, A. H. "The League's Disarmament Activities and the Washington Conference," *Political Science Quarterly*, March 1922, pp. 1–24.
Abbott, E. H. "Britain at the Conference," *The Outlook*, November 2, 1921, pp. 335–37.
——. "British 'Propaganda' and French 'Imperialism'," *The Outlook*, January 11, 1922, pp. 51–53.
——. "France at the Conference," *The Outlook*, October 19, 1921, pp. 247–49.
——. "Japan at the Conference," *The Outlook*, October 12, 1921, pp. 209–11.
——. "Simplicity, Honesty, Honor," *The Outlook*, November 23, 1921, pp. 462–65.
——. "Stop-Now Policy," *The Outlook*, November 30, 1921, pp. 508–11.
——. "Strategy of Peace," *The Outlook*, December 28, 1921, pp. 678–80.
——. "Washington Conference a Year After," *The Outlook*, December 13, 1922, pp. 649–50.
"America, Britain and Japan," *New Republic*, July 6, 1921, pp. 152–54.
"America's New Triumph," *Literary Digest*, December 24, 1921, pp. 16–17.
"America's Reply to Japan's Protest," *Current History*, August 1924, pp. 881–89.

"Anglo-Japanese Alliance, The," *The Outlook,* July 6, 1921, pp. 408–9.

"Anglo-Japanese Alliance, The," *Review of Reviews,* August 1921, pp. 204–5.

"Anglo-Japanese Alliance, The," *Round Table,* December 1920, pp. 87–97.

"Anglo-Japanese Alliance, The," *Trans-Pacific,* April 23, 1927, p. 6.

"Anglo-Japanese Alliance and the League of Nations," *The Nation,* August 10, 1921, p. 160.

"Arming the World?" *The Nation,* January 16, 1924, pp. 51–52.

"Arms Conference in Action," *Current History,* December 1921, pp. i–xxxvi, 375–88.

Aston, G. "Japan and Singapore," *Nineteenth Century and After,* August 1923, pp. 177–87.

Ballou, S. "French Point of View," *The Outlook,* January 25, 1922, pp. 136–37.

Batault, G. "Le pacificisme et le problème du Pacifique," *Mercure de France,* December 1, 1921, pp. 309–43.

Bedford, A. C. "The World Oil Situation," *Foreign Affairs,* March 1922, pp. 96–107.

Blakeslee, G. H. "Mandates of the Pacific," *Foreign Affairs,* September 1922, pp. 98–115.

Bland, J. O. P. "After Washington: The Future of the Pacific Problem," *Atlantic Monthly,* December 1922, pp. 843–53.

———. "Plain Truths about China," *English Review,* February 1927, pp. 145–54.

Bliss, T. H. "What Is Disarmament?" *Foreign Affairs,* April 1926, pp. 353–68.

Boulger, D. C. "Anglo-Japanese Alliance," *Contemporary Review,* September 1920, pp. 326–33.

Brailsford, J. A. "Anglo-Japanese Alliance, An Australian View," *The Nation,* August 31, 1924, p. 234.

"Briand's Bid for Eternal Peace," *The Literary Digest,* May 14, 1927, p. 11.

Bridge, C. A. G. "The Pacific Problem," *Spectator,* July 23, 1921, pp. 103–4.

"Britain's Grave Chinese Problem," *The Literary Digest,* February 12, 1927, pp. 16–17.

"British and Japanese Policy in China," *Living Age,* January 15, 1927, pp. 111–16.

"British Policy at Washington," *Living Age,* December 3, 1921, pp. 580–88.

"British Policy in China," *Asiatic Review,* January 1927, pp. 17–21.

Brown, P. M. "Preliminary Disarmament Conference," *Current History,* July 1921, pp. 601–3.

Bryce, J. "Case for the Conference," *Living Age,* November 26, 1921, pp. 503–6.

Buell, R. L. "Again the Yellow Peril," *Foreign Affairs,* December 1923, pp. 295–309.

——. "British Barriers against the Japanese," *Current History,* September 1924, pp. 962–67.

Butler, N. M. "L'État actuel des esprits aux États-Unis," *Revue des Deux Mondes,* August 15, 1921, pp. 780–89.

——. "Les devoirs des États-Unis," *Revue de Paris,* December 1, 1921, pp. 488–500.

Bywater, H. C. "The Limitation of Naval Armaments," *Atlantic Monthly,* February 1922, pp. 259–69.

——. "Naval Construction in Japan," *Scientific American,* January 1922, pp. 25–26.

——. "A Sequel to the Washington Conference," *Atlantic Monthly,* February 1923, pp. 240–49.

——. "Singapore Naval Base," *Forum,* May 1926, pp. 700–707.

Carter, W. H. "Japanese Exclusion, Its Political Effects," *Current History,* April 1925, pp. 30–33.

Casenave, M. "The Naval Needs of France," *World's Work,* March 1922, pp. 558–60.

Castex, R. "Piracy," *Living Age,* March 18, 1922, pp. 654–57.

Cecil, E. A. R., Viscount. "American Responsibilities for Peace," *Foreign Affairs,* April 1928, pp. 357–67.

"China," *Round Table,* September 1925, pp. 674–91.

"China and the British Proposals," *Round Table,* March 1927, pp. 287–95.

"China and the Pacific Pact," *Literary Digest,* January 28, 1922, p. 19.

Chirol, V. "Washington Conference and the Pacific Problem," *Contemporary Review*, February 1922, pp. 147–57.

Cogniet, A. "Les enseignements de la guerre navale et les raisons techniques de la Conférence de Washington," *Mercure de France*, October 15, 1923, pp. 414–50.

"Comment on the Four-Power Treaty," *Review of Reviews*, January 1922, pp. 85–87.

"Conférence de Washington, La," *Revue de Paris*, November 15, 1921, pp. 439–48.

"Conference of Friends, Not a Mass Meeting," *The Independent*, March 25, 1922, pp. 302–3.

"Controversy over Yap Island," *Current History*, April 1921, pp. 108–10.

"Correspondence on Yap Issue between Japan and America," *Asian Review*, May–June 1921, pp. 392–401.

"Debate on the Treaty," *The Outlook*, March 22, 1922, pp. 453–54.

Degouy, J. B. "Après Washington et après Gênes," *Revue des Deux Mondes*, June 1, 1922, pp. 639–66.

De Kerguezec, G. "French Naval Aims," *Foreign Affairs*, April 1926, pp. 369–82.

"Delegates to the Washington Conference" (Progress of the World), *Review of Reviews*, December 1921, pp. 565–67.

Dennett, T. "American Policy in the Far East," *Current History*, July 1923, pp. 598–602.

Dennis, A. L. P. "New Russo-Japanese Treaty Explained," *Current History*, May 1925, pp. 240–44.

Dewar, G. A. B. "British Recognition of Soviet Russia," *Foreign Affairs*, December 1924, pp. 313–19.

"Disarmament at Deadlock," *Literary Digest*, May 7, 1927, pp. 16–17.

"Disarmament Snags at Geneva," *Literary Digest*, June 5, 1926, pp. 14–15.

Dolliver, J. P. "Significance of the Anglo-Japanese Alliance," *North American Review*, May 1902, pp. 594–605.

Dolsen, J. H. "Thorny Problems of China and the Powers," *Current History*, November 1926, pp. 221–30.

Dubosq, A. "Les relations Sino-Francaises en face de la question d'Extrême-Orient," *Mercure de France,* September 15, 1921, pp. 657–67.

Dulles, A. W. "Some Misconceptions about Disarmament," *Foreign Affairs,* April 1927, pp. 413–24.

Dulles, F. R. "French Problems in Indo-China," *Current History,* May 1927, pp. 197–202.

"Emergence of Yap, The," *Current Opinion,* April 1921, pp. 443–47.

"Empire and the Alliance, The," *The Nation* (London), July 9, 1921, pp. 531–32.

"Empire, the Fleet, and Japan, The," *The Nation* (London), June 25, 1921, pp. 459–60.

"Entangling Alliance and What It Might Lead To," *Current Opinion,* May 1922, pp. 581–83.

"Europe's Distrust of the Washington Conference," *Current Opinion,* November 1921, pp. 558–60.

"Fanciful Fears," *Independent,* February 25, 1922, p. 191.

"Fight on the Treaty," *Current Opinion,* February 1922, pp. 152–55.

Fiske, Rear Admiral B. A. "Limitation of Armament, Uncensored Statement," *Harpers,* July 1925, pp. 129–38.

———. "Strongest Navy, Reply to Wester-Wemyss and Admiral Sims," *Current History,* July 1922, pp. 557–63.

"France Signs Up for Naval Peace," *Literary Digest,* July 28, 1923, pp. 14–15.

"France's Demand for Submarines," *Literary Digest,* January 7, 1922, pp. 7–9.

"French Navy and Army Today," *Literary Digest,* February 11, 1922, pp. 34–35.

"French Chagrin at Washington," *Literary Digest,* January 28, 1922, p. 20.

Gardiner, A. G. "The Prospects of Anglo-American Friendship," *Foreign Affairs,* October 1926, pp. 6–17.

Gardiner, W. H. "Naval Fleet Ratios," *Review of Reviews,* March 1924, pp. 305–8.

———. "Naval View of the Conference," *Atlantic Monthly,* April 1922, pp. 521–30.

Gardiner, W. H. "Some American Naval Views, *Fortnightly Review*, March 1, 1923, pp. 353–73.

———. "Why Japan Would be Mistress of the Sea," *World's Work*, December 1921, pp. 212–17.

Gaunt, Sir G. "Singapore," *Nineteenth Century and After*, September 1923, pp. 359–62.

"Geneva," *Round Table*, December 1926, pp. 37–55.

"German Distrust of French Friendship," *Literary Digest*, April 16, 1927, pp. 18–19.

Gerould, J. T. "Disagreement at Conference on Naval Disarmament," *Current History*, August 1927, pp. 792–96.

———. "Disarmament Negotiations," *Current History*, May 1927, pp. 267–69.

———. "The Failure of the Three-Power Conference," *Current History*, September 1927, pp. 945–49.

Glasgow, G. "Lord Cecil at Geneva" (Foreign Affairs), *Contemporary Review*, June 1926, pp. 781–85.

———. "Naval Disarmament," *Contemporary Review*, March 1927, pp. 386–88.

Grattan, C. H. "Australia and the Pacific," *Foreign Affairs*, October 1928, pp. 144–49.

Hedges, F. H. "The Foreign Grip on China," *Current History*, November 1923, pp. 288–94.

Hinds, Capt. A. W. "Sea Power and Disarmament," *North American Review*, November 1921, pp. 588–93.

"Hope of the Treaty," *The Independent*, March 18, 1922, p. 272.

Hornbeck, S. K. "Has the United States a Chinese Policy?" *Foreign Affairs*, July 1927, pp. 617–32.

———. "Principles and Policies in Regard to China," *Foreign Affairs*, December 1922, pp. 120–35.

Huddleston, S. "France, Her Politicians, and the Washington Conference," *Atlantic Monthly*, December 1921, pp. 830–42.

Hudson, M. O. "International Problems at Shanghai," *Foreign Affairs*, October 1927, pp. 67–88.

Hughes, C. E. "The Foreign Policy of the United States," *Current History*, January 1924, pp. 575–83.

Hughes, H. "China in Anti-Foreign Mood," *Current History*, July 1925, pp. 618–20.

"Human Aspects of the Conference," *Review of Reviews*, January 1922, pp. 41–51.

Hurds, A. S. "Britain's Naval Policy," *Review of Reviews*, August 1921, pp. 201–2.

———. "Is the Washington Naval Treaty Doomed?" *Fortnightly Review*, January 1923, pp. 13–27.

———. "Naval Scares in the United States," *Fortnightly Review*, August 1924, pp. 211–26.

———. "Washington Conference and the Naval Issue," *Fortnightly Review*, November 1921, pp. 717–26.

———. "Washington Naval Standards; War Fleets of Four Million Tons," *Fortnightly Review*, January 1922, pp. 106–21.

"Is France Getting a Fair Deal?" *Current Opinion*, February 1922, pp. 157–61.

"Is the Four-Power Treaty an Alliance?" *World's Work*, February 1922, pp. 349–50.

"Island of Yap, America, and the Far East," *Review of Reviews*, November 1919, pp. 540–41.

Iyenaga, T. "How Japan Views the Arms Conference," *Current History*, April 1922, pp. 22–25.

"Japan as Its Own Island," *Literary Digest*, January 7, 1922, pp. 10–11.

"Japan's Attitude toward Russia," *Literary Digest*, February 23, 1924, p. 23.

Kawakami, K. K. "The Hidden Conflict at the Three-Power Naval Conference," *Current History*, October 1927, pp. 106–11.

———. "Manchuria: the Crux of Chino-Japanese Relations," *Foreign Affairs*, April 1928, pp. 379–94.

———. "Turmoil on the Yangtse: a Japanese View, *North American Review*, March 1927, pp. 47–54.

Kinney, H. W. "Puzzled Japan," *The Outlook*, August 24, 1921, pp. 641–42.

Knox, D. W.; Wygant, B. B. "Five-five-three," *The Outlook*, December 13, 1922, pp. 668–71.

La Bruyère, R. "France's New Army and Navy," *Current History*, April 1926, pp. 21–26.

———. "French Naval Ideas," *Atlantic Monthly*, June 1922, pp. 826–33.

La Bruyère, R. "La Marine française et le désarmement (Avant la conférence de Washington), *Revue des Deux Mondes,* November 1, 1921, pp. 118–32.

———. "Notre détresse navale," *Revue des Deux Mondes,* August 15, 1921, pp. 881–94.

Lauzanne, S. "The Affections of France," *The Outlook,* August 17, 1921, pp. 599–600.

———. "France, the good Milch Cow," *Forum,* June 1922, pp. 461–66.

———. "Why France Will Back Up America at the Washington Conference," *The Outlook,* August 24, 1921, pp. 640–41.

Lawton, L. "Evasions of Washington," *Fortnightly Review,* February 1922, pp. 292–99.

Le Chartier, G. "Choses vues à Washington," *Revue des Deux Mondes,* December 15, 1921, pp. 913–30.

"Les États-Unis et la paix," *Revue de Paris,* August 1, 1921, pp. 666–72.

"Limitation of Armament," *Review of Reviews,* August 1921, pp. 199–202.

Lippman, J. "Why France Cannot Disarm," *Current Opinion,* March 1922, pp. 317–20.

Longford, J. H.; Theodore, E. G. "Anglo-Japanese Alliance," *Living Age,* July 24, 1920, pp. 202–7.

Looram, M. L. "Yap," *The Outlook,* November 12, 1919, pp. 310–12.

Low, A. M. "The Anglo-Japanese Alliance," *Forum,* April 1902, pp. 196–206.

McCall, S. W. "The Washington Conference," *Atlantic Monthly,* March 1922, pp. 386–94.

McElroy, R. M. "New Immigration Law over Japan's Protest," *Current History,* July 1924, pp. 648–52.

Mah, N. W. "Foreign Jurisdiction in China," *American Journal of International Law,* October 1924, pp. 676–95.

"Maintaining the Navy's Efficiency," *The Outlook,* October 4, 1922, pp. 177–78.

Maxey, E. "The Anglo-Japanese Alliance," *Arena,* May 1902, pp. 449–54.

Mayo, L. S. "Putting the Navy to the Test" (Chapter from the Diary of John D. Long), *Atlantic Monthly,* February 1923, pp. 209–18.

Mills, O. L. "Our Foreign Policy," *Foreign Affairs,* July 1928, pp. 555–72.

"Net Results of the Washington Conference," *Current Opinion* March 1922, pp. 291–93.

"New China Boycott of Japan," *Literary Digest,* June 23, 1923, pp. 19–20.

"New French Submarine Programme," *New Statesman,* December 31, 1921, pp. 360–61.

"Not Allies but Friends," *The Outlook,* April 5, 1922, pp. 536–37.

Obregon, A. "Washington Conference," *English Review,* January 1922, pp. 73–76.

Okamoto, T. "American-Japanese Issues and the Anglo-Japanese Alliance," *Contemporary Review,* March 1921, pp. 354–60.

Oulahan, R. V. "Personnel of the Arms Conference," *Current History,* November 1921, pp. 185–93.

"Our Yap Protest as Seen in Japan," *Literary Digest,* April 30, 1921, pp. 17–18.

"Pact of Paris, The; Opening a New World Era," *Literary Digest,* September 8, 1928, pp. 5–7.

Pasvolsky, L. "Russia Takes Over Vladivostok," *Current History,* December 1922, pp. 499–501.

Peffer, N. "Intrigue at Washington; an Inside Story," *The Nation,* January 18, 1922, pp. 64–65.

———. "Jockeying at Washington," *The Nation,* December 21, 1921, pp. 724–25.

———. "The Menace of the Anglo-Japanese Alliance," *The Nation,* November 9, 1921, pp. 529–30.

Pennypacker, J. W. "Britain, America, Japan, and Yap," *The Nation,* May 4, 1921, p. 664.

Piesse, E. L. "Japan and Australia," *Foreign Affairs,* April 1926, pp. 475–88.

Pollen, Sir A. J. H. "The Submarine," *Foreign Affairs,* July 1927, pp. 553–66.

Ponsonby, A., and Watney, C. "Washington Conference," *The Nation* (London), October 8, 1921, pp. 49–50.

"Power of Simple Truth," *The Independent*, December 31, 1921, p. 344.

Pratt, W. V. "Case for the Naval Treaty," *Current History*, April 1923, pp. 1–5.

"Press of Paris, The" *Literary Digest*, February 11, 1922, p. 73.

"Progress of the Arms Conference," *Current History*, January 1922, pp. 699–744.

Quigley, H. S. "China's Relations to the Great Powers," *Current History*, September 1926, pp. 866–71.

———. "Extraterritoriality in China," *American Journal of International Law*, January 1926, pp. 46–68.

Quigley, W. "Foreign Concessions in Chinese Hands," *Foreign Affairs*, October 1928, pp. 150–55.

Rea, G. B. "Facing the Facts," *Far Eastern Review*, September 1922, pp. 565–68.

Rogers, L. "Books on Disarmament and Pacific Problems," *World's Work*, December 1921, pp. 218–21.

Roosevelt, F. D. "A Democratic View" (of our Foreign Policy), *Foreign Affairs*, July 1928, pp. 573–86.

Roosevelt, N. "Russia and Great Britain in China," *Foreign Affairs*, October 1926, pp. 80–90.

Rosen, F. "Vale the Anglo-Japanese Alliance," *Living Age*, February 11, 1922, pp. 325–27.

Ruffe, R. de. "Le Problème Chinois, *Mercure de France*, April 15, 1927, pp. 257–83.

Saulsbury, W. "American Naval Efficiency," *Current History*, April 1922, pp. 32–33.

Scammell, J. M. "Policies and the New Armament Competition," *North American Review*, October 1923, pp. 448–54.

———. "The New British Naval Base at Singapore," *Current History*, December 1923, pp. 114–18.

Schornstheimer, G. "America's Present Naval Organization," *Current History*, October 1923, pp. 131–34.

———. "Armies and Navies of the World," *Current History*, April 1924, pp. 161–62.

———. "The Case against the Naval Treaty," *Current History*, June 1923, pp. 401–6.

———. "Our Navy Unready for War," *Current History*, January 1923, pp. 624–31.

"Secretary Hughes Explodes a Bomb" (The Conference), *The Independent*, November 26, 1921, pp. 209–11.

"Seminole." "Singapore Naval Base," *The Outlook*, May 13, 1925, pp. 65–67.

"Senate and the Treaties, The," *The Outlook*, March 8, 1922, pp. 370–72.

"Senatorial Game of Reservations," *Current Opinion*, April 1922, pp. 435–38.

"Shidehara Insists on No Interference," *Trans-Pacific*, October 18, 1924, p. 13.

"Shidehara States Position on China, *Trans-Pacific*, February 19, 1927, p. 16.

"Sidney." "The White Australia Policy," *Foreign Affairs*, October 1925, pp. 97–111.

Simonds, F. H. "The Arms Limitation and the League," *Review of Reviews*, April 1927, pp. 377–85.

———. "From Washington to Geneva," *Review of Reviews*, February 1922, pp. 147–54.

———. "The Washington Conference," *Review of Reviews*, December 1921, pp. 599–605.

———. "What the Conference Achieved," *Review of Reviews*, January 1922, pp. 33–41.

———. "What Was Gained at Washington," *Review of Reviews*, March 1922, pp. 261–71.

Sims, Rear-Admiral W. S. "Status of the United States Navy," *Current History*, May 1922, pp. 184–94.

"Singapore," *The Outlook*, May 13, 1925, p. 51.

"Singapore and Washington," *The Nation* (London), May 12, 1923, p. 186.

Singh, St. N. "The Anglo-Japanese Alliance," *London Quarterly Review*, January 1921, pp. 87–95.

Smith, C. H. "What Happened in Siberia," *Asia*, May 1922, pp. 373–78, 402–3.

Spear, L. Y. "Battleships or Submarines?" *Foreign Affairs*, October 1927, pp. 106–15.

Stead, A. "Anglo-Japanese Agreement from Japanese Point of View," *Contemporary Review*, March 1902, pp. 437–45.

Street, O. "Reduction of Armaments and International Guarantees," *The Outlook*, November 23, 1921, pp. 465–67.

"Submarine Controversy," *Spectator,* December 31, 1921, pp. 881–82.

Sullivan, M. "Afterthoughts on the Conference," *World's Work,* April 1922, pp. 589–96.

———. "The Conference First and Last," *World's Work,* March 1922, pp. 550–57.

"Treaty Triumph in the Senate," *Literary Digest,* April 8, 1922, pp. 12–13.

Tsurumi, Y. "The Difficulties and Hopes of Japan," *Foreign Affairs,* December 1924, pp. 253–65.

Turnbull, A. D. "The United States a Second-Class Naval Power," *Current History,* March 1924, pp. 969–83.

"V." "An English View of Anglo-American Relations," *Foreign Affairs,* December 1922, pp. 59–70.

"Vers le désarmement," *L'Illustration,* January 16, 1926, pp. 42–43.

Villard, O. G. "Arms Conference; Its Balance Sheet," *The Nation,* February 15, 1922, pp. 184–85.

———. "Briand's Failure," *The Nation,* December 7, 1921, pp. 641–42.

———. "The Conference Near the Rocks," *The Nation,* December 28, 1921, pp. 746–47.

———. "Publicity and the Conference," *The Nation,* January 18, 1922, pp. 65–66.

Walker, J. B. "Naval Strength of the United States, Great Britain, and Japan," *Scientific American,* November 1921, pp. 11–13.

"Washington Conference," *Spectator,* November 19, 1921, pp. 657–58.

"Washington Conference Made Absurd," *World's Work,* July 1924, p. 239.

Wester-Wemyss, Lord Admiral. "And After Washington," *Nineteenth Century and After,* March 1922, pp. 405–16.

"What Japan Thinks of Singapore" (from a Japanese Correspondent), *Spectator,* May 2, 1925, pp. 710–11.

"What the Conference Has Achieved," *Current Opinion,* January 1922, pp. 1–6.

"Where Our Navy Is Ridiculous," *Literary Digest,* September 15, 1923, p. 24.

Wickersham, G. W. "Has the Conference Succeeded?" *Forum,* January 1922, pp. 54–63.

Wilson, P. W. "First Month of the Conference," *Current Opinion,* January 1922, pp. 27–31.

"Workability of the Four-Power Pact," *Literary Digest,* December 24, 1921, pp. 5–8.

Wright, Q. "Powers' Differences on Chinese Conflict," *Current History,* March 1927, pp. 898–906.

———. "Powers' New Attitude toward China," *Current History,* February 1927, pp. 751–53.

———. "Tense Situation in China," *Current History,* April 1927, pp. 127–29.

———. "Washington Conference," *American Political Science Review,* May 1922, pp. 127–29.

Wright, Q. and Quigley, H. S. "Progress of Peking Tariff Conference," *Current History,* January 1926, pp. 609–12.

Wu, C. C. "Foreign Relations of the Chinese Nationalist Government," *Foreign Affairs,* July 1928, pp. 668–70.

Yang, S. K. "China Abrogating Unfair Treaties with Powers," *Current History,* February 1927, pp. 699–703.

"Yap and the Cables" (Progress of the World), *Review of Reviews,* April 1921, p. 359.

"Yap and Djambi," *The Outlook,* May 11, 1921, pp. 45–46.

"Yap for Yappers," *The Nation,* September 6, 1919, p. 328.

"Yap Question, The," *The Japan Review,* April 1921, p. 95.

Young, R. "Anglo-Japanese Alliance," *Contemporary Review,* July 1921, pp. 8–19.

JAPANESE MAGAZINES

Chuo Koron (Central Review).
Gaiko Jiho (Revue Diplomatique).
Kaizo (Reconstruction).
Kokusai Chishiki (International Knowledge).
Taiyo (The Sun).
Toyo Keizai Zasshi (Oriental Economist).

INDEX

INDEX

Acton, Admiral, asks that American plan on aircraft carriers be modified for Italy, 96

Agenda of the Washington Conference, 24–25, 335

Aims of the Washington Conference, vii, 24–25

Aircraft: report of committee, 99; subject of, intrusted to subcommittee of experts, 99, not included in proposal of United States for limitation of naval armament, 361

Airplane carriers: definition of, 379; limitation, 27, 96–99; proposal of the United States regarding, 359; replacement of, according to treaty agreement of Five Powers, 371–72

d'Alte, Viscount, on the Four-Power Pact, 131–32; representing Portugal, 164

Amami-Oshima and the Bonin Islands: fortifying of, 84–85; inclusion of, in Naval Treaty, 87, 91

America, see United States

Anglo-Japanese Alliance: comments regarding termination, 125–30; history of, 115–21; subject of renewal of, 7–9; titles and authors of articles on, 134–37

Archimbaud, L., on the Four-Power Pact, 121, 133–34; on the Naval Treaty, 140

Ariga, Dr. N., on extraterritoriality in China, 268

Arms conference (Five-Power Arms Conference): failures and accomplishments of, 100; foremost problem of, 60; organization of, 26–28; results of, 347–48

Associated Press, report of, on French demands for allotment of capital ships, 60; see Press, American

Australia, friendly with Japan since the Washington Conference, 350

Auxiliary combatant craft: agreement on, at conference, 96; American plan for, at Geneva Conference, 148, 150; British plan for, at Geneva Conference, 148–49, 150; Japanese plan for, at Geneva Conference, 149; limitation, 27, 37, 81, 147; summary statement of situation of, before the Geneva Conference, 147–48; United States proposal for limiting and replacements, 357–61

Bakan Treaty, 178, 341

Balfour: capital-ship proposal, 55–58; comments on Briand's speech regarding French land armaments, 101; concurs with American and Italian delegates on limitation program, 65; criticises China's demands for sovereign independence, 253–55; explains Great Britain's two kinds of leased territories and her views on restitution, 264–65; extends to China equal responsibility regarding international commitments and publicity of small transactions, 239; interprets Briand's letter regarding

Balfour (*Continued*):
  ratio of capital ships as assent, 69–70; letter to Dr. Sze on terms of release of Weihaiwei, 266; official response for Great Britain at second plenary session, 40–42; parallelogram scheme, regarding *status quo* definition, 86, 88; remarks on achievement of Naval Treaty, 111; requests assurance from China on retaining French co-director general of post offices, 209; resolution on arms embargo restriction, 261; seconds Viviani's committee proposal for Chinese questions, 217–18; states principle of Great Britain regarding China, 162; suggestion for drastic reduction of submarines and prohibition on building large-sized ones, 72–73, 76–77; tenders services on issue of Shantung, 285; termination of Anglo-Japanese Alliance, 125–26; tripartite treaty between America, Great Britain, and Japan, 120–21; *see* "Big Three"

Bandits, *see* China

Barry, Robert, attacks France for failure to make a premise similar to Great Britain on leaseholds in China, 265–66

Bau, M. J., on Chinese opinion of open-door doctrine, 192; on signing the Treaty of Commerce, 169

Beatty, Admiral, 47

Belgian Treaty with China, 223

Belgium, member of the Washington Conference, vii, 10 (*see* de Cartier, Baron)

Bibliography, 403–25

"Big Three": agreement on Four-Power Pact, 121; application of capital-ship ratios considered by, 53 f.; capital ships, provisional agreement reached on ratio of, 46–47; interviews on capital ships, 46–60; meetings of, 27, 47; provisional agreement reached on ratio and fortifications, 54, 58–59; *see* Balfour, Hughes, Kato

"Bill of Rights," China's, 160, 341

Birkenhead, Lord Chancellor: legal view of, on Anglo-Japanese Alliance, 7

de Bon, Admiral, disagrees with Hughes's interpretation of Briand's letter on acceptance of ratio of capital ships, 69; refutes British views on merit of submarines as defensive weapon, 77; states French needs for aircraft carriers, 97; states French views on armament limitation, 61–62, 63

Bonin Islands, *see* Amami-Oshima and the Bonin Islands

Borah, Senator: amendment offered by, to the Naval Bill, 5

Borden, Sir Robert: discusses fourth article of Nine-Power Open-Door Pact, 196; discusses lack of governmental authority in China, 249–50; proposes a drafting committee to resolve on Chinese demands, 218

Boxer Uprising, 173, 185; French indemnity from, 342

Briand, Premier: on land-armament situation in France, 101; reply, in part, to Hughes's letter regarding French counter-proposal on limitation of armament, 68–69; speech at inaugural session of the conference, 38; speech at the second plenary session, 43–44; sympathy with Chinese problems, 163–64

British Empire, *see* Great Britain

Bryce, Lord, opinion of, on Anglo-Japanese Alliance, 129

Buell, Dr., on the Four-Power Pact, 133

Bywater, H., on the Naval Treaty, 145–46

Cables, conference on: former German cables, 326–27, 392; relation to open-door policy, 331; rights defined on Yap, 338–39; Shantung Treaty provision, 392; Yap, the center for, in the Pacific, 334

Capital ships: abandonment of construction program, Hughes's proposal, 35–36; agreement of United States, Great Britain, and Japan, 359–97; American plan for, 58–59, 60, 104–5, 353–57; Balfour's proposal for Great Britain, 55–60; "Big Three" provisional agreement, 27, 54, 58 f.; discussion on, 63–71; France, on scrapping and replacement, 106, 370, 376; French views, 61 f.; Hughes's proposal on replacement, 36 f.; Hughes's proposal to Japan, 54–55; Italy, table of replacement and scrapping, 377; most important task of Washington Conference, 46; negotiations regarding, 47–59; provisional agreement on ratio of, 395–97; replacement tonnage, "Big Three" agreement on, 59; replacement treaty of Five Powers on, 371–79; scrapping of, 106, 369–71, 373–78; United States, replacement and scrapping, 373; *see* "Mutsu," "Super-Hoods"

de Cartier, Baron, states position of Belgium on problems of China, 163; in regard to the Hankow-Peking Railway, 257

Castex, Captain, views of, as exposed by Lord Lee, 79; repudiated by French delegates, 79–80

Cecil, Lord, on auxiliary craft at Geneva Conference, 150–51

Changchun Conference, 322

Chatfield, Rear-Admiral, 47

Cheng, S. G., on tariff provisions in treaties, 171–72

China: army, resolution advising reduction, 248–51, 345; bandits, 224–26; cancellation of war zone, 274, 291; conditions in, 223–29, 349; demands presented at conference, 159–61, 252–53, 296, 345–46; diplomatic standing before Washington Conference, 340–41; electrical installations, 231–36, 344 (*see* Radio stations); extraterritoriality, 202–7, 220, 268, 345–46; Far East and Pacific Conference, statements regarding, 155–66; foreign relations and domestic policy, 155–59; German relations, 180, 181; international commitments, 235–41, 246–47, 344–45; inter-power agreements, 248–66, 296; invited to attend the conference, 23; Japanese troops in, 212–19, 344, 388;

China (*Continued*):
Kiaochow, *see* Kiaochow; leased areas and embargo on arms, 260–66, 344, 346; Nationalist Government, 349; party to open-door policy, 200, 201, 343; post offices, 207–11, 219, 344; principles of conference on, adopted, 165–66, 342–47; problems attended to by conference, 29, 341–47; program at Paris Conference, 279–80, 295–96; radio stations in, 233–35, 246, 344, 392 f.; railways, 181, 190–91, 250–51, 294, 345, 389–90, 394; responsible for failure of Special Conference, 176–77; "restrictive stipulations" on, 258–59; Russian relations, 179, 180, 181, 186; Shantung, *see* Shantung; "spheres of influence," 257–59, 343, 346; Treaty, Chinese Tariff, 398–402; treaty with Japan on South Manchuria and Eastern Inner Mongolia, 293–95; treaty with Japan on return of lease of Kiaochow, 265; views of delegates regarding demands, 161–64, 253–59; *see* "Bill of Rights," Chinese tariffs, Chinese Ten Points, Koo, Liaotung Peninsula, Open Door, Open-Door Treaty, Twenty-one Demands, Sze, Wang, Yen

China Year-Book, 1928, observation of, on resolution of Special Conference, 176

Chinda, Count, on mandatory rights and cable question, 331–32

Chinese Eastern Railway Company, 179, 236; China made responsible, as trustee of, for fulfilling the financial obligations to powers, 247, 345; problem of, introduced by Hughes, 241–42; report on, 242–44; resolution pased by Committee of Delegates regarding, 246

Chinese Tariff Treaty, 398–402

Chinese tariffs: American government signs treaty regarding, 177; articles of treaty regarding, 174–75, 342; brief history of, 168–74; considerations of conference, 175; *likin*, 173, 174, 175, 342; railway tariffs, 259–60; ratification of treaty regarding, 175; Revision Commission of treaty regarding, 175; Special Conference on treaty, 175–77; treaty regarding, 174 (*see* Chinese Tariff Treaty)

Chinese Ten Points, third of, 252

Clyde, Paul H., lx

Commitments, international, *see* China

Committee of Fifteen, 27–28, 60

Committee of Naval Experts, 47, 48

Committee of the Whole: Arms Conference, 26–27

Committee of the Whole, Conference on the Far Eastern and Pacific Problems: adopts, criticizes, and amends Root resolution, 165–66; adopts resolution of drafting committee regarding electrical installations in China, 232–33; first meeting of, 159; presented with China's "Bill of Rights," 160–61

Committees of the Washington Conference: *see* "Big Three";

INDEX

Committee of Fifteen; Committee of Naval and Legal Experts; Committee of the Whole; Joint Committee; Program and Procedure; Senior Delegates; Subcommittee of Naval Experts of America, Great Britain, and Japan; Subcommittees of the Conference on the Far Eastern and Pacific Problems; Technical Committee

Conference on the Far Eastern and Pacific Problems, characterized as a "Conference on China," 155; organization of, 28–29

Coolidge, President, calls Geneva Conference, 147

Coontz, Admiral, 47

Cordier, H., 178

Covenant of the League of Nations, Article 8, 3–4; *see* League of Nations

Curzon, Lord, 8–9

Czecho-Slovaks, *see* Siberia

Dairen Conference, 322, *see* Kwantung

Daughters of the American Revolution Building, scene of the inauguration of the conference, 34

Delegation, American: report of, in estimating the action of the Conference, 347; report of, to President Harding, on friction in the East centering about China, 159; views on Naval Treaty of, 110–11

Delegations, foreign: views of, on French demands on auxiliary craft, 95–96; views of, on Hughes plan, 38–40

Dennis, Professor, indictment of Anglo-Japanese Alliance by, 128–29

Discriminatory exclusion of the Japanese, a problem to be settled, 349–50

"Dollar diplomacy," 179

Estimate of the conference, 347–50

Far Eastern problem: approach of American Government to the Four Powers on, 9–10; board created to deal with, 343; conditions concerning, since the Conference, 349–50; interests of British Empire, America, and Japan in, 20; steps taken by British Empire to interest the United States, China, and Japan in, 7–9; *see* Conference on the Far Eastern and Pacific Problems

Five-Power Arms Conference, vii–viii, 3–152; *see* Arms Conference

Formosa, specified in Naval Treaty, 87, 91

Fortification and naval bases in the Pacific region: agreements of "Big Three" regarding, 27, 54, 58–59, 83; faulty character of provisions on *status quo*, 83–84; islands to be included in agreement, 84–93; Japan's demands on *status quo*, 46; *status quo* zone, by terms of Naval Treaty, 92–93; term of treaty regarding, fixed at fifteen years, 109

Four-Power Pact: achievement of the Conference, viii, 113;

Four-Power Pact (*Continued*): authorship, 124–25; criticisms of, 130–34; effect of, 138–39; history, 121–25; loose language in, 83; object of, 123; origin of, 113–15; relation of, to Portugal and Netherlands, 125, 131–32; supplementary treaty, 124; text of treaty, 121–23

France: auxiliary craft demands, 94–95; capital ships, allotment of, American plan, 104–5, 354–55; communiqué to, to partake in conference, 10; concession of "six years" naval holiday, 94; consent to ratio of capital ships, 94; demands of, regarding capital ships, 104–5; reception of, at conference, 15, 20; relations with Japan, since Conference, 350; scrapping and replacement of ships, 106; submarines, demands on tonnage, 94 (*see* Treaty in Relation to the Use of Submarines and Noxious Gases in Warfare); success of conference made to depend on, 63; support of Japan on issues regarding Shantung and German islands north of the Equator, 278–79; treaty on capital ships, 368, 376; views on Naval Treaty, 140–41; *see* "Big Three," de Bon, Four-Power Pact, Sarraut, Viviani

Garret, John W., Secretary-General of the Conference, 25

Gases: conference rules on the prohibition of use of poisonous, 72, 81, 82; critical estimate of treaty on, 139–40; Treaty in Relation to the Use of Submarines and Noxious, 383–85

Geddes, Sir Auckland, comment of, on resolution of Hughes regarding open-door policy, 193; fifth resolution to inter-power agreements regarding China added by, 256–57; resolution with declarations on railway tariffs in China, 259–60; says Great Britain is prepared to publish all the commitments it had with China, 236

Geneva Conference, 147–52, 348 f.

Gerard, M., on significance of the fall of Tsingtao, 272

Germany: loses extraterritoriality in China, 223, 333; relations with China, 180, 181, 186; *see* Cables, Kiaochow, Mandates, Shantung, Witte

Great Britain: Agreement regarding naval limitation, 59; airplane carriers and airplane allotment, 359; alliance with Japan on *Status quo* of Far East, 187, 278; American plan on capital ships, 104 f., 355; answer to Hay "circular note," 183; auxiliary combat craft allotment, 157; capital ships, allotment of, 104–5, 355; communiqué to, to partake in conference, 10, 11, 13–14; Geneva Conference plan, 148–49, 150; Naval Treaty, effects of, on *status quo* of British Empire, 92; Naval Treaty, on capital ships, 366–80; relations with Japan since the conference, 350; scrapping and replacement of capital ships, 106, 356; submarines, views on, 73–74, 80,

81; view of, on termination of Anglo-Japanese Alliance, 127, 130; *see* Anglo-Japanese Alliance, Balfour, "Big Three," Four-Power Pact, Geddes, Hongkong, "Super-Hoods," Provisional agreement, Weihaiwei

"Group" interviews, unique practice introduced at the conference, 32–33

Guam, application of Naval Treaty to, 91, 92

Hanihara, refusal of, to China's demands for restitution of leased territories with explanation of reasons, 263–64; reply of, to Dr. Sze's challenge regarding Japanese troops in China, 213, 214–15, 216; reply to Chinese demands to abrogate treaties with note that subject is one for Japan and China to settle alone, 259; Japan's reasons stated by, for refusal of withdrawal from foreign control of China's post offices, 210; Japanese view of sovereign rights of treaty making stated by, 255–56

Hara, Premier, interview of, on proposed conference, 16

Harding, President; conclusion of opening address to conference of, 34–35; invitation of, to Japan, to attend conference, 21–23; statement of construction of term "insular-possessions and insular dominion," 123; statement of, at close of conference, 347

Harriman scheme, 189

Harvey, George, expresses pessimism over a tripartite agreement between America, Great Britain, and Japan, 120

Hawaii, application of Naval Treaty to discussion of, 85

Hay, Secretary, circular notes of, 182, 185, 188; on the "open door," 183–84; telegram to Buck, 184

Hongkong, in provisional agreement, 83; *status quo* clause includes, 92

Hoover War Library, ix

House, Colonel, 331

Hughes, Charles Evans: American plan to limit aircraft carriers, 96; on China's proposal for withdrawal of Japanese troops from China, 213, 216 f.; on Chinese railways, 250–51; delegates invited to general discussion on Chinese question, 161; explanation of "Big Three" agreement to Arms Conference, 60–61; on French counter-proposals, 63–64; French delegation's proposal on limitation of craft other than capital ships requested, 70; on international commitments affecting Chinese interests, 235; on international principle involved in visit and search in attacks on merchant ships, 76; letter to Briand on international armaments, 67 f.; new schedule to meet demands offered by, 97–99; note to British, French, Italian, and Japanese governments on validity of mandatory rights of Japan over Yap, 332; open-door policy, 192, 193–

Hughes, Charles Evans (*Continued*):
94, 195, 300–301, 304–5; permanent chairman of conference, 25; plan for Japan's allotment of capital ships, 54–55; plan proposed by, for reduction of armaments, 35–36; plan for replacement tonnage of capital ships, 36–37; publicity for international commitments, 235–36, 241–42; reply to criticism of American proposal on submarines, 74; revision of original scheme of tonnage of submarines, 77; Shantung issue, 285; Siberia, American expedition to, explained, 316–19; on treaty demands of China and the province of the committee regarding, 255; on Twenty-one Demands, 300–301, 304 f.; United States policy of land forces explained, 100–101; Yap, status of, settlement announced by, 335; *see* "Big Three"

Inauguration of the Washington Conference, 34–45
Institute of Pacific Relations, 350
International commitments, 235–41, 246–47, 344–45
Ishimaru, Lieutenant-Commander, on the Naval Treaty, 144–45
Italy: allotment of capital ships to, 104–5; American plan for capital ships, 354–55; communiqué to, to partake in conference, 10, 15, 20; and the Naval Treaty, 368 f., 377; principle of parity with France, 77–78; scrapping and replacement of capital ships, 106, 377; six-year "naval holiday" concession, 94; stand against arms embargo restriction in China, 261; *see* Schanzer

Japan: alliance with Great Britain on *status quo* of Far East, 187; American plan for, 354–59; anti-Bolshevist campaign, 310–11; auxiliary craft, plan for, at Geneva Conference, 149; capital ships, American plan of allotment, 104–5, 354, 355 f.; communiqué to, to partake in conference, 10, 13, 15–23; conditions of acceptance of ratio on capital ships, 46 (*see* "Mutsu"); decisions regarding, at Washington Conference, 343–44; diplomatic standing before the Washington Conference, 340–41; discriminatory exclusion of, in United States, 349–50; fortifications, *see* Fortifications and naval bases in the Pacific region; Korean conspiracies, 312; land forces, reduction of, 103; mandatory rights, *see* Mandates; Maritime Province, precaution taken in evacuating, 312–14; Naval Treaty provisions, 369, 378; program and issues at Paris Conference, 279, 280 f., 332; relations with nations since the Washington Conference, 343–44, 349–50; reply to Secretary Hay, 185; Russo-Japanese War, 188; Russian relations, present, 322; Sakhalin, *see* Sakhalin, Shantung, Siberia; South Manchurian Railway Company, 189, 191, 224 ff.; statement on conditions in China, 223–29; submarines, agreement with France and Italy on, 75 ff.; support of open door, 189 f.; treaty with China on lease of South Manchuria and Eastern Inner Mongolia, 293–95; troops in China, 212–20, 344, 388; twenty-one demands, 191, 274–75; vital interest in Pacific and Far Eastern questions, 20–21; Yap, 29, 334 (*see* Yap); *see* Anglo-Japanese Alliance, Four-Power Pact, Hanihara, Kato (Admiral), Kato (Baron), Kiaochow, Provisional Treaty, Shidehara, Tokugawa

Joint Committee, 28

Jusserand, Ambassador, 80

Karnebeck, Jonkheer van, 131; on interest of Netherlands in Chinese problems, 164

Kato, Baron: agrees with Italian demands and presents Japanese, 97; Article XIX of the Naval Treaty given by, 90; Balfour's parallelogram scheme rejected, 86, 88 f.; on the Hughes plan (interview), 40; on Japan's terms of acceptance of Hughes plan, 51–53; on limitation of armament (interview), 19; member of "Big Three," 27; "notes" proposed by, 89–90; official view of Hughes plan, 42 f.; on Shantung, 285; "victim" of domestic politics, 85–86, 90; *see* "Big Three"

Kato, Vice-Admiral, 47; public statement of, 48

Katsura, Premier, memorandum of, to Harriman, 189

Kawakami, K. K., on the Four-Power Pact, 134; on the wisdom of causing Japan's participation in the war, 271

de Kerguezec, Gustave, on the Naval Treaty, 141

Kiaochow: pre-conference attempts to restore, 281–85; terms of treaty on Shantung regarding, 386–88, 391, 393, 394; treaty on lease of, 265

Knox neutralization proposal, 190

Kolchak, Admiral, 309, 313

Koo, Dr.: China's position regarding Chinese Eastern Railway Company, by, 246; on Chinese tariffs, 167 f., 173 f.; Chinese Ten Points recalled by, 252–54; debate by, at the Paris Conference, 280; foreign leaseholds in China, 261–62; publicity of international commitments in China asked by, 235

Korean conspiracies against Japan, 312

Kowloon, 92

Kurile Islands, 93

Kwantung, Province of: Dairen Conference, 322; Japanese refusal to relinquish right to lease of, 263–64

Land-force limitation of Arms Conference, 100–103

Lansing-Ishii notes, 139

Lauzanne, Stephane, 11–12; articles in *The Outlook*, 12; *see* Bibliography

League of Nations (*see* Covenant of the League of Nations): machinery for armament limitation of, 4; principle of, on

League of Nations (*Continued*): mandates, 336–37; reply of Supreme Council to the United States' position regarding decisions of the League on mandates, 329

Leases: *see* China

Lee, Lord, on reduction of submarines, 73–74; on Italian claim for aircraft carriers, 96–97; on modification for Great Britain, 97; on views of Captain Castex, 79

Liaotung Peninsula, Russian lease of, in the hands of Japan, 344

Likin, see Chinese tariffs

Limitation of armaments: origin of idea, 3–9; plan for, beginning of, vii; proposal of the United States for naval, 353–61; Treaty on, 362–82

Lloyd George: on Japanese mandate over German islands, 325; on renewal of Anglo-Japanese Alliance, 7–9

Lodge, Senator: speech of, at fourth plenary session of conference, 114; on termination of Anglo-Japanese Alliance, 127

Loochoo Islands, 93

MacMurray, J. V. A., 238; on Twenty-one Demands, 291

Makino, Baron, 280

Mandates: American Government on, 327–29; given to Japan, 333; principles of the League of Nations on, 336–37

Maritime Province, 312–14

Matin, Le: British Premier, 12

Millard's Review, 212–13

Moore, F., on Siberian campaign, 319, 321

Morse, H. B., on Sino-Japanese War, 158; summary of China's modern relations with Western nations, 156–58, 340

"Most - favored - nation clause," 173, 177

"Mutsu": American plan to scrap, 354; Baron Kato's statement on, 50–51; discussion of "Big Three" regarding, 53–56, 58–59; Naval Treaty retains, 369; permission asked for substitution of the "Settsu," 46; Provisional Agreement regarding, 395

Nationalist Government, 349

Naval armament, reduction of: documents on, 353–82; Geneva Conference on, 147–52, 348–49; League of Nations provision for, 4; proposed by Hughes, 35, 36

"Naval holiday," declared for ten years, 59; modified to six years for France and Italy, 94; proposed by Hughes, 37

Naval and Legal Experts, Committee of, 28

Naval Treaty: Article XIX, 83, 90–91, 92–93; construction, 104; effect and estimates of, 138–39, 141–47; limitations of craft other than capital ships, 107; number and caliber of guns, 107–8; number and tonnage of ships, 105; opinions on, 110–12; provisions for execution of terms, 108–9; provisions for war, 110; scrapping specifications, 106; term of pact, 109–10; text of, 362–83; views of nations, 140–46

INDEX

Netherlands, member of the conference, vii; relation of, to Four-Power Pact, 125, 131–32; *see* Van Karnebeck

Neutrals and non-combatants, rulings protecting, passed by the conference, 81–82

New York Times: on "feelers" by President Harding regarding international conference for limitation of armaments, 6; text of the treaty regarding Yap, 335

Nikolaievsk, massacre at, 310, 314 f.; American view of occupation of Sakhalin in retaliation for, 317

Nine-Power Open-Door Pact, 192–201

Official Gazette of Japanese Government, 237

Okuma, Premier, 302

"Open diplomacy" feature of the conference, 26, 29–33; wisdom of, questioned on American-Japanese relations regarding the Island of Yap, 334

Open-door policy: in Anglo-Japanese Alliance, 1902, 187; China a party to, 200, 201, 343; entente of Russia, Germany, and Great Britain, regarding, 186; final test of, 188; Hay, on, 183–84; misunderstanding of, 185–86; Open-door Treaty, 251–66, 343; opinions on, 184, 192, 200–201; Portsmouth Treaty on, 188–89; principle of, 178–92, 195; Sino-Japanese treaties, note of United States on violation, 298–99; South Manchurian Railway violates, 191; technical declaration of, by Hay, 188; in Washington Conference, 192–201; *see* Cables, Nine-Power Open-Door Pact, China

Opium War, 168, 169

Organization of the conference, 26–29

Outlook, The, see Bibliography

Pacific and Far Eastern Conference, viii–ix, 155–350

Pacific Treaty, *see* Four-Power Pact

Pact of Paris, 152, 350

Papuan Bay, 92

Paris Conference: Chinese program at, 278–80, 295; Japanese program at, 279, 280–81

Pescadores, to be specified in Naval Treaty, 87, 91

Philippines, application of Naval Treaty to, 91, 92

Portugal, member of the conference, vii; *see* d'Alte

Pratt, Captain, 47

Preliminaries of the Washington Conference, 3–23

Press: American, reception of, to proposal for the conference, 11; attitude of, on cable question and Island of Yap, 334; divided opinion of, on resolution regarding China, 166; enthusiastic over the achievements of the Conference, 348; "group" interviews granted to correspondents, 32 f.; popularity of delegates largely determined by, 3; pros and cons of American-British-Japanese alliance, discussed by, 121; *see* Associated Press

Program and Procedure, Committee on: of the Arms Conference, 26; of the Conference on the Far Eastern and Pacific Problems, 28–29
Proposal of the United States for a Limitation of Naval Armaments, text of, 353–61
Provisional Agreement between the United States, British Empire, and Japan, 395–97
Publicity, principle of: on international commitments in China, 235–41; on notes exchanged by the League and governments on Yap, 334–35

Radio stations: foreign, in China, 233–35, 246, 344; provisions regarding, in treaty on Shantung, 392–93
Reboul, Colonel, on the Four-Power Pact, 134
Records of the conference, character of, 32
Roosevelt, President, 188
Root, Elihu: on impasse regarding solution of Chinese Eastern Railway problem, 245; on principle of "spheres of influence," 257; resolutions of Committee of the Whole on China formulated by, 165; on submarine rulings, 82, 140; on withdrawal of foreign post offices in China, 208
Root-Takahira notes, 139
Rozanov, General, 313
Russia: extraterritoriality rights in China lost by, 223; present relation to Japan, 322, 350; relations with China, 179, 180, 181, 186; demands on China, 188; war with Japan, 188; see Chinese Eastern Railway Company, Siberia
Russo-Chinese Bank, 179

Saint-Pierre, Abbot Charles Irénée de, 3
Sakhalin: American views on, 317–19; massacre at Nikolaievsk, 310; military occupation of, by Japan, 314–15, 322
Sargent, A. J., on opium question, 169; on railway concessions in China, 181; on tariff provisions in treaties, 171
Sarraut, Albert: on Article 4 of Nine-Power Open-Door Pact, 194; on "Big Three" agreement, 61; French counter-proposals defended, 65–66; on French demands on auxiliary craft if she accepts capital-ship ratio, 78; guaranties on auxiliary craft asked, 71; refusal of both British proposals on submarines, 74–75
Sauerwein, Jules, on official attitude to the conference proposal, 15
Schanzer, M. (Italian Delegate): assent of, to Hughes plan, 43; on the Four-Power Pact, 130–31; on Italian land forces, 101–2; Italian support pledged in considering Chinese problem, 163; Italy's public opinion explained by, 64–65; on Lord Lee's characterization of submarines, 75; on parity of fleets, 62–63
Schornstheimer, G., on the Naval Treaty, 143–44
Scrapping, see Capital ships

Seibold, Louis, on reception of Hughes plan in inaugural session of the conference, 38
Semenoff, Ataman, relations of, with Japan, 313–14
Senior Delegates, Committee of: of the Arms Conference, 26; of the Conference on the Far Eastern and Pacific Problems, 28–29
Sessions of the conference: inaugural, 25, 34–45; open, 25–26; plenary, 39; second plenary, 40–44; third plenary, 100–103; fourth plenary, 113
"Settsu," *see* "Mutsu"
Shanghai, agreement of, 173
Shantung: agreement by China and Japan on, 29, 155; résumé of the issue, 267–85; return of, ceremony at, 288; Shantung Treaty, terms of, 275–77, 286–87, 343–44; Sino-Japanese "conversations," 285–86; *see* Treaty for the Settlement of Outstanding Questions Relative to Shantung
Shidehara, Baron: draft resolution of open-door policy as new definition, 195; on governmental and private commitments in regard to Japan's agreement to publicity, 236; Japanese declaration on Siberia, 311–16; language difficulties pointed out, 237–38; on Twenty-one Demands, 296–98, 304
Siberia: criticisms of American expedition to, 319–20; inter-Allied expedition to, 306–11; Japanese expedition to, 320–22; question of, at the Washington Conference, 346–47

Sims, Admiral, 6–7; on the Naval Treaty, 142–43
Sino-Japanese war, turning-point in Pacific history, 158, 178
Smith, C. H., on Kolchak fiasco and support of it by Allies, 319–20
South Manchuria and Eastern Inner Mongolia, treaties regarding and developments from, 293–96, 305
South Manchurian Railway Company, 189, 191; tables on bandits attacking, injuring, and arrested within the zone of, 224, 225, 226
Special Conference, 176–177; *see* China
Subcommittee of Aviation, 28
Subcommittee of Naval Experts of America, Great, Britain, and Japan, 27
Subcommittees of the Conference on the Far Eastern and Pacific Problems, 29
Submarines: allotment of, as proposed by Hughes, 77, 81; Balfour's views, 72–73, 76–77, 80, 81; critical estimate of treaty on, 139–40; French views on, 76–77, 78–80, 81; Italian views on, 77–78; Japanese views on, 78, 81; question of abolishing, 28, 76, 77, 80; rules governing use of, 72, 81–82; tonnage limitation abandoned, 94; *see* Treaty in Relation to the Use of Submarines and Noxious Gases in Warfare, A
Sullivan, Mark, on Anglo-Japanese Alliance, 127–28; criticism of French stand on armament limitations, 102–3

"Super-Hoods": American proposals on, 46, 55–58, 354; *see* Capital ships, Great Britain

Sze, Dr.: appreciation of foreign interest on behalf of China, 164; on Article 4 of the Nine-Power Open-Door Pact, 196; data on Japanese troops in China, 212–13; on electrical installations in China, 231–32; on foreign grants in China, 207–8, 211; reply to Hanihara on Japanese troops, 215

Takahashi, Premier, 85–86
Tariffs, *see* Chinese tariffs
Technical Committee, 245
Temps, Le, article by Jules Sauerwein, in, 15
Tokugawa, Prince, 31; on entente cordiale between America, Great Britain, and Japan, 120; speech of, at inaugural session of the conference, 38–39; on termination of Anglo-Japanese Alliance, 126
Treat, Professor P. J., on America's position regarding Hay's note, 183; on the Anglo-Japanese Alliance, 130; on effect in China of concessions of China to Japan, 295; on history of Chinese foreign relations and her domestic policies, 155–56; on policy of South Manchurian Railway, 191; on secret alliance between Russia and China, 179; on Shantung rights, 267–68, 270; on Twenty-one Demands, 292–93
Treaty of Portsmouth, from standpoint of open door, 188–89
Treaty in Relation to the Use of Submarines and Noxious Gases in Warfare, A, 383–85
Treaty for the Settlement of Outstanding Questions Relative to Shantung, 386–94
Treaty between the United States of America, the British Empire, France, Italy, and Japan, Limiting Naval Armament, A, 362–82
Tripartite agreement of the Arms Conference, 58–59, 114, 120–21
Twenty-one Demands, 191, 274–75; China asks abrogation of, 259; present status of, 344; study of the history of, 289–303; summary of the views of, expressed at Washington Conference, 303–4

Underwood, Oscar, on financial condition of China, 167; formal presentation of resolution requesting China to reduce her army, 249
United States: airplane carriers and aircraft, American plan for, 359; allotments, auxiliary combatant craft, American plan, 357; capital ships allotments, 58–59, 60, 104, 105, 355, 367; communiqué to Powers to participate in conference, 10, 11; 16, 17, 21–23; Czecho-Slovaks release of, 307–8; Geneva Conference, 148, 150; mandates, stand on, 327–29, 333; Naval Treaty, 92, 373–74; Netherlands, note to, on Four-Power Pact, 132; open-door policy, note to China and Japan on, 298–99, 300 (*see* Open Door); opinion in, on Japanese conditional note, 17–19; relation with Japan

since Washington Conference, 349; scrapping of ships, 106; submarines, American plan, 72, 77, 358–59; termination of Anglo-Japanese Alliance, official and unofficial views on, 126–30; treaty with China on tariff autonomy, 177; withdrawal of American troops and railway experts from Siberia, 309–10; *see* Four-Power Pact, Harding, Hays, Hughes, Knox, Open Door, "Mutsu," Proposal of the United States for a Limitation of Naval Armaments, Provisional Agreement, Yap

Uyeda, Captain, 47

Van Karnebeck, on the Four-Power Pact, 131
Versailles, Treaty of, signed, 333
Viviani, René (for France): on conditions relative to withdrawal of foreign control of post offices, 209–10; refusal of China's demands not to use legation electrical installations for commercial purposes under existing conditions, 232; subcommittee on extraterritoriality suggested, 217

Wang, Dr.: on cancellation of notes on Japan's Twenty-one Demands, 259, 296, 298–300, 304; on extraterritoriality, 203–4; "spheres of influence," 257
Washington Post, estimate of, on the Washington Conference, 348
Weihaiwei, 181, 265, 266
Wester-Wemyss, Lord, on the Anglo-Japanese Alliance, 129, 133; on the Naval Treaty, 141–42, 145
Weyl, W. E., on the "open door," 184
Wheeler-Bennett, J. W., 3
Wilson, President, reservation of mandates agreements of League of Nations relative to Yap, 325–26, 333, 339
Wilson-Lansing reservations, 325
Witte, Count, on his instruction to his agent in China, 180
Woodhead, H. G. W., 288

Yap, agreement reached regarding, 29, 334 f., 347; articles of the treaty discussed, 337–38; historical study of, 323–34; nature and scope of treaty, 339; preamble of treaty regarding, 335–37; unusual diplomatic procedure in controversy on, 334
Yen, Dr.: on China's difficulty to agree to resolution to Chinese Eastern Railway resolution and asks for reservations on, 244–45
Yuan Shi-kai, 303

OCT 3 1989

JX
1974
5
I4

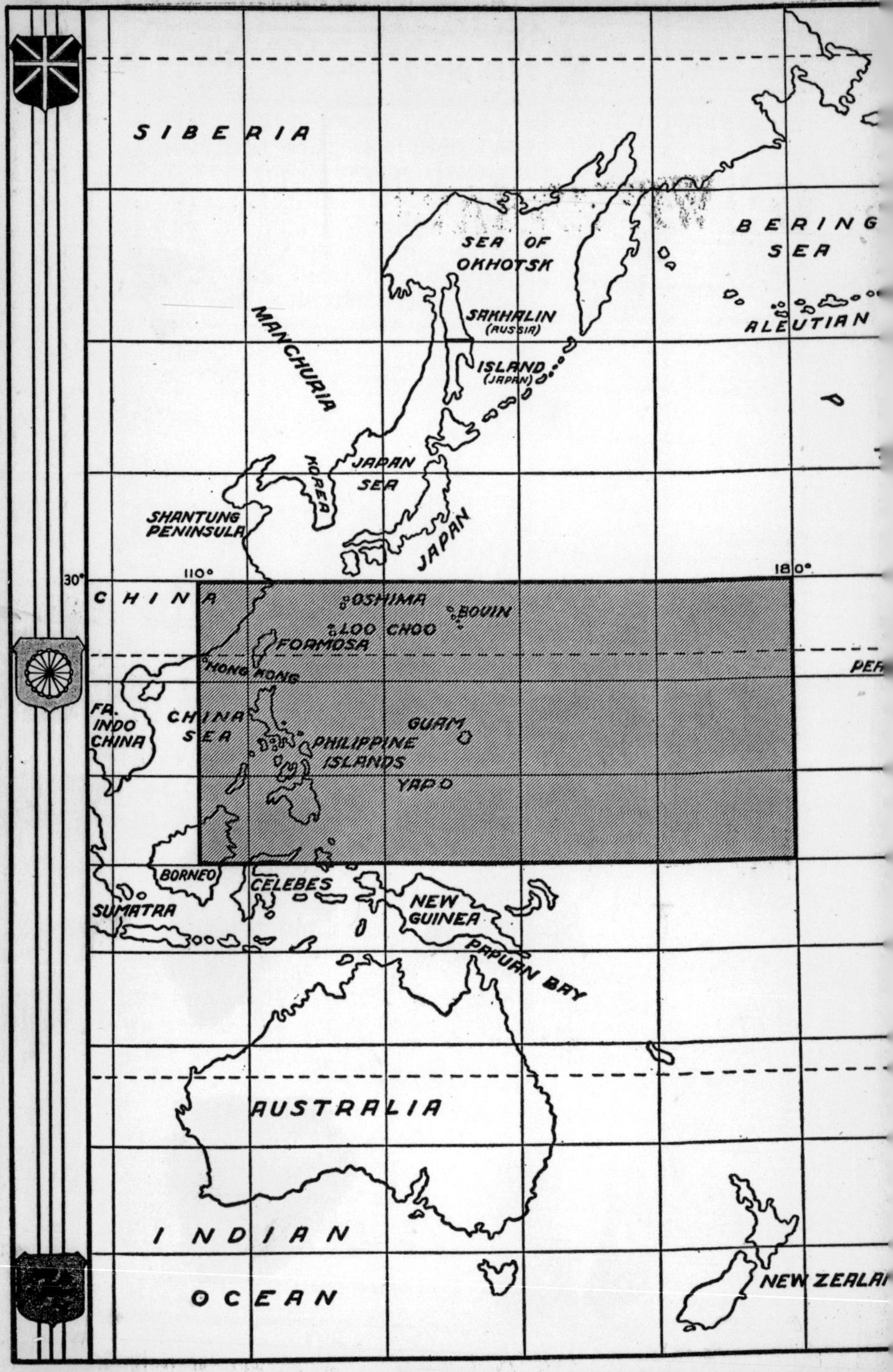

SIBERIA
BERING SEA
SEA OF OKHOTSK
SAKHALIN (RUSSIA)
ISLAND (JAPAN)
ALEUTIAN
MANCHURIA
KOREA
JAPAN SEA
JAPAN
SHANTUNG PENINSULA
110°
180°
30°
CHINA
OSHIMA
BOUIN
LOO CHOO
FORMOSA
HONG KONG
FR. INDO CHINA
CHINA SEA
GUAM
PHILIPPINE ISLANDS
YAP
BORNEO
CELEBES
SUMATRA
NEW GUINEA
PAPUAN BAY
AUSTRALIA
INDIAN OCEAN
NEW ZEAL